Running the Show

DATE DUE

Running the Show

The Essential Guide to Being a First Assistant Director

Liz Gill

ELSEVIER

Amsterdam • Boston • Heidelberg • London • New York • Oxford
Paris • San Diego • San Francisco • Singapore • Sydney • Tokyo
Focal Press is an imprint of Elsevier

Focal
Press

Cover image and illustrations by Stephen Daly.

Focal Press is an imprint of Elsevier
225 Wyman Street, Waltham, MA 02451, USA
The Boulevard, Langford Lane, Kidlington, Oxford, OX5 1GB, UK

Notices
Knowledge and best practice in this field are constantly changing. As new research and experience broaden our understanding, changes in research methods, professional practices, or medical treatment may become necessary.

Practitioners and researchers must always rely on their own experience and knowledge in evaluating and using any information, methods, compounds, or experiments described herein. In using such information or methods they should be mindful of their own safety and the safety of others, including parties for whom they have a professional responsibility.

To the fullest extent of the law, neither the Publisher nor the authors, contributors, or editors, assume any liability for any injury and/or damage to persons or property as a matter of products liability, negligence or otherwise, or from any use or operation of any methods, products, instructions, or ideas contained in the material herein.

Library of Congress Cataloging-in-Publication Data
Gill, Liz.
  Running the show : the essential guide to being a first assistant director / Liz Gill.
    p. cm.
  Includes index.
  ISBN 978-0-240-82146-7
  1. Motion pictures–Production and direction–Handbooks, manuals, etc. I. Title.
  PN1995.9.P7G442 2012
  791.4302'3–dc23

                                                              2011049129

British Library Cataloguing-in-Publication Data
A catalogue record for this book is available from the British Library

For information on all Focal Press publications
visit our website at www.elsevierdirect.com

12 13 14 15   5 4 3 2 1

Printed in the United States of America

To
Breda and Elsie

Contents

Contents

Contents

Acknowledgments

I'd like to offer my sincere and unlimited thanks to Breda Walsh, Elsie Walsh, Conor McCarthy, Annie Gill, Betsy Gill, Michael Gill, Neil Winterlich, Oorlagh George, Seamus McInerney, Bryan Thomas, Noelette Buckley, Tim Bird, Thomas Whelan, and Elsie Lau at Entertainment Partners, Sahar Moridani at the DGA, Elizabeth Moseley at SAG, and Ken Segna at Starz Encore.

And especially Dennis McGonagle, Lauren Mattos and Anne McGee at Focal Press, for green-lighting, producing and distributing this book.

Preface

A few years ago, a friend of mine who had worked on my team for many years got her first job as a first assistant director (AD). We spent an afternoon in my kitchen with the script of her project and her computer, going through all the basics as well as the more complicated stuff. She had a good idea of what was involved, but wanted the reassurance of a more experienced person to guide her through her first steps. In a sense, this book is my way of being that person at the kitchen table for all those who are about to embark on the adventure of Firsting a shoot and, whether they know a little or a lot, want the support of an encouraging friend for their first time out.

This book is also for anyone with an interest in the movies who wants to know how they really work. Very few civilians (that is, people who don't work in the movie business) have even heard of a first assistant director, never mind key Second, Second Second, etc. Yet these team members are the backbone of the shoot and the ones who, in the most immediate sense, keep the show on the road. In fact, with a good cameraman, script supervisor and first, you can go a long way without having a director at all! So while I would hope other first ADs might enjoy reading it (and having very different opinions), this book is aimed at people who are considering a career in film, or who want to know more about the realities of life as a first AD. I hope it might also be useful to other members of crew and even cast who want to understand how a production actually works. Knowledge is power!

Although it's an invisible job (in movies onscreen, the director is always the one who calls "action" or tells the extras where to stand), being a first AD is actually one of the most interesting and challenging jobs on the planet, and it can be very well-paid, too. No two days are ever the same; you're always at the very heart of the action; and you can contribute hugely to the quality of the end result. It does require talent and skill, some of which can be learned—like scheduling, production systems and paperwork—and some of which is innate but can be improved—like being a good team player, people manager, diplomat and leader. Ultimately, the first AD can make the difference between a good film and a bad one, providing crucial expertise and support to the director and the producer, inspiring the cast and crew, maximizing time so the focus is on the story, and protecting the safety and welfare of the whole unit. Moreover, it's a creative role, not only directing the background action, but also sometimes giving a performance that would put the cast to shame! It's a rewarding, collegiate and exciting job: from breaking down the script to directing the director, the first is the timekeeper, logistics expert, navigator, ambassador and first mate. Anyone who works in film and TV can tell you just how critical the first is, the hub of the operation who literally runs the show.

This book is written for English-speaking readers, who generally will work under either the North American or the UK system (which extends to Ireland, South Africa, Australia, New Zealand, and beyond), and when

I use the term UK, it refers to all of these places as well. I generally use North American work practices as a primary model and point out differences of protocol as we go. Where I have put an alternative term in parentheses, it's generally the name used in the UK system—for example, for a second second (third) AD. However, no matter where you're shooting or for what kind of project, the ultimate objective is the same: to get it in the can. For this reason, film crews from around the world, even without sharing the same language, can work together more or less smoothly. The principles are global, even if local color changes from place to place. If you learn your craft well, you can work anywhere.

For simplicity's sake, in this book I'm using the model of a low-budget feature film, as this is a standard example that most other projects can refer to; if you have more money, just multiply everything accordingly, and TV programs, short films and others can also extrapolate from this prototype. I use interchangeably the terms First and first AD, but in every case they signify the first assistant director. Most of the book is divided into two parts, broadly prep and production; most elements, naturally, are covered in both sections, and I apologize for any repetition, but sometimes the same information is relevant in different contexts, and this was my intention.

I'm grateful to have worked for some of the best directors in the world: Martin Scorsese, Barry Levinson, Todd Haynes, Jim Sheridan and Kevin Reynolds, among others. But I've learned as much, if not more, from the first-timers. In any case, whether you realize it or not, you learn from every job you do, but it's only when you're on the next job that you realize what you've learned. Either way, it's like driving a car: first you read the theory, then you get behind the wheel. We all continue to learn on the job, and that's one of the beauties of this occupation—you never know everything, which keeps it interesting. While the best teacher is experimentation (and especially failure!), I hope that you can save yourself some heartache and learn from my mistakes. I welcome your comments or thoughts on the Running the Show website and Facebook page. Ultimately, the way a first does their job is as personal and unique as every individual—there are bound to be things in here that you disagree with, or would do differently, and so much the better. It's a role, and every actor interprets the script in their own way.

Page One

Occasionally, you'll hear a crew member with an exasperated tone and a roll of the eyes refer to someone's error as being "page one." I have always yearned to see this mythical page, on which the original commandments of filmmaking are laid out for all to see. Having not yet unearthed the lost ark, I've created one myself, hoping that others will add to it in future editions. In the meantime, to get the ball rolling, here are some of the primary rules that seem to fall under this elemental jurisdiction:

a) Don't stand in doorways (poetically expressed on New York shoots as "move or bleed").

b) Don't talk during takes; that includes whispering, mouthing, or large physical gestures.

c) Change Change Change: that's the movie business, love it or leave it.

d) Never assume—anything.

e) Admit when you've messed up—as early as possible.

f) Never say, "I don't know," say "I'll find out," and do.

g) It's better to be looking at it than looking for it.

h) No live ammo, real alcohol, real violence or real sex: the point is to create an illusion, real life is for documentaries.

i) Never film anyone without a signed release form (or the equivalent).

j) Every day this side of the grass is a good day.

k) It's only a movie: it'll all be all right in the end, and if it's not all right, it's not the end.

And now for Page Two.

Chapter 1

Pre-pre-production

It is not the ship so much as the skillful sailing that assures the prosperous voyage.

George William Curtis

What Is an Assistant Director?

Francois Truffaut said that making a film is like going on a sea voyage: you start out hoping for a pleasant journey and you end up clinging on, praying to survive. This may be an extreme example, but the metaphor of the ship is accurate, and in this scenario the assistant director (AD) is the first mate. The director may have the vision of the destination, the production manager may be calculating the budget, but the first mate has to be the director's support, the producer's representative and the crew's inspiration; if you don't keep the director encouraged, the producer informed and the crew happy, you will end up shipwrecked, keelhauled or facing a mutiny. I've seen all three happen, and they're not pretty.

An assistant director, first of all, is very different from an assistant to the director. "Assistants to" can end up doing practically anything the director wishes, from the most personal errands such as picking up laundry to liaising with the editor to making dinner reservations. In any case, a production can move seamlessly forward with no assistant to the director whatsoever. Without a first AD, however, you won't have a schedule or a communication system, and without these two things there's no show. You can have a first-time director carried by a good first AD, you can have a first-time producer educated by a First; but with a bad First there will be a catastrophe, and, joking aside, people can actually die.

As we go through the stages of what the job requires, the details of exactly what a first AD does will become clearer, but for now suffice to say the First creates and manages the schedule, runs the set, and executes the director's vision within the parameters of the production's resources. The first AD is largely responsible for making sure that the day's work is completed, directs the background action, supervises crowd control and maintains communications between the director and the crew. The First's currency is time, and a good First makes things happen in the most efficient way possible, like the manager of a highly efficient factory. Rather

1

than producing widgets, however, this company manufactures emotional responses in the psychologies of an audience; naturally enough, then, the First is managing egos, ideas, vulnerabilities and artistic personalities, while trying to make it all happen yesterday at the mercy of the weather, the public or the claustrophobic environs of a soundstage. At best, it's like being a conductor leading an orchestra in Bach's most beautiful concerto; at worst, it's like trying to control a class of sugar-fueled three-year-olds let loose in a paint factory. In any case, it's never dull; no two days are ever the same and every job is unique. It's the ultimate collaborative process, in which the first AD manages the balance between creativity and forward motion.

The entire job is about anticipating where delays or problems could occur and taking steps in advance to prevent them. That's really it. Across the departments, under all the circumstances, with all the personalities: what can possibly go wrong and what can you do to make sure it doesn't? It's a good job for someone who suffers from anxiety and impatience. Anxiety helps you foresee any potential disaster, and impatience means you're going to solve it quickly. Again, though, this is all internal; the mask of a First is unflappable, steady, and in control, no matter what's going on inside. Leadership is not letting them see your fear, otherwise known as grace under pressure.

How Do I Start?

If you've ever tried to figure out how to turn a script into a shoot, you've already begun the process of being a first AD. Naturally, the more you know about the way a film shoot works, the better your ideas of how to plan the production are going to be. A film unit is a hierarchal structure, almost military in style, and this isn't because filmmakers are fascists but simply because it works. It's the most efficient system we have developed over the past 100 years to get the film through the gate (or capture the information, if you want to get digital about it!). Most ADs begin at the bottom rung of the ladder (as a PA or trainee), and despite the fact that the freelance world of filmmaking is completely unpredictable, it can be comforting to understand that if you want to be a first AD there really is a pretty clear-cut career path, even if it doesn't feel that way at the time.

The first step is getting a job, any job. No matter what department you actually want to work in, the hardest part of the whole film industry experience is getting that first job. You might assume that the word "job" implies that you will actually get paid, but that isn't necessarily the case. You have to be willing to shovel elephant dung for free—literally—to have any hope whatsoever of working in the business. In fact, if your goal is to get rich or famous, please look elsewhere. Inside every person on a film set, including the caterers and even the surliest electrician on the truck, somewhere exists the romantic child who was first dazzled by the silver screen. We're here because we love what can happen in a darkened room full of strangers; or because we were entranced and delighted by what we discovered at the movies; or because we were consoled or entertained or distracted or inspired by some sound and image we might no longer even remember. Even in the most grizzled cynic's heart is this childlike love of the cinema; if this doesn't ring a bell with you, then you'll save yourself and everybody else a lot of heartache if you find something else to do with your one wild and precious life. If you have a choice, you're in the wrong game. This business is for obsessives, dreamers and poets, people who simply cannot live in any other world. You have to be willing to put up with long hours, bad pay, disgusting food, verbal abuse, freezing cold and baking heat, and still keep smiling. I'm not saying that you won't get the odd job that is a complete pleasure, or one freak shoot that is actually as much fun to work on as all the stars say it is when they're being interviewed, but generally it's a tough slog no matter what you're being paid, and you need to have some love or madness in your heart to get you through. Consider whether you want to get up at 4:30 a.m. six days a week for eight weeks to stand in the snow for 12-hour days. If you can't face that, go elsewhere. (And if you think I'm exaggerating, have a look at how the Directors Guild of America (DGA) itself describes the job in their trainee program at www.trainingplan.org— not for the faint-hearted!)

If you're still game, you simply need to get in anywhere that will have you. Most cities (and unless you're an auteur and plan to write, direct, star in and edit your film yourself, you will have to be in a city) have some kind of filmmakers' association that may also publish a journal of some sort. I used to look in New York's theatrical newspaper *Backstage* to find short films to work on for free; now Mandy.com has similar listings online (for a list of other online resources, see www.runningtheshowbook.com and *Websites and Other Resources* at the end of this book.). There are film co-ops, alliances, independent film associations, and even film schools that need people willing to pitch in. Either way, get in the door, work your butt off, and word will go out that you're worth hiring. Eventually you'll get paid.

You then work your way up the ladder: production assistant, known as a PA (or trainee AD), Second Second (or Third in the UK), second AD, and finally First. The only odd thing about this career ladder is that being great at one job doesn't necessarily mean you'll be good at others. I hated being a second AD. Detailed paperwork is really not my strong suit; I'm worse still supervising makeup, hair, wardrobe and nervous actors, and luckily for the industry I did only one job as a Second (unless you count one where I was fired). Being a Second Second, however, really is the step below being a First and requires similar skills, so you can learn everything that can be learned from watching in this role. The important thing is not to be impatient about your progress; once you make the step up, it can be harder to step back, so a general suggestion would be to upgrade when someone offers you a job in that higher grade, as will inevitably happen if you prove yourself in the one you're in.

A job on a film crew is an invitation to the most exclusive party in town. There are no passengers on a set, and everyone is depending on you, regardless of whether you're the director or a PA. The job you're doing is the most important job you'll ever do, not a means to an end, but the end in itself. Ultimately, what we all want is to make a good show—whether we're running coffees or calling action isn't the issue—the idea is to serve the ultimate good of the project, and leave your own agenda at home.

Getting the Job

Once you get to be a First of any description you may be well-known and sought after, but no matter how good you are, you will still need to audition for the director. This is sensible; a certain amount of chemistry is required for this to be a successful relationship, and a director should get to choose—or at least approve—the first AD or there will be one immediate excuse for things to end in tears.

This audition (or meeting, as they're euphemistically referred to) is important to get right. Ideally, the First will have been able to read the script beforehand and prepare notes on it to have to hand at the meeting, which the producer and/or an assistant may also attend. Even if you don't have the script, you can trawl the Internet and anyone you know for information about the director and producer. Any details you can get are important, especially their work-style, their previous work and how it was received. They may ask what you're working on or what your last job was; even if it was a real stinker, find something positive to say. Don't be negative, as this shows disloyalty, and no one wants to think you might go on to badmouth them all over town.

What I usually try to do once the small talk is out of the way is to actually begin the working process by asking questions. Not tough questions that are going to put the director on the spot (for example, how do you plan to shoot the ghost sequence?), but general questions ranging from how they like the mood on the set to whether they've worked with the cast before to general ideas about anything tricky in the script (generally, tricky involves stunts, special effects, children, animals, etc.). Again, you're not expecting them to have all the solutions at this stage; for various reasons many decisions may not have been made yet. Ideally, you're encouraging the director to share their ideas with you, and offering thoughts and options about what might work. If you can give them useful information, you'll be perceived as valuable. You can casually mention the way you like to have the extras supporting the main action of the scene, and how strong the team is that you bring with you. At all times, you are to be positive about the script. You'd be surprised how much it means to the people hiring you—everyone is still insecure about how good (or not) the material is, and even when they don't expect much from the script, it's reassuring to have someone being positive about the possibilities. Even if it's a turkey, there must be something you can find about the project that's good, or else why work on it? As Joan Holloway in *Mad Men* once said, "An interview is the chance to be intelligently enthusiastic about the job and convince them that you're the right person for it." If you've already begun the process of eliciting the director's desires and discussing ways to put them into practice, you're potentially much further down the road of actually working together than the other candidates. Toward the end of the interview, the conversation will probably turn to dates, and you should make it clear (briefly) if you have recently had a meeting with another production and if there could be a clash. Don't rule anything in or out at this stage—it's all just talk for now, and dates do sometimes shift.

Assuming you get the job, only then will you discuss the exact dates and the money. Because Firsts generally don't have agents, it's down to you to negotiate these things yourself. If during the follow-up conversation (which will happen with either the producer or production manager) you should discover that you have a scheduling conflict, you should let them know the second this becomes clear. One thing that will get you blacklisted is jumping ship: committing to a project, and then bailing out. It's not just rude, it's infuriating, and I have refused to work with people after they've done this to me. It erases your reputation for being trustworthy, and in such a trust-dependent business that can be fatal. If a First can't be relied on, they're no good to anyone. The rule of thumb is to be completely honest and transparent about what your previous commitments are, and then you won't end up in a muddle. My strategy is to behave as I would if I were invited to two dinner parties on the same night: I don't jump ship, I just go to the one I was invited to first. I may miss out on some fun, but my conscience is clear.

This transparency extends to your salary negotiations; trying to play one job off against another financially will lead to big problems. For one thing, production managers talk to each other, and even if they're not friends they commonly pick up the phone and confer over what they're both offering you. No matter how big a city you're working in, in this business it's a small town. The other aspect to this is that if you're dealing with a respectable PM or producer, the figure they're quoting you will be what they have budgeted for, and they often have very little leeway. Other crew members such as sound or camera technicians may bring gear with them that can provide a little wiggle room in relation to their rates ("box fees" or "allowances" they're sometimes called), but ADs don't bring equipment with them (unless they own their own walkies, which is unusual and would probably be a separate deal), so the rate is the rate and probably won't change by more than a hundred bucks at best.

If you really can't work for what they're offering, say so and walk away. If you sign on for that rate, that's the end of the conversation. One thing producers hate is any crew member trying to renegotiate deals later on. Whatever you commit to stands for the whole job, unless some unforeseeable major change affects the entire shooting structure.

It's important to agree in this conversation when overtime, if any, kicks in. (This will feature strongly later for the First when creating the schedule; for now, we're only talking about personal conditions.) ADs are often classified as being in the production department, but even when they're not, they're expected to work long hours without additional pay for extracurricular meetings or other requirements. ADs generally work from at least an hour before call time, through lunch, and for a short time after wrap (unless there's an additional recce or meeting planned), all-inclusive.

Once you have an understanding, you enter that charmed era when you have a job lined up, but haven't started it yet. This is the time to pack as if you were about to embark on that wonderful ocean cruise. Do all your laundry, say goodbye to your friends and family and stock up on foodstuffs—it's going to be a bumpy ride.

Chapter 2

Pre-production

Give me five hours to cut down a tree, and I'll spend three hours sharpening the axe.

Abraham Lincoln

Pre-production, or prep, is in many ways the most important part of the shoot: there is still time to solve problems and it's much cheaper to do so now rather than later. Prep is about imagining the worst-case scenario and doing everything possible to avoid it, and so requires imagination, communication and execution. Most of this imagining stays private, but those elements that involve taking action will be shared. And no matter how much planning you do, there will always be surprises and disasters. The difference between a good First and the one the crew wants to string up is whether these disasters are self-inflicted. A film set is a great place to create total chaos, confusion and bad feeling; how much of this you get is determined by how well you prepare. If you know the script, know the schedule and know the director, you will handle the Acts of God more gracefully, and this is really what you are being paid to do. A clever monkey can create a schedule, but it can take a genius to make it work.

For the purposes of this book, let's imagine as an example a six-week shoot with a four-week prep for the first AD. This is typical of a lot of low-budget feature productions, but of course there are any number of variations—there's no such thing as a normal shoot. You should be able to adapt this model to whatever scale of production you're working on. A TV show is more compressed (seven days prep and eight shoot days per episode, for example), while a studio feature might shoot for over 100 days. On any size production, the minimum amount of prep time for the First is four weeks per six weeks of shooting. And I mean minimum. (The DGA publishes the prep time requirements for ADs and PMs on their website.) If someone is asking you to do your prep in less time, they either have a schedule done already, which means you'll be taking responsibility for someone else's work, or else you're going to be expected to work 16-hour days producing a schedule in a hurry that's inevitably going to have some mistakes in it. So hold the line. You don't need eight weeks prep for an eight-week shoot unless you enjoy completely redoing all your work over again, as the script and locations are invariably going to change that far from shooting. So let's imagine that you have four weeks until D-Day, or that we are starting at Day One minus four weeks, what is commonly known as Week Minus Four.

WEEK MINUS FOUR (WEEK ONE)

The Production Office

The size of the production department varies from project to project, but it will usually be your first point of contact with the show, typically through a call from the production manager (PM) or line producer (sometimes also called production supervisor) to check your availability. These titles are often interchangeable, and there may be one or the other, or both. If you have both, the line producer will be overseeing bigger picture concerns and the production manager will cover the day-to-day detail of the shoot. Sometimes, there may also be a unit manager, who is occupied predominantly with the logistics of the operation: catering, parking, and the general overlap between the production and locations departments, which impacts greatly on the ADs. Assistant directors, in North America, are officially part of the production department, and this should be borne in mind to negate any tendency to create an "us-vs.-them" situation, which is unhelpful on both a professional and personal level. Even if the coordinator is the kind who appears put-upon, overworked and resentful of any and all requests, the ADs need to embrace the office as part of their team, including them in their information dissemination and appreciating their help. Up to and including certain elements of the shoot, most production information is distributed through the production office, and it's your job as a First to make sure information gets out smoothly; even just from a self-interest point of view, they should be your allies and friends.

There can be any number of producers with various descriptive titles. Generally, if there are multiple producers you need to ascertain who makes the decisions, or at least takes responsibility for the decisions, and work primarily with them. An associate producer can be anyone from the producer's girlfriend or boyfriend, to someone who was instrumental in raising some of the finances, and who you may never meet. An executive producer is usually someone directly involved in the financing, or if in TV, from the broadcaster, and who may visit the set occasionally; likewise, an executive in charge of production is often someone from the studio, network, production company or other investor, who will also typically "drop by" the set once or twice, often around lunch break. This person can be an asset if they come from a production background and understand the technical elements, or a hindrance if they interfere with the creative process and request and issue script rewrites very late in the day.

Let's assume for the purposes of this example that the production we're working on has a producer and a production manager (this is generally the minimum, although sometimes producers are forced, through lack of resources, to PM the job themselves).

The producer and PM will either have their own offices or share one, while the production office will be the domain of the production office coordinator (POC) and his/her team. Your first morning will usually begin with making friends with the POC and his/her assistant—the assistant production coordinator, or APOC—and a trainee or office PA. Some jobs might have a production secretary (an assistant to the production manager) or a travel coordinator (just what it sounds like!).

After saying hello, you'll get a copy of the unit list/crew list (the names, contact details and job titles of all the crew on the job so far), the cast list (if there is one at this stage), a vendor list or contact sheet and any other relevant information from the office, especially the production calendar (Figure 2.1), which we will discuss more later in the chapter, in the section titled "Week Minus Three."

By the time you start the job, the POC will have created a pre-production schedule for the weeks leading up to the start of the shoot. If the shoot involves filming in multiple countries, or cast or crew are traveling from abroad, these elements will be in place on the calendar, as well as most heads of departments' (HOD) start dates, travel, and any casting sessions. You'll have a look at this and see if there is any time penciled for rehearsals, tech scouts or tests, and have a brief chat about how those dates were chosen and what works best. The production office retains control of the prep calendar throughout the prep period, while the ADs and the other departments (especially the second AD) feed information into it through the POC.

I would request at this stage that weekly production meetings be added to the calendar, on the same weekday every week (sometimes a Tuesday morning at 9 a.m. is a good time, and when people start saying they're too busy this can be pulled back to 8 a.m.). Either way, I make sure that these meetings are on the calendar and happen every week, as they're critical to a good prep period. It's also critical that the director attend them, and the coordinator will have the best information on how that will be possible.

The coordinator will also have all the scoop on any actors who have been cast at this point, and a rule of thumb is that The Office Knows Everything. They know if someone is already being difficult about their accommodation, their deal or their lunch, and all the drivers, who listen to everything that goes on, talk to the girls (and boys) in the office. This is not gossip (unless you repeat it—not to be advised), but rather valuable professional information, no matter how much it sounds like snooping. Anything you know about the cast before working with them can be useful to the production later; you want them to be happy and arriving on time.

The AD's office is often shared with the locations department, and some locations crew should already be working. Once you've met them and gathered any information they have about the locations (and they will have a fair amount already in terms of potential sets and restrictions), you should do a quick trip through the rest of the departments and see who is on board at this point.

The other departments who may have started before you will mostly likely be accounts, art department and costume/wardrobe. You will say hello to accounts, and sort out your paperwork, start form, and so forth; art department, where you will want to spend about 20 minutes meeting everyone and getting their general views on any possible challenges and solutions—and, if possible, their experience thus far of the director; and wardrobe—depending on the size of the job, and if it's period, they may already be working away. At this stage, you probably won't have much to discuss with costume beyond a social visit, unless they've already met or worked with any of the cast.

Just letting these people all know you're on board is the first step in uniting disparate departments that may be physically separated from each other. Then you can have lunch! Production generally isn't responsible for feeding you during prep, although you will learn a lot about the scale of the production from the standard of the coffee…!

Generally, no sooner will have you walked in the door and sat down at your desk than you will get a call or a message from the casting director asking for a schedule. It's a little sneaky to try contacting you directly, but it's commonplace. In my experience, the less direct contact you have with the casting director the better: no good

'FAB TV SERIES'

Pre-Production Diary   As of 19/08/11

Week	Mon	Tues	Wed	Thurs	Fri	Sat	Sun
−3	**22 AUG** Set up Production Base at The Factory PM: Producer meeting with Line Producer, POC and APOC	**23 AUG** Tues 9AM Production Meeting Director Script Work	**24 AUG** Wed Production Accountant 10AM Art/props show & tell To start: Distribute locked script 2–6PM: Casting @ The Production Office	**25 AUG** Thurs Rehearsals @ The Prod Office *TBC–Jack, Jill, Granny* 4PM–Director - First AD Meeting	**26 AUG** Fri Rehearsals @ The Prod Office *TBC–Hansel & Gretel*	**27 AUG** Sat	**28 AUG** Sun
−2	**29 AUG** Mon To start: Second AD Director of Photography Assist Costume Designer Rehearsals @ The Prod Office *TBC–Jack, Jill, Hansel, Gretel* *Stunt Coordinator joins rehearsal*	**30 AUG** Tues Rehearsal room in Production Office not available PM Scout: Dir, DP, Prod Des, Locations	**31 AUG** Wed Rehearsals @ The Prod Office *TBC–Hansel, Gretel & Big Guy (if cast) to join*	**1 SEPT** Thurs 10AM Art/props show & tell Rehearsal room in Production Office not available	**2 SEPT** Fri Tech Scout–Day 1 of 2	**3 SEPT** Sat	**4 SEPT** Sun
−1	**5 SEPT** Mon Tech Scout–Day 2 of 2 Fittings To start: Script Supervisor Sound–0.5 wk Stand by Prop 2nd 2nd AD Extras Co-ordinator Accts Assist Gaffer Make-up Hair Transport Co-ordinator	**6 SEPT** Tues Fittings–incl. Gretel 7:30 AM Production Meeting 11AM–Read Through PM–Rehearsals @ The Prod Office *TBC–Jack, Jill, Hansel, Gretel* *Stunt Coordinator joins rehearsal*	**7 SEPT** Wed Fittings AM - Production Meeting PM–Rehearsals @ The Prod Office *TBC–Richard, Peter, Catherine & Ogre to join*	**8 SEPT** Thurs Fittings 10AM Art/props show & tell Check Camera Equipment To start: (Focus Puller/1st AC) PM CAMERA TESTS– To include SFX champagne	**9 SEPT** Fri Fittings Trucks Loading To start: Camera Trainee	**10 SEPT** Sat	**11 SEPT** Sun
SHOOT / 1	**12 SEPT** Mon 1st Day of Principal Photography To start: Boom Op Art Dept Trainee Make-up Assistant Hair Assistant Pass Van Driver	**13 SEPT** Tues	**14 SEPT** Wed	**15 SEPT** Thurs	**16 SEPT** Fri	**17 SEPT** Sat	**18 SEPT** Sun

Figure 2.1 *The production calendar*

can come of it. All communication should go through the POC or producer, and when you eventually have a schedule that can be shared with the casting director, it will be the producer who approves it and provides it. And never, never, NEVER deal directly with an actor's agent or an actor, even if you're sleeping with them! The best way to get in trouble or make it for everybody else is to tell an agent or an actor anything, even if it's the truth.

Typically, you won't have even gotten to do your first pass at a schedule before someone is looking for it. This is normal: do not be pressured. If they wanted a schedule last week they should have hired you to start then. It takes at least three days to do a six-week schedule, and can be more, depending on the script. No one should expect anything before the end of the first week.

Reading the Script

After meeting everyone, you need to find somewhere quiet where you can actually read the script in peace. In many cases you will have read the script before you start work, and even though reading it at that stage is technically unpaid, it's worth doing for your own peace of mind. The first time you read a script, don't break anything down: just read it straight through, in one sitting, making notes only about story points you don't understand or thoughts on character. Try to read it as an audience will see it, and understand what it is you are all trying to make. It should be obvious what genre the material is, and I'm wary of combinations such as comedy-thriller; they often become neither one or the other.

As soon as you get your script you want to put your name and phone number at the top of it—you don't want to lose this, as it will have some important notes on it very soon. You also don't want to lose it because it's confidential. Even if it's not watermarked with your name on it (so that if it leaks, they'll know who to blame), you're responsible for keeping it safe. Think of it like a soldier and his gun.

The next day—ideally—read it again, this time with your tools (a pen, maybe some highlighters). Some people like to highlight all the elements in a different color: cast, extras, props, effects, vehicles, etc. I find this cumbersome and it depends on how much time I have. It does make it easier down the road when you're shooting, as with a quick glance at your script you know what's required for the scene, and certainly in the early days of your career I think it's a useful exercise. However, if the script pages are changing frequently it becomes a chore; it's something everyone has to personally decide. I would strongly recommend highlighting on your first few projects and then evaluating how it's working when you have more experience. See Figure 2.2 as an example. (A color version of this figure can be found on the companion site.)

During this second pass, I'm writing lists of questions for the various departments: How is this being done? Who is responsible? What has been done so far? And many others. As I'm going, I organize my questions into categories by department: director, producer, designer. It's worth keeping these categories going throughout the project, as you will often need to get six answers from someone in a very brief conversation and there isn't time to rifle through your notes while someone waits. You'll notice that I'm asking HODs these questions; HODs expect to be asked questions directly by the First, and overall they're the first person in the department you should talk to, unless it specifically refers to something being managed by someone else (the art director often manages the art department schedule, but unless the designer tells you not to ask him/her about scheduling issues, you should always start at the top). If you look at Figure 2.3, which contains notes

Jack and Jill meet in the hall: she's shocked to see him here, he was supposed to be on the hill with a pail of water.

She runs, and he takes off after her.

105   EXT. PRECINCT - MORNING (CONTINUOUS)   105

Jill runs down the sidewalk.

When she sees Jack chasing her, she runs across the street narrowly avoiding being hit by a car, and struggles to get her keys to her own parked car.

Jack chases her, but a woman's dog chooses this moment to have a pee and Jack has to leap over the leash stretching across the sidewalk.

Jill pulls out into a gap in the traffic.

Jack runs after her, then hails a taxi and jumps into it.

106   EXT. STREET - MORNING (CONTINUOUS)   106

Inside the cab, there is a very surprised passenger. Jack flashes his ID at her and the driver.

                    JACK
          Police. I need you to follow that
          car.

                    DRIVER
          Oh, come on - they only say that in
          the movies!

                    JACK
          This is a movie!

                    DRIVER
          No, it's not, it's a Fab TV Series.
          That's what it said on my call
          sheet.

Jack can see Jill's car getting further away.

Figure 2.2 *An example of a highlighted script page*

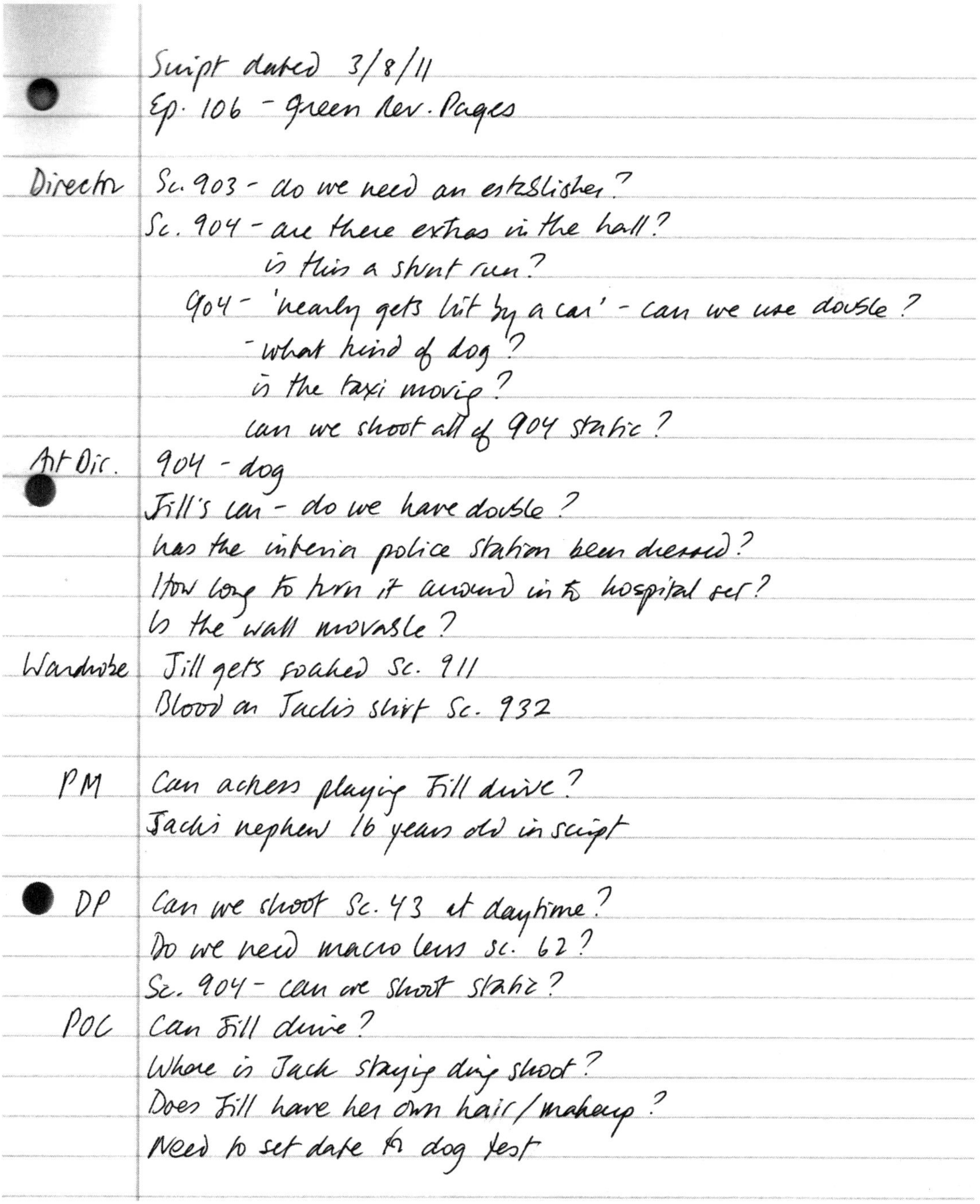

Script dated 3/8/11
Ep. 106 - Green Rev. Pages

Director | Sc. 903 - do we need an establisher?
Sc. 904 - are there extras in the hall?
     is this a stunt run?
   904 - 'nearly gets hit by a car' - can we use double?
    - what kind of dog?
    is the taxi moving?
    can we shoot all of 904 static?

Art Dir. | 904 - dog
Jill's car - do we have double?
has the interior police station been dressed?
How long to turn it around into hospital set?
Is the wall movable?

Wardrobe | Jill gets soaked Sc. 911
Blood on Jack's shirt Sc. 932

PM | Can actress playing Jill drive?
Jack's nephew 16 years old in script

DP | Can we shoot Sc. 43 at daytime?
Do we need macro lens sc. 62?
Sc. 904 - can we shoot static?

POC | Can Jill drive?
Where is Jack staying during shoot?
Does Jill have her own hair/makeup?
Need to set date for dog test

Figure 2.3 *An example of a page from my notebook after reading the script*

from the first pass, you'll notice that sometimes I have the same question for more than one person—perhaps the director and the DP—and there are some notes that aren't questions. Especially as you start to get more information in, it's crucial to keep passing it on.

In a perfect world, you may have gotten to do both these reads before you start on a Monday morning. If not, they still need to be done. The third time you read the script is when you start doing the breakdown. I'm old enough to remember doing this by hand, where script changes really meant starting from scratch, so I appreciate the joys of the electronic age.

A breakdown just means transferring the information in the script into a schedule format. It's a very useful process to go through for a First, as you get familiar with what's required in a very intimate way. If you are being asked to work on the basis of someone else's schedule and there is already a breakdown in existence, it's still crucial to go through this process yourself as it's the only way you will really understand what's required.

Here's one crucial fact to know before you type one word, however: Is the script locked? This is the question to ask everyone you meet on your first day in the office—the coordinator, the PM, the producer, the director and the writer (and in TV a writer may well also be a producer). If there is any doubt that the script is locked, then you start campaigning.

Let me be clear about what I mean about a script being locked. This does not mean the director will not change the stage directions, the actors will not change the dialogue and the editor will not change the scene order. A locked script has nothing to do with the content of the scenes: it is entirely about scene numbers. When you do your breakdown, create the schedule and that schedule is distributed, everyone on the crew will be doing their own breakdowns and notes referring to those scene numbers. If a script is not locked and a scene is deleted or added, the scene number of every subsequent scene changes, and everyone's breakdowns become inaccurate and must be re-done. There is never enough time to do this and people become very unhappy. Writers and directors (and sometime producers) resist declaring a script "locked" as if they are then iron-bound and cannot make any further changes, but in fact this is a purely technical issue that has no effect on their lives (ask the writer or director if they care what the scene number is) but massive effect on everyone else's (ask an art director to re-do their entire breakdown and watch them cry).

Once a script is locked, any subsequent changes are issued on colored paper by the production office. In the USA, they go in order white, blue, pink, yellow, green, gold, buff, salmon, cherry, white (this time known as "double white"), and back to blue ("double blue") if you're on a frequently changing show—the number of producers is often a guide to how many new script pages you might expect. (In the UK, they start with blue, then move on to pink, and so on. In TV, many companies use their own custom colors; it doesn't matter to the First once you know what the system is.) A good coordinator will attach a cover sheet describing what the changes are, and on the pages themselves there will be an asterisk beside every change—again, that way you'll know if it's simply a dialogue change or whether there is now a bar-room brawl. It's a system that works perfectly when properly implemented.

One final note as regards the color of the revised pages being issued: there is a difference in practice between the USA and the UK systems on this point, which I will touch on briefly here, even though the US method is becoming ever more pervasive (and with good reason, as it is simpler to understand). In the US, each new batch of script pages are all issued on the same color paper, with the date and color of the page at the header of every page (the color will be written out, "GREEN," as when you're making a photocopy you might not have handy access to green paper). On some UK productions, the color of the page will depend whether that page itself was changed before, in which case the set of new pages, even though they're distributed at the same time, will all have different colors. For example, let's say that last week there were changes on pages 2, 6, and 10. This week, there are changes to pages 6, 10, and 43. In the US system, this week you will get a batch of pages that are all green. In the UK system, you would get a blue page for page 43 and green pages for pages 6 and 10, as they are moving into the second layer of the color scheme. In practice, for the first AD it makes very little difference as to which system is being used (although this latter practice makes life very tough on the production trainee, who is trying to keep track of which color each page should be!) as long as the system is coherent and consistent. But it's worth asking the question of the coordinator in the beginning as to which system is being used, and if there is a choice, I would push for the US practice as there is less opportunity for confusion.

If the scene has become longer due to the change, let's say page 30, additional pages will be added as required and called 30A, 30B, etc.—this means they can be slotted into the master shooting script without disturbing the subsequent order. If the page is deleted, it may still be issued but marked as "OMITTED" so that people understand what has happened to that page. If a page is shortened, the new page will reflect that in the normal page number space: page 15 might become page 15–16, for example.

Likewise, the all-important scene numbers are handled the same way: if there is a new scene added between scenes 101 and 102, that new scene will be numbered Sc. 101A. If you need to add another scene between 101A and 102, that becomes 101B. If you need to add a scene between 101 and 101A, that new scene becomes 101aA. Again, if a scene is deleted, its scene number is still preserved, and OMITTED is written beside it. This means scenes won't "fall off" the schedule or off people's breakdowns, but that every scene is traceable and that scene numbers are always maintained. This may seem like boring technical information, but it will save you literally hours of work if the system is used correctly—truly boring is having to change scene numbers scene-by-scene because the script wasn't properly locked!

The nightmare scenario is when a writer or director refuses to lock the script, keeps tinkering away and eventually a new "white" script is released. It's called white, as the name implies, because it's effectively an entirely new script, with—most importantly—new scene numbers. This renders pretty much redundant all the work that has been done on the schedule up until this point. An entirely new breakdown must be created, which requires the same amount of time as the first one. As you can imagine, this sends most departments into a mild panic as they then need to either re-create their own breakdowns or wait for the new one to come out. A strong producer will not allow this to happen, but even on larger-budget pictures I have seen producers who don't understand the consequences of not locking the script early enough: stress, confusion, mistakes, and a complete waste of many people's time. While everyone scrambles to process the new information, they're not doing the other crucial work required at this time, so stress levels skyrocket and people will have to work longer hours to catch up, meaning they're worn out before the shoot even begins! Am I emphasizing strongly enough how important it is to "lock" the script?!???

Figures 2.4 and 2.5 show examples of a title page and script after revisions.

```
                  Madeup Film Productions Ltd

                    Fab Series Season 1

                    Production Office
                     Happy Studios
                       A Street
                    A Town, A State

                    + 555 123 4567

                    + 555 123 4567
```

Fab TV Series Ep. 9

by

A. Genius

SHOOTING SCRIPT - 22nd September 2011

PINK SCRIPT - 28th September 2011

PLEASE NOTE THIS IS A LOCKED WHITE SCRIPT - ALL
FUTURE REVISIONS WILL BE ISSUED AS COLORED PAGES

BLUE PAGES - 8th Oct 2011
12, 13, 18, 18A, 18B, 29

YELLOW PAGES - 13th Oct 2011
18A, 18B

GREEN REVISIONS - 29th Oct 2011
28, 28A, 29, 32, 33, 39, 45, 45A

Figure 2.4 *An example of a title page after revisions*

901   <u>OMITTED</u>   901

901A   <u>OMITTED</u>   901A

902   <u>OMITTED</u>   902

903   INT. PRECINCT, HALL - MORNING   903

Jack and Jill meet in the hall: she's shocked to see him
here, he was supposed to be on the hill with a pail of water.

She runs, and he takes off after her.

904   EXT. PRECINCT - MORNING (CONTINUOUS)   904

Jill runs down the sidewalk.

When she sees Jack chasing her, she runs across the street
narrowly avoiding being hit by a car, and struggles to get
her keys to her own parked car.

Jack chases her, but a woman's dog chooses this moment to
have a pee and Jack has to leap over the leash stretching
across the sidewalk.

Jill pulls out into a gap in the traffic.

Jack runs after her, then hails a taxi and jumps into it.

905   EXT. STREET - MORNING (CONTINUOUS)   905

Inside the cab, there is a very surprised passenger. Jack
flashes his ID at her and the driver.

                         JACK
                Police. I need you to follow that
                car.

                         DRIVER
                Oh, come on - they only say that in
                the movies!

                         JACK
                This is a movie!

                         DRIVER
                No, it's not, it's a Fab TV Series.
                That's what it said on my call
                sheet.

Jack can see Jill's car getting further away.

                         JACK
                Are you going to follow the damn
                car or do I have to drive myself?

                         DRIVER
                You can't drive, you're main cast.

The passenger looks at her watch.

Jill looks back and can't see Jack anywhere. She relaxes.

                Fab Series Ep 9 GREEN REV PAGES 29th OCT 2011   1A.

905   CONTINUED: 905

Figure 2.5 *And a page from the script itself*

Breaking It Down

Assuming that you have a locked script, you may then begin the breakdown that will eventually become the schedule. In the old days, we hand-wrote a breakdown sheet for each scene that contained all of the information about what was required. A synopsis of this information was then transferred to a 17-inch, narrow strip of cardboard (hence the name strip—more on this later) that could be moved around on a big, accordion-style frame called a stripboard. I'm delighted to say that those days are gone and everything is now done electronically; one of the greatest advantages of the electronic system is that you can save various versions of the schedule. It's analogous to the difference between cutting on film or digitally—in the old days on film, if you made a change, remembering what you had before was challenging, and restoring it was labor-intensive. Now, you can have as many versions as you like at your fingertips, and compare them with the click of a mouse. I mention the old style method simply as an explanation of how the vocabulary of scheduling arose.

The industry-standard scheduling software is from Entertainment Partners and is called Movie Magic Scheduling (if you ever had to do a board the old way, you'd agree that it's magic!). It can be downloaded from www.entertainmentpartners.com and costs about $US500, which sounds steep but it's an inevitable cost. There is the option of a free trial, and the purchase comes with two applications, so you could split it with someone unless you want it on two computers of your own. Subsequent upgrades cost another $200–300 depending on your system. Either way, there's no alternative and it's worth every penny. (There are other softwares out there but I've never been on a production that used them—multi-camera shoots do use different techniques to create camera cards and vision-mixing scripts, but for now we're just talking about "single-camera" production.)

Whether you're a first AD, PM or line producer it's part of your job description to own and be able to use Movie Magic, and I highly recommend it to Second and second second ADs as well, both because you may be called upon to make a few tweaks for a First who can't leave the set, and to familiarize yourself with it so that it's not a complete shock when you become a First yourself. It's easy to install and you'll be guided through the steps by the program. I'm not writing a Movie Magic manual, I'm just going to describe how I use the software. Movie Magic offers technical support, but they're in LA, which isn't always practical from a time-zone point of view. I've always found other Firsts or PMs to be most helpful when it comes to questions or difficulties, and the next time you may be able to help them!

Now, assuming you have that famous locked script, you're ready to start your breakdown. Every First has a different method of breaking down, and this is how I do it:

First, create and save a new Movie Magic file with the name of the project. (If you have already made a schedule for another job, or have another First's template and you like the preferences that are set up, you can create a schedule template from that version and use it here.) Then, under the heading "Schedule," enter "Stripboard Manager" and create a schedule called "Script Order." I would then also create another called "Schedule Order," so you can clearly distinguish between the two. Now go back to "Script Order" to begin.

Most scripts will exist in Final Draft (a screenwriting program, also industry-standard), in which case some of the grunt work can be done for you. If you don't own the Final Draft software, the production coordinator usually does. Ask her/him to save the script as "Movie Magic" and this will create a file that you can then import into your schedule. Certain elements will translate into your breakdown sheets: scene headings and numbers, speaking cast and page lengths, for example. But this is not a replacement for any of your attention—you'll still need to be painstaking about these elements and everything else, but it saves some typing and in this game every second is precious. (If the script exists only in Screenwriter software, you can export it from within the script to a .sex file, which can then be imported to Movie Magic Scheduling.)

The Breakdown Sheets

A breakdown sheet is simply a page that reflects every possible element referred to or implied in the script, as in Figure 2.6. The most important are interior/exterior, set, day/night and the cast, and most of these will have transferred electronically for you. This is, I stress, no substitute for doing your own breakdown: cast won't be reflected unless they speak, and very few writers use the screenwriting software in such a way as to be perfectly transformed into a schedule. One needs to comb painstakingly through every detail of the hard copy of the script; a tiny mistake now can lead to major confusion and cost later, so it requires patience and a

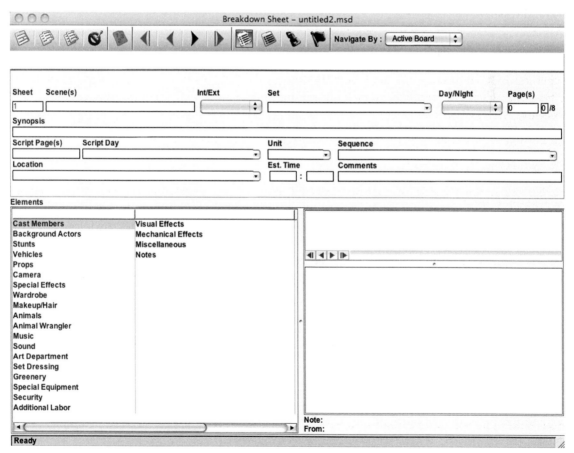

Figure 2.6 *An empty breakdown sheet*

methodical, steady approach. This is why it's best done locked away on one's own—interruptions or distraction are really not welcome at this stage.

This part of the process is mechanical, and, truth be told, pretty tedious. You are simply transferring the information in the script to the breakdown sheet. I start at the first breakdown sheet and sometimes use the "Add Breakdown Sheet" shortcut, the little image of a page on the top left side of the toolbar. You can also click "Action" and then "Add Breakdown Sheet," and there is also a keyboard shortcut beside this command.

In all of the sheet categories you can "add a new element" by simply typing in the new name followed by a semicolon (;) or choosing an existing one by clicking the arrow on the right of the category name. It's very easy to create a new name but not add it to the sheet (it has to be done in two separate actions), and it's even easier to remove an element from the sheet with an inadvertent click of the mouse, so I re-emphasize how painstakingly this must be done—it's not a rush job.

As you go, you will collect another long list of questions for various departments, so I always have beside me a notebook with names in the margins and spaces for the questions beside them. That way, you're consolidating information and every time someone sticks their head in the office you can get a concise briefing from them of what you need. Some things, of course, may not be answerable at this stage, so they will go on the next list and continue to travel from list to list until they have been answered. (This is the same system I use in Figure 2.3.)

There are many categories on the breakdown sheet, some of which are never used and can be ignored from the start. Some contain information that is very detailed and possibly going to change, while there are certain elements that the PM and the rest of the company are desperate to get information on, so it's important to prioritize the elements. These are the ones, in breakdown sheet order, that I make sure to include in the first pass:

Scene Number

Scene numbers may be generated automatically if you have imported the script. Even so, you should keep an eye on them as you move through the breakdown to be sure they correspond correctly. (I have never known anyone to use the Sheet Number function, except in a case of re-ordering all the sheets after some kind of major change or mistake.) If, as is often the case, the writer has neglected to create a new scene when the character(s) move from int. to ext. or any other location, you'll make a note of this and pass it on to the POC. The scene will either be broken up in the script, and a new scene number with an "A" following it, for example, issued as a script change, or you will describe the scene as Scene 101 (part 1 of 2) and Scene 101 (part 2 of 2). I like to include how many parts there are of a particular scene, and this can be abbreviated to appear as PT 1/2 on the schedule.

Some scenes will become broken into sections by virtue of the fact that they are to be shot across different locations, while remaining part of the same scene. This is particularly common in an action scene, where, for example, in Scene 43 a character runs to the edge of a cliff, sees their child drowning in the sea below, rushes down to the beach, enters the water and rescues the child. This scene could have five or more parts: the parent on the cliff, the POV of the child in the water, the beach, the sea, a swimming pool or tank, and so on. These sections would be designated as "Parts," and I would always reflect them as such—for example "Sc. 43 – PT 1 of 5," "Sc. 43 – PT 2 of 5" and so on. If you always specify which part it is of a definite amount of parts (as opposed to simply saying Part 1, Part 2, etc.) you (and the script supervisor) can tick them off the list (and the schedule) as you go, without a part dangling somewhere unnoticed.

Another point about scene numbers is that on episodic TV, it's useful to use the episode numbers to preface the scene numbers—for example, the first scene of episode 1 would be 101, the third scene of episode 2 would be 203, the sixth scene of episode 8 is 806, etc. (It's rare that an episode would have more than 99 scenes, but in this case you could start using As and Bs.) It's a visual shorthand that lets everyone know exactly to which episode scenes on the schedule correspond.

INT/EXT

As mentioned earlier, it's very important to look out for scenes that start outside and move in, or vice versa, which the writer hasn't broken up. Even if a scene changes location and both are interiors or exteriors, it's important to delineate them as two scenes. (It's very common to have confusion around this issue in relation to car shots. We'll go into more detail later, but the more clarity you can assign to whether the camera is inside or outside the car the better.) The same rules apply as described above, even if all of the scene parts are interior or exterior.

Set

This means the scene heading, the story name of the location. As you work through the script, you will often discover that the same set has been given a variety of descriptions throughout the script. For example, someone's bedroom could be described in scene headings as

INT. FAMILY HOME, SHELLEY'S BEDROOM
INT. SHELLEY'S BEDROOM
INT. HALLWAY OUTSIDE SHELLEY'S BEDROOM
INT. SHELLEY'S ROOM

You get the idea. It's often the case that you might have several subsets within one overall set, such as rooms in a family home, areas of a hospital, etc. What I recommend is to assign a uniform description to the overall set, with the sub-set following this title. For example:

INT. FAMILY HOME, SHELLEY'S BEDROOM
INT. FAMILY HOME, KITCHEN
INT. FAMILY HOME, LIVING ROOM
EXT. FAMILY HOME

And so forth. The beauty of this system is that the designer, location manager, and everybody else know immediately that these sets are all related from a story point of view (even though they may be shot in separate locations). It gives a unity to a number of disparate elements.

As you continue the breakdown, you will need to keep track of each of these scene headings so the coordinator can then amend them in the script. There will be a number of such technical changes to be made; this is not something the writer needs to do, as it's a purely logistical change and the office will be better at maintaining the system and will send the writer the new script pages.

Day/Night

In most cases this is obvious, but often doesn't come through electronically in your import. (Writers frequently include the day/night title as part of the scene heading rather than as a separate element.) The only categories accepted by Movie Magic are Day, Night, Morning, and Evening. If a scene heading says "evening," "dusk," or "morning," always check with the director and DP (hopefully at the same time) what time of day that scene should ideally be shot. It's not always possible, but you can try to accommodate their requirements. At the very least, you need to determine how each defines "evening," as for some people this means late afternoon or dusk, while for others, it's night, and it can cause serious problems if you assume. If the director or DP wants it to be dusk or magic hour, while this can't be reflected within the Day/Night element on the breakdown sheet, what I recommend is adding it in the Sequence element, where you can create your own elements (as with the cast, just type in your title followed by a semicolon), or under Notes.

Pages

The page count should have come through in the import. The script supervisor will do their own count and this will be the official standard, but meanwhile you need accurate estimates. Script pages are divided into eighths and described as such: 1/8, 1 2/8, 3 6/8, etc. Most lower-budget movies will need to shoot about four pages a day (sometimes up to about seven depending on the material), TV movies shoot five to six, and TV series six to seven. A 1/8 page scene might entail the famous "the cavalry comes over the hill," or 5 pages might be two people sitting in a room. There are no hard and fast rules, but if you have a day that's less than three pages or more than 8 you will need to really examine if it's using the time properly. Once the script supervisor provides the final tallies, you (or someone on your team) will need to ensure that all the schedule page counts conform to his/her breakdown.

Synopsis

Here's where a certain sensitivity and intelligence can prevail. Essentially, you're trying to communicate the action in the scene: Harry punches Tom, or Mary tells Bill she's pregnant. (An aside on story—you can tell the film is going to struggle if you are having a hard time synopsizing the scenes!) They need to be brief and evocative, the way someone would describe the scene in shorthand—"the waterfall sequence" or "Maddie gets dressed." What we don't need to know is the emotional content or the story point: it's all about Action, and needs to be short enough to fit comfortably on the strip (you'll see very quickly the synopses that are too long when you look at your stripboard). The best way to do this, I find, is to read the scene through and then imagine a one-line synopsis, rather than describing it beat by beat.

Script Page

In standard drama I have never seen this element used or necessary, and in any case it will import if you have taken the script from Final Draft.

Script Day

Script Day, or Story Day, is a vital tool for continuity and will be reflected everywhere from the break-down sheet right through to the daily call sheet—but don't try this at home. This is definitely a category that you'll leave blank until the script supervisor starts, as it is an art in itself distinguishing how each day should be labeled. You also don't want to have to be keeping up with script changes on this element. So on your list of questions for various crew, under script supervisor you will now have "Page Lengths" and "Script Day."

Unit

This only applies once you get into second unit, beauty unit and such like, and these usually occur later into the shoot. If you know that there is an aerial unit doing landscape shots, by all means add it in, but until there's a good reason it can be left blank.

Sequence

Some scripts work across various time periods or locations (*The Hours* or *Traffic*), or may have scenes that are categorized as "fantasy," "flashback," "dream," and so forth. To reflect this, I would either add a category for each under "sequence," or be sure that it's included in the set description of each scene, so that people can tell with a glance at the strips which zone the scene takes place in. (Not only will there be slightly different elements required for each sequence, but you will also be able to see at a glance whether you're chopping and changing between them unnecessarily, thereby requiring costume or hair/makeup changes, for example.) I prefer the Sequence function, as it can be seen at a glance on a Strip (as long as you later add that box to your Strip Design, see Figure 2.15) and later you'll be able to group them together more easily.

This is also often a category that comes into play if there is second unit or a reshoot scenario. A typical example would be a separate, stand-alone "second" unit (meaning with its own director, DP, and first AD, and various other crew drawn from the main unit or elsewhere) that is responsible for delivering a number of scenes that constitute a sequence. In a case like this, it's worth identifying on the breakdown sheet that that particular scene is part of this sequence. However, you will rarely have this information on your first pass.

Location

Where you know it, enter it. Not the exact address, however, but the neighborhood or street name, or if it's in a studio, which stage. These locations may change as you go on, but whatever information you have to hand is critical and should be reflected, however vague it may be at this point, in this category.

Est Time

Even on TV shows I have never had to enter this information on a schedule, as the script supervisor is responsible for it and usually has their own way of communicating this information. The script supervisor and POC will work out their own method for the production reports.

Comments

As broad as it sounds! This may be where you choose to reflect that it's to be shot at dusk, or there's a specific wrap time, or children or animals involved. However, most of these elements can be reflected in the other categories on the sheet, or in the Notes section, so it's really a matter of personal taste rather than necessity. I don't use it as a rule but other Firsts might.

To recap, for most of the above categories you can create your own content by either selecting a choice from the drop-down menu, or typing in your information followed by a semicolon (;). The beauty of all of these categories is that they can be reflected on the strips and the breakdown sheets. The advantages of this will be seen more clearly later.

Elements

We now move into the Elements, and this is where prioritizing really comes into play. Unless you're shooting a film that's set in the jungle and filmed in a studio, or one of the lead characters is a florist, you will rarely use the category "greenery"—but there will always be that first time! A number of categories are absolutely crucial to the schedule (and, hence, the budget), and others are rarely used but handy, just in case. The critical elements for the first pass of the breakdown are Cast, Background Actors (or Extras), Vehicles, Special Effects, Special Equipment, and Additional Labor. If you're really under pressure, a schedule with just these elements will allow the PM to get a pretty realistic shape on the budget. As we go through one by one, I'll identify the ones that can wait until the next pass, and those you will use rarely, if at all. This approach is useful if you are in a rush—and you almost inevitably will be! So I'll go through them in breakdown sheet order.

All of these elements are discussed in more detail in later chapters; for now I'm just outlining their aspects in relation to the sheets and the first pass of the schedule. In the following categories you can "add a new element" by simply clicking on the element heading, or select an existing one from the drop-down list.

Cast

The important thing at this stage of the process is to ensure that the breakdown sheet is absolutely, 100% accurate when it comes to cast in a scene. The single biggest mistake a First can make is not to have the correct cast on set, and this can happen easily enough to give an AD cold sweats at night. Electronic is beautiful, except when it goes wrong.

The first place that cast can get dropped from the scene is in the importing process—if a character doesn't speak, they won't be listed as present in the scene. So a big part of the first meeting with the director (after the first draft schedule is done, but before it is distributed) is to double-check that you have the right cast in the scenes. This sounds obvious, but better to be pedantic than caught out. Especially in an ensemble drama, it may be implicit or assumed that a certain character "would be" in a particular scene. It is not good to find this out on the shoot. Besides the effect on the story, cast are booked and paid for the number of days worked, and if they weren't originally scheduled to work it won't be budgeted for, or the actor may not be available. (On a job I joined last-minute as a troubleshooter, working from someone else's schedule, we pulled two actors from their beds at 5AM to rush them a two-hour car drive to our location. I had an anxious wait, with 100 extras in period costumes and a contingent of the nation's army ready to shoot with these actors. Never again!)

The other issue to watch out for here is repetition: the writer may have made a typo so that MOTHER and MOTHRE are reflected as two different characters. If you are importing, MOTHER (O.S.) or MOTHER (V.O.) or MOTHER (CONT.) will be misunderstood as separate characters (instead of off-screen, voice-over or continued, meaning simply that the character speaks twice in a row). Try to weed out as many of these mistakes as you can before you begin by searching for the element in the schedule ("Edit," "Find," then add the element, the character name), then referring to the script to check whether the character is entirely O.S. or, perhaps, whether they walk into the room and need to be included in the scene. Once you have checked all the scenes, you can delete the mislabeled element entirely (back into "Element Manager," tick the box beside the character name and click on the red "Ø" symbol in the toolbar).

Another point to be aware of is when you have several actors playing the same character, as will happen if the character ages, let's say, from 6 to 60. You might designate these characters as JOE (AGE 6), JOE, and JOE (AGE 60), leaving out the age designation in the character name for the one who claims the majority of screen time (in this example, most of Joe's story happens when he's 30, say). It's an important fact to double-check with the director or producer if there is any ambiguity about when the transition from one actor to another occurs. You'd be amazed at the number of professional scripts that have characters aged across their childhoods at ages 5, 7, 10, 12, 16, 18, etc. Unless the producers are going to cast different actors who resemble each other perfectly for each age, what happens is that they're amalgamated into a child, a teen, and very occasionally a young adult (or even the star pretending that they can still play 22…!).

When you get confirmation from the director, write it onto the scene in your script (not just on a note to yourself) and also inform the coordinator, as s/he needs to add them to the next set of script pages. Wardrobe, makeup, hair and props, at the very least, need to know when this character appears and be prepared for it.

Check, and check again, that you have all the cast required on the sheet. And even when you're absolutely certain, beware! If you click on the Cast Members element heading, and then click a little lower on any name, it will add or remove that character from the sheet and is easy to do accidentally. Before I issue any schedule, I insist that some poor person—either the second AD, if they have started, or the production trainee, if there is one—go scene-by-scene through the script to make sure that the cast and the schedule correspond. This is one of your central responsibilities as a First, and there are very few other people you can blame if you get it wrong.

Background Actors

This is a polite word for extras. In your first pass at the schedule you should check with the PM whether they want you to add guestimates of figures in this category. You may not know the size of the bar-room set, but it's safe to imagine that you will need 10 people there, unless the script indicates full or empty. I would describe this as "10 × bar-room crowd." In another scene, I might say "10 × hospital crowd"— the main thing is that if you put the figure first, you can generate calculations and totals more easily down the road. Even if there is a "man in a hat," I would call him "1 × man in hat" to keep the figures in a neat, easy-to-read column. Extras are expensive and add up quickly, so a good first AD gets the most mileage possible out of them and understands how the different lenses can affect the impression of crowding.

Special extras are those extras who are expected to do more than simply reflect light; sometimes, they might even have a line or two. In the USA, there is a strict limit as to how many words they can speak, and no extras may be spoken to directly by the director without being entitled to a supplementary fee. In any case, they should be added to the sheet with as descriptive a character name as possible: LAUGHING MAN, for example, in capitals, to denote that they have a status separate from the crowd. Beware of writers who like to call people "cackling hag" or "fat man"—I usually ask the coordinator to get permission to change these to less offensive terms that still refer to the same person. I have heard ADs telling people on the phone "you're playing the CACKLING HAG" and it's not a great diplomatic maneuver, besides unnecessarily hurting people's feelings!

Stunts

Basically, anything that involves someone moving any quicker than a walk is a stunt. This may sound prissy, but this is your job. Certainly, at this early stage when everything is still possible, it's really important to point out to all concerned whenever a run, jump, fall, fight and so forth are occurring in the script. Sometimes people simply don't realize the scale of physical activity until it's demonstrated to them in the breakdown; either way, stunts are expensive and time-consuming and the earlier discussions begin about how they are to be managed and filmed the better. (For more discussion about stunts, see the sections on stunts later in this chapter and in Chapter 3.)

The stunt category is simply a description of the specific action (Tom punches Harry); but any time you add a stunt to the sheet you must also add a stunt coordinator in the Additional Labor category. (Some PMs prefer that they go into the Cast category as they get paid like cast members, just check with them first.) You also need to ascertain from the director whether stunt doubles are required for the actors, or whether picture doubles (that is, non-stunt performers who are just lookalikes) can do the job. There's a big price difference, so it does matter. And, of course, you will need to add a number of Stunt Performers, who will also go into the Cast category as either their picture name or your own description (Arthur Stunt Double or Punched Man in Bar, for example).

Vehicles

This is another critical area that the PM will want information on ASAP. The obvious vehicles are the cars where characters have conversations (even if that's a donkey cart) as they are specified in the script. Every locality has its own lingo for what you call a vehicle that appears on screen (picture car, action vehicle, etc.), likewise the rig or truck that tows it (insert car, process car, low-loader, tow-rig, etc.). It doesn't matter what you call it as long as you establish at the start clearly which term you're using for each element, and stick to it.

Depending on your budget, each of these vehicles may require a low-loader or camera mount (add that to Special Equipment) with a driver (add that to Additional Labor), possibly a police escort (add to Additional Labor and check with locations) and possibly a mini-generator for lighting (check with the DP and then add to Special Equipment). There may also be an additional grip or electrician called in on the day to pre-rig. If you're doing a street scene, there's every chance that the art department will want to add other vehicles, either parked or also driving, and you will most likely require a follow vehicle, usually a van, to transport all of the support crew who can't get on the tow rig. You see how much gear and personnel are involved, and we haven't even pulled out yet! This is why the PM wants to figure out as early as possible what the vehicle requirement is, and you will often have to think about combining scenes that contain vehicles into particular days (although even this can create more complications as you can only pre-rig and shoot on one low-loader at a time). On lower-budget shows, and those shooting with smaller cameras, many of the car interiors will be shot from within the car, which has its own considerations.

The more clarity you can assign to whether the camera is inside or outside the car, the better. Often, it may be possible to amend the script so it reflects what's actually happening. You may have a scene that is headed "EXT. STREET – NIGHT," yet all of the action takes place inside the car, in which case it becomes "INT. CAR - NIGHT." The more specific the director and the script can be at this early stage the better.

You'll also eventually need to think about who is driving other vehicles if the art department is going to provide dressing cars, and those drivers will need to be included in the extras count, as well as put through wardrobe, makeup and hair (especially if it's a period film). The figures for all of these things will be constantly changing, as the PM tries to lower costs and the director wants to increase production value. These elements can change until literally the night before, so as always, the practice of the First is to embrace change, while making sure everyone else hears about it.

Props

This element can be minimalist at this stage of the game. If people are screaming for a schedule, only include the props that are important story beats or emphatically referred to in the script. Everything else can be added in your next pass. The art department will have their own breakdown, and as the script gets more defined you can add these elements—or even, if need be, have someone in your department add them if you're too busy. The rule of thumb is if an actor carries it, it's a prop, and if they wear it, it's wardrobe. The issue of something like a wooden leg should be claimed (and is often avoided) by both. A prop like this should be in the first pass. Also, you should take note of which props should be backed up by a duplicate or "repeat" in case of damage. If it's a critical prop, you will need to have more than one available.

Camera

You probably don't need to worry about this yet—additional or unusual camera elements will be covered under additional equipment, and unless a scene takes place underwater you probably won't have that information this far from the shoot.

Special Effects

Nowadays, almost everything that involves special effects also involves visual effects, and it's the First's job to ascertain who is doing what. Sometimes, despite all your determination, you end up on the set with a disgruntled prop man expected to achieve the effect, but you really want to work it out in advance. Based on the script, anything that involves an action prop could be considered a special effect, from champagne spilling out of a bottle to a building exploding. If an actor needs to "fly," a car flip over or even a rubber blade be retractable, these are all special effects. For the time being, put anything that could remotely be construed as an effect in this category. This is another area that the PM will be looking at closely, so they need to know the worst-case scenario early. You also need to talk all of these through with the director, as his/her idea of what s/he wants may be very different from what's on the page. If this is the case, you need to discuss it with the producer before informing the POC, as these changes relate to content rather than format. Special effects are costly and time-consuming, and if it is agreed that it's a special effect, you'll need to add the number of technicians required to the breakdown under Additional Labor. As with stunts, the Special Effects category is a description of the action required. There will most likely be Additional Equipment and depending on the level of risk you might also have a medic (Additional Labor) and an ambulance (Special Equipment) standing by.

Wardrobe

Only costume issues referred to in the script need to be noted now; for example, if something happens to the costume during the scene, such as getting ripped, stained, burned, etc., you will need to liaise with wardrobe about how many "repeats" you will have of the costume, usually somewhere between three to six. You should then make sure that the director and DP are aware of this as early as possible, as three to six repeats may be fine for one angle, but they may need another and this discussion needs to happen well before shooting. It's sometimes the case that the garment, even after it has been damaged, can be repeated, but that's a bonus rather than something you should plan on. If you catch these things early enough, costume won't establish the actor in a costume that can't be repeated, but without mentioning it clearly you can't assume that they won't, accidentally or otherwise.

Makeup/Hair

Again, this only needs to be added if there is something unique or special mentioned in the script, and can be added on the second pass of the schedule, as makeup and hair people probably won't start work for another few weeks anyway. If you're doing a fantasy film where half of the cast are in prosthetics, then even this might not make it onto the sheet, as it becomes almost standard. This category is really for one-offs: blood, sweat, tears, beards, wigs, etc.

Animals

These should be reflected early as they are significant cost and time elements, and always have to come with an Animal Wrangler. No matter how small or manageable the creature might be, it needs a dedicated handler. Even if the dog belongs to the director, it needs to be decided beforehand who will bring it to set, mind it and return it home. Particularly if it's the director's dog, you don't want it sitting in a hot car for 12 hours with no one dedicated to watering and feeding it. No matter how much the director loves the dog, s/he will have other urgent issues on their mind, and that goes for any member of the shooting crew. It might not need to be a highly trained technician, as it would have to be for a wild animal (I'll never forget the day on a set in California when the coyote wrangler showed up missing three fingers—not very reassuring), and rats, flies, cats, and so forth all need handlers who can deliver the required action and should have demonstrated their ability to do so at a test during the prep period. The easiest non-exotic animals to work with are dogs and horses; cats and birds are the most difficult.

Music

This element would only feature on a breakdown sheet if the actors or action related to a particular track, which would require playback equipment. If so, this gear would also be listed under Special Equipment and Sound. In a case like this, you should also make sure to have a conversation with the coordinator, to check that s/he has secured permission to use the track (source and copyright clear); the director, to ascertain whether a choreographer or musicians are required (and if so, the coordinator will need to be informed, as well as these people being added to the Additional Labor category); and the sound recordist, to ensure that s/he is either bringing the gear or production are providing it. The coordinator will also need to liaise with whomever is providing playback equipment to ensure that the format of the music is correct for the type of equipment being provided, and that it will synch correctly with the images, which requires a call to the post-production house or sound editor. This may not sound like a First's business, but if you're standing on the set while the sound mixer is saying s/he can't play the track because it's the wrong format, it becomes your problem. This type of issue will require a lot of follow-up, so it should stay on your list until the mixer has assured you that s/he can play the music correctly and that the post-production supervisor (or their equivalent) has signed off on it. This will probably be in the last week of prep.

The other scenario is when live musicians are going to play; typically, you will record their music separately either before or after the scene, and use a little of that recording as playback to give the actors the tempo and volume level before the dialogue starts (you never record dialogue over music, unless you don't plan to edit it). This is a technical sound issue and can swallow up time, so needs to be prepared for. Ideally, the track will be recorded elsewhere, and only played back and lip- or music-synched on the shoot. You might, alternatively, include this information in the Sound category.

Sound

Probably not something to worry about on the first pass, but if there's a specific requirement you'll need to follow it through, as described above, to ensure that it doesn't hold you up on the shoot. Sound effects referred to in the script are almost never provided on the set, although if the actors are supposed to react to the sound of an explosion or machine-gun fire it's helpful to them to provide a drum or some other prop that can stand in as a motivation. It needs to be something that doesn't resonate, as if it does it will potentially bleed into the dialogue, evoking complaints from the sound mixer. Most sound heard on the finished film—a radio playing, music, etc.—is laid down in post and is never recorded married to the dialogue.

Art Department and Set Dressing

I have rarely, if ever, added much information to these categories and again, unless there is something specific called for in the script it would certainly not be in my first breakdown. Most objects relating to art department would fall into the props category—set dressing is stuff like furniture, wallpaper, etc., that you would expect to find when you walk onto a "dressed" set, and that you wouldn't expect to move on camera. In the normal course of events, the First and the set dresser rarely meet, especially during the shoot. The art director will supervise the dressing crew, and will come to you if there is a problem with the schedule from their point of view.

Greenery

This refers to any plants or trees that aren't already on the original location—rarely something for the first pass.

Security

This will be covered by the locations department, and the planning and paperwork for this is usually handled directly between the locations department and the PM. There will be situations where you might request it yourself—particular neighborhoods or extensive lock-offs—but as these are location-dependent they probably won't be on your first pass.

Additional Labor

This is one of the biggies in terms of cost, so you want to be sure that, if anything, you have over-estimated rather than under-estimated what's required. On your first pass you might have only the generic requirements referred to in the sections on Vehicles or Animals; this category will be changing constantly, and it's very important that you keep up to date with it. Ultimately you'll be responsible for these people being on the call sheet and the set, so you need to continuously liaise with the various departments to make sure that they're booked and informed as to what their roles may be. Anyone working who isn't on your daily shooting crew needs to be reflected here on the schedule, as the accounts department doesn't like surprises.

Anytime there is a stunt or special effect, I add a medic under Additional Labor, so that it comes up for discussion during prep. Likewise, if there is any water work, I add a boatman and safety divers; with special effects, potentially an ambulance. I would add the largest number of people or things you think could possibly be needed. This is the first pass, not the final shooting schedule, and it's a great way to get the conversation started about what might be necessary on the day.

Visual Effects

More and more shots are becoming visual effects shots, even if it may not appear that way from the script. This is an important part of your conversations with the director as it has a massive impact on the amount of time a scene may take, in some cases saving you hours (as you don't have to wait for sunset), and in others, costing you hours (as you wait for a giant bluescreen to be positioned or lit). It's very important that you understand the purpose of the VFX shot and how it works, and it's also important that the VFX supervisor, or whoever is going to be making the shot work in post, is present on the set to approve whatever is being done. If I know of a visual effects shot, I will automatically add this person to the Additional Labor category so that the conversations in relation to this can begin early. Some PMs may also want you to add VFX to the Sequence category, so that it will be obvious on the schedule how many VFX shots or scenes are in the script and schedule.

Mechanical Effects

These elements would generally be covered in either Art Department or Special Effects. If something in the script fits into this category, make sure it's in the first pass of the breakdown as it will need to be figured out and tested as early as possible.

Notes

This is one of the most useful elements in the whole sheet. Everything tricky, unusual, or just plain interesting can be flagged here, from "Sound Playback Equipment" (just to remind everybody) or "must be shot at magic hour" to "location closes at 4 p.m." Often, things like "20× wetsuits required" or "Camera platform in tree" would go in here, as there isn't a category for Production but there are elements they need to manage. It's an important record and way of disseminating bits of information that could otherwise get lost in the shuffle or simply forgotten. These will probably be amended the closer you get to production, so in the first pass of the breakdown you might have very few; after the tech recce, the category may be packed. Either way, make them as clear as possible in the sheet, but don't forget to also discuss them personally with the person responsible.

Red Flags

This is a relatively new function in Movie Magic that allows you to create reminders that appear on the Stripboard when your elements have conflicts. This can be a godsend if you have 30 cast, and 10 of them have availability issues. Theoretically, this will help to avoid potential scheduling disasters, although you shouldn't need to be relying on this to save you!

Add Images

You can attach images—such as Storyboards, location photos, or actor headshots—to your breakdown sheets, which is useful for stunt sequences, after a tech scout to remind everyone which way you're looking, or on commercials, when the frame on set needs to match the approved storyboard.

Finally

Once your breakdown sheets are complete (see Figure 2.7 for an example). The first thing to do is to save this version of the schedule board as the Script or Story Order (click on "Schedule," then "Stripboard," then "Board"—see Figure 2.8, where I used a fake TV show as an example, to demonstrate episodic TV scene numbering. This schedule starts on a Sunday, as the location was only available then.

To recap, there are certain elements that have a big effect on the budget and at which the producer/PM will be looking right away; these are the elements that I'm sure to include on the first pass: Cast, Extras, Vehicles, Special Effects, Visual Effects, Special Equipment, Stunts, Animals, and Additional Labor. The rest of the elements are generally less important and costly, or may change, so I would leave these to the second pass. Depending on time (mine), money (whether I have help), and the practices of the other departments (art department and wardrobe may not depend on your breakdown), some may never be filled in. This will really depend on the specific nature of the production.

I always print out the strips in story order as a handy reference, and offer PDF and hard copies to production and the other departments, which they often appreciate. Then I save it (within the "Stripboard Manager," not as a separate file) again as "Schedule 1" with the current date. Every time I make a change and print it out I create a new version, with the date, and if I'm issuing more than one in a day (hopefully not!) then I add the time as well.

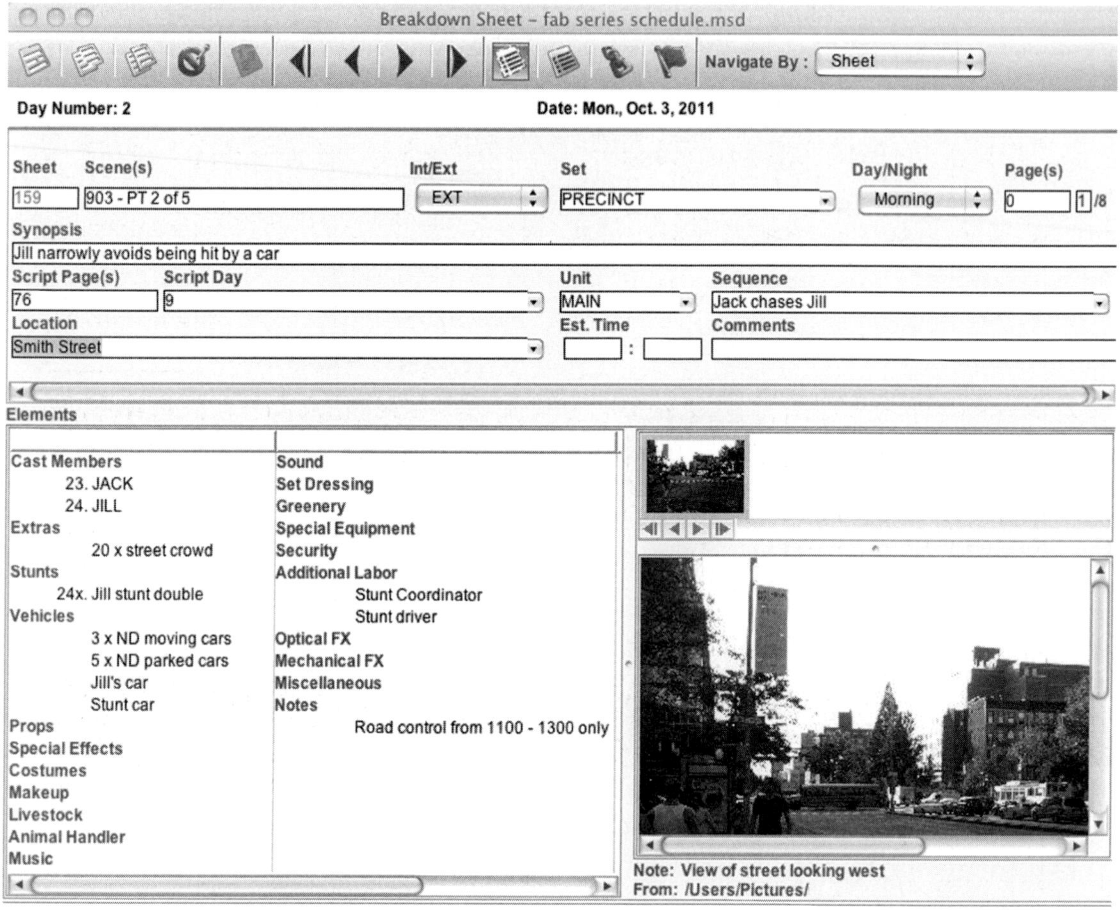

Figure 2.7 *A completed breakdown sheet*

After I have compiled all this information into the breakdown sheets (which could take 2 or 3 days to a week, depending on how many scenes there are in the script and how elaborate they are), I add the information to the Production Calendar (within the schedule, as opposed to the one the POC manages). This calendar reflects the shooting schedule—the start date, days off, etc. To open it, click "Schedule," "Calendar Manager," then double-click on "Default Calendar" to reveal and edit the blank Calendar. I would call this by the name of the show, and when I need to do variations, I title each with the reason for the variation ("Fab Series, version starting April 5th," for example). No one will see what you call it; it only exists to reflect within the schedule what your start date and rest days will be. You just type in the Prod Start date and click on all of the rest days and away you go.

I then enter the Production Information, so that when I print out any schedules the title of the show will appear. Under "Design," click "Production Info," and enter the title of the project (I've never needed to fill

FAB SERIES DEMO - EP 1 STRIPS IN SCRIPT ORDER						
101 Ocean	INT	LIFE BAR Opening sequence	Day	2 4/8	pgs.	1, 2, 3, 4, 5,
102	EXT	UNIVERSITY Students criss-cross like fishies	Day	1/8	pgs.	
103	INT	UNIVERSITY CLASSROOM Tom flirts with Isolde	Day	1 2/8	pgs.	1, 8
104	EXT	UNIVERSITY Clara sees Tom and Isolde	Day	6/8	pgs.	1, 4, 8, 13
105	EXT	TOM'S HOUSE Tom finds Clara on his steps	Evening	3/8	pgs.	1, 4
106	EXT	DAIL BUILDINGS Clara meets Angie	Evening	1	pgs.	2, 4
107	INT	ANGIE'S HOUSE Angie feeds her fishies	Evening	4/8	pgs.	2
108	INT	UNIVERSITY Tom and Larry discuss Renee	Night	1 1/8	pgs.	1, 7, 10
109	INT	CLARA'S BEDSIT Clara rings Angie	Night	2/8	pgs.	4
110	INT	ANGIE'S HOUSE Angie and Red get Clara's call	Night	2/8	pgs.	2, 3
111	EXT	MISS JULIE'S BAR Clara enters the bar	Evening	2/8	pgs.	4
115	INT	MISS JULIE'S BAR Clara meets Angie	Evening	2/8	pgs.	2, 4
117	INT	MISS JULIE'S BAR Angie asks Clara about her past	Night		pgs.	2, 4
118	INT	NIGHTCLUB Tom feels ancient	Night	2/8	pgs.	1, 8
119	INT	ANGIE'S BEDROOM Angie and Clara make love	Night	1/8	pgs.	2, 4
120	INT	TOM'S KITCHEN Tom is in love with Isolde	Morning	1 4/8	pgs.	1, 8
121	EXT	ANGIE'S HOUSE Angie and Clara kiss	Morning	2/8	pgs.	2, 4
122	INT	RED'S FLAT Red finds a toothbrush	Morning	1/8	pgs.	3
123	INT	VAN Angie thinks of Clara	Day	1/8	pgs.	2
124	INT	RED'S FLAT Red places the toothbrush in an envelope	Morning	1/8	pgs.	3
125	INT	DIVINE HOUSE Angie's interview is distracted	Day	1	pgs.	2, 14
126	EXT	MERRION SQUARE Red runs up the steps	Morning	1/8	pgs.	3
127	INT	MERRION SQUARE OFFICE Red passes the receptionist	Day	3/8	pgs.	3
128	EXT	MERRION SQUARE Red's bike is locked	Morning	2/8	pgs.	3
129 Ocean	INT	LIFE BAR David calls Red	Day	2/8	pgs.	5
130	EXT	MERRION SQUARE David frees Red's bike	Night	5/8	pgs.	3, 5

Figure 2.8 *An example of the strips in Script Order, with the scenes numbered as in an episodic TV show*

in any of the other categories, but you can if you wish). That's the first breakdown pretty much complete. By now, I'll have a long list beside me of questions for everyone on the crew, particularly the director.

Meeting the Director

Let's imagine that on Monday morning you started work; hopefully, by Wednesday afternoon you have your first proper meeting with the director. You need to get at least 45 minutes of his/her time, which will be hard to do. It's best to go via the POC (who controls the production calendar) to schedule a time between casting, script meetings, location scouts, etc. This is important, because the schedule is at a standstill until this happens, and if the producer understands this they will help make it happen, if need be.

I'm a First who likes to understand the director's desires before I start trying to talk them into something faster or cheaper. I see this first director meeting as a fact-finding mission, where I can collate their ideal scenario for every situation. Once I have all this information, I know how to inform the producer if there is something I feel is simply beyond us, or needs more conversation. But part of this meeting is to build collaboration and trust, and if you're always seeing everything simply from your own perspective the director won't believe that you have the interests of the bigger picture at heart (and s/he's probably right!). It's important to understand the director's vision, as you will spend most of your time interpreting and communicating it to everyone else, so no matter what alarm bells are ringing in your head, be supportive, curious and encouraging; this is your new best friend for the next few weeks or months, so you want to start off on the same team.

Unless the director has nothing to do that evening, this is a very time-pressurized chat. You really need to get through your list, but you also need to let them feel comfortable working with you. Bear in mind that some directors see Firsts as killjoys, who want to force them into commitments they don't want to have to make; these directors also sometimes bring their personal attitudes to authority (and potentially their parents) into the mix. Other directors understand your role, and will give you very direct answers as they don't have a lot of time and they need to get the information out quickly. You will know very early on what kind of director you're dealing with, and your approach will have to accommodate that reality.

Let's assume here that you're dealing with a mature adult who wants to make decisions and give you answers. There are a few areas that you need to cover above all else: cast, extras, stunts, vehicles, special equipment, and special and visual effects. I'm not saying you get every last detail about each subject—that could take hours. But you need enough to put a shape on the schedule, and you need to get it really fast. The best way to do this is to be sure your questions are specific and appropriate, and as simple as possible: yes/no is ideal. You don't need to understand the characters' motivations or the story arc—not at this meeting (if you want to discuss that over dinner, great). You need as many facts as you can get in a short time.

What I usually do is go through the questions in script order. This is easier for the director to imagine, and your questions are probably in chronological order as you have broken down the script that way. This is the last time you'll be able to enjoy that continuity, so make the most of it! It's not quite a "page turn" unless you literally have questions about every scene, which would be a little worrying. At this stage, identifying the nomenclature of the special extras (remember "cackling hag"?), the special extras' responsibilities (and whether the role requires a day player, that is, a proper actor, or whether an extra really can do it), and the ballpark figures you're adding for crowd should all form part of this initial meeting with the director.

It's true that in the early days of prep many locations won't be decided upon, and so it's impossible to say with certainty how many extras will be required. However, if you know it's a busy street scene and lasts 30 seconds, you'll probably need 40 people. If it's an almost-empty bar, that will be different from a dance hall and you can hazard a guess that you'll have 5 in the bar and 50 in the dance hall. I find it more productive to have ballpark figures in mind for each scene, which you can then run past the director, rather than asking them to come up with a figure for every scene. Extras cost a lot and production and accounts will be asking you for the numbers.

Some directors will want to double all of the extras numbers, either because they're inexperienced (and think more is always better) or because they're very experienced, and know that the producers will eventually cut the extras numbers way back and they want to start from somewhere high enough to cut. An experienced director might ask for at least a third more than s/he actually believes s/he will need. Even if the numbers s/he is saying seem wildly exaggerated, it's not your job to argue the toss, unless you're expressly asked your opinion. Your role is to (in this case) keep your mouth shut, record all the figures the director tells you, and then add them up. Later on, you will go through the draft schedule and see which extras can be "recycled"— that is, re-dressed from one scene to the next, see whether there are any adjustments you can make to minimize extras' figures (such as consolidating these scenes on the same day), and then report to the PM what the figures are. (There is an "extras report" section in the Movie Magic scheduling program, but it cannot, of course, take into account your recycling process, so it generates terrifying and untrue figures.)

After the PM has climbed down from the ceiling, s/he will either talk to the producer, or at the next opportune moment talk to the director. Often, they will tell you to tell the director that you're way over budget on extras, but this isn't, strictly speaking, your job. The PM will need to determine exactly how far over the extras budget you are, and by how much the numbers need to reduce. This over-and-back will continue through prep right up to the shoot, as locations are locked down and the director and producer struggle to balance production value and the bottom line.

You will need to get a sense of how the director plans to cover any scenes in cars, trains, planes, etc., and any other special or visual effects and stunts: literally scene by scene. You will want to record everything the director says, probably by hand on your notebook in such a way that you can later transfer all the information to the schedule, and to refer to later in case you can't remember how a decision came about. This is your record of events and you may need it later.

You also need to understand from the director what the shooting style of the show is (Lots of coverage? Long lenses? Many takes?), particularly in relation to coverage. If you are shooting TV, in a two-person scene (or "two-hander") you can generally assume that you will be getting a wide shot (often the master), a closer two-shot, and some angle (be it over-the-shoulder or clean) on each actor, so typically a minimum of three to four shots. On a feature, the director may have a plan to cover everything in one roaming tracking shot, which at first glance sounds quicker but in fact is generally at least as time-consuming, as every tiny detail has to work in one take and can result in a very high number of takes (as well as leaving the editor very few options). The director doesn't have to know how they plan to cover each scene, but if you can get a sense early on of any scenes that require long tracks, cranes, numerous setups or other creative choices, you can try to budget your time for these scenes accordingly.

You can glean this information in two ways: by asking the question straight out, and by listening closely whenever s/he talks about a scene. If you have a scene that continues from interior to exterior, or vice versa, you need to understand whether they intend to play that as continuous, or if you can cut between the two.

Finally, you need to loosely agree on what tests will need to be done, and which tests filmed, before shooting; whether and how s/he wants to rehearse; and I like to end the meeting by asking about what it is they like and don't like about Firsts, or what they most want from you. If they're not a first-timer they will have worked with various Firsts before and often have strong opinions. Besides doing the job well, some directors don't like "screamers," others don't like Firsts who are too laid-back, and so on. You also want to get as much information as possible about the cast and the director's relationship with them—have they worked together before and is there anything that might be useful for you to know? If they can't tell you anything, so be it, but sometimes a small detail can allow you to advise your team much more effectively. What's not interesting here, however, is your opinion—you want to glean information, not share it, and generally it's a good idea to keep your own counsel at all times except where you really need to speak out.

As you talk these things through, you will very quickly get a good idea of what the director is going to be like on the set. Some directors avoid making any decisions, saying that they'll decide later. This is a bad sign. My least favorite expression in the English language is "we'll suck it and see." This quickly translates into "it'll suck." The most important thing you need from any director in prep is decisions. As they say, any decision is better than no decision, and a decision can always be changed or amended, but without one nothing can happen. If a director is resisting making decisions, you will need to evaluate how this relates to their level of experience, and if it starts to delay your ability to do your job, you'll need to have a chat about it with the producer. On a big-budget project, directors often have the latitude to simply ask for all the elements to be provided and make their decisions on the day. This is expensive, and simply isn't an option on lower-budget projects or TV.

This meeting may be your only chance to sit down one-to-one with the director before the real whirlwind begins, and it allows them to tease things out or think things through without an audience, so it's important to make the most of this time together. You want to, as always, be encouraging, supportive and informative, as well as offering them ideas in the form of questions. I really don't care whose idea it was, as long as it makes the most sense, and directors, who are often insecure, appreciate being able to appear in control and still get the benefit of your experience and imagination. Depending on your relationship with the producer, and their relationship with the director, after this meeting is a good time to have your first chat with the producer about the results of your meeting. The bottom line is that you want to make friends and get information, and should be able to do both. It's also no harm to be enthusiastic about the script and the project: it can make a big difference to a director's fears and anxieties to know that there's someone who also believes in the project. Directing is a very lonely job, and sometimes an ally can make all the difference.

Here is a checklist of things you need from the director in prep:

- Relations with the cast
- Extras numbers
- Special extras castings and approvals
- Approach to vehicles, stunts, and special or visual effects

- Shooting style—e.g., long tracking shots, multiple setups for coverage, cranes, dollies, static, etc.
- Agreement on elements to be tested, on camera and in person
- Style of set—quiet or military
- Location, art department and wardrobe choices
- Information on familiarity with DP, cast, producer, script supervisor, etc.
- Dietary, coffee and other preferences
- Previous experience and any pet hates

After this meeting you'll want to input all the information you've collected and share it with the PM, production office, and any other relevant crew members. Do another trawl through the departments—locations, art department and production (and costume if they're around)—and collate any other info they may have for you. And now, you're ready to start the schedule!

THE FIRST SCHEDULE

If one does not know to which port one is sailing, no wind is favorable.
Lucius Annaeus Seneca

Creating a schedule is like doing a jigsaw puzzle in mercury: there are millions of pieces that have to fit together and they're constantly changing. The best approach is to try to look at this as fun. I'm not saying you have to like crossword puzzles or sudoku (I hate them both), but you do have to have the kind of mind that likes teasing order out of chaos. And being a little bit obsessive doesn't hurt! Firsting is never recognized as a creative element, but it takes every bit as much imagination and perseverance as any sculptor put into their marble block. The difference is, nobody ever says "What a beautiful schedule!" but they will certainly point out what's wrong with it. So maybe Firsts are just artists with tougher skins. Whatever you need to believe to keep your sense of humor…!

To be pedantic about it, a schedule is an arrangement of the breakdown sheets into their shooting order, as distinct from their story order. Every director I have ever worked for wants to shoot as much as possible in story order, and I have only seen it happen on one occasion, when the director was the wife of the producer! (And even that changed once we started filming.) Everyone would like to shoot chronologically, and no matter how much time and money you have it's basically impossible. Even if it were possible, it would usually be the most inefficient and expensive way of filming. Shooting out of sequence can take getting used to—I once had a first-time director ask me how we could possibly shoot the scene on the plane before we shot the character buying his ticket—but experience is a great teacher and, like driving a car, it soon becomes automatic.

If you're wondering where to begin, there is a lazy-man's trick that can put a shape on a schedule with a few simple moves—but this is an automated function, and, as no mental effort whatsoever goes into it, it should be treated with the respect it deserves. Movie Magic can group together all of the sets for you. Simply click "Stripboard," then **Actions**, then **Sort**. In the little window that comes up, click on **Add**, and then **Sheet**; scroll down to "Set," the third in the list. Voilà—all of the strips relating to a certain set are grouped together.

You can then, if you are so inclined, again from the Stripboard menu, click Actions, Auto Day Breaks, and in the window that appears choose a "maximum page count per day." The nature of your production will dictate what you need to achieve. You could simply divide the number of pages in the script by the number of shooting days, and round this up as a ballpark figure; 120 pages divided by 20 days means you need to shoot an average of 6 pages a day, for example. Obviously, some 1/8-page scenes take a day, while a 4-page scene might be done in a morning, but it will give you a basis to work from.

I would always double-check, before I show the schedule to anyone, that all of the scenes in the script are reflected on the schedule. It's easy to do this if you have already printed out your script order and you can go scene-by-scene in 10 minutes. No matter how careful you are, the only downside of working electronically is that it is possible to accidentally delete a strip, or misplace it.

From there on in, it's just plain graft; you arrange the strips into the logical order based on the sets, cast and special equipment, trying to keep the exteriors at the start of the schedule and the interiors at the end, if that's possible or logical in your particular circumstances.

Sets, Locations, and Stages

The first element in creating a schedule is the set—the name of the location in the story. Naturally enough, you want to "shoot out" any set, filming every scene that happens there in one block, rather than coming in and out of somewhere repeatedly. (The only time you might do this is when you have a "standing set," that is, one that is accessible and dressed for the entirety of the shoot, and is being used as weather cover, or if it needs to be re-dressed for story reasons.) The set will be either on a location or on a stage.

Locations—anywhere not constructed in studio—will always have some restrictions: a bar might be Monday nights only; in someone's home you may have to be out by 8 p.m., a public library might give you permission for only four hours, and so forth. It's worth entering these restrictions on the schedule in the Notes section or by creating a red flag. You should also enter the name of the location onto the breakdown sheet itself.

Shooting on a stage or studio, where the sets are built by the art department, also poses its own issues. If you're using the same space for two different sets, one will have to be struck and the other built before you can shoot on it. Or a set may need to be aged, painted or otherwise re-dressed for story purposes. The art director will have a good idea of the turnaround time required for the various sets, but will need to get a sense from you as early as possible the order in which the sets will be required. It's possible that the room King Leopold sweeps out of will be only a memory by the time you shoot the hallway he walks into, and they may both stand on the same spot in the studio. Space in studios is always at a premium, no matter how big they are, and you also want to avoid the situation of a set being built or struck in the same stage as the one you're shooting in, due to the noise and other disruptive elements.

Cast Deals

Unless you're making a completely animatronic film with computer-generated voices, your schedule is largely driven by actors' availability and working conditions. (There is the occasional situation where a location is so unique and restricted that the production will cast around the location, but this is extremely rare, such as a military base or a church that permits filming only once a year.)

There are basically three kinds of arrangements you need to factor into the schedule. The first, and most convenient, is the **picture deal** or buyout, in which the actor has signed on for the entire shooting schedule. Producers usually try to get the two leads to sign these kinds of deals, but for various reasons don't always succeed, and so you might end up with **weeklies**—that is, actors contracted to work on a weekly basis. This is relatively straightforward from a scheduling point of view, as it's a broad, immovable stroke that ring-fences certain scenes into a certain time frame.

The third category is **day players**. Just as it sounds, these are characters whose parts may not require a full week's filming. However, in the US, to pay an actor for three days' work costs the same as a weekly rate (based on union minimum wage agreements), so if an actor is required for three days, the producer will hire the actor for the week. This allows the production a little more flexibility, but because the producer always needs to save money, you need to reduce these days or weeks into as few as possible by consolidating any scenes in which a day player appears. While you're doing your breakdown, the producer may be negotiating with the actors' agent, and they don't want to book an actor for three weeks to discover that they're only needed for two. These weeks also then need to be consolidated. We'll talk later about the Day-Out-Of-Days (DOOD) that reflects the actors' workdays and their "drop/hold/pick-up days," but for now you can assume that you want to book the actor in one block, rather than scattered across the schedule.

If the actor is to work on selected days, the casting director will nominate **"on-or-about"** dates. These provide a slight element of flexibility, in that you can adjust the actor's shoot date to fall one day before or after the nominated date, hence the name: the days before and after the day "on" provide the "about." To capitalize on this freedom, you would never nominate a Monday as your on-or-about date, but rather the Tuesday, even if you plan to shoot the scene on the Monday. Nominating the Tuesday gives you the option of the Monday and the Wednesday as possible shoot dates with that actor (assuming you're not shooting on the Sunday). Equally, you would nominate a Thursday rather than a Friday, as this gives you the Wednesday and the Friday to play with (assuming you're not shooting on the Saturday). It doesn't mean that you can work the actor for three days, but that you can pick a working day on either side of the nominated date you want him to work. It's easier in practice than it sounds here! These "on-or-abouts" will only be given at the last possible moment, because once you have committed to these dates they will cost money to change.

The tricky bit for your schedule is when, as often happens, the producers pull a favor or otherwise inveigle a higher-profile actor to do a smaller part—"just a couple of days." That actor has no incentive to work around you, and in fact feels like s/he's doing you a favor, so you can end up in the bizarre situation of scheduling an entire shoot around a character who appears in three scenes.

The UK system is slightly different when it comes to weekly and daily players. If an actor works more than a day in one week, or even only one day but you want flexibility in relation to which day in that week, the producer pays a weekly "engagement" rate, and a token daily "production" rate per days worked within that week. If the date is solid (and if you're at a certain budget level), you can nominate and pay for a date which is less than an engagement rate and a production day rate, but isn't flexible. There is more explanation of the agreement with British Equity on the PACT website (www.pact.org). Most often, it will be the weekly players who dictate how you organize the shoot. In any case, every time someone is cast (or drops out, or is replaced) you have a new set of parameters that will dictate the order of things. At this stage in the game you probably won't have anything on paper from the casting director (via the POC), but it's from him/her that you'll get whatever information there is thus far about the actors' availability. The bottom line for your schedule is that cast dictates the shape of it; if a day player's availability for a single day just isn't working out, the production will, in the worst-case scenario, re-cast. But all other elements generally work around cast availability and working conditions.

Deal memos, or **casting advice notes**, are short-form actors' contracts that should have the fees whited out before you receive them (Figure 2.9). They will specify the actor's terms, including their workdates, pay, credits, availability for post-production ADR and publicity, and the special stipulations. These "stips" often specify whether the actor has exclusive ground transport (that is, whether they have to share a car with another actor) or other, more unique requirements, including availability for rehearsals, personal hair/makeup artists, assistants, air travel entitlements, per diems (if applicable), and even, sometimes, dietary requirements. These will often affect the second AD's day-to-day life more than yours, but you do need to be aware of them. Although these are legally binding documents, they are only a synopsis of what the contract will spell out. You may not have received any of these, depending on how far casting has progressed, but the office will pass them on to you as they are confirmed (which may require amendments to your schedule).

Although the strength of the actors' unions varies from place to place, the guidelines and practices of the Screen Actors Guild (SAG) must be among the most comprehensive in the world. For this reason, it's worth understanding the broad strokes of the SAG rules, and, if necessary, extrapolating from them elsewhere. See Figure 2.10 for some additional points to clarify regarding the cast and extras.

SAG—The Screen Actors Guild

SAG is in many ways the most important union for any production, as even on the lowest-budget projects, where the entire crew may be nonunion, the actors will almost always be SAG members. SAG represents actors, background actors, stunt coordinators and performers, singers, puppeteers, pilots, dancers and even, sometimes, swimmers and skaters, and SAG rules will dictate many of the parameters of your shoot.

SAG divides filmmaking practices into a number of tiers, based on the budget level. For example, films can range from shorts (under $50,000), to ultra low-budget (less than $200K), to modified low-budget (less than $625K), to low-budget (less than $2.5 million). (These figures are accurate at the time of writing; you can check current information online.) There is no low-budget agreement for TV production, which falls under the Basic Agreement, also applicable to features with budgets over $2.5 million. You'll never see the production budget of your show, but you will know at which level you're operating, and your Second will also be sure to conform to the relevant SAG requirements.

The main conditions are adequate facilities (dressing rooms, toilets, etc.), the length of the **shooting day** (no more than six hours from breakfast to lunch and six hours from end of lunch to wrap), **overtime** (150% of the daily rate for the first four hours after twelve worked, 200% after that), whether a sixth consecutive day can be worked (and at what rate), whether and how the drop/pickup rule applies, and turnaround.

CASTING ADVICE NOTE
"FAB SERIES"

Casting Productions, 25 Woods & Trees Avenue, Big City, Some State 00700
www.casting.com

Date:	2nd October, 2011
Artiste:	**Diva Queen**
Character:	**Jill**
Character No:	23
Address:	1 Actors Place, Actorville, CT
Telephone:	555 904 0017
Agent:	**Hard Bargana, Ten Per Cent Management**
Address:	Unit 22, Green Hills, Actorville
Phone:	**555 453 4446**
Email:	Hardb@10percent.com
Production Company:	Fab Series Ltd.
Production Office:	A Street, A Town, Productionville
Phone:	555 353 1601
Fax:	555 353 1601

Principal Photography:	Sunday 2 October to Fri 12 November 2011 inclusive
Dates Artiste is not available:	**15-18 October inclusive**
Period of Engagement:	2 days on/about 12thNov, 04thDec
Remuneration:	$1000 per day
Total Guaranteed Payment:	$2000
Buyout:	**One (1) network transmission, three (3) repeat transmissions (including a repeat within 7 days of broadcast) and Rest of World (all world television including basic cable and theatric, except USA, and all world non-theatric rights) for All Media Worldwide, in perpetuity, now known or unknown and includes payment for all services and all rights.**

Special Stipulations:

Schedule:	**Shooting 5 day week**
Ground transport:	**Non-exclusive to and from set, no more than one other passenger**
Air travel:	**Economy. On a favored nations with other cast.**
Accommodation:	**Best available self-catering accommodation/guest house/hotel**
Per Diems:	**The Company will provide per diems of $40 dollars per day, on a favored nations basis with other cast**
Dressing Room:	**Shared**
ADR:	**At Half Daily Rate less Use Fees.**
Rehearsals:	**$100 per session for 3 sessions.**
Billing:	**Shared 5 th Credit if Front Credits are used.**

Signed: _____   Signed: _____

Manager . On behalf of the **Artiste**   On behalf of the **Producer**

Date: _____   Date: _____

Figure 2.9 *An example of a very basic actor's deal memo*

<u>Cast and Extras</u>

Is the production SAG signatory and if so, under which tier: Theatrical, Low Budget, Modified Low Budget, Ultra Low Budget, Short film, Student film; network TV or basic cable?

If there are to be any minors employed, the governing laws and practices in place (local and federal)

Individual cast deals: length of engagement, availability, rehearsals, sole transport, nominated days, special stipulations, turnaround, stand-ins, body doubles, nudity and dressing rooms

Extras: required SAG figures and nonunion totals

Figure 2.10 *Additional points to clarify regarding performers*

Drop/pickup—or the "consecutive employment" rule—is waived under the low-budget agreement, but in the basic agreement, if you have a day player working days spread across the schedule, you have to pay them for the "hold" days in between, unless there are more than 10 hold days in a row. This obviously has a big effect on your schedule, as you don't want to be paying for any hold days if you can help it. (In the UK system, hold days don't apply, unless the actor is a member of SAG contracted by a US company, working abroad.)

Turnaround is defined as the time between the actor being released on set and expected to report the next morning, specified as 12 hours. Within the designated production zone (for example, seven miles from the production base), the turnaround can be reduced to 10 hours every fourth consecutive day. There is also a 15-minute dispensation for removing makeup and wardrobe (if no assistance is needed), unless on an overnight location. Performers are entitled to a weekly rest period of 56 hours (or 54 if their call time is after 6 a.m. the next day). On a six-day location week, this is reduced to 36 hours. If turnaround is encroached on (that is, "crunched," or broken), known as a "forced call" or rest period violation, the penalties are such that most productions will do their best to avoid it: either a day's pay or $900 for day players, and a day's pay or $950 for weeklies, whichever is less. Even if the production is willing to pay, the actor will have to be asked, and may refuse.

If the actor in the last scene of the day is also required for the first scene the next morning, ADs and PMs start to get twitchy about releasing the actor. This can lead to the unfortunate situation in which one actor may have to deliver all of their lines to a taped "X" on a lamp-stand, because the other actor has been wrapped to preserve their turnaround. If you can't wrap the actor, you will have to "push" the call time for the next day later, which has obvious knock-on effects for all the departments (it's no fun trying to re-schedule 100 extras at 9 p.m.). So while there's still time, both in prep and during the shooting day, the Second will be helping you try to maintain turnaround.

The actors' **timesheets**, known as "Exhibit Gs," are an integral part of this process, and once they are filled in by the Second, the actor must sign off on them so they can be delivered to SAG to prove that the company is conforming with regulations. (See Figure 2.11.) If there is a discrepancy between what is on the call sheet and the Exhibit G, the second AD will need to be able to explain this both to the actor and the PM.

Production Time Report Exhibit G 6 14

Figure 2.11 *The SAG Exhibit "G"—Actors' timesheet*
Reprint of the Production Time Report—Exhibit G, courtesy of Screen Actors Guild. Forms are revised periodically; contact Screen Actors Guild for the most current version of the forms or visit www.sag.org/productioncenter http://www.sag.org/productioncenter.

The term **Taft–Hartley** originates from legislation passed by the US Congress in 1947, but its meaning in relation to film production is when someone is used in a SAG role who is not a member of the union. A typical case would be if the director's mother, for example, is chosen for a part, and the production has to make the case to SAG in prep as to why this person is uniquely qualified, more than a SAG member, to take this job. The conditions SAG recognizes for such a situation are as follows:

> Member of a recognized "name" specialty group
> Important, famous, well-known or unique persons portraying themselves
> Military or other government personnel used due to governmental restrictions
> Special skill or unique physical appearance
> First employment of a person who has training/experience as a professional performer and intends to pursue a career as a motion picture performer
> Child under the age of 18
> Owner or operator of special or unique vehicle or equipment
> Employed as stunt coordinator
> Employed as body double for scenes requiring nudity or sexual conduct
> Background actor adjusted for non-script lines

It can happen that the director, on the set, decides that he wants to give a nonunion extra a line or a part, as per the above "adjustment," with a penalty to be paid by the company. To keep producers honest in relation to such penalties, SAG insists that a security deposit, known as the bond, whose amount is proportional to the number of actors and extras working on the film and at least $10k at the time of writing, be deposited in advance of filming at a bank designated by SAG. After wrap, and all the performers have been paid, SAG will deduct all penalties and fines the union is owed by the production and return the remaining bond, with interest accrued, to the production.

The most important thing to remember when dealing with SAG is to be totally honest and transparent. If SAG suspects that there is anything untoward occurring, they will order the actors not to report for work in a heartbeat, and I have seen a production halted because a producer lied to SAG and was outed, unknowingly, by the second AD who was telling the truth. Not a good situation to have your whole unit in Death Valley, in a hotel, on a work stoppage. No actor will disobey SAG, even if they wanted, and given the flexibility that SAG has in dealing with any and all sizes and shapes of production, they should never need to.

SAG also has the right to visit any set to observe (not to say police) the proceedings, and this is particularly common on low-budget features when children are working, as they may perceive this to be where shortcuts might be taken.

When an actor is out of standing with the union due to overdue payments of contributions and fees, it's known as a Section 12; the actor will need to redeem themselves with the union within 48 hours of their employment, or the producer could be the subject of a Union Security Violation claim.

In the UK and Ireland, extras are members of Actors' Equity, which, unlike in North America, represents actors from the worlds of theatre, film and TV. Any extra who is being paid is a member of this union, which is not as onerous to join as the US Equity or SAG, and the only nonunion extras would typically be friends or family. Generally, extras can say up to 5 or 6 lines and become a "featured" extra, which gives them a slightly higher rate but nothing like as much of an adjustment as with SAG. However, if the part is speaking or recurring, you really should be casting a day player for performance (Figure 2.10).

Minors

Another important consideration in this first, big-picture pass of the schedule is **child labor**. Unless a person under 18 is either married, in the armed forces, legally emancipated or has completed state education requirements, they are considered minors. SAG has comprehensive guidelines relating to the care and working conditions of minors, but in all cases local law takes precedence over SAG and you'll need to get the legal parameters from the PM. The SAG rules as regards minors' working hours are as follows:

Maximum Minors' Working Time

Ages	Time at Workplace	Time Working	Rest/Education	Total Including Meals
15 days – 6 months	2 hrs	20 mins	100 mins/0	2 hrs
6 months – 2 years	4 hrs	2 hrs	2 hrs/0	4.5 hrs
2 – 5 years	6 hrs	3 hrs	3 hrs/0	6.5 hrs
6 – 8 years	8 hrs	4 hrs	1 hr/3 hrs	8.5 hrs
9 – 15 years	9 hrs	5/7 hrs	1 hr/3 hrs	9.5 hrs
16 – 17 years	10 hrs	6 hrs during schooldays; 8 hrs on holidays or if graduated	1 hr/3 hrs	10.5 hrs

For every child under the age of 16, a parent or guardian must be within sight or sound and there must also be a studio teacher present. If the child is between 15 days and 6 weeks, there must be a nurse for every three children, and between 6 weeks and 6 months, a nurse for every 10 children. Travel time is considered part of the workday, unless it is an overnight location. The workday itself must happen between 5 a.m. and 10 p.m., unless there is prior permission for an exception confirmed in writing by the authorities. On a school night they must be wrapped no later than 12:30 a.m.

Minors are not allowed to work more than six consecutive days, (although a day spent in school or travel doesn't constitute a workday). Work hours exclude meal periods but include school time, and there are limits to how much schooling they may receive: 4 hours for those under 6, 5 hours for grades 1–6, and 6 hours for grades 7–12. There must be one teacher to every 10 children, 20 if they are all in the same two grades. There is the same 12-hour turnaround required for children as for all SAG actors.

In addition, no dressing rooms can be shared between minors and adults, and if a child feels that some action is unsafe, no matter what the opinion of the ADs, parent or stunt coordinator, the child cannot be required to perform the action.

There are times when a parent will be quite casual about their child's working life, but that's not something to be admired. The schedule must reflect the legal parameters of the child's working day and adhere to them. Often, what this means is filling out the days where children work with scenes in which they don't appear, or with other children.

It's crucial that you check at the beginning of every job exactly the age of the child playing each role (not the age in the script, as typically we try to hire children who are older than the age they're playing to avoid as many of these restrictions as possible), and then get your updated, accurate information about the nature of the legal restrictions from the producer or production manager. The thing about child labor is that it's not simply part of a deal arrived at with the crew, and therefore negotiable, but enshrined in law and enforced. SAG or other bodies will send out inspectors to ensure that child protection measures are being observed, and aside from the ethical considerations of abusing children, your shoot can be closed down if you're not obeying the letter of the law. Not on your watch!

Crew Deals

A large part of your crew deal will already be determined by the SAG tier that you're working under. However, remembering the golden rule "never assume," you will need to sit down with the PM to ascertain, at the minimum, the terms of the crew deal, as shown in Figure 2.12, and you can add to this depending on the nature of your production.

Every job has its variations. A typical US shooting day would be 6 hours from call to lunch, then another 6 hours from lunch to wrap. Many crew members have to show up anywhere from 1.5 hours to 30 minutes before this time. Add on breakfast and travel time and you're looking at a 14-hour day, easily. These conditions can be truly punishing, especially if (as in a place like New York) you're dealing with either extreme cold or extreme heat.

UK film and TV shoots might work 5-day weeks, with 5 hours from call to wrap and 5 hours after lunch, with some TV series alternating between 5-day and 6-day weeks, what's known as an 11-day fortnight, or even continuous 10-hour days without a lunch break. There may also be the issue of national holidays to contend with. (There are more elements discussed in the section titled "International Variations" in Chapter 3.) In short, every job is different, and you'll need to get the parameters from the PM before you start arranging your strips. If you're on a union shoot, the unions themselves will have specific parameters.

The **Directors Guild of America** (DGA) is the union to which directors, assistant directors and production managers might belong. There are two tiers within the DGA agreement, low-budget and basic, and the terms and conditions of each are spelled out on the website and are generally in synch with SAG rules.

To become a member of the DGA you have to demonstrate a specific number of days worked on DGA projects; for example, 260 days as a first AD, proven by call sheets, pay slips, letters from employers, production reports, and so forth. Once you join you will be entitled to earn significantly more money (including pension and welfare provisions) and work under better conditions. However, once you join, you can't go back to working nonunion, so you need to be certain that you'll be offered enough DGA work to make the transition successful. DGA guidelines are, for the most part, common sense protections, and can be viewed at www.DGA.org.

There is also the DGA trainee assistant director scheme, a highly competitive but excellent way to be apprenticed onto DGA shoots, which you can find at www.trainingplan.org/. One of the DGA's most enforced rules is that if the director is union, so must be the PM and the ADs, so if you're not in the union it can rule you out of working with any director beyond a certain level. If a show becomes signatory while you're on it, however, you can become an "incumbent," but still have to accumulate the required days to be eligible to join.

The International Alliance of Theatrical Stage Employees, Moving Picture Technicians, Artists and Allied Crafts of the United States, Its Territories and Canada, or **I.A.T.S.E.** (often pronounced Yat-see), is a labor

What's the Deal?

The information you need from the PM or Line Producer

<u>Your own deal</u>: your weekly rate, as well as when and for how much any overtime may be; car allowance, phone bills, gas, mileage, per diems, hotel rooms or any other possible payments you may be entitled to

<u>Elements that will affect the schedule:</u>

How many weeks the shoot will be, and how many shooting days in a week

How many shooting days the producer expects to see

The length of shooting day: the standard call time to wrap time (for example 8AM - 8PM), and the number of shooting hours before and after lunch

Meals—lunch breaks and the late breaks: how long the breaks are, and who gets paid meal penalties if they're late

The difference (if any) in the deals with the various departments (especially cast, electricians, camera department, grip/standbys, etc.) regarding the shooting day, overtime, turnaround, meal breaks, night shoots or holidays. (You don't need to know how much anyone gets paid, just what the parameters are.)

Night shoots/late calls—any overtime or penalty payments for split days or night work? What are the required rest periods following night shoots?

Turnaround time for cast and any union or nonunion crew; does turnaround apply from wrap to call, or door to door? Also check turnaround in the case of a night shoot before a rest day or weekend, as well as standard weekend breaks.

The nature of the deal for hair, makeup, wardrobe (they will often have agreed to work a certain amount of time before call and after wrap and you need to know how much is included in their weekly deal)

Travel time / mileage (does the travel time get added to the length of the shooting day, and are people being paid for this time and/or a rate per mile?)

Overnight accommodation, per diems and any other distant location agreements

Are there any penalties for work on Sundays? Are there any national holidays occurring over the course of the shoot, and if so are they days off or workdays? What is the premium, if any, being paid for those days and is a premium being paid to everybody?

Are there any additional issues—transport, cultural or language specifics—that need to be factored in?

Figure 2.12 *Important aspects of the crew deal*

union representing technicians, artisans and craftspersons in the entertainment industry, including live theater, motion picture and television production, and trade shows. IATSE members, like those in the DGA, are entitled to weekend turnaround, meal penalties, travel time payments, medical and dental benefits, and RRSP plans. Most crew on a union shoot will be IATSE and the PM will have the most up-to-date information on what the parameters of your particular show are.

In SAG-designated "Production Cities," you will only find nonunion crews on lower-budget projects, but in the 21 "right-to-work" states, employees can decide for themselves whether to join the union or not, regardless of the other union members. This makes it easier for producers to hire nonunion crews, even on larger-budget shows. All unions prohibit their members from working under nonunion conditions, and they will be fined or even discredited from the union should they do so.

The beauty of SAG agreements is that if you're conforming to them, you're more than likely observing the regulations of the **other unions** as well. Outside of the US, every country has its own unions and you would need to familiarize yourself with the local conditions through the indigenous line producer or PM. However, shooting in another country does not relieve US union members from their obligations, or producers from their obligations to such employees. The DGA and SAG, in particular, will fine their members if they receive information that a DGA director is not employing a DGA first, for example—even in South Africa or Ireland. In this case, it's the union member who will be penalized, and SAG and the DGA have extensive guidelines about their rules, both on distant locations in the USA and around the world.

Every film and TV union in the world has guidelines on wages, overtime, night and weekend work; meal breaks and penalties; job descriptions and minimum staffing requirements; travel and distant location wages and entitlements; hazardous work allowances; union dues and fringe benefits; and insurances, subcontracting and arbitration proceedings. As always, the person to ask about any of these issues is the PM.

Continuous Days/French Hours

Imagine you're shooting on a beach, and there is a 7-hour window between tides in which you can shoot. If you have to break for lunch after 6 hours, you're going to lose at least 1 hour of your possible shooting time, as well as whatever time it takes to get to and from the unit base from the set. Or you're working with an actor who simply has to make a flight that evening, or you're shooting a daylight scene in a northern clime and the sun rises at 9 a.m. and sets at 4 p.m. These are just some examples of situations in which it makes sense to make use of a continuous day.

A continuous day is essentially a day in which the crew and cast don't stop for lunch, but work straight through, typically a 10-hour day without stopping. (In the US, to schedule so-called "French Hours" you need to get approval from 51% of the crew.) The production would be expected to provide a proper meal available for two hours (in the US, and all day in some other places), and as the First you would be trying to make sure that the camera crew do actually get to eat at some point, presumably while waiting for lighting or another department to complete some task. It's also commonplace for the craft services to be augmented, particularly if they're normally pretty sparse. If you go even a minute past your 10 hours, the company is liable for massive retroactive meal penalties.

In the UK proper, it is now common to work a 10-hour day without an official lunch break. This can be tough when working outside or under difficult, hot or cold conditions, but has advantages in terms of protecting actors' turnaround, combating the difficulty of regaining momentum after lunch, and providing more time "off-the-clock," especially for those departments whose pre- or post-shoot duties add an hour or two to their workday. Some productions, particularly TV shows, prefer to retain the lunch breaks and work a sixth day, arguing that this reduces the health and B safety risk of fatigue, but the continuous day is now the norm for feature films and may soon become standard on TV, too.

In France, continuous days are commonplace, but when they do break for meals they are seated and served a full meal, including wine. Every territory has its own standards, and this is another area to be clarified in your PM meeting regarding the crew deal.

Generally a continuous day is a really useful option under certain circumstances, but as it also shortens by at least an hour the total on-camera time available, it needs to be reserved for special situations. If it looks like a solution, I would put it on the schedule and add it to the Sequence section so it will be visible on the Strips (Figure 2.12).

Special Equipment

The final major factor in the schedule (as if there wasn't enough to be getting on with!) is special equipment. We'll talk more about the specifics of working with special equipment on the set in Chapter 3, but for now you need to identify when you will be using an expensive bit of gear—a camera crane, low-loader, motion-control camera or rain machines, for example—and try to schedule all of the scenes that require it together. This is rarely possible, and will prompt the question of whether it can be afforded for every scene that it's requested. This is a question the PM will have with the director—you never need to discuss money—all you have do is flag the requirements, share the information and budget the time accordingly.

Other Considerations

A first AD is always trying to avoid confusion and make sure all information is well distributed and crystal-clear; the worst AD, and one who will oversee a mutiny, is one who creates confusion. Sloppiness in relation to tiny mistakes like cast numbers is psychologically destabilizing as it affects the company's trust, and time-consuming and expensive, as every moment explaining or correcting something costs money. Change is constant but it must be well-motivated, not accidental. And in the haste to issue a schedule, little typos can wreak havoc. You will have to check and double-check the schedule yourself, as in the early days your team won't be on board yet.

The first pass of the schedule will group all scenes by **set**, and then by **interior/exterior**. Generally, I would put all the exterior scenes at the beginning of the schedule, and all the interior scenes at the end. Particularly if you have a bulk of material in one location—a house, say, or a set in a studio—it can be useful to have this all as a block at the end. This also creates a potential option of weather cover.

Weather cover is, as it sounds, a plan "B" for when your preferred location, for whatever reason (including weather) is impracticable and you need to move somewhere else. Let's say there is a wedding scene that absolutely demands sun—normally, you would make the decision regarding weather cover as close as possible to the shoot day, but still with enough time to re-schedule extras, etc., should the day change. It's important to reflect on the schedule what the weather cover scenes are for particularly weather-dependent shoot days, so people can be prepared. The worst-case scenario is when the forecast is wrong, you show up to shoot and get rained out, snowed on (or blown away—which is happening more and more recently, as climate change yields greater winds, making work with cranes or at height impossible). If you have to go to weather cover on the day, it's always a scramble and eats up valuable time, so it's really not desirable to call it on the morning of the shooting day. Unfortunately, it sometimes happens. But for your purposes in scheduling, if you have a big block of scenes in one interior location at the end of your shoot, this is the material you might consider first for having on stand-by as weather cover for other more weather-dependent scenes, particularly if they don't involve many day players or extras.

Another starting point you will consider on your first schedule is **night shoots**. You generally don't want to start with nights, but rather to work toward them at the end (unless you're starting in late May, for example, when the nights are getting shorter). A night shoot is when you shoot past midnight and can be expensive, attracting night shoot penalty payments in some jurisdictions. In many cases you can still shoot in the dark by having late calls, or as they're also called, **split days**, in which you might shoot day scenes in the afternoon, break for lunch at dusk and shoot the night scenes when it's dark, up until 11:30 p.m., leaving half-an-hour for wrap time. Obviously, time of year will have a big impact on the exact shooting times available (especially in northern climes). The other big implication of a full night shoot is that in most countries you have to provide a rest day afterwards. The details of this will change from show to show and country to country, but generally there is a 36-hour minimum turnaround required between a night shoot and the next shooting daytime shooting day. Either way, you want all of the night shoots to happen in the same week, and as far down the schedule as possible.

If you have **stunts** and/or big action scenes, it's ideal to schedule them in week 2 or 3 if possible, when everyone still has some energy but they've had a week to work together and come together as a unit.

You should also bear in mind any large **crowd scenes**—if there is a big sequence (like a wedding) or a couple of stand-alone scenes that have big crowds, they should be grouped together as much as possible. Extras can be recycled (or re-dressed, and re-hair and makeup-ed) from one scene to the next, which will save money for production. Again, this is something to double-check with the PM as they will have the up-to-date information and final decision on whether it is cheaper to keep a crowd of extras for the day and into over-time, or to bring in a new batch to complete the day.

As mentioned before, what the director and cast would like is to shoot the whole script in **chronological order**. While this is rarely possible, what you can do is try to maintain chronological order at least within each day. Again, this first pass is the ideal-world scenario, so do have a look to see where you can place the earlier scenes before the later ones.

Finally, your **first day** of production should be a "light" day—that is, one that is definitely achievable—without too many unit moves, stunts or a sex scene. It takes at least a day for the cast and crew to gel into a team, from understanding how others work to simply knowing who everybody is, so it's good not to put this fledgling unit under too much pressure. Ideally, the first day will have a relatively small page count and involve scenes that are expository rather than hugely emotional. Another tip is to deliberately film an excessive amount of

coverage. The most common note back from executives is to shoot more coverage, so if the first day's rushes contain angles from every possible direction, they will relax somewhat on this score. This is a point that is, I find, sometimes useful to make to first-time directors before shooting starts, especially in TV.

The Shooting Schedule and the Strips

The breakdown sheets that you have produced, and arranged as per the requirements of the script, sets, cast and special equipment, form the basis of the **shooting schedule** (Figure 2.13). A print-out of this document is what you will distribute at production meetings, as it will list all of the elements required for each scene in schedule order. The format I prefer is "Shooting Schedule #2," which you can access by clicking on "Print/View," then "Reports," then "View" or "Print." (If you want to amend or design your own report format, in the breakdown sheets click "Design," "Report Layouts," and work away.) As with the strips, I like to make a couple of tweaks to the design, putting a horizontal line between the title of the picture and the first sheet's information (Design, Report Layouts, Shooting Schedule #2), as well as adding the Sequence and Script Day here, too. I also delete (by cutting) any categories that I know I won't use (e.g., Music, Greenery, etc.), as the idea is to try to get as much information onto each page as possible.

However, when people are looking for the "schedule," what they're generally referring to is the **stripboard**, or **one-line schedule** (see Figure 2.14). As described earlier, this harks back to the days of pen and cardboard, and is the single most important document the First will issue. This is, effectively, the master schedule, and the First has sole responsibility for making sure it is accurate and achievable. The schedule, combined with the script, creates the movie.

To look at your strips, click on "Schedule," then "Stripboard." There you will see reflected some of the information you entered on the breakdown sheets: Scene, page count, set, synopsis, Day/Night, and Cast IDs. You can design these strips in any way you like and every First has their own little tricks. I always work on the 14″ Horizontal, which I find prints out the best—you access it by clicking Strip Layout at the top of the board.

I like to **customize the format** of the strips by clicking "Design," "Strip Layouts," and then clicking the box beside Horizontal C. The one thing I always add to the Strip Design is "**location**" underneath the scene number, so you can always be sure that the scenes in the same location are kept together and everybody can see at a glance what they are, and whether a move is required. You do this by clicking on the box that says "sheet #," at the top left of the strip template, and "cutting" it, the way you would cut (as in, cut and paste) text in any word-processing document. I then do the same for the box that says "sheet." (I always delete the sheet number from the strip, as this is unnecessary information in my experience. The only time I've used them is if, for some reason, my script order board has disappeared, and a way of re-creating it is to sort by sheet order. But this is extremely rare.)

I also make sure to add the "**sequence**" box—although it won't be on every strip, the ones it is on will be important. There is usually a space for this after the "set" box or "synopsis."

I then drag the two boxes on the bottom left, the ones that say "page," up to where the "sheet" boxes were, then click on the line symbol above them to draw a line underneath these boxes by dragging the cursor across (see Figure 2.15). I then click back on the arrow symbol above the "pages" boxes, click "location" from

END OF DAY #1 - 3 Total Pages

SHOOT DAY #2 -- Monday, October 3, 2011

Scene #903 - PT 1	**EXT**	**PRECINCT**	**Morning**	1/8 Pgs.
of 5	*Jack chases Jill*			

Cast Members
  23.JACK
  24.JILL

Extras   **Additional Labor**
  20 x street crowd   Stunt Coordinator

Stunts
  Jill runs fast

Vehicles
  3 x ND moving cars
  5 x ND parked cars

Notes
  Road control from 8AM - 10AM only

Scene #903 - PT 2	**EXT**	**PRECINCT**	**Morning**	1/8 Pgs.
of 5	*Jill narrowly avoids being hit by a car*			

Cast Members
  23.JACK
  24.JILL

Extras   **Additional Labor**
  20 x street crowd   Paramedic s/by from 11:30

Stunts   Stunt Coordinator
  24x.Jill stunt double   Stunt driver

Vehicles
  3 x ND moving cars
  5 x ND parked cars
  Jill's car
  Stunt car

Notes
  Road control from 8AM - 10AM only

Scene #903 - PT 4	**EXT**	**PRECINCT**	**Morning**	1/8 Pgs.
of 5	*Jill pulls out into traffic*			

Cast Members
  23.JACK
  24.JILL

Extras
  20 x street crowd
  Jill driving double
  Woman with peeing dog

Animal Handler
  Dog handler

Livestock
  Peeing dog

Vehicles
  3 x ND moving cars
  5 x ND parked cars
  Jill's car

Notes
  Road control from 8AM - 10AM only

Figure 2.13 *Shooting Schedule #2*

FAB SERIES DEMO SCHEDULE DATED SEPT 1, 2011						
129	INT LIFE BAR		Day	2/8	pgs.	5
Ocean	David calls Red					
234	INT LIFE BAR		Day	1 6/8	pgs.	4, 5, 6, 13
Ocean	Leo thinks Clara is cool					
666	INT LIFE BAR		Day	6/8	pgs.	4, 5, 13
Ocean	Leo is angry at Clara					
616	INT LIFE BAR		Night	3/8	pgs.	1, 5, 8
Ocean	Tom gives Isolde the Rilke					
585	INT LIFE BAR		Night	5/8	pgs.	4, 8
Ocean	Clara and Isolde date					
SUNDAY SR 7:09 SS 18:06 UNIT CALL 11AM						
--- END OF DAY 1 -- Sunday, October 2, 2011 -- 3 6/8 pgs.						
903 - PT 1	EXT PRECINCT		Morning	1/8	pgs.	23, 24
Studio 5	Jack chases Jill					
903 - PT 2	EXT PRECINCT		Morning	1/8	pgs.	23, 24
Smith Street	Jill narrowly avoids being hit by a car					
903 - PT 4	EXT PRECINCT		Morning	1/8	pgs.	24
Smith Street	Jill pulls out into traffic					
904 - PT 2	INT TAXI		Morning		pgs.	12, 23
Smith Street	Jack's POV of Jill's car					
903 - PT 3	EXT PRECINCT		Morning	1/8	pgs.	23
Smith Street	Jack nearly trips over a peeing dog's leash					
904 - PT 4	INT TAXI		Morning		pgs.	24
Jones Street	Jill sees that she's not being followed					
903 - PT 5	EXT PRECINCT		Morning	1/8	pgs.	12, 23
Smith Street	Jack hails a cab					
904 - PT 1	INT TAXI		Morning		pgs.	12, 23
Smith Street	Jack says "follow that car"					
904 - PT 3	INT TAXI		Morning		pgs.	12, 23
Smith Street	Jack argues with the taxi driver					
COMPANY MOVE TO BRIDGE STREET						
131	INT DAVID & ROSIE'S FLAT		Night	1	pgs.	5, 6
Bridge Street	Rosie has on new knickers					
MONDAY SR 7:06 SS 18:08 UNIT CALL 11AM						
--- END OF DAY 2 -- Monday, October 3, 2011 -- 1 5/8 pgs.						
734	INT DAVID & ROSIE'S FLAT		Morning	4 3/8	pgs.	5, 6
Bridge Street	Rosie throws David out					
243	INT DAVID & ROSIE'S FLAT		Evening	3/8	pgs.	6, 11
Bridge Street	Helen arrives with champagne					
404	INT DAVID & ROSIE'S FLAT		Night	2 3/8	pgs.	5, 6
	David and Rosie fight					
612	INT DAVID & ROSIE'S FLAT		Night	2/8	pgs.	5, 6
	A horrible silence					
634	INT DAVID & ROSIE'S FLAT		Night	4/8	pgs.	5, 6
	David dreams about Red					
901	EXT ROSIE'S APARTMENT		Night	5/8	pgs.	6, 7, 12
Bridge Street	Larry and Rosie get out of the cab					

Figure 2.14 *The strips, or one-line schedule, in schedule order*

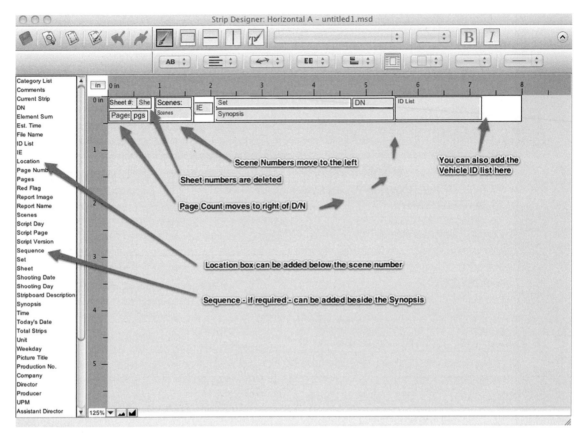

Figure 2.15 *Customizing your strips*

the menu on the left-hand side, and drag this into the space below the pages boxes. The font of this "location" box may need to be adjusted to match the size and style of the rest of the strip (the font options are in the toolbar on the right). One last option is to add the **Script Day** beside the Day/Night box, which is very helpful when you're in production. It does mean that you have to cut your "timings" boxes on the extreme right, and drag everything else (including vertical lines) to the right to create space, but even though it's fiddly it's worth it in the end.

It's a question of personal taste, but I also like to cut the box that contains the word "scenes," and enlarge the "scene number" font size and bold it. This helps me visually see the scene number at a glance when scanning through the strips in a hurry.

The Day-Out-Of-Days

The Day-Out-Of-Days (DOOD) is an unwieldy term for a chart in grid form that shows how many days a given actor/vehicle/animal or any other element is required over the course of the schedule (Figures 2.16 and 2.17). The cast DOOD is the Holy Grail for the ADs, production, casting and wardrobe. It's worth checking

Report created Oct 3, 2011
11:20 PM

"FAB SERIES"
Day Out of Days Report for Cast Members

	Month/Day	10/02	10/03	10/04	10/05	10/06	10/07	10/08	10/09	10/10
	Day of Week	Sun	Mon	Tue	Wed	Thu	Fri	Sat	Sun	Mon
	Shooting Day	1	2	3	4	5	6			7
1.	TOM	SW	H	H	H	H	W			H
2.	ANGIE									
3.	RED		SW	H	H	H	W			W
4.	CLARA	SW	H	H	W	H	H			H
5.	DAVID	SW	W	W	W	H	W			W
6.	ROSIE	SW	W	W	W	W	W			W
7.	LARRY			SW	W	W	H			H
8.	ISOLDE	SW	H	H	W	H	H			H
9.	KATE									
10.	RENEE									
11.	HELEN			SW	H	H	W			W
12.	TAXI DRIVER		SW	W	H	H	H			H
13.	LEO	SWD								
14.	MRS. DEVINE					SWD				
15.	GROOM					SW	H			H
16.	LUCY									
17.	INTERVIEWER									
18.	MOTHERCARE ASSISTANT									
23.	JACK		SWD							
24.	JILL		SWD							

Figure 2.16 *Page one of the cast Day-Out-Of-Days*

Report created Oct 3, 2011
11:21 PM

"FAB SERIES"
Day Out of Days Report for Cast Members

	Month/Day	11/07	Co.						
	Day of Week	Mon	Travel	Work	Hold	Holiday	Start	Finish	TOTAL
	Shooting Day	24							
1.	TOM			10	6		10/02	10/21	16
2.	ANGIE			8			10/11	10/31	8
3.	RED	WF		9	5		10/03	11/07	14
4.	CLARA			10	9		10/02	10/26	19
5.	DAVID	WF		9	1		10/02	11/07	10
6.	ROSIE			9			10/02	10/12	9
7.	LARRY			6	5		10/04	10/18	11
8.	ISOLDE			7	8		10/02	10/20	15
9.	KATE			4	3		10/11	10/31	7
10.	RENEE			4	5		10/11	10/21	9
11.	HELEN			5	2		10/04	10/12	7
12.	TAXI DRIVER			5	13		10/03	10/26	18
13.	LEO			3	7		10/02	10/26	10
14.	MRS. DEVINE			3	3		10/06	10/28	6
15.	GROOM			2	2		10/06	10/11	4
16.	LUCY			1			10/13	10/13	1
17.	INTERVIEWER			1			10/12	10/12	1
18.	MOTHERCARE ASSISTANT			1			11/06	11/06	1
23.	JACK			2			10/03	10/28	2
24.	JILL			2			10/03	10/28	2

Figure 2.17 *The last page of the cast Day-Out-Of-Days*

the cast DOOD after every version of your schedule; click "Print/View," "Day out of Days," "Cast," "View" to see the characters' "spread." As depicted, the DOOD will reflect each cast member in their schedule number order, and show WS (Work Start), W (Work) and WF (Work Finish), with a total number of days at the end. Depending on your SAG tier, you may need to reflect when an actor is on Hold (H), or, when there is a gap over 10 days between shooting days, WD (Work Drop) and WP (Work Pick-Up). Additional abbreviations are R (Rehearse), T (Travel), SW, (Start Work), W (Work), D (Drop), P (Pickup), Travel (M), / (Holiday) and WF (Work Finish). If someone works for only one day, this would be reflected as SWF (Start Work Finish).

You'll immediately see if you have a character working one day on every week, or at the very beginning and very end of the schedule, neither of which is ideal, and you'll start moving the strips around to improve these actors' spreads.

The first column of the cast DOOD will also reveal if you have any characters doubling up, or any typos in character names.

You now need to carefully **number the cast**, and this is a political act. At this point you may or may not have deal memos from the coordinator, which may specify which cast number the cast member will be known by. There are occasions on which a certain actor, by virtue of their fame or clout or agent, will work only a few days on the project, but will still be designated Number One.

If there isn't a political issue, you have a number of choices as to how to number them. In Eve Light Honthaner's *The Complete Film Production Handbook* she relates the system that first AD Lou Race uses to number cast. After the first 4 or 5, which are dictated by occurrence or billing, he uses 13 for a villain or comic relief character; round numbers (6, 8, 9) for women, and straight numbers (7, 10, 11) for men (with all due respect to political correctness). He also keeps couples together (Mr. and Mrs. Smith would always be 16 and 17, for example), and members of a group such as three café workers or gangsters would also have consecutive numbers, so that if one is missing it's obvious and can be checked to ensure that it's deliberate. To number your cast, go to "Breakdown," then "Element Manager," where you can assign a character a board ID by double-clicking on that character name, adding the number and ticking "Lock ID" as in Figure 2.18.

You can also simply allow the characters to be numbered in order of occurrence—click "Element Manager," and beside the "Sort By" label choose "Occurrence" from the drop-down menu. As deals are done and the script evolves, so cast numbers may change. When you get information about particular cast numbers, you can lock that number to the cast member to avoid embarrassment later. In any case, you will lock all of the cast numbers before you issue the first Day-Out-Of-Days. Once you have issued your first schedule, NEVER change these numbers again. They have gone out into the world, so you want to make sure these numbers are locked. Even if a character is deleted or added, these original numbers must remain the same, or a memo explaining the change must be issued with the next schedule.

The most controversial aspect of the schedule is the cast DOOD; it will depend entirely where you are in the casting process as to whether this DOOD is shared with the casting director, or whether this information is retained, and either way it's not your decision or something you need to have a view on: this is purely a production call. The producer will have the casting director book actors on the basis of this document, and the First's job is to ensure that actors' days are consolidated into the minimum amount of time.

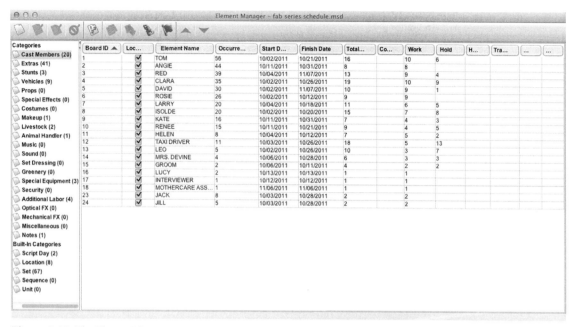

Figure 2.18 *The Element Manager*

Consultation

As soon as I have a pass of the schedule that accommodates the main cast issues to date, I talk it through with the location manager and art director to incorporate their requirements. To do this, I would give them both a copy of the Strips in the morning, and sit down with them both at lunchtime to talk it through. They'll have plenty of notes by then, and it's best to get them to go through it together with you, as solutions to one's issue may create one for the other.

Publishing the Schedule

Once the schedule is in a condition to distribute, you will want to add a few more details before sharing it. **Banners** are helpful tools that look like day breaks but are not automated or linked to the calendar. Because they have to be created and moved manually, I don't add them until right before I distribute. To create a banner, while in your Stripboard click on the strip where you want the banner to appear, then click Actions, Insert Banner. You then have the option to insert whatever text you prefer. The first banner is a headline at the top of the schedule—the name of the project, and "schedule dated 1/1/12," for example. Other useful banners indicate a Company Move, the sunrise and sunset times for that day, and the provisional call times. If you have a Travel Day, Rest Day or other day, that gets a Day Break as well as a banner. I put the banner immediately above the day break (which is always at the END of the shooting day), and generally have one for every day.

Finally, when printing out, if you print the banners and day breaks as white text on black it uses up a lot of ink on your printer and the photocopiers, etc. It's greener and easier to read if you go into Design, Strip

Colors, then click on Day Break Strips, Background, then White on the palette. You must then click on the Text button, and choose Black from the palette. You can then do the same thing for the Banner Strips, and when you print out, your strips will be much more popular in the production office. You also, when printing, have the option in the print box to uncheck the Header Board. I would print this as it provides an easy reference for who the cast numbers refer to, but prefer to move it (once printed) to the last page of the schedule rather than the first page, as not everyone is interested in it. I also only print the scheduled area— the unscheduled area should only be for scenes that have been cut; every scene you need to shoot must be contained within the schedule. If it's second unit, designate it as such with a banner and a day break, within the scheduled area of the strips.

Before you print anything out, do use the Print Scaling function to squeeze more information onto the page before you print your reports. The zoom tool makes it easier to see what will fit onto the page before you print.

Once you have all of the elements in place, and a workable version of the strips that fits the script into the time allocated, and you have gathered all the information you can at this stage from the various departments and addressed it as best you can in the schedule, you are ready to issue your first pass.

As mentioned earlier, all **distribution** of documents happens through the production office. You should never try to share any paperwork yourself, as there will inevitably be someone who doesn't get it and will be annoyed about it. There are exceptions—for example, if you want someone to look over something to double-check it or give their opinion privately—but otherwise everything goes through the POC. So with your beautiful, shiny new schedule, print it out and give her a hard copy, and also email her/him a PDF version of the strips, shooting schedule and DOOD for cast and any other elements. The coordinator will then make sure it goes to all relevant people. To create a PDF of any of these documents, go into File, Print/View, choose the format you wish to print, then click print. In the next print window on the bottom left will be a button called PDF; first Save as PDF, then email this PDF to the POC.

It's helpful to look at the schedule as a continuous work-in-progress, a living, changing, evolving creature that will never be set in stone until the last shot is completed. However, you need to be a bit clever about when you issue new drafts. The first one is critical, but you won't be issuing a new one every time you make a change. Schedules follow the same color-coded pattern as script pages, and if you can indicate what the major changes are on a cover sheet so much the better. It requires a judgment call to determine when new schedules need to be issued, and this is a decision that will be made in conjunction with the PM. But whatever you are issuing, from a memo to a schedule, it should go through the production office. Even if a producer has asked you to send them a draft version, it's no harm to let the POC know that that is happening and copy them. Everything is the POC's business, and you want to be sure you and s/he have a constant and open line of communication.

By the end of your first week you will hopefully have produced a schedule that is sturdy enough to distribute and discuss, ideally at the production meeting at the beginning of Week Minus Three (Week Two). If the schedule has changed over the course of the week—and it almost inevitably will have—a general rule of thumb in terms of distributing the schedule is to offer the new version just before each production meeting. At least that way you can be sure everyone is getting it at the same time, and you can explain to the group what the changes are and the reasons for them.

The Bond Company (Part 1)

One of the parties most interested in the schedule is the bond company. A completion bond is basically an insurance policy the investors take out to ensure that the film that is delivered corresponds to the film they financed, and if the film is abandoned, that they are reimbursed for losses. The bond company generally doesn't have any interest in the quality or content of the film, but they are very interested in the budget and schedule, and, as the shoot progresses, whether the schedule is being maintained.

TV shows and studio pictures generally don't have bonds, but any feature film over a two-million-dollar level is probably going to have one. If so, the bond company will need to approve you as a First, and this can be a little bit of a catch-22: to first a bonded film, you need to have firsted a bonded film. At the time I did my first bonded film, I had firsted numerous nonunion features and I had a very experienced producer and director who were willing to endorse me as a First. If you have done plenty of TV, especially for reputable broadcasters, you should also have no problem getting bonded. The bond company will also have approval over the director, DP, line producer/PM, and sometimes even the gaffer (chief electrician), and their say is final.

If the film is bonded, certain key members of the cast and crew will need to be medically examined and passed as fit by a doctor, and also agree to refrain from "hazardous activities," such as horse-riding, motorcycling, skiing, etc. This usually applies to the director, DP and one or two main cast.

Generally, the bond company is invisible and often in another country. However, if you or the director are first-timers, you may receive a personal visit during prep. Either way, the bond will be poring over your schedule, and will require the director to sign a contract that s/he commits to fulfilling that schedule as planned. This is important to remember when dealing with a director who appears to think that the schedule is the First's or the producer's problem, as sometimes happens. In fact, s/he is committed to making the days, and is at least as legally responsible as you are.

Most of the paperwork generated by production is provided to, if not designed for, the bond company, who will notice very quickly if you're not making your days (completing the work on the call sheet). The best situation is a totally invisible bond company, with whom you have no contact, and if all is going well you won't. In the prep period all you have to do is provide the schedule, possibly meet the representative very briefly, and be sure that the director is aware of their responsibilities.

WEEK MINUS THREE (WEEK TWO)

It is amazing how much people get done if they do not worry about who gets the credit.
Swahili proverb

In this book, we're working to a four-week prep period, so the first two weeks involve creating the schedule, meeting the director and communicating with the production team, art department and locations (among others). There may be script revisions, casting, location scouts (which you will not attend—these are for the designer, director and possibly the director of photography (DP) if s/he has started), and potentially meetings between the director and other heads of department who haven't been hired yet. If you're very lucky, this time will be quiet, while busy. Plenty of information will be flowing toward you, but unless there's a financing crisis afoot everyone is as calm as they will ever be.

You'll see that a number of the following section headings are followed by "Part 1"—this to reflect that they are being covered from the perspective of pre-production and to differentiate them from "Part 2," which happens during the shoot. There is a degree of overlap between their requirements as elements on the breakdown sheets, in prep, and on the shoot, and I recommend that readers engage with all three to get a complete picture.

Once your head comes up for air from the schedule (or possibly while you're still in it), you'll also be contributing to the pre-production calendar (Figure 2.1). The POC will already have indicated on this document when any new crew are starting, as well as any other events that are known at this point.

The Production Calendar

Several elements may need to be added to the production calendar: besides the weekly **production meetings** that are hopefully already marked up, it's time to start thinking about camera, hair, makeup and wardrobe **tests**, as well as any **animals**, **stunt rehearsals**, **visual effects**, **special props**, etc. Basically, anything that is more involved than a simple dialogue scene should be examined to determine whether a test would be required and possible.

At this stage, you'll know when the DP is starting, and most of these elements will revolve around his/her schedule. It is ideal for the director to attend these tests; however, if s/he is in rehearsals or casting they can be shown the recorded results afterwards. If main cast are involved, however, the director must be present.

The director will also need to be scheduled for weekly **art department meetings** to look at all of the props to be used during the shoot (these meetings are weekly because there will be new elements being sourced all the time, and the props people will need to offer up replacements and alternatives for whatever the director may have rejected at the first meeting). There may also be drawings to approve, sets under construction, or any other design elements the director needs to see. What you are trying to ensure is that the director is never seeing something on set for the first time when it could be wrong and create a delay or worse, and I feel responsible if this situation is allowed to occur. These director–art meetings are sometimes known as "**show and tells**," and they should be clearly marked on the production calendar and organized by the First personally. I also try to attend these meetings when possible, as it's the only way to be sure a) that they're happening and b) where potential issues might arise. Of particular concern would be props that involve some kind of mechanical or other effect. There is a real potential for a gap between props and special effects, or props and wardrobe, and I view it as the First's job to make sure nothing slips through these gaps.

As well as developments with script, cast and locations, a lot of the main crew are going to be coming on board, and it's often a chance to have your first **production meeting**.

Production Meetings

I can't over-emphasize how important production meetings are, but if you don't run them properly they will waste people's time and attract resentment or even no-shows. I'm going to provide an example of how

I would run a production meeting in an efficient and effective manner. Let's assume that this is the first time that everyone on the production is in the same room together.

On the table will be copies of the **one-line schedule**, or strips, and the **shooting schedule**. The shooting schedule is the expanded version of the strips, which reflects all of the elements on the breakdown sheets. You can print this out for yourself beforehand and read through it, to ensure that it reflects all of the information you have to hand at this point, as well as being easy to read and well-formatted.

The production office will be responsible for providing enough copies of both; I would check that they can print on both sides of the page, and that they start this process in plenty of time, ideally the evening before. It's typical that under time pressure the printer/photocopier gets jammed or breaks down. They will provide water and make sure there are enough glasses and chairs, but as always, it's a team effort, and you should be checking that this happens and moving furniture with them, if need be.

First, I make sure the meeting starts on time. I might give a 5-minute grace period for people to settle in, but I want to start as I mean to continue and demonstrate to people that time will be managed punctually. I sit at the head of the table, with the producer and director on either side. We start by going around the table, each person saying their name and what their role is on the picture. I then offer the director and the producer the opportunity to say a few words, which is usually a "welcome to the show and we're so glad to have you" type of speech; sometimes the director will describe very briefly what, for them, the film is about and why it is they want to make it. I encourage directors to do this, especially if the film is one that is personally meaningful to them, as it reminds us why we're all here.

The first thing I say is that we are going to go through the schedule as quickly as possible; if there is a point that concerns everyone, it should be mentioned here as we go through, otherwise it should be saved for a private conversation afterwards. Repeat: only issues that affect everybody at the table need to be discussed now. If at any point a conversation is digressing into a particular department's sole concerns, it is up to the First to interrupt and suggest that this be clarified later.

I then very briefly remind everyone of the context we are working in, depending on the financiers. Whether it's for a studio or an independent, TV or cable, there will be a safety policy, and I will remind everyone of its main points and the fact that under law in most countries people are responsible for the welfare of themselves and others. If something goes wrong, we are all personally liable, not just the production company. If there are any other overall concerns, such as working extensively with children or on location, I will very briefly describe them, but time is of the essence: you need to get through this meeting in about 1.5 hours, or people's energy and attitudes will flag.

I also allow myself a very short personal message: we are all in this together and we are all on the same team. This is an opportunity to make a great film, and to be good human beings. One whiner can ruin the party for everyone, so if you have a problem bring it to me or the relevant person, otherwise keep it to yourself. We want to stay positive, regardless of the circumstances. It will make for a better shoot and a better film. And we treat each other with respect, if not love. This usually gets a laugh, but it's actually what I think! Either way, you make it clear that this is a place where abusive language or behavior is unacceptable and there are procedures in place to deal with it if it arises. (Unfortunately, verbal abuse is a common enough element on a minority of productions and I have never seen bullying or just plain nastiness reprimanded if it's coming from a producer or director. However, if you've said in advance that it won't be tolerated, at least you have some moral ground should you need to take someone on.)

The other thing I mention is my pet peeve of the crew troubling the director for information that I could provide. Please ask me first: if I don't know, I'll either find out or refer you to the director. But s/he has enough to worry about without repeating information, and that's why I'm here.

You then talk straight through the schedule, using the shooting schedule as your guide. Anywhere there is anything unusual—special effects, stunts, vehicles, etc.—you point this out and carry on. You'll also highlight now if there is an unusual call time, an encroachment on turnaround, or any other circumstances that people should be aware of in advance. Don't go at completely breakneck speed; people do need to process what you're saying as well. And they will ask questions as you go. This is the best opportunity for people to get the director's views, and the beauty of it is that there is a room full of witnesses. While you are running the meeting, most of the questions will relate firstly to logistics, and then to the director's vision. The director him/herself may have some questions as well, as they start to understand exactly how the shoot will go.

Many of the questions that are raised at this meeting won't get answered. Either way, you should be writing everything that comes up on your own shooting schedule, so that you can input the new information and chase up that which is outstanding. You will also probably spot mistakes on the schedule, or other people will have better ideas. This is what the process is about, and if you can welcome this as collaboration instead of getting defensive, the crew will continue to help you throughout the shoot. It's not a contest. If you keep things moving and it's over within two hours, it will serve to unite and inspire confidence from the crew that this production will be efficient and friendly, and that can be a self-fulfilling prophecy.

Before breaking up the meeting altogether, while you have everyone in one room it's worth quickly scanning through the rest of the pre-production calendar as well, to advertise any tests that need to happen and make sure everyone is aware of the next production meeting.

Directing the Director (Part 1)

Inexperienced directors are sometimes unsure how to prepare, as in the early days of prep they are not being barraged by endless questions. If asked, there are two exercises I would advise any director to undertake: firstly, to plot out the character map of the project—that is, where every character is in their emotional journey in every scene, and what are the two action verbs that the director is going to offer the actors to remind them of this on the set. Even the most experienced directors can come a cropper when dealing with the actors on set, as no one else can help them in this area. It is for the director, and the director only, to liaise with the actors in relation to their character arc. And it can be really difficult at 7 a.m. in the rain shooting way out of sequence to remember where you are in the film. Actors expect a director to be able to remind them where they're coming from and going to in the story, and if the director has a brief note on their script to help them remember, the cast will feel safe and protected. If they lose this sense of trust and start to doubt that the director is totally clear about their role in the big picture, the director will become isolated, ignored, even resented, and it's very hard for anyone to recover from that. If the director's and actor's views of their motivation in the scene are different, that's fine—that's the creative process. But if the director is flailing for an answer and doesn't honestly know, they're dead.

The other activity I would recommend to any director in prep is to draw the movie—literally, go shot by shot imagining the film. No one ever needs to see these drawings, and they certainly don't have to be able to draw, but the process of envisioning the film, and discovering the issues and questions this raises, is invaluable. Script problems, character issues, camera, location and prop ideas will all result from this imagining; no one else ever needs to know how the director thought it all through, but think it through they must, and it's difficult to do without a systematic method. (A book that is enormously helpful to directors plotting their film is Bruce Block's *The Visual Storytelling*, which imparts all of the tools of composition and how to use them to create emotional responses in the audience.) This may not sound like the first AD's department, but sometimes subtly imparting a preparation method, particularly to a first-timer, can help them and the movie.

During prep, you want to have your list of director's questions to hand at all times, so if you do catch the director in the kitchen or hallway you can get the answers to six things in one session and not have to pester them constantly. I would build it into your day that you touch base with them every morning or evening—it may be simply to say "Hi" and ask if they're all right, but it's almost certain that you'll have a few questions as well. Good questions will get them thinking about what they want while there's still time to organize it, and offer them solutions: "Would you like to shoot that from outside? Do we need to think about having a double for that scene? Do you want Actor Y in that scene?"—all of these examples may be suggestions that you are diplomatically presenting as the director's idea.

Depending on the director's preferences, the Second will liaise with the coordinator about the rehearsal location and the director's schedule, which should all be reflected on the production calendar. Due to budgetary constraints, rehearsals are under increasing pressure, but the director still needs to meet up with the actors before shooting. This can have a massive impact on the schedule and so, in a subtle and skillful way, you want to make sure this happens. Without any initial conversations about the character and his/her objectives, this discussion can end up happening on the set, in front of an impatient crew. Even a low-budget (around a million-dollar) movie costs about 50¢/second to run, so every second of chat is extremely expensive.

Very often, this initial director–actor meeting will take place as an informal conversation over coffee or dinner. If the director can meet with each actor and simply go scene by scene through the script, this can even be more productive than a conventional rehearsal, as it leaves room for creativity on the day, while addressing the big picture issues. While these meetings may not technically be classified as rehearsals, they are still a part of production and the coordinator or Second's responsibility, as s/he will be the one organizing taxis, reservations, etc.

A little-advertised fact about directors is that they are very often terrified, and by nobody more than the cast. Few directors come from the theater, where they develop a deep understanding for and solidarity with the actors' work. Rather, they may come from advertising, graphic design, visual effects, stunts, writing or any number of other disciplines that have little or nothing to do with directing actors, and many directors assume an attitude of dictatorship as the default position. Actors, meanwhile, having suffered such attitudes more often than they would care to remember, are understandably wary of directors; after all, it's their faces and bodies the world judges. So the relationship can begin on delicate ground, and often deteriorates.

One step a First can take to help improve this situation is to encourage the director, especially a first-timer or one who doesn't particularly like actors, to engage with them as much as possible before filming. This can be entirely social; it really doesn't matter if they ever talk about the script, but the more time they spend in each other's company the more comfortable they'll be on the set. The reality is, they're actually in the same department: despite the titles, the assistant directors are not uniquely the director's team—in fact, the actors and the director are what's known as the Talent. At least, on the topsheet of a budget, they are all "above the line" (the line being literally a line that divides the "creative elements"—script, cast—from the technical—crew, equipment, etc.). Like the cast, directors get driven to and from work, and lunches are delivered to them. They are, as much as the actors, the stars of the show. The more a director realizes that the actors are his colleagues, and creates in them the illusion that they are all on the same side, the more rich and trusting the relationship will be.

The other tasks you want to gently guide your director to do (beside casting, which will already be being supervised by the producer) is to engage with the crew—especially art department, locations and wardrobe.

Art Department

The size of the art department will depend on the budget and scale of the picture, but traditionally you will find at least these personnel:

Production Designer: the head of department who oversees the entire look of the film, as depicted by sets and props. As much as possible, the production designer and costume designer should be working together closely.

Art Director: the production designer's second in command. On some jobs there will be an art department coordinator; in the absence of this person the art director will manage the department in a hands-on, nuts-and-bolts way, including the budget and art department schedule. They will supervise any draftspeople who may be creating the plans for sets to be built, and they may also stand by on set when the designer is not present, ensuring that the designer's vision is being fulfilled. There may also be a **stand-by art director** for expressly this role.

I would always ask the art director if they have any plans of the sets—even when they're not constructing sets, they may still have maps they have made, and these are really handy when you're recording camera positions (especially in big crowd scenes). In the days of Google Maps you can generally create your own maps of exteriors, but whatever they can give you will be useful.

Construction Manager: takes any plans from the draftspeople and manages the crew—carpenters, plasterers, riggers and painters (scenic artists)—to build the sets and strike them after use.

Set Dresser/Decorator: responsible for adding all additional detail to the sets: furniture, props and all other dressing that create the environment of the set. The decorator will typically have a crew who ensure that the sets are dressed on time and undressed after usage. Much of the dressing will be rented and will need to be returned as soon as possible.

Prop Master (short for Property Master): there are two kinds of props: dressing props (as described above) and action props—that is, the props handled by the actors. The prop master is responsible for sourcing and managing all of the action props, under the supervision of the designer. The prop master may be overseeing a team of buyers, who, despite the title, may be renting props and set dressing, as well as the on-set stand-bys.

Stand-By Props: usually a team of two who are on the set during filming, managing all art department requirements. They look after the action props, resetting drinks, chairs, newspapers—anything that is moved during the take. They also work to the art director's instructions if any set dressing needs to be changed or moved.

There may be any number of other additional art department members, but these critical roles above are like HODs in their own rights, and need to be kept informed.

As a First during prep, most of your contact and conversations will be with the art director, who is responsible for the scheduling of the art department activities. The art director will advise you whether a plan is possible—for example, can a set be "turned around," that is, redressed to appear in another time period or as another set altogether, or not? Can a location be painted or dressed in time? Do they need more time to build? All of these issues will be imparted by the art director.

You will also need to engage with the prop master to ensure that the director gets to see everything that will be used on set before the shoot. The designer and art director should be informed of and invited to any "show and tells," and will also have their own separate demonstrations to the director of any models, plans or photos that relate to sets being built. It's important for the First to attend these meetings, as despite the fact that most of the talk may be about color schemes or wallpaper, there may be a comment relating to whether a wall "floats" (that is, is movable) or whether a sink is "practical" (that is, actually works), and that can have a bearing on the schedule or the scheduling of scenes during the day.

The art department is one of the first departments to begin work on the project and will always be on board before you. They'll often be able to share useful information about the practicalities of the shoot and the personalities involved on the crew.

Locations and Scouts

The locations department will also already have started by the time you come on board, although there may as yet be only one or two people in the department: the head of department is the **location manager**, and they would probably have engaged an **assistant location manager** or a **scout**.

Early on, the manager or the scout would have started photographing possible locations to show to the director. The locations the director likes will be visited, which is also known as a scout. The difference between a scout and a tech scout (or a recce) is that a scout is simply an initial visit to determine whether the location is suitable. The tech scout is made to a location that has been chosen by the director, booked by the location manager and is now ready to be prepared by the crew, usually a short while before filming. There is no point in a First going on a scout unless there is either a very strong possibility of an unusual location being used (for example, a dam or airfield), highly delicate stunt or safety work being performed there, or the scripts are late and you are delayed in creating the schedule (or, as seems to be a pernicious new trend, the director chooses not to go on the tech scouts). The scout group will often consist of the director, location manager, the production designer, and the DP (if s/he has started work). Generally, the First is not required at this stage and has more pressing work to do. However, a lot of useful information may come out of the scout, which is why it's very useful to touch base with the director and whoever accompanied them to find out anything that may have been decided or discussed. You may not want to attend these scouts, but you do want to glean whatever information comes out of them.

At this stage you'll also be working with locations to schedule the tech scouts (or tech recces) and planning the transport and schedule for these days with the location manager and PM. These recces should be happening at the beginning of the next week (Week Minus Two) and will hopefully take less than three days in total. The tech scout needs to include any locations that are confirmed, with a priority on traveling in a geographically logical sequence, and at roughly the time of day when you plan to be shooting there, if possible.

Costume

Some directors, particularly those coming from a commercials background, will engage enthusiastically with the costume department from an early stage. For others, it wouldn't even occur to them to have a conversation. You want to ensure that the **costume designer** is getting enough information from the director to be able to work productively, and, as with props, you want to facilitate the wardrobe department in terms of presenting their ideas as early as possible, whether this be in the form of sketches, "mood boards," or actual costumes.

You also want to ensure that the production designer and costume designer are working in synch; this can be a delicate relationship, and it may require diplomacy to arrange open and constant communication between the departments. Sometimes it's easier to liaise with the art director and the **wardrobe supervisor** (the art director's equivalent in the costume department), as they understand the vision of their HODs without, perhaps, the emotional attachment. At the very least, you want to be sure that both departments are aware of the dominant colors being employed by the others—you don't want the actress showing up in a red dress to sit on a red couch, which I have seen happen. (The annoyed actress was sent off to change, the costume department had to race out to buy a new dress and we lost 45 minutes shooting time, which made it very much my problem and a good lesson.) If the director isn't sharing the information regarding colors and styles, as always, you need to be sure that the information is still being exchanged.

The second AD, once they begin, will liaise with the wardrobe department about **costume fittings**, and the makeup and hair departments about tests. If the actors are union members, there will be the requisite paperwork and formalities. Actors are often booked very close to shooting time, and costume will probably have been begging and/or screaming for weeks about getting measurements for the actors. By the time the Second starts, hopefully the actors have been booked and are available to be scheduled for fittings.

It's difficult to facilitate it so the director is available to attend these, as they often happen at his/her busiest time. What I recommend is that the actor and the costume designer go through all of the costumes themselves alone, before the director arrives at the end and they do a brief fashion parade. Naturally, some of the big stars will not consent to this, but if they're that big a star you will have a stand-in anyway, who could model the clothes if the director and the actor don't get to be together for this process. However, that's the worst-case scenario. The fittings are really valuable not just to show the director the clothes, but to continue to develop their relationship and the actor–director creation of the role. Clothes make the character, very often, and the most emotional arguments can happen over a frock. The director should be involved with this process as much as possible.

The best-case scenario is to show the director the costumes the previous week, so the designer doesn't sell the actor something the director hates. This shouldn't take more than an hour and can save huge amounts of time and drama. Ideally, the production designer would be part of this conversation to head off any awkward coincidences. Once the final decisions are made, the production designer should be provided with photos of all of the major costumes. As always, the First is trying to ensure that there are no surprises on set.

Storyboards and Shotlists

As indicated earlier, I think it's a useful exercise for a director—especially one with less experience—to draw the entire project, for their own purposes. Storyboards, on the other hand, are designed to share, even if they're little more than crude stick figures. There are two areas for which I always try to encourage the production of storyboards: **sex scenes**, and **stunts**. It's common enough to have storyboards, even professionally produced, beautiful comic books, for stunt and action sequences, and in my view sex scenes are equally fraught. A lot of embarrassment can be avoided, and a better scene can result, if they are planned as intricately as any other complicated sequence. Storyboards should be distributed to everyone who might possibly be interested, and sometimes even attached to the call sheet so everyone has a reference on the day. Naturally, the actual set and action will differ slightly from the storyboard, but it should be only slightly or you will need to advise the producer.

From a storyboard, the First or the director can produce a shotlist. I prefer to do this myself, as I can put realistic timings beside it. On commercials the shotlist is often produced well before the shooting day, whereas on TV drama or features there is rarely a shotlist for a standard scene until it has been rehearsed. I then create a shotlist that we can all refer to during the course of the scene.

Previz has now become an industry tool on bigger-budget productions, an abbreviation of Previsualization. It's an animation software used to plan shots and sequences, like an animated storyboard. (Commercials frequently use "animatics" for the same purpose, draft animations that depict the shots and timing that the ad will ultimately possess.) It's highly effective in providing an opportunity for conversations to happen in prep instead of on the set, particularly for sequences involving stunts or visual effects. If there are a number of such sequences, the show might actually have a previz department with an office in the production base.

Sex Scenes and Nudity (Part 1)

Unless you're a voyeur, sex scenes are an opportunity for embarrassment, discomfort, and if you really get it wrong, lawsuits. The best approach, as always, is to elicit exact information from the director—the more specific the better—about what has to happen, and to make sure he has informed the cast, if not actually rehearsed it.

According to SAG rules, performers must be advised of any nudity before the first audition or interview. In any case, by the time you're on board the producer should have advised the actor's agent as to what's required. If a body double is to be used, the performer must agree to both the extent of the nudity and the physical contact, in writing.

In Part 2 I describe the management of a closed set, but in the prep period your main concern is to ensure that the actors are all fully informed of what is desired—and this has to come only from the director or producer, it's not a conversation the ADs should be involved in, besides advising wardrobe, makeup and other departments as to the technical requirements. I highly recommend sex scene rehearsals as much as stunt rehearsals. If something is going to be awkward or embarrassing in private, imagine it with 20 people watching under hot lights and a time pressure. It's best to get the cringe-factor dealt with in advance.

Stunts (Part 1)

As described in relation to the breakdown sheets, anything an actor does that involves a little more than walking can reasonably be considered a stunt. A lead actor on a major TV series recently insisted that he could jump from a three-foot wall without needing a stunt double, and the director insisted the same. After six takes, the actor felt a little twinge in his foot. They continued for another three takes. The next day, while doing a straightforward sword-fight, he slipped, and the weakness in his foot caused him to fall awkwardly, fracturing his leg. He finished the shoot in a cast and all of his riding and fighting scenes, of which there were many, had to be rescheduled for six months later as he had back-to-back filming commitments. This pickup week cost over three million dollars. Much of this was covered by insurance, but besides the cost it also affected the broadcast date, the look of the show (most of the other actors had cut their hair by the time of the re-shoot, requiring hair extensions) and a continuity challenge, as it was now a different season and the foliage had changed. All this because he jumped from a three-foot wall. You get me?

It's not forbidden for actors to do a certain amount of action work—it certainly sells the drama better, and many of them enjoy it. The crucial thing is that it be supervised by someone who understands intricately both what works for camera and the limitations of an actor's body. For all their beauty, they are often not in perfect shape: a body sculpted in a gym can lack endurance and flexibility. A stunt coordinator is responsible for choreographing and supervising whatever action is necessary and will cast the stunt performers.

SAG divides stunt performers into three categories:

- Stunt Doubles, who may perform only for the character they are designated to double and who are engaged on a daily basis;
- Utility Stunt Performers, who may double for any character or perform any other stunts required; they are engaged on a weekly basis only;
- ND Stunt Performers, who may perform any generic stunt work, but who may not double for a character without being engaged with an additional Stunt Double contract; ND Stunts are engaged on a daily basis.

As described, a stunt can range from jumping from a low wall, to shooting flaming arrows on horseback or falling from a skyscraper. A number of shots will form the sequence, and it is the First's job to ascertain as early as possible what the shots are, which of them involve the actor and which can use picture doubles or stunt doubles. The difference is as it sounds—a picture double is someone who resembles the actor and can substitute for them in non-stunt action. The stunt double is a stunt performer who resembles the actor as much as possible, but their proficiency with stunts is the most important thing. The difference in these two roles is reflected in their costs: a picture double could be anyone, such as an extra, who can be dressed and bewigged to resemble the actor and execute the action—such as driving or as a passenger in a car, or walking in a very wide shot, etc. The stunt double will be able to crash the car, run over rocky ground, fall, and so forth. Stunt performers are categorized as cast, with the same requirements and treatment.

It is not permitted for a stunt coordinator to perform in the stunt themselves, as this would compromise their ability to oversee and anticipate danger. Thus, for any stunt, there is always a coordinator and usually a stunt double, as well as the actor and possibly a picture double. The main concern, at all times, for the first AD is the health and safety of all concerned.

Any stunt, no matter how large or small, should be presented to the director (and hopefully the producer and DP) before filming. Particularly with fight scenes, the director will have some number of changes or ideas they would like to see incorporated. If this doesn't happen in advance, you can either have the director's vision compromised, or changes on set, which are both costly and dangerous. Most people have heard the infamous story of the fatal accident on the set of *Twilight Zone*. It seems clear from court records that what led to the actors being killed was on-set amendments to the pre-agreed action. In this case, the request was to bring the helicopter lower; it could be anything else, from making the car drive faster, the performer stand closer, etc. These changes to the plan are what lead to accidents.

If the stunt has been tested (and I would recommend photographing the test) in advance, these conversations and decisions should have been addressed in a calm and orderly way. If it's in the middle of a night shoot, weeks into the shoot, the "gag" isn't working and the director is shouting orders, it can be difficult to keep control of what's happening. Situations like this can be the biggest test a first AD has to face. The First is often the person on the crew with responsibility for health and safety, and this is an enormous responsibility. No one working on a film or TV should ever be hurt, especially during a prepared stunt.

The First must have an open and honest relationship with the stunt coordinator and special effects coordinator, as well as any other HODs directly involved in the action. If a director is looking for changes, they must first be discussed and the professional advice of the coordinators adhered to. I have been in situations where I have faced the dilemma of not being happy with facilitating what the director wants, and it is a fine line when you can hold your ground if you think something is unsafe: do you walk away, or stand by and do your best to reduce the risks? On my first feature as a First, I believed that a fight hadn't been properly prepared and I left the room in protest. Moments later, the actress was screaming in agony from a dislocated shoulder. My leaving hadn't made her any safer, and I now wish I had prevented the scene from going ahead without proper precautions. Each situation is unique, but when it comes to the welfare of the cast and crew it is imperative to err on the side of caution. Certainly, the producer must be called to set if you are unhappy at any time. A serious amount of pressure can be brought to bear on the First, including threats to their job. But a crew is dependent on the First's protection, and although getting fired might seem like the worst possible event at the time, it won't stop you from working again. What I perceived to be dangerous situations were the only times in my career that I have called "cut" before the director.

Special Effects

Special effects is another vast term that covers anything from a massive explosion to a pop-gun firing. Certainly, any time you're dealing with explosives (no matter how tiny), it's a job for special effects, and they also control the elements of nature: fire, wind, rain, water, snow and the destruction these forces can cause.

Special effects supervisors are supported by a team, with whom they work regularly, and this continuity allows them to develop practices that improve the safety and efficiency of the production. Testing, and filming the tests, is an essential part of the preparation, as making adjustments on set is both expensive and dangerous (as with stunts). Doing a test on set and filming that does not count as prep and is a really bad idea, as I learned to my chagrin, and nearly lost my hearing in the process.

If you have a company health and safety officer, they will evaluate the hazard and write up a risk assessment for what's involved; if you don't, you will have to do this yourself, and will need to get all available information from the SF/X supervisor and his or her team.

A standard SFX requirement is **rain**. Rain bars are generally mounted either on stands or cherry pickers, and draw their water either from an approved hydrant, body of water or water bowser. If you are using a bowser, there is obviously a limited supply before the bowser needs to be refilled, so the best method is to have two bowsers that can be used in rotation to keep a near-constant flow. Locations will secure such refill permission, if required—you can't just stick a hose in a lake.

Generally, a number of rain bars, placed at varying distances from the camera, can be individually controlled to increase or decrease the volume of flow. On the shoot day, wind direction and intensity will have a big effect, but test first anyway. As with the props show and tell, it is always better to be discussing a specific object rather than an idea—the director's notion of a color or what constitutes heavy rain (for example) can only be properly understood in relation to a demonstration. No matter how seemingly obvious the effect, it needs to be tested, and if the test yields changes or improvements, it needs to be shown to the director again.

The reason I'm emphasizing this so heavily is because the most expensive time on set is spent waiting for something to be done, or discovering on camera that something doesn't work. It will cost either in terms of time, money or the director's vision. Either way, if it happens, the producer will justifiably be asking you why this wasn't tested beforehand. In a worst-case scenario, or when circumstances don't allow any other option, something may even be tested on the morning of the shoot day itself. Whatever it takes, the director and DP should know what they're going to be filming before it arrives on set.

In my experience, there are several methods of creating **snow**. The old-fashioned way, which I hope is not used any more, is a kind of sticky confetti that is an absolute nightmare to remove, especially from small leaves or gravel. More recently, I have seen a very effective use of ash to create falling snow, while a foam was used for creating snowbanks and drifts. If the snowbanks need to be larger, this may become an art department issue, where they will be constructed and covered with a snow-like substance. Whatever material is being used, it's important to test not just its look but especially how it is removed and what its environmental impact may be—these substances are often chemically intense and need to be evaluated before someone's precious garden is buried under a foot of it.

Any kind of **fire** is a safety issue; flame bars are a controllable means of placing flames within a set and gas burners are often used in fireplaces to give a flame effect. If the set itself is supposed to be on fire, or if anyone is to be on the set when such flames are burning, they may need to be stunt doubles. If a person needs to wear a flame suit, so as to appear as if they are actually on fire, this is necessarily a stunt person. Despite the specially constructed nature of a fire suit, and the application of fire-resistant gel on the performer's skin, s/he can still be burned simply by the reflected heat of the flames. There is a very strict time limit as to how long a performer can be in close proximity to fire, which you need to make clear to the director and DP well before filming takes place.

Needless to say, there must always be fire extinguishers in strategic placements around the set, recently checked and ensured that they are the correct extinguisher for the nature of fire involved. There should be at least one specially designated meeting before production to talk through the details of the SFX involved, with the producer, director and the DP present, so that any questions or requests can be accommodated in time.

Other flame effects, such as outdoor fires, the classic fire in a garbage can, or the burning sconces sometimes seen in mediaeval castles, are also care of special effects. A hazard of these, of course, especially on a sound stage, is the smoke they give off, which is allegedly safe but nonetheless gets stuffy. Whenever possible, it's up to the First to ensure the set is adequately ventilated; very often a window or door can be left partially open without affecting the lighting and be closed for sound only during the takes.

The only fire-related element I can think of that can be delegated to a prop assistant is candlelight, within reason, say, on a normal-sized dining room table. Even then, precautions must be taken to ensure that the candles are drip-proof and are not going to drop hot wax on an actor or the furnishings; are in steady, well-balanced candelabra, and that there has been official notice made to production that candles will be used (they may need to report this to the insurance company). If an actor needs to walk with a candle, their hand and wrist must be protected, and the candle only handed to them immediately before the take, and removed by props upon cut.

Wind is generally a pretty straightforward effect to create. Depending on the force and area required, there are a number of tools available, ranging from smaller hand fans and "mole" fans, to larger standing fans to airplane propellers that can be wheeled into position on large trolleys or small trucks. The greatest potential danger from wind machines is the dust and debris that can get into people's eyes, particularly if there is a call for leaves or other bits of stuff to be blown through the air. In this case, everyone on the set should be equipped with a pair of protective goggles, and as few people as possible should be in a risky position. Such wind machines make a huge noise, and can render any dialogue unusable.

We will talk later about working in tanks and underwater, which strictly speaking don't involve special effects. SFX **water** would involve something like the construction of a waterfall or other mechanical effect that is beyond the purview of the props department. As with all such constructions, if an actor is to be engaged in action with it, additional care must be taken to identify the risks involved and take steps to diminish them. Either way, the safety of the crew must be a priority at all times, and the worst-case scenarios explored. Damage to sets, and of course proximity to electrical cables and equipment, have to be evaluated and supervised whether or not cast are involved in the action.

When it comes to **explosives**, SFX guys (and so far in my experience, they have all been guys) would prefer to overdo it than underdo it. Even on big-budget productions, SFX coordinators have been known to cause serious damage as a result of overdoing an explosion as they don't want to be embarrassed if it becomes, literally, a damp squib. So tests should take place in a controlled environment, where even if the SFX supervisor has overdone the impact to the power of 10, nobody can get hurt. My advice is to discuss at length the amount of explosives involved, and to require a demonstration in a safe, controlled area before anyone goes near the location or the shoot day.

Equally if not more hazardous, if smaller in scale, are the tiny explosives, or **squibs**, used for bullet hits, which are generally built from using minute amounts of gunpowder or the equivalent, which explodes, bursting a small balloon-like container of blood. They are potentially dangerous for actors to wear; however, it is often the case that actors, rather than stunt doubles, will actually take such a bullet hit. The reason these are more dangerous is that they are by definition closer to the actor's skin. The first step is to ensure, with the costume department, that the actor will have sufficient protection between their skin and the squib itself (maybe this is why you rarely see someone with their shirt off taking a hit?). Even at that, bullet hits often involve a certain amount of physical action, and care must be taken that these protective layers won't slip during the course of the shot. The actor also needs to be careful that they don't, in the course of the action, press their hand or arm against the squib at the moment of the hit, or they could be burned—this should all be addressed in rehearsal. Costume also needs to be involved with this discussion to ensure that there are sufficient repeats of the costume and that the color will be light enough to show the bloodstain effect.

One other illustration of how things can go wrong—on a job I know of, a legendary (for all the wrong reasons) SFX coordinator wired up the lead actor for a number of bullet hits across his chest. The decision was made to break for lunch, and for the hits to be filmed first thing after the break. While all the cast and crew went to eat, the director and SFX coordinator stayed back to discuss the shot further. The SFX coordinator had a small control panel that sent electrical signals to all of the squibs so they would happen in a very quick sequence. "How does that work?" asked the director. "Well," replied the SFX man, "all I do is flip this little lever here," and he demonstrated, forgetting that the actor was completely wired, having his lunch in the studio canteen. As the actor's squibs exploded and blood splashed out he screamed with terror and pandemonium broke out. Page One?

SFX are often related to stunts; for example, in a gun battle the stunt coordinator will need to liaise with the SFX team regarding where a squib is to be attached. At any stunt rehearsals that might involve SFX, the SFX team should be present for the final presentation to the director and DP. If you are getting resistance from SFX to this (as can often happen if they are extremely busy on the shoot) you need to advise the producer/PM so they can make the decision whether to insist that they be there, or let them be absent. Either way, in this case if they don't attend and something goes wrong it has been the producer's decision.

SFX also overlap with stunts during the use of "**breakaway**" glasses, tables, chairs, etc.—objects that have either been pre-rigged to break, or entirely fabricated out of a soft substance that resembles another. Sugar glass, for example, is often used for glasses or bottles that are supposed to break over someone's head, and while they're generally harmless they can still hurt if used incorrectly and need to be properly supervised.

If an amount of **smoke** is required that is larger than one prop person with a machine can achieve, it falls under the auspices of special effects (certainly, if it's exterior smoke—for example, mist on a landscape—that is beyond props' remit). If there is to be smoke employed, SAG rules dictate that main cast must be notified in writing of its usage. It's useful to fulfill this obligation, as again, you don't want to find out on the shoot that the leading lady has asthma and won't work with smoke!

The most important thing to remember, no matter how large or small the stunt or effect, is that it's only a movie and there is no excuse for anyone getting hurt, ever. This isn't just my opinion, it's the law.

Health and Safety

Unless someone else has been so designated, the first AD is the person responsible for the safety and welfare of the cast, crew and public, a massive responsibility. Health and Safety, in many territories, is the one area of the law in which you are guilty until proven innocent. It's not just the production company or the producer or director who will be fined or imprisoned (although they may be as well), but you, personally, no matter your role on the production, are liable for any and all costs and consequences that may occur if it can be proven that you could have done something to prevent an accident, and didn't. The law may not be quite so penurious in North America, but it is no harm to behave as if it is. We all have a duty of care to each other, and if we see something we believe to be unsafe, no matter how apparently insignificant, we are obliged to take action to eliminate the risk or inform the first AD, who may do so.

Of course, everyone should be concerned from a moral and humanitarian point of view that no one gets hurt. But the legal and financial aspects of an accident are equally daunting. It's quite amazing how few accidents happen on sets, given that they are extremely dangerous workplaces. Not only are there usually significant amounts of electricity being used, but the equipment involved can be extremely heavy, work is often at night in locations that are not designed for filming (cliff tops, beaches, public roads), and there is generally a lot of travel and transport. The main precaution against accidents is common sense; but when fatigue sets in, and hurry on top of that, people can be tempted to cut corners, and that's when accidents happen. Your job as a First has dual responsibilities: you need to make things happen as quickly as is humanly possible, but you also need to be sure they're being done safely, and this latter trumps the former. If you ever, as a First, ask someone to do something unsafe you may conceivably go to jail. If concern for your fellow man doesn't make you considerate, hopefully fear of imprisonment will!

Some productions can afford to hire a dedicated health and safety officer, which makes your job a thousand times easier as they will prepare the risk assessments (see Figures 2.19 and 2.20) that are required for insurance and that will be attached to the call sheet. Risk assessments (RAs) are created in liaison with the stunt coordinator and/or SFX coordinator, production manager, and any other relevant parties. It's important to discuss in prep who will produce the RA for the shoot.

A safety statement is the company policy on safety; generally, everyone will have had to sign a form guaranteeing that they have read the statement, and they should be posted in areas of high traffic (such as beside craft services) for everyone to read. At the production meetings and on the morning of the first day of the shoot, the first AD may welcome everyone by reminding them of the conditions under which they will work, as detailed in the safety statement, and in practice to always look out for each other's welfare. I would remind the crew who the safety officer is, ask them to immediately report anything they see that they feel might have hazardous implications, and ask them to take responsibility for each other.

In some locales, it's now required by law that in every workplace there must be a first-aid kit, a fire extinguisher and someone trained in CPR (hopefully you). Part of the Second Second's job is to know exactly where all three elements are at any time, and in a car at unit base is not the place. Every time you enter a new location, you must know where the fire exits are and that they are accessible. In any location with unique conditions, the First is expected to make a brief safety statement at unit call relating to any details of health and safety; it reassures everybody to be reminded, and it takes less than a minute to do so.

<u>**Location Risk Assessment**</u>

Shoot: **Happy Productions "Fab Series"**
Shooting Location: **Smith Street, A Town, A State**
Filming Date: **Monday, October 4, 2011**

Main Risks Identified:
1 scene involving precision driving – a stunt double is nearly hit by a car
1 scene involving stunts – a stunt double jumps over a dog's extended leash

There are further shots involving cast in the cars being towed by a process car.

We will also have 1 x 18k light on a cherry picker for lighting purposes.

Control Measures to Minimize Risks:
1. The roads used for all of the day's shots are closed to public access and controlled exclusively for filming.
2. The precision driver, director, DP, first AD and producer will walk through the two precision shots at 10 a.m. before unit call and confirm the action.
3. All crew to wear high-visibility clothing.
4. All standby vehicles and crew cars will be parked on a separate section of the road that will not be used for filming. All crew not directly involved in the filming of the sequence to stand by at the unit base.
5. Precision driver, artists and any crew traveling in action vehicles to wear seatbelts.
6. **No filming will take place until the precision driver and first AD are satisfied that the conditions are safe to do so.**
7. The light and cherry picker will be pre-rigged during daylight hours.
8. The light and cherry picker will be supervised by a single crew member for safety throughout the shoot.
9. The gaffer will alert the DP and first AD if he feels that the wind conditions are unsafe. The cherry picker will either be lowered to a height that is considered safe by the gaffer, or stood down completely, in this event.

<u>**Studio Risk Assessment**</u>

1- Access and egress is good, there are four doors, one in each corner of the studio plus two scene dock doors.
2- There are ample fire extinguishers; these are placed strategically within the studio.
3- All fire exits must be kept clear and tidy and open whenever there are crew and artists working in the studio and walkways free from any obstruction.
4- The electrical mains cupboard must be kept accessible at all times, should an emergency shutdown be necessary.
5- All floor areas to be kept uncluttered and swept and tidy at all times.
6- All electrical equipment and circuits to have M.C.B. or R.C.D. protection.
7- A fresh water cooler to be provided.
8- Additional fire extinguishers should be placed strategically within the film set.
9- All portable electrical appliances must have a current up to date test label.
10- Equipment on the set to be stored in a sensible way, keeping walkways clear for any emergency evacuation.
11- All mains cables to be installed overhead on the scaffolding provided at all mains distribution outlets. Extensions should where possible be kept to one side and when crossing doorways taped or matted.
12- Working lights to be installed above and around the set for safe working and safe access and egress.
13- A medic to be on set at all times during filming.
14- The extraction fans to be used whenever there is a turnaround.
15- Scaffolding to be earth bonded.
16- Lighting stands to be weighted down with sandbags for stability.
17- Artists and crew to be informed of emergency procedure and the Assembly Point.

Figure 2.19 *Some elements to address on risk assessments—even in a studio, there are always some hazards*

Risk Assessment

Title: Name of the production			Producer: Name	Date of assessment:
Scene No(s). & Description				

Describe here the activity, method of participation, including any props, sets or other structures involved. Where appropriate include drawing(s) and screenplay extracts, tech scouts and the like:

HAZARDS: (what might go wrong)	RISK: (e.g. H = High)	PRECAUTIONS: (risk elimination/reduction)	RESIDUAL RISK:	WHO IS AT RISK:	RESPONSIBILITY:
	Medium		Low	Cast and Crew	Name (First Assistant Director)

Signed and agreed by:

Line Producer name: Name	Signed:	Date:
Copy to: Cast, Crew, Insurance Company		

Figure 2.20 *A sample risk assessment form you can add to as appropriate*

One of the most important contributions a First can make to health and safety is keeping the set productive but calm; if people are rushing, nervous, or worried they're going to get screamed at, they don't work well and are more prone to be clumsy and bumbling. I certainly don't work better when I'm stressed off my head. One example is when we were working outdoors and a swarm of bees approached. Before they arrived, I just asked everyone to be perfectly still and quiet; we all froze, and they flew innocently past us. If someone had screamed, "Bees! Duck and cover! Run!" I guarantee you there would have been at least one sting. Calm and steady isn't just a personal style, it's actually safer for all concerned.

Health and safety are often well-managed when it comes to stunt and special effects work, as generally risk assessments are detailed and required by insurance providers, and a great many conversations happen to ensure that all possible steps have been taken to minimize the hazards involved. In these cases, also, you are relying on the expertise of the practitioners, as well as your own judgment, to ensure that what is planned will be safe. Anytime there is any action required that does pose a safety risk, I request a stand-by medic, if there isn't one already on the crew. At the very least, you need to have done a worst-case scenario talk-through with your team, so that if an accident happens everyone knows their role.

The DGA recommends the "Safety Passport" and it's useful to share this with your team, but most health and safety behavior is simply common sense of the "don't run with scissors" variety. It's the little things that will get you. Doing a stunt or special effect, everyone is focused on safety. Accidents often happen in situations that aren't obviously dangerous, and this is where you and your team need to be vigilant. Besides reminding everyone at the production meeting that everyone is responsible for each other, you need to be constantly alert to any potential hazards. Simple things like gear being left in a pathway; a cabinet door open at eye level; a mat on a wet floor; slicing a bagel into one's hand; slipping on steps coming out of a truck; falling in the ice, or dropping something on one's foot. The worst car accidents I have heard of have always been caused by fatigue. And a big part of this comes under the heading "don't touch my stuff"—one should only lift something at the express invitation of the person from the department to which it belongs. There are methods for lifting cases and c-stands; they're heavy and will hurt your back if you do it wrong.

Even on the most high-profile movies accidents can occur. A cameraman died on *The Dark Knight* when the car he was filming from hit a tree. You can bet that every possible step had been taken to ensure his safety and that of everyone on the crew; and yet two children lost their father that day. The biggest danger on a set is complacency; if your stunt coordinator or SFX supervisor is treating you as if you're just uptight, you need to be on them like spandex. A stunt or SFX shot is not the time for casual confidence, or "trust me's."

If it looks or feels unsafe, it probably is. We'll talk more later about specifically hazardous activities, but the bottom line is that you, as the First, have final say on what is an acceptable risk from a safety point of view. If you are unhappy, but still being pressured to allow something to occur, it's your responsibility to inform the producer, make your concerns known and insist that he or she makes the call on whether to proceed. If work goes ahead, you must do everything in your power to make sure everyone is protected. It's not that directors are inhumane maniacs who will risk life and limb (other peoples') to get the shot—although some of them are!—but their job is to get the most exciting, dynamic, visual shot they possibly can. Your job is to support them in that, while making sure nobody loses an eye.

Extras

For a start, they're not called extras anymore—it's politically incorrect, and SAG calls them background actors. In the UK, they're background artistes, if you don't mind. But I grew up with extras and I use the term here confidentially, just between us. You may, too, as long as it's not within earshot of any extras!

Extras are generally sourced one of two ways: either through an agency, which allows the second AD or POC to simply supply a list of the numbers required and their descriptions (age range, race, preferred clothing colors or other general notes depending on the context of the scene they will appear in); or by the AD team. If the ADs are sourcing the extras there will need to be an extras coordinator and often one or two assistants, depending on the size and nature of the show. If it's contemporary, it's relatively straightforward to organize the required background artists. If it's historical, then the extras may each need to come in for fittings during prep, when they will be dressed and photographed. Male extras on historical dramas are often asked to grow their hair, both cranial and facial, for the entire time of the prep and shoot, so that the hair and makeup departments have options to work with. Naturally, any teeth braces, facial tattoos or piercings are unacceptable in this context.

Ideally, the production will be using an experienced extras casting agency, and once you've solicited from the director what you need, you can pass this on to the agency and they'll do the rest. The agency gets paid on commission for the number of "man-days," or days worked by the extras they represent, so there's no disadvantage to getting them your lists as early as possible during production. Depending on the size of your show, the lead time can range from 2 weeks (contemporary, low-budget) to 8–10 weeks (for a period script with fittings, etc.). The Second or Second Second will liaise with the agency during prep and into the shoot, keeping them advised as early as is practicable about call times and/or changes. The SAG tier of your shoot will dictate how many SAG extras you must hire before you can supplement this figure with nonunion (cheaper) extras. On a low-budget feature, the first 30 must be SAG, including stand-ins; on a short-form TV show, the first 21.

If an extra is *booked* for work and cancelled, they have to be paid for the day. If their *availability is checked,* they can be stood down for free, but they may or may not then be available. If they are already working and booked for the following day, they need to be cancelled by 4:30 p.m., or else they're due another day's pay. If the cancellation is after 4:30 p.m. and is the result of an event so catastrophic as to elicit an insurance claim, they will be paid a half-day. They can be given a weather-permitting call, which means that if they are sent home within two hours after arrival they get half a day's pay; if it was a standard call, they get the full day's wages.

Background actors must be told at the time of booking if there is to be any rough or dangerous work, extreme weather, water or smoke, and if they are to have their hair cut or be fitted for prosthetics, or if nudity is required. Nudity rules are the same as for main actors: closed set, no photos. If they haven't been warned, they can refuse and still get paid for the full day. Nude body doubling is paid at the cast daily rate.

Extras also get paid extra if they have to get wet, wear body makeup, a skull cap, "hair goods," grow their own beard or provide their own wardrobe or props. If they will be required to take a hit, literally, as in, wear an SFX squib, they become a day player and have to consult with stunts and/or SFX.

There are six categories of background actor as defined by SAG:

- General Background: exactly as it sounds
- Special Ability Background Actor: anyone with a disability, or doing something athletic, dancing, amateur singing, driving that requires a special license, card dealing, and so forth
- Stand-In: an extra used as a substitute for the cast for lighting and camera purposes; these may then also be used as background actors
- Photographic Double: when a double is actually photographed as a replacement for an actor—such as a drive-by, or extreme wide shot—payable at the Special Ability rate
- Day Performer: if they say one line, they're recategorized as Day Performers, with the commensurate rise in pay (they are technically now cast)
- Omnies: Extras who make indistinct sound, or walla, in a crowd shot, such as a restaurant or bar scene.

Extras are more expensive than they appear at first glance: besides their daily rate and overtime, if it is a period project, they may need to come in for a wardrobe fitting or hair/makeup adjustment before the shoot, and they also will need to be fed at about 20 dollars a head, notwithstanding the craft services costs. If an extra receives direction from the director, that adds to their daily rate, and if they have any special action or are given a line of dialogue it goes up again. For this reason PMs are highly vigilant about extras' figures, as they can very quickly soar to thousands of dollars for only a few extra bodies.

Besides the regular background actors, you may have **featured extras** that you will need to cast differently than the general background. If you have an extras coordinator or an agency, they will select a few options for the director, offering photographs and details. More than likely, it will be you as the First presenting these options to the director, sometimes with the EC present to answer any questions s/he may have. If the special extra has to do a particular kind of action, or if they are going to be working as a body double for main cast, whenever possible I will bring the person in to meet the director—usually for under 3 minutes—simply to be seen and approved in costume to avoid any drama later.

If the extras you do have on set aren't all highly visible and really earning their keep onscreen, you can expect the displeasure of the PM and producer in your personal direction. I have heard producers go ballistic when more extras are called than are seen, and it is up to you to have the right amount on set and on screen.

SAG requires every show to have a minimum number of extras who are union members, depending on the scale of the show. Extras who are union members are entitled to basic benefits such as a clean, well-lit dressing room or "green room," or holding area (now they're starting to sound like cattle), and overtime after the first 12 hours (time and a half for the next 2 hours, then double time after that). Since union extras have a higher base rate of pay and receive more benefits than non-union members, a production will usually only hire the minimum number of union extras. If a non-union extra is asked to say a line, they then become "Taft-Hartley"-d, will be paid more, can join SAG and the production is fined.

If you're shooting far enough away from a SAG-designated "production city," you are no longer obliged to use union extras (each city is different so you have to check on a case-by-case basis). And I have to say, UK extras seeing the above rules would weep with envy; things have improved, but there are cases I know of where extras are mistreated but in my opinion, if the rules don't get you, karma will!

There are also guidelines of professional conduct for extras, and two of these I wish every background artist would remember is that quiet on set means silence, and "do not ask to leave early, and do not leave early." Why can't we all just get along?

Tests and Retests

I've never met a test I didn't like. They're awkward to arrange, cost money and are often resisted, but to my mind they can provide the single biggest saving—of time and money—that is possible in advance.

The first thing to test, if possible, is the actors' look. This is generally the leading lady, who very often has an opinion about what she feels looks best on her, not only in terms of costume, makeup and hair, but often lighting. I heard one actress during a test say to the very experienced lighting cameraman that she had gotten a list from the previous DP she worked with of the lighting he did for her that she liked, which she would be happy to provide. Needless to say, the DP was less than grateful for the advice, but he was able to demonstrate to her that he could make her look even more beautiful than the last guy, and she went away happy. This confrontation, which could have happened on set and cost a grand a minute as everyone waited around, increasing the pressure on both parties, leading to frayed nerves and potentially harsh words, could happen in the test with a degree of privacy that allowed both to come to a resolution. Whatever the aesthetic merit of the occasion, it was certainly invaluable to the production.

Leaving aside the insecurities of aging actresses, the test is also an opportunity to ensure that the main parties involved are in agreement regarding the look of the film. It's a chance to test the lenses, and the hair, makeup, lighting and any costume issues. If there is a special costume—The Red Dress, for example—it's worth making the effort to make sure it looks on camera the way everyone wants it to look. Costume may not have this exact garment ready, but they should be able to offer a stand-in version for the test. Sometimes lighting can show a shimmer in a fabric that isn't visible to the naked eye; stripes or a heavy weave can moiré (or "buzz"), while colors also can react differently under lighting or on film or HD. And yes, most actors do actually have a "good side," even if they don't know it, and it's worth knowing in advance even if it can't always be accommodated.

Visual effects are increasingly common, and what should be tested in prep is not necessarily the elaborate post-production process or any CGI, but what may reasonably be expected to be created in-camera. Shutter speeds, slow-motion, unusual modes or moves, any lighting effects—everything visually unusual needs to be experimented with now.

I'm also fixated on testing animals: I can't tell you the total hours of my life I must have spent waiting for a dog or cat or fly to do a "simple" trick on command. I have to say I would actually challenge anyone to get a cat to do a trick of any description! But even a standard request such as a dog sitting or lying down can take an hour in the unusual circumstances of a film set, so it's worth bringing the dog and its handler to wherever you're testing (the ideal scenario would be on the actual location) and making sure it works. For one thing, the dog is often slightly different than the director expected, and this conversation can happen while there's still time to adjust. It's also a chance to judge whether the action is physically possible—if the creature can't do it with 10 people watching, it definitely won't with 50. You'll also get to evaluate the handler—you can tell quite quickly whether this is someone who just loves animals, or is a trained technician who understands what the camera requires. If it's the former, it's time for a replacement. It sounds harsh, but so is a "trainer" feeding a puppy treats until it vomits and still not getting the shot. This test doesn't have to be filmed, but the director has to see it, so if s/he can't make it, it needs to be recorded on some kind of video to be played back for approval.

Likewise, any kind of special effect should be shown to the director and DP beforehand. Any mechanical effects or special builds must be viewed in advance. If they can't be seen during prep, they need to be seen at least 3 days before the shoot date. If that doesn't happen, and it arrives on set and it's wrong, it will be your fault.

If a demonstration of any kind isn't exactly right, I would be wary of accepting a verbal reassurance that it will be amended and perfect on the day. Retests are every bit as important as tests—I want the director and DP to see exactly what's going to happen, and be happy with it. If not, action needs to be taken—off-set—so that we don't end up with a unit standing around while something is tweaked. Problems can happen at any budget level; on the bigger budgets people tend to get even more hysterical, so it's not safe to assume (ever!) that just because an SFX or VFX person is highly experienced that they don't need to demonstrate exactly what's needed in advance.

The camera crew probably won't start until the last week of prep, but as you can see there are many things that can be tested without the actual camera, and that last week is the time for the retests.

Prep Week Two (Week Minus Three) Checklist

By the end of this second week, you should have:

- A revised version of the schedule
- Ballpark extras' numbers and numbers of special extras/body doubles
- Some locations decided upon and the tech scouts scheduled
- The first production meeting
- Tests
- "Show and tells" with the director and art department, props, costume
- An updated production calendar reflecting production meetings, tech scouts, casting, show and tells with art dept, props and costume, and tests
- Some cast confirmed

WEEK MINUS TWO (WEEK THREE)

You've got to be very careful if you don't know where you're going, because you might not get there.
Yogi Berra

Now it's getting busy. This is the time when the pace ramps up, and you can feel a noticeable difference in the atmosphere and the amount of people buzzing around the Production Office. People are in earlier, and leave later. Departments that have started work will now have more of their crew on board, and you'll be getting more and more questions and information about the schedule. This is a time when every bit of new information you receive must be passed on to anyone it might affect, as well as being entered into the relevant category on the breakdown sheets (if the information doesn't fit into any obvious category, list it under "Notes" so it can still be discussed at the production meetings).

By now, hopefully, your DP is on board and talking to your director and designers; script changes have been incorporated, scouts are happening, actors are being cast, and everything is moving along happily.

If this happens, crack open the champagne: you're on an ideal shoot. It's unusual, to say the least, and there are any number of possible things that could be happening during this week. You need to be sure that the things that are definitely happening are the production meeting, the art and props show and tells and the tests. There will be new information for you every day, and all of this will need to be continually added to the schedule.

The Current Schedule

At this stage, there will be a lot more information you can add to your breakdown sheets: revised figures and information for background actors, stunts, vehicles, special effects, animals, special equipment, additional labor, visual effects and notes. You may also now have detail to add to categories that didn't feature on the first schedule: props, camera, sound, and so on. There may be more information you can add to the elements such as sequence or unit, and most importantly I would ensure that the Locations box is filled in—even if it's not confirmed—and if it hasn't been selected, simply put a "TBC." This makes it clear on your one-line schedule which locations remain outstanding, and the relative proximity of confirmed locations. You may also now have some cast availability issues to add to your Red Flags.

You will also probably be getting some new script pages—it's important to keep track of the elements that are being added and removed, and the page counts, as these will have a big impact on the shape and size of your days.

Every time you issue a new schedule, be sure to save it as another version (in Stripboard Manager), and amend the banner across the top, stating the date the schedule is being issued. You also, at this stage, can hopefully be refining the banners under each day break with the provisional call times and sunrise/sunset times.

Tech Scouts

A tech scout, or recce (pronounced "rekkee," short for reconnaissance), is a chance for the technical heads of department to visit all of the shooting locations with the director to prepare for shooting there. The required personnel, besides the First and director, would be the production manager (PM), director of photography (DP), production designer, construction manager (if you're building sets), art director and possibly the set decorator, gaffer (chief electrician) sometimes accompanied by the best boy (second electrician), the key grip, location manager, transport captain and/or facilities manager, the sound recordist and the second second AD. If production can afford to have a health and safety officer attending the recce to compile notes for your risk assessments, that's of huge benefit. The special effects (SFX) and visual effects (VFX) supervisors, stunt coordinator and horsemaster might rendezvous at points along the scout in particular locations where their services will be required. It's worth checking with the PM first, as there is a cost issue involved with their time that you need to observe. However, once the PM has arranged that they may be present, it is up to you to liaise with them beforehand about what you agree they need to see, and to decide on the rendezvous locations.

By now your second AD should have started (if not during Week Minus Three), and will need a day to read the script and comb through the shooting schedule to make sure they both correspond. The tricky thing is that his/her first day may often be the first day of tech scouts, so you may only be able to communicate by phone when s/he begins. If you have any kind of budget, the Second and Second Second will go on the tech scouts too.

Ideally, the tech scout happens as proposed here, at the beginning of Week Minus Two. It's often the case that the locations simply aren't secured in time for this to be possible, or all of the crew haven't started yet. Even if a few of the locations haven't been completely locked, I would strongly recommend having the tech scout in the second last week. The very latest is the beginning of Week Minus One, but every day that it creeps later gives you less time to adapt to the new requirements (and there will always be new requirements that arise from a tech scout) and communicate these changes to the rest of the crew.

The location manager will create the tech recce schedule, which you need to be sure to look at in advance and make sure it makes sense from your end. For example, you want to be looking at locations as close as possible to the actual time of day you will be shooting them. You will also want to start with the locations that are the most complicated and/or involve the greatest number of scenes. Or you may want to group scenes together that all require stunts, so you can limit the amount of time the stunt coordinator will be required to join you. Either way, you will want to discuss the tech recce schedule in enough time for the location manager to adjust or improve the running order. This is the only occasion when someone else will be creating a schedule, but as a First you will still need to stand over the logic of the decisions being made.

Tech scouts typically start very early, as there is usually a lot to pack in. The crew will meet at a central location, often the production office, and travel together in a minibus (of course, there can be variations to this, but generally it's inefficient to travel in a convoy and parking can be an issue unless you happen to be shooting a film whose locations are all within walking distance of each other). Those people who are joining the recce at particular locations will travel separately from the minibus and this will be reflected on the schedule—the term O/T refers to "own transport." It sounds like overkill, but it's important to remind the coordinator (who will be notifying the crew about the time and departure location) to ask those attending to bring weather gear. It is easy to imagine, when you're in prep, that you don't need to wear waterproofs if you're only going to visit a location. But if you're in the countryside you'll need boots, and even if you're in the city you don't want to be standing in the rain for 15 minutes with no jacket. Whatever the weather, sandals or flip-flops are not appropriate footwear and some locations require specific safety boots. An AD should never have to be told to bring rain gear, but it's incredible to me how many directors don't even own weather gear, never mind wear it! (I was on one shoot where the director was too vain to be seen in waterproofs—this was in Ireland, where rain is not uncommon. By the second week of the shoot the director had a cold; by the third week he was really sick, and by the fourth week he had pneumonia; shooting stopped, there was an insurance claim, the actors were going to be out of contract: it was a major situation. That's why sometimes even the director's socks are your problem. You need to keep him or her warm, dry and healthy insofar as you and everyone else can, to keep the show on the road.) So even if it looks like a sunny day, everyone needs a raincoat!

Before the tech scout, the First should have a very good idea of what will take place in each location. If there is a particular location that has a lot of scenes or a lot of extras, it's best to visit it in advance with the director and DP. However, it can happen sometimes that this will be your first time seeing the location. If it's a set, the art department might have floor plans that you can copy and provide to everyone on the recce, and if it's an exterior location you may be able to blow up and print an image from Google maps. These maps, even if they're only hand-drawn, are very helpful as a reference, particularly if discussing a location after visiting it.

The First effectively leads the scout and keeps it moving, as you will on the set. As soon as everyone has disembarked from the bus, you should gather their attention; firstly, to inform them of any location or safety issues, and then to the director so that s/he can describe the action and how s/he plans to shoot it. After the director speaks, the crew will then break into a number of smaller conversations—the director and the DP, on which you eavesdrop every word; the DP and the gaffer, some of which again will be useful for you to hear; the grip and the PM, the director and the designer, etc. As you gain experience, you learn to hover unobtrusively, and to sense which conversation has more relevance to you: that is, to the schedule.

Unfortunately, directors are sometimes not so decisive or clear. I once turned to an Oscar-nominated director at the scene of a very complicated stunt sequence and asked him to explain to us all what he had in mind, and he simply said "No." Whether he knew what he was going to do or not, he wasn't going to commit to anything in advance. He simply wanted a 20-yard platform built out into a lake, onto which we could maneuver a 50-foot Technocrane (being brought in from another country), and three 25-foot bluescreens. The DP then added to this a lighting crane (also known as a cherrypicker or condor) to hold a 20K lamp. At this stage we had about $50,000 worth of special equipment hire and additional personnel required, with no definite plan! Not a PM's dream scenario, but this director had the clout to go unchallenged. When we arrived on the day with our 50 extras and 10 horses all in period garb, as well as four lead actors, sub-aqua unit, stunt performers, stunt doubles and special effects team (not to mention the track mats—iron sheets that had been laid across a field to bring the trucks in), the lack of information continued, meaning we couldn't work ahead. It was only when the director announced what the next shot was that we could bring the horses, extras and cast into position, which took much longer than if we had been able to prepare in advance.

I prefer the school of director (typical of a BBC TV background) who understands exactly what the purpose of the tech scout is. They will often request a few minutes to walk it through privately with the DP, if this is either of their first time there. Then they will walk through the action for the crew, demonstrate the camera positions, and be able to answer questions about which area forms the dead zone, that is, where the **trucks** can be parked. This is always the first question from locations and facilities, and is critical. Occasionally, a director will want to shoot "360," that is, to be able to look around 360 degrees. The question then is whether this happens in one shot, or whether the scene can be broken into angles and, after completing the shots looking in one direction, then move the trucks and look the other way (again, a time-consuming method that everyone will resist but is sometimes necessary).

The second question is generally for you: "What time will we be here?" You should have a rough idea from your schedule the general **time of day** you plan to shoot: early morning/late afternoon, etc., or you may even have a specific time like 11 a.m. This will have a big impact on the lighting requirements, and you may get a request from the DP to schedule it at a different time of day, depending on the sun path or other lighting elements. You may be able to do that easily, or it may be impossible—there may be an actor issue, location restriction or director request that dictates why you have the day in that particular order and that scene at that time. The more information you can provide the better, and if you're not sure just say you'll see what you can do. You will also need to know from the DP if s/he is going to require blackouts on windows or doors, and be sure that the PM is also aware of this as it will involve time and labor.

Once you have gathered what you can from the director, DP, gaffer and grip, you should confer with locations and the second second AD about where the trucks are parking, whether and where there is a place for extras holding (if required) and where actors can change or rest if there aren't trailers or Winnebagos (it all depends on the budget). If the actors are being housed near set, try to see the facilities or have the Second Second check it out—the accommodation will often be inadequate and you will need to flag this to the PM early to avoid hysteria on the morning of the shoot. You also need to know where lunch is being served, either by caterers or a local facility, and how long it takes to get there.

It's very common to have what's known as a **unit base**, where the actors' trailers, catering, wardrobe, make-up and hair trucks, and the mobile production office are all parked up. This might be at some remove from the set, where the stand-by trucks (camera, electrical, generator, sound, props, construction) will be parked. There needs to be transport between the two areas, usually coordinated by the transport captain at the requests of the key second AD. As a First, you need a realistic understanding of the distance between the two at all times of day. One of the trickiest juggling acts for a First on a shoot day is calling the actors to set, particularly if they're traveling from any distance. They hate waiting on set, and everyone else hates waiting on them, so there's a lot of skill and a bit of luck involved in arranging things so that any waiting is kept to a minimum. There's also the issue of crew travel time at lunch to and from set to the unit base, which eats into the length of the shooting day and must be planned in advance.

Finally, if you have been joined by the VFX, SFX, stunt coordinator or horsemaster, the director, with the DP and First, must talk them through exactly what's involved. The easiest time to answer questions about any of these elements is now: standing on set with everyone present. It's important to allow time in the tech scout schedule for this conversation to be in-depth and thorough, as the next time you will all be gathered in this place is on the shoot. It's much easier to agree on blocking areas and action when you are all physically there and able to contribute any ideas or concerns at once. It will be up to you as a First to decide whether a particular piece of action actually demands a stunt rehearsal in situ, which will happen outside of the tech scout timeframe, or a special effects test. There may also be a case wherein it is useful to have a stand-in for the actor (usually the second second AD or the PM) and potentially to shoot some video for everyone to refer to after the fact. You'd be amazed how much physical space changes in the memory, even for directors: rooms or landscapes look very different after the fact in the mind's eye, and this can lead to confusion or misinterpretation. The time spent hammering out the details on the tech scout is priceless, although the First must judge when the conversation can be continued on the crew bus.

Finally, you must determine access and egress for both people and equipment: whether the trucks can actually park adjacent to the set, or whether equipment needs to be "hand-balled" (that is, carried) an unworkable distance. Sometimes quad bikes (ATV's) or buggies and trailers can be arranged to bring the gear from the truck to the set, for example, if you're shooting on a mountain-top or beach. If this is the case, you will need to allow for it in your call times, by possibly giving relevant departments earlier calls to facilitate loading out and in. This decision can only be made in conjunction with the PM, as there are cost implications either way.

Before you leave any location, you should have worked out:

- Which areas are "set" and which are "dead"
- Where the work trucks will park
- Where the unit base will be in relation to the set
- Where the actors and extras will be held when off-set (but not at unit base)
- What lighting or weather conditions may impact on filming
- Whether traffic or the public is to be contained or diverted
- Any additional equipment or personnel required, including blackouts
- Whether any visual effects, special effects or stunt work is to take place, and if so, exactly how this will be executed. Likewise any work with animals
- Is a "house electrician" or any other personnel from the location required
- Are there any local activities that could interfere with the shoot (cleaning, gardening, deliveries, sports events, etc.)
- Is access with heavy equipment difficult or time-consuming
- How much time is required or available to dress (and strike) the set
- Whether it can be used as weather cover

The longest conversation during the tech scout will usually be between the DP and the gaffer, so you will need to sit on them a little bit to keep them moving. One trick to keep the momentum going is to get everyone else back on the bus, so the DP and gaffer feel that they are keeping everyone else waiting. This sounds mean, but you will have a lot to get through, and there may be a certain amount of talking they can do en route to the next location. (You do need to stick to the scout schedule, as location owners will be expecting you to be on time.)

These in-between travel times are very useful opportunities for you to liaise with the PM and be sure that you both have the same understanding of what gear or additional labor is required. You will also probably have a long list of questions for the director and DP, either directly resulting from the scout or not, and this is when you have them both together as a captive audience: trapped and available to interrogate together (!), which is a huge asset to determine if they are thinking the same way.

You will hopefully see that your director and DP are sitting together, or at least close by, and communicating freely and openly. If every time you enter a location they instinctively move to different sides of the room, you're in trouble. This is perhaps the most critical relationship on the crew, certainly for both of them, and if there isn't a trust, or at least respect, between them, it's not going to be fun or fast. It's remarkable how rarely directors get to work with the same DPs—mainly because as DPs work on more movies than directors, their schedules are often incompatible, and you are frequently in a situation where they are working together for the first time. Some DPs have large egos, and think that the camera is the most important aspect of the film. It's an understandable point of view, but in fact the audience's emotions are the most important thing, and this resides mainly in the director's guidance of the actors, which is being observed by the camera but shouldn't be dictated by it. No one will generally say this out loud, and there are DPs who like to try to run the show and compete with the director, and there are directors who allow themselves to be bullied. You need to suss out very early on how to negotiate this relationship, as you are the third element in the triangle.

Lunch is usually a working lunch (organized by locations and paid for by the PM), during which you need to be sure that you are always within earshot of the director, and as time goes by you will develop an uncanny ability to tune in whenever they are expressing an idea or request, no matter what else is going on.

By the end of the day, everyone will be exhausted and the discussions will become shorter, which is why it's best to schedule your most important locations early in the day. When everyone else goes home, your work begins—you need to enter all the new information onto the breakdown sheets, and experiment with the various requests you have received to rearrange strips, etc. You will also probably have some information to pass on to other departments. If it's getting late, you can send them an email, and then a text message to say you've sent an email. It's worth recapping, in an email, to the PM all of the information that you've gotten out of the day, and what steps you've taken to address it.

Depending on the script and the show, tech scouts may last one day or several. Either way, by the end of the recces, you need to turn around a schedule in double-quick time that reflects all of the new information and changes, in time for the final production meeting. There will often be resistance to this production meeting, as people are now running out of time. However, this meeting is absolutely crucial, and every head of department and their second in command (at least) needs to attend. It should be scheduled for very early morning (8 a.m. or even 7:30) so people can be finished by start of business. There are so many reasons to do this meeting that they are impossible to list, but, for example, it means that the crew who haven't met will be in the same room, this is the chance for final answers from the Director, and the director, PM and producers are now signing off on a plan. It's one way of bringing order to what can feel like chaos, and is an important opportunity for the First to indicate the type of ship s/he is going to run: calm, orderly, efficient and fast. You are in command, and you will direct your troops in a fair and disciplined manner. We will discuss more about this final production meeting in the section on Week Minus One.

One final note about the tech scout: it is a well-worn truism that if you have a beautiful, sunny day on the scout it will rain on the shoot (and vice versa). So if it's howling a gale when you're on the recce, don't lose heart, but be particularly sure that you still get as much information as you possibly can before people run for the bus. And be happy: it will be sunny when you come to shoot.

Running Your Team: the Assistant Directors

Being a head of department means being responsible for your team: when they do well, when they screw up and when they need help. As the Japanese proverb has it, one arrow can be easily broken, but not a bundle of ten.

The size of the AD team will vary dramatically based on budget, cast, extras, and other requirements, but the very smallest team that can function is three people: the First, the Second and the Second Second (or Third, in the UK system). Even if the whole movie only involves two actors in one location, you need these three people. The Second is indispensible—you need a call sheet, cast wrangler and production report—and without a Second Second you're going to have to do their job, and then who's doing yours? Any attempt at savings in this area is a false economy, costing the production far more in time, money and quality than the price of the wages for a few weeks.

Depending on the show's budget, you may have multiples of these roles: there may be a key Second and additional Seconds, as well as numerous PAs on set and at base. Let's assume that you're going to have a small but effective team—a Second, a Second Second and two PAs—one to assist at base with the Second, and one to be on the set. If the budget is really tight, it'll be the same PA running between the base and the set (it's not by accident that they're often called runners in the UK). As the head of department, your role is not simply to tell (or ask) them what to do, but to train them, and hopefully help them to become better at their jobs as they go. As always, the best way to lead is by example, and if you need to correct something, try to do it in private and with the overall good of the project in mind.

The second AD should start at least two weeks before the first day of the shoot, while the Second Second should get a week's prep, and the PAs will start on day one. This all reflects the official time for which they're getting paid. But if they're not coming straight off of another job, it's good to get them the script, a schedule and a unit list in advance. If they have any time to look at it before they start, it'll prevent an intense prep period from feeling overwhelming.

Depending on the nature of the job, there may be an extras coordinator, or even a whole team to service this area. They will start at least two weeks before the shoot, and while they work somewhat independently, they are still part of the AD team and should be included in your plans and meetings. Too much information never killed an AD!

The Second AD

It's really important that your Second be a team player, and one who communicates with, if not befriends, the production office. The coordinator and the Second are doing analogous jobs—one on set, and one in the office—and they should operate hand in glove. I have seen too many productions where the office viewed the set as a chore, and vice versa, and that doesn't help anyone. There are still some coordinators who like to chain-smoke and complain, but I hope those days are mainly gone. The whole show depends in so many ways on the production office, and your Second needs to understand that and treat them with the respect and collaboration they deserve. The Second's biggest challenge, like the First's, is to behold the wood and the trees simultaneously: to micromanage every tiny detail, while maintaining an awareness of the big picture.

A Second needs to be someone who obsesses over detail for its own sake; who abhors typos and other technical errors and takes pleasure in perfection. They also need to be a highly trained diplomat and psychologist, who can cajole, encourage and, if necessary, manipulate highly sensitive and vulnerable children, also known as actors. A good Second will end up knowing intimate details about all of the cast, but will never enter into storytelling or gossip. When the Second begins, the first thing I like to have him/her do is check my shooting schedule against the script, both to check that all the scenes are in the schedule, and also particularly in relation to cast, to make sure there isn't a character added or dropped from a scene, as it's also extremely easy to accidentally do that, too.

They will usually have a number of questions after that task, and very often will you have to talk them through on the phone if you're out on a scout. But at some point you need to sit down in person and give them the scoop on the director, the DP, other crew, and what you know thus far about the cast. All your opinions and ideas you should never share with anyone else go to the second AD. This may feel therapeutic, but really it's about giving them a crash course in the personalities involved, because much of the Second's job is about managing these personalities.

Once they have checked the schedule, they then need to examine the actors' deal memos (also known as casting advice notes (CANs), or booking slips—see Figure 2.9), to take note of any special stipulations; for example, who gets exclusive ground transport, and any other particularities of the actor's deal, especially nudity clauses and the like. Also crucial to the Second is whether rehearsal times and fittings are included in the deal, as the immediate requirement is to schedule these accordingly and feed them into the production calendar. Once the Second comes on board, they are the only person who should have direct contact with the cast, other than the coordinator (who manages travel and accommodation). Everyone else, including the director, should go through the second AD to make any kind of arrangements. The First will have already discussed rehearsals with the director—some directors don't require them, while others will actually want to rehearse on set, and, failing that, to use a fully marked-out rehearsal room.

During the shoot, the second AD creates the call sheets, liaises with all of the departments about upcoming work, facilitates communication between the office and the set, and produces the first draft of the production report, recording crew "out" times and any other additional information. They supervise the cast getting through hair, makeup and wardrobe and to set; they're often the first in in the morning and the last to leave at night. Like the POC, the Second provides the "invisible hands," without which the whole operation would grind to a halt. The Second also has to be able to inform the office of the first setup of the day; lunch break; first shot after lunch; progress through the day, and wrap time. They will also alert the office about any injuries or equipment failure. The office can then distribute all of this information accordingly.

Once you start shooting, the Second will generally only come to set to deliver or discuss the call sheet, and they often really don't like being on set if they can help it. The Second generally doesn't deliver the cast to the floor themselves; that escort role would typically be handled by the Second's PA, and the set PA often meets and greets the cast and shows them in. This is both to keep an eye on the cast so that they don't go AWOL or take a smoke break, and because it can sometimes be quite tricky to find the set down dark corridors filled with cable. Ideally, the AD escorting them will carry a small mag light for cases like this.

The Second Second AD and the Extras Coordinator

Whether both of these roles are filled during prep depends on the budget and nature of your production. In an ideal world, the Second Second (or Third) will start in time for the tech recces and have a good knowledge of the locations before shooting. If you have several Seconds, you will differentiate by having a key Second and subsequent Seconds.

During production, the Second Second will also usually look after the walkie-talkies, distributing them at the start of the day, collecting them at the end, and making sure they're charged overnight.

Depending on the number of extras involved, there may also be an extras coordinator (EC)—sometimes an entire team—especially if it's a period film and the background artists need to be brought in for fittings before the shoot. Ideally, this is all handled by an extras agency, who the production will provide with a list based on your breakdown.

Occasionally, if the extras required are contemporary and minimal, the Second Second will do the extras coordinating in prep, and hand over to another AD once shooting begins. Either way, it is your job to ensure that the team has all the information they need. The chance to get the director's views on extras is in early prep before things get really hectic, and only the First will be around then. As things change (and they will, as the producer tries to bring down extras numbers and locations begin to have an impact on what's required), you need to keep feeding this information to your team. It's unlikely that the director will have much direct contact with the Second Second or EC, so as always you are the communications bridge between them, and should be present if they present options to the director. Typically, this happens in the form of photographs the director can approve.

During the shoot, the Third will be instrumental in directing extras and we'll discuss that more later. There are often a number of special extras—basically, any extra referred to in the script who has to have a particular look or action. These extras will be offered up to the director in photos for her or him to choose which ones they like. Equally, picture doubles may be shown to the director, often dressed in costume and hair/makeup as part of the test week so that the director has signed off on them and can't have a fit when they show up on the day. The Second would supervise the coordination of this, while again you would be present at the viewing to ensure that everything runs smoothly and in case there are any further instructions.

Production Assistants

Filmmaking is the ultimate team sport, and if you're antisocial or a solo operator, you're in the wrong game. Two of the basic requirements for working in film and TV are: a) having a good attitude—that is, smile when your heart is breaking—and b) initiative—as in, move the paint can out of the doorway without being asked. In fact, these qualities are required in any and all occupations I can think of, and while they are sometimes god-given they can also be learned and practiced; in film and TV they have particular nuances and implications.

Attitude is very simple: you stay positive and never let them see you cry. Initiative is a little more sophisticated, as its evil twin is interference and potential disaster. Initiative sounds like it requires originality of thought, when in fact what it requires is perfect empathy. Useful initiative is when you are able to think like the person directly above you in the chain of command and can anticipate their needs. Interference is when you think something would be a good idea and act on it. Until you gain a certain level of experience, even the best-intentioned action can be annoying. For example, as a PA I saw that the art department had to replace books on a shelf. I eagerly leapt in to "help," and was gently informed by the production designer that the books were in fact continuity and had been removed from the shelf in a perfect order. What she didn't have to point out was that I had wrecked the system and they were now going to have to decipher from some blurry photos which books went where. I was lucky—I could have been screamed at in front of the whole crew, and justifiably. So it's not about leaping in—in fact an AD should never touch a prop or anything else without being asked to; what I should have been doing was seeing what the First needed, without having to ask, even if it was simply a glass of water. The issue of initiative will recur throughout the chapters, but my simple advice is to study the behavior of your head of department so you can anticipate their needs: this is the greatest blessing a First can have, and isn't that hard to learn if you intend to.

This practice of empathy extends to other crew and cast members—if you see someone struggling to open a door because their hands are full, open it! Filmmaking is one of the few areas I know where you can help as much as you can without people thinking you're weird or kissing ass. Everyone on the unit is your colleague, and you want to make their lives as easy as possible—but only after making sure that your own duties are completed.

One other rule is never to leave your post without informing the person who put you there and, following on from this, if someone asks you to do something, tell them what you're doing and be sure they want you to stop doing that. I don't want an AD who's so willing that they abandon the duty the Second has given them to do something for me.

In the UK system, the actors' stand-ins are also part of the AD team as PAs; in the US, stand-ins are a separate entity (this is covered more in the section on Extras).

If you're on your first job, or on a freebie, you need to work like you're being overpaid, not like you're doing someone a favor. Interns cost the company money, as they eat lunch and drink coffee, so they're not a blessing to production, despite what they might think. I heard a great line spoken by an intern who was lucky enough to be allowed to work on a low-budget feature with one of the country's top directors. The production designer saw this intern reading a book—first mistake—and asked him to help her moving boxes. His response? "I won't get to Hollywood lifting boxes." Never mind Hollywood, he wasn't invited back the next day. Page One.

The worst kind of PA is the one who thinks they should be directing, and are too good to be making coffee. Getting tea and coffee may seem menial, but as with any "menial" task it's an opportunity to demonstrate that you can do it well. I recommend to every PA that the first time they get a beverage for anyone—director, producer, cast, even, yes, the first AD—they write down exactly how they take it (milk, sugar, etc.) so they never have to ask again. If required, I'll make the director a coffee myself—no one is too good to shovel the elephant dung. My motto throughout my working life, whatever job I happen to be in, is to do it to the best of my ability, and that worked for coat-checking and waiting tables just as well as running a show. Part of my horror of film schools is that they produce an annual crop of auteurs who have no interest in or ability for the reality of filmmaking, and think they know everything about cinema. Your ambitions are irrelevant until someone asks you what they are; the only ambition of any importance is to learn, to work very hard and to serve the project to the best of your ability. In a way, the filming unit offers a community that in many ways fulfils the noblest aspects of concerted labor and common dedication to a greater cause. Ego and self-interest are a hindrance, even to a director, and to a PA or any AD they're career suicide. I will fire someone who is lazy and smart over someone who is keen and dim. And if you're working in LA, you will get fired very easily. Not to scare you, just a word to the wise. As Tom Whelan, DGA Production Manager, advises every new PA: "Show up on time, do what you're told, and don't ask when you can leave." How hard can it be?

The most important aspect of being a good AD is projecting "a sense of calm". Both to the crew in general and to every individual you come in contact with. A film set can be a very intense, stressful environment and I find people do their best work when they are calm and can think clearly. Not necessarily relaxed - there is too much work to be done in a short period of time to be relaxed – but calm. I think this is equally true for a PA or a director but most of all it is true for an actor. I think the one thing an AD can do above all else is to create a calm, supportive environment on set for the director, the cast, and the crew to create that magical moment when the camera is rolling.

Being a good AD is like being a good parent. People look to you for a sense that you are in control of the situation, you are anticipating what is going to happen next. There is a big difference between talking loudly so everyone on set can hear you convey a piece of information and yelling. When someone is yelling they are telling everyone they have lost control and for an AD that is a fatal error. If there is one person on a film set who needs to be in control of what is going on around him or her it is the AD.

Timothy Bird, DGA First AD

The AD's Meeting

The problem with communication is the assumption it has been accomplished.
G. B. Shaw

Besides the final production meeting, I find it crucial to have a separate AD's meeting before the start of the shoot. This meeting must involve everyone who will be in your department—it's vital to gather your team so you can ensure that you are all working in the same way. The team represents you, and so you need to instruct them in how you want them to behave.

I always invite locations to this meeting—they can rarely attend en masse, but if the assistant can join you for an hour it's phenomenal the amount of difficulties you can avoid by talking through—quickly—the main issues at each location.

Ideally, the ADs can attend the main production meeting (even if they haven't officially started). As you go through the schedule they can compile a list of questions to go through afterwards, as well as becoming familiar with the HODs and the other ADs (you don't always get to bring an entire team from one job to the next).

The production meeting is to talk through the issues that apply to everybody present. At the AD's meeting, you can go through the schedule again, but this time with a view to the issues they need to focus on: where the set is in relation to the base; actors' and extras' holding facilities; any special equipment or requirements; if there's car stuff, what your plan is, in as much detail as you have at the time; even the location of the bathrooms. I'd rather spend three hours in this meeting than see a mistake later on.

The first thing the unit expects from the AD team is information: what's going on, when and where. Even a PA on their first day on a film should have read the script at least once and understand what the requirements are for the scenes that day. If the first call sheet is ready, it's useful to talk through the scenes and their requirements in shooting order, explaining to the team what is needed, when and why. However, just because you have shared this information doesn't mean the PA should involve themselves in its management; if there is ever a question over whether information is sensitive, it probably is, and the PA should always check with their immediate superior as to whether to pass it on.

An AD never says "I don't know"—especially if they don't! What they say is "I'll find out," and they do, as fast as possible. When obtaining information, the best way to go is to the person directly above them, who will either know or tell them who to ask. The request should begin by stating who needs to know—this will determine how the information is directed, that is, in the relevant context. If a PA asks me which direction we're looking (as in, the camera is looking), it makes a big difference whether it's the location manager or the designer who is asking, and I don't want to have to spend the five seconds asking "Who wants to know?" (Fifty cents a second!)

The ADs are walking information booths and should keep themselves constantly informed as to what's going on. A good First calls the relevant information over the walkies: for example, "wide shot completed, moving on to coverage, three shots remaining in this scene, first is a mid-shot on Angie…standing by for rehearsal… scene 101 complete, moving on to scene 56, and so forth." Most of the crew will get this information over the radio, but there will be people who are either not on walkie or who for other reasons haven't heard, and the ADs should be able to inform anyone as to what is going on. I have heard of one AD whose habit is to answer a question like "where are we at?" with a shrug and "I've no idea," and I would never hire her on that basis alone.

There is no such thing as "not my problem." In the absence of someone else, everything is an AD's responsibility. If there's a problem in the locations department, or production have messed up, it's the AD's job to help in any way possible. ADs shouldn't rush in, but should work to whatever the relevant head of department needs; it's simply courtesy to help a makeup artist open the door of the trailer, point people in the direction of the set or tell facilities if there's no toilet paper. My point is that an AD should never brush off a request of any kind, no matter how far it may seem to be from their job description. The unit needs to function as a single organism, not a disparate collection of departments, and the ADs should lead by example.

Speaking of courtesy, being brusque, loud or bossy is the quickest way to lose friends and alienate people. No one likes being ordered around, particularly by some youngster who has only been in the job a wet week, and it's really important for ADs to be polite to everyone they're dealing with, under any circumstances. There is no excuse for being rude to anyone, including extras. Some people seem to be attracted to AD-ing because they want to boss people around or enjoy shouting; these are the ADs no one likes to work with. There is the occasional director who likes to have a real pig of a First, as it makes them look nice, but this isn't the kind of director I want to work with. There's no reason why information and directions can't be passed on with manners and even a sense of humor. It makes for a much happier working environment.

In the AD meeting I reiterate the importance of safety, and that the ADs are responsible for minding everyone and making sure the workplace is as safe as possible. Keeping doorways clear, making sure there is adequate lighting, checking that cables are covered, that areas off-set have work-lights—very tiny things can save someone from a broken ankle. They should also know where the nearest hospital is (it should be on the call sheet, but they shouldn't have to look it up—every day, they need to check before call time). There is a

General Code of Safe Practices for Production at the CSATF website (www.csatf.org/bulletintro.shtml) and you should read it yourself and distribute it to your team before every job.

As well as being tuned in to what's happening at present, the AD's job is to think ahead. A good AD is always looking to the next scene, the next set, the next location, and ensuring that everything is in place to make the transition as smooth as possible. As a First, I will already be doing all that, but an AD who has the minibus parked up facing the right direction with the driver in his seat ready to go, without me having to ask them, is an AD I will hire again.

The only time you say you know nothing and won't find out is when talking to the press. Even if it wasn't spelled out in your deal memo, you have no authority to make any statement whatsoever on behalf of the production, and your only option is complete silence. Some unscrupulous journos will behave like members of the public and try to wheedle information out of the PAs, the greener the better. Especially if you're locking up pedestrians on the street, beware of anyone asking questions. You don't even want to give away the title, so the best response is "I'll see if I can get someone to answer that for you," and instead, inform the First that there may be press present. If they admit to being press, tell the First and await instruction.

Likewise, social media. Don't EVER tweet, post or otherwise upload any information about or images of your working life. Not only are you violating copyright, it's a really dumb thing to wreck your career over. One TV show I worked on had huge media interest in the climax to an ongoing storyline that had gripped the nation. The "reveal" scene was being shot in a location so secret that most of the crew were only provided with the address on the morning of the shoot. That day, one of the lead actors didn't like his lunch, and tweeted a photo of it to his followers. Within an hour, the paparazzi had the place surrounded and the word was out: it was easy for them to track the location of the photo, and the surprise ending that the whole production had spent months building toward was ruined. Don't let it be you.

It's important to know when to ask questions; if you're given an instruction, you must be certain that you understand exactly what the person requires. If they're using vocabulary you're not familiar with, ask them to explain, at the risk of being annoying. It will be more annoying if you bring them the wrong thing. But questioning the decision behind the instruction is not a good idea. One PA on a job recently told the Second Second he didn't think it was important for him to lock up a door that led onto the set, went on to tell wardrobe that he didn't like the actor's sweater and finished by advising the director that he thought the actress was playing too drunk. You know where he is now? I don't.

A big mistake less-experienced crew can make is to be over-enthusiastic in regard to the social and romantic possibilities. A film crew can feel like a big party, packed with fascinating, attractive people. Some newbies join a crew and end up going out every night after work, having affairs and an all-round fabulous time, but they will be tired and distracted at work and chances are, won't be hired again. It's a very tough business and you don't want to mess up your first—and possibly only—opportunity. If yours is the love affair of the ages, it can wait until wrap.

The only mistake worse than sleeping your way through the crew is getting intimate—in any way at all—with the cast. The cast are strictly off-limits for even the most platonic friendship; any contact beyond the immaculately professional will get you into big trouble before you know it. There is a very clear line and my simple advice is DO NOT CROSS. Again, if you think you're destined for a great friendship or romance, explore it at the wrap party, not before. Anything to do with the cast is highly political, and if you don't know that well enough to stay away from them, your days are numbered.

ADs need to be courteous, quiet, dependable and smart; if they have a sense of humor, that helps, too. If they're taking a bossy tone with anyone on the production, particularly someone junior to them, this needs to be stamped out immediately as it creates a very bad atmosphere and can have a contagious effect. There is no complaining, especially about changes to the plan, long hours, hot, cold, or bad food—not even to each other, never mind anyone else. They can bore their partners or their cats with the whining—the production is the place for Positive Mental Attitude, as much of a performance as that may have to be. Anyone with eyes will see if they're soaking wet or sweating and admire their stoicism, if they can just get on with it, and everyone higher up in the production has probably gone through exactly the same hell and survived it.

One last word: never sit down. ADs don't sit. If you want to sit, go into another department. And when you're asked for something, you don't stroll at your own pace—but don't run, as that's dangerous. You move as fast as you safely can, a brisk walk or a controlled jog, as you would if you were part of a surgical team who needed a tool.

Yes, I said a team. Teamwork makes the dream work! Problems, concerns or difficulties need to be shared, and mistakes confessed to as early as possible. Everyone's human and things will happen—they only turn into disasters when someone tries to cover them up or blame someone else. No matter how experienced one may be, every job is an education, and by acknowledging mistakes and focusing on fixing them, rather than finding someone to blame, a creative solution will be more quickly found. If everyone on your team is informed, punctual and polite, you're ready for showtime.

Week Three Checklist

- Tech Scout
- Production Meeting
- Prop Show and Tell
- Camera, Hair, Makeup, Wardrobe Tests
- Scripts finalized
- Second AD begins and schedules rehearsals and fittings

WEEK MINUS ONE (WEEK FOUR)

Coming together is a beginning. Keeping together is progress. Working together is success.
Henry Ford

This is crunch time—there may still be huge schedule changes happening, while the tech scouts might still be taking place, as well as some final tests and rehearsals. Locations are being finalized, new script pages issued, cast confirmed and crew joining the ship. It's your last chance to tie up any loose ends, and everyone else on the crew is in the same position. It's a week of long hours and excitement (not to say pressure), the last chance to batten the hatches before the ship sails. Everyone is looking to the First for information, and you and your team are disseminating everything you know at the fastest possible speed.

Meanwhile, one of the most important things your Second will be working on is the call sheet. The shooting schedule is the breakdown sheets in schedule order; it's the document you've been using at production meetings and tech scouts, and reflects every bit of information you currently possess. This report is the basis for all of the production call sheets.

The Call Sheet (Part 1)

The call sheet (Figures 2.21, 2.22, 2.23 and 2.24) is the daily bible; if it's not on the sheet, it won't be on the set. Every little detail, from crew to equipment to time of lunch, will be in black and white for all to see. At the bottom is your name: every day, you sign off on everything that is required. If something doesn't appear on set, you are responsible.

On the last day of the last week of prep, the first call sheet will be issued; for some reason, no matter how clear it has been for weeks what the first day's shoot will entail, the call sheet is almost always issued very late in the day. It's a bit like a wedding: no matter how long it has been planned for, there's always a last-minute panic.

Each territory has its preferred format, and I recommend going with what the locals are familiar with rather than trying to get them to work to a different system. In the US, the individual call times for each crew member are listed right there on the sheet. In Europe, it's really just the scenes, cast, and special requirements that make the front page. There's now even an iPad app for call sheets! The particular format you're using doesn't matter as long as the information is clear and quickly visible. Beyond this, every Second will have their own little individual foibles.

One very important note is that call sheets are highly confidential, privileged information, and must be guarded with the appropriate care. If they leak out to the press or to interested parties, your shoot can suddenly become a nightmare, swarmed with paparazzi or crazy fans. Although they should never list actors' personal information, even their character name and transport can be useful to a tabloid editor, and on a project where you're trying to keep the ending or other plot devices secret a call sheet can blow your cover completely. They should never be left lying around, any more than a script or a unit list, and it's worth reminding the crew of this when you start, particularly if there is anything the production wishes to protect.

Every sheet will list the project's title, and it's important also to have the contact info for the production office right up front. The call sheet number will correspond to the shoot day—if it's call sheet 13, it usually means it's the 13th shooting day. If there is a second unit shooting simultaneously with main unit, it may appear as 13A or 13X.

The first thing to check is the **call time**—this is the one thing everyone on the crew looks to see and is the single most important piece of information. Just below the call time will be the time from which breakfast is

PRODUCTION OFFICE:	**FAB SERIES**	Monday, October 3, 2011
Happy Studios A Street, A Town, A State (555) 123-4567 (tel) (555) 234-5678 (fax)	MAIN UNIT	**Day 2 of 24**
PRODUCTION COMPANY: Fab Series Company, Movie Makers Rd., Pictureville, A State (555) 345-6789 (tel) (555) 456-7890 (fax)	CALL TIME **10AM** SEE BACK FOR INDIVIDUAL CALL TIMES	Sunrise: 05:33 Sunset: 21:28 Weather: Partly sunny, Winds from the NNW at 16km/h, 22°
Director: John Doe Exec.Producer: Joe Soap, Jane Doe, and any number of others Co-Producer: Guy Fawkes Associate Producer/Writer: Some One Writer: I. Scribe Writer: A. Scribe	SHOOTING CALL **11AM**	**Nearest Hospital:** Our Lady of Perpetual Misery Mercy Street, A Town, A State (555) 987-6543

NO FORCED CALLS, PRE-CALLS, MEAL PENALTIES, OR OVERTIME WITHOUT PRIOR APPROVAL OF UPM. ALL DEPTS WITH PRE-CALLS MUST NDB.
NO VISITORS ON SET / NO PERSONAL CAMERAS ON SET / NO SMOKING ON SET

PLEASE NOTE STUNT REHEARSAL SC. 103 (2/5) TO BE HELD AT 10AM ON LOCATION 2

SET/DESCRIPTION	SCENE	CAST	DAY	P/gs	LOCATION
EXT. PRECINCT Jack chases Jill	103 (1/5)	23, 24	9	1/8	Loc 1: Studio Five Standbys trucks only to park at location.
EXT. PRECINCT Jill narrowly avoids being hit by a car	103 (2/5)	23, 24, 24x	9	1/8	Loc. 2: Smith Street
EXT. PRECINCT Jill pulls out into traffic	103 (4/5)	23, 24	9	1/8	Loc. 2: Smith Street
EXT. PRECINCT Jack's POV of Jill's car	104 (2/4)	12, 23	9	1/8	Loc. 2: Smith Street
EXT. PRECINCT Jack nearly trips over a peeing dog's leash	104 (3/4)	23, 23x	9	1/8	Loc. 2: Smith Street
INT. JILL'S CAR Jill sees that she's not being followed	104 (4/4)	24	9	1/8	Loc. 3: Jones Street
16:00 – LUNCH					
EXT. PRECINCT Jack hails a cab	103 (5/5)	12, 23	9	1/8	Loc. 2: Smith Street
INT. TAXI Jack argues with the taxi driver	104 (1,3,/4)	12, 23	9	1/8	Loc. 2: Smith Street
COMPANY MOVE TO BRIDGE STREET					
EXT. DAVID & ROSIE'S FLAT Rosie has on new knickers	131	5, 6	N1	1	Loc. 4: New Street
TOTAL PAGE COUNT				1 5/8	

#	CAST	CHARACTER	STATUS	LEAVE	REPORT	REH	SET	NOTES
12	Moustache Mann	Taxi Driver	WF	11:30	12PM	12:30	1PM	Van
23	Diva Queen	Jill	S	08:45	09:15	10AM	11AM	p/up
24	Hunk E. Guy	Jack	W	9:30	09:45	10AM	11AM	Van
5	Bigg Girle	Rosie	SW	3PM	3:30	4PM	5PM	p/up
6	Sum Guye	David	SW	3:30	3:45	4PM	5PM	Van
23 x	Daree Deville	Jill Stunt Double	SWD	09:30	09:45	10AM	11:30	O/T
24 x	Butch Fella	Jack Stunt Double	SWD	09:30	09:45	10AM	11:30	O/T

m=minor

STAND INS & ATMOSPHERE:	SPECIAL INSTRUCTIONS:
STAND INS: JILL #23 - (Shirley) RPT TO WARDROBE @ 10:15 JACK #24 - (Dave) RPT TO WARDROBE @ 10:45 **SC. 103, 104 – EXT. PRECINCT** 24 x ND Street 1 x Taxi Passenger 1 x Lady with Peeing Dog **26 TOTAL BG**	**ART:** Sc. 903 (1/5) False door into Precinct **PROPS:** Dog Pee, Leash **ANIMAL HANDLER:** Mary McNamee, owner of "Piddles" **CAMERA:** Sc 903, 904: Arri 435, Split Diopters, Sc.903: Iconix **VEHICLES:** 4 x ND extras' cars, Jill's car, Jill's car double; 5 x ND parked cars **ADDL LABOR:** Stunt Coordinator, Precision Driver, Picture Car Driver, Medic **STUNTS:** Jack jumps over leash, Jill nearly hit by car
HOLDING / CATERING	**BASE CAMP/CREW PARKING**
The Nearby Building Smith Street, A Town	Studio 5, Backlot, Happy Studios

ADVANCE SCHEDULE

TUESDAY, OCTOBER 4 - UNIT CALL 10AM

SC.	SET/DESC.	DAY	CAST	PAGES	LOCATION
734	INT DAVID & ROSIE'S FLAT Rosie kicks David out	D4	5,6	1	Bridge Street
243	INT DAVID & ROSIE'S FLAT Helen arrives with champagne	D1	6, 14	5/8	
404	INT DAVID & ROSIE'S FLAT Rosie kicks David out	N3	5, 6	1 3/8	
612	INT DAVID & ROSIE'S FLAT A horrible silence	N5	5, 6	1/8	
614	INT DAVID & ROSIE'S FLAT David dreams about Red	N6	5, 6	6/8	

PM/UPM: PENNY PINCHER	FIRST ASSISTANT DIRECTOR: ME TOO	2ND AD: SMART COOKIE (555) 987-6543

Figure 2.21 *A US call sheet, page 1*

	DEPT.	LV	RPT	NAME		DEPT.	LV	RPT	NAME
FAB SERIES			**CREW CALL: 10AM**				**DATE: MONDAY, OCT 2, 2011**		
*** NO FORCED CALLS, PRE-CALLS, MEAL PENALTIES, OR OVERTIME WITHOUT PRIOR APPROVAL OF UPM. ALL DEPTS WITH PRE-CALLS MUST NDB. ***									
	PRODUCTION – SET			CH. 1, 2, 4		**ART DEPT./CONSTRUCTION**			
1	Director	09:00	9:30	J. Doe	1	Production Designer		O/C	
1	Producer		O/C		1	Art Director			
1	Co-Producer				1	Art Dept. Coordinator			
1	Assoc. Producer				1	Graphic Designer			
1	Writer				1	Art Dept. PA			
1	Writer								
1	1st AD				1	Construction Coordinator			
1	Key Second AD				1	General Foreman			
1	2nd 2nd AD				1	Foreman			
1	Key Set PA				1	Prop Maker			
1	Set PA								
1	Set PA					**SET DECORATING**			
1	Set PA				1	Set Decorator			
1	Addl PA				1	Lead Person			
					1	Buyer			
1	Script Supervisor				1	Buyer			
					1	Set Dresser			
	PRODUCTION - OFFICE				1	Set Dresser			
1	Production Supervisor								
1	Production Coordinator				1	On Set Dresser			
1	Asst. Prod. Coordinator								
1	Production Secretary					**SCENIC**			
1	Travel Coordinator				1	Scenic Charge			
1	Office PA				1	Painter			
1	Green Compliance Org.				1	Painter			
	CAMERA			CH. 6		**LOCATIONS**			
1	Director of Photography				1	Location Manager			
1	A First Asst Camera				1	Asst. Location Manager			
1	A Second Asst Camera				1	Location Scout			
1	B Camera/Steadicam Op				1	Location Scout			
1	B First Asst Camera				1	Location Scout			
1	B Second Asst Camera								
1	Camera PA					**ACCOUNTING**			
1	Still Photographer				1	Production Accountant			
	DIGITAL IMAGING				1	1st Asst. Accountant			
1	Digital Imaging Technic.				1	2nd Asst. Accountant			
					1	Payroll Accountant			
	VIDEO				1	Accounting Clerk			
1	Video Assist								
						ASSISTANTS			
	GRIPS			CH. 8	1	Asst. to Producer			
1	Key Grip				1	Asst. to Director			
1	Best Boy Grip				1	Asst. to Co-Producer			
1	Dolly Grip								

Figure 2.22 *A US call sheet, the back page*

1	Company Grip					**CASTING**				
1	Addl Grip					1	Casting Director			
						1	Casting Associate			
1	Rigging Key Grip					1	Casting Assistant			
1	Rigging BB Grip									
SET LIGHTING				CH. 7		1	Extras Casting			
1	Gaffer					1	Extras Casting Assistant			
1	Best Boy Electric									
1	Electric					**POST PRODUCTION**				
1	Electric					1	Editor			
1	Addl Electric					1	Post Production Consult.			
1	Genny Op					1	Sound Designer			
						1	Post-Prod Sound Mixer			
1	Rigging Gaffer					**PICTURE CARS**				
1	Rigging BB Gaffer					1	Picture Car Captain			
SOUND						**TRANSPORTATION**			CH. 3	
1	Sound Mixer					1	Transpo. Captain		O/C	Eamon Target
1	Boom Operator					1	Transpo. Coordinator		O/C	
1	Utility					1	DOT Compliance			
						1	15 Pass Van		Per ET	
PROPERTY				CH. 1		1	15 Pass Van		Per ET	
1	Prop Master					1	Honeywagon		Per ET	
1	Asst Prop Master					1	Star Trailer		Per ET	
1	Addl Props					1	2-Banger		Per ET	
						1	H/M/W Truck		Per ET	
COSTUME						1	Camera Truck		Per ET	
1	Costume Designer					1	Grip Truck		Per ET	
1	Asst. Costume Designer					1	Electric Truck		Per ET	
1	Wardrobe Supervisor					1	Prop Truck		Per ET	
1	Key Set Costumer					**CATERING**				
1	Set Costumer						Caterer			Yummy Food Inc.
1	Wardrobe Intern					1	Chef			
HAIR						1	Sous Chef			
1	Hair Dept. Head					1	1st Assistant			
1	Key Hair Stylist					70	Crew Breakfast	Rdy	@10AM	
1	Hair Stylist					25	BG Breakfast		@10AM	
MAKEUP						70	Crew Lunch		@4PM	
1	Make Up Dept. Head					25	BG Breakfast		@4PM	
1	Key Makeup Artist					**CRAFT SERVICE**				
						1	Craft Service			
ADDITIONAL PERSONNEL						1	Craft Service Asst.			
1	Dog Handler						Addl Craft Service			
1	Precision Driver					70	Craft Service for Crew	Rdy	11AM	
1	Process Car Driver					25	Craft Servce for BG	Rdy	11AM	

TRANSPORTATION PICKUPS

PU D. QUEEN (#23)	HOME	08:45	Merc	
PU H. GUY (#24)	HOTEL	09:30	Merc	
PU M. MANN (#12)	HOTEL	11:30	Van	
PU J. DOE (DIRECTOR)	HOTEL	09:00	Van	

Figure 2.22 *(Continued)*

CALL SHEET

Director.............................John Doe
Exec. Producers.................Joe Soap, Jane Doe,
      and any number of others

Co-Producer......................Guy Fawkes

Second A.D.........................Smart Cookie (555) 234 5678
Location Manager..............Map Maker (555) 345 6789

FAB SERIES

MAIN UNIT

Happy Studios
A Road, A Town
A State
(555) 123 4567

Date:	**Monday 3 October 2011**
Day:	**2** Out of **24** Days
CREW CALL:	**11:00**
Breakfast:	**10:00**
LUNCH:	**16:00**
Sunrise:	**05:33** Sunset: **21:28**
Weather:	Partly sunny, Winds from the NNW at 16km/h, 22°

Loc. 1 = Studio 5
Loc. 2 = Smith Street
Loc. 3 = Jones Street
UNIT BASE: Studio 5, Backlot

PLEASE NOTE STUNT REHEARSAL SC. 103 (2/5) TO BE HELD AT 10AM ON LOCATION 2

SET/DESCRIPTION	SCENE	CAST	DAY	P/gs	LOCATION
EXT. PRECINCT Jack chases Jill	103 (1/5)	23, 24	9	1/8	Loc 1: Studio Five Standbys trucks only to park at location.
EXT. PRECINCT Jill narrowly avoids being hit by a car	103 (2/5)	23, 24, 24x	9	1/8	Loc. 2: Smith Street
EXT. PRECINCT Jill pulls out into traffic	103 (4/5)	23, 24	9	1/8	Loc. 2: Smith Street
EXT. PRECINCT Jack's POV of Jill's car	104 (2/4)	12, 23	9	1/8	Loc. 2: Smith Street
EXT. PRECINCT Jack nearly trips over a peeing dog's leash	104 (3/4)	23, 23x	9	1/8	Loc. 2: Smith Street
INT. JILL'S CAR Jill sees that she's not being followed	104 (4/4)	24	9	1/8	Loc. 3: Jones Street
16:00 – LUNCH					
EXT. PRECINCT Jack hails a cab	103 (5/5)	12, 23	9	1/8	Loc. 2: Smith Street
INT. TAXI Jack argues with the taxi driver	104 (1,3,/4)	12, 23	9	1/8	Loc. 2: Smith Street
COMPANY MOVE TO BRIDGE STREET					
EXT. DAVID & ROSIE'S FLAT Rosie has on new knickers	131	5, 6	N1	1	Loc. 4: New Street
TOTAL PAGE COUNT				1 5/8	

	CAST	CHARACTER	P/U	M/U	HAIR	WARD	LINE UP	SET
12	Moustache Mann	Taxi Driver	11:30	12:00	12:15	12:30	12:45	13:00
23	Diva Queen	Jill	09:00	9:15	10:00	10:30	10:45	11:00
24	Hunk E. Guy	Jack	10:00	10:30	10:15	10:30	10:45	10:00
	STUNTS	CHARACTER	P/U	M/U	HAIR	WARD	LINE UP	
23x	Daree Deville	Jill Stunt Double	o/t	10:15	10:45	11:15	10:00	11:30
24x	Butch Fella	Jack Stunt Double	o/t	11:15	11:30	11:45	10:30	12:00
Sc. 903 (2/5)	Jimmy Speed	Stunt Driver	o/	10:45	11:00	11:15	10:00	11:30
	DOUBLES	CHARACTER	P/U	M/U	HAIR	WARD	LINE UP	
Sc. 904 (2/)	Serena Divine	Jill Driving Dbl	o/t	10:30	11:00	11:30	11:45	12:00
	EXTRAS	CHARACTER	P/U	M/U	HAIR	WARD	LINE UP	
Sc. 903	1	Lady with peeing dog	o/t	10:00	10:15	10:30	10:45	11:00
Sc. 903	20	Street crowd	o/t	10:00	10:15	10:30	10:45	11:00
Sc. 904	1	Taxi passenger	o/t	11:30	11;45	12:00	12:30	11:30
Sc. 903-904	4	ND drivers	o/t					11:00
	STAND-INS	CHARACTER	P/U	M/U	HAIR	WARD	LINE UP	
All Scs	Samantha Lookalike	Utility	o/t	10:30	10:30	10:30		As Req/d
All Scs	Joe Alias	Utility		10:30	10:30	10:30		As Req/d

First Assistant Director: Liz Gill (555 2523846)	2nd Assistant Director: Lisa Lovemyjob (555 763 7764)	2nd 2nd Assistant Director: Richie Richards (555 956 3854)

Figure 2.23 *A UK call sheet, page 1*

REQUIREMENTS	
Camera	As per Oneyed Jack – DOP/Operator (555-9356463): Sc 903, 904: Arri 435, Split Diopters, Sc.903: Iconix
Grip	As per Bear Hanlon (555-8112401) Sc.904: Slider, Sc.903 (2/5): Giraffe Crane on set from 14:00, crane op Marty Mechanic, additional grip John Geranium (555) 253 2699
Sound	As per Power Toole (555 867 1246): Sc. 131 playback of answering machine message
Dog	As per Tony Canine (555-2539415) Sc. 904 peeing dog
Stunts	As per Bill Fallover (555 989 1234) Sc. 904 wire rig & safety platform required; Jill double kneepads and elbow pads required; crash mat; Jill and Jack Stunt Doubles to be WMH'd @ main unit base
VFX	As per Look Nsee: Sc.131: Rosie morphs into lingerie model
Script Supervisor	As per Kathleen Continu
Art Dept/Construction	As per Mad Genius: Sc 903 (1/5) False door into Precinct
Props/Set Dressing	As per Lyndon Johnston: Sc.131: baton (rubber); Sc.903 (3/4): dog pee kit
Costume	As per Mah Vellous: Sc.903, 904 Jill and Jack Double Costumes, Jill Double Rubber Sole boots, 2 x crew on standby
Make-Up	As per Dee Vine: Sc.903, 904 Jill and Jack Double, 2 x crew on standby
Hair	As per Dee Corcoran: Sc.903, 904 Jill and Jack Double 2 x crew on standby
Vehicles	As per Eamonn Target: Sc. 903/904 4 x ND extras' cars, Jill's car, Jill's car double; 5 x ND parked cars
Medic	As per Chancer Mullen (555-1619016 on channel 14) on set from 11:00
Production	As per Denis Adset: 8 x Walkie Talkies on charge for 2nd Unit in A/D's office. Ecologist Faith Wilson to stand by on set from 9AM
Facilities	As per Eamonn Target (555-6019700) – 1 x Star Trailer, 1 x 2 Banger, Dining Bus & Honeywagon and Facilities Genny, up and running at Unit Base from 10:00
Catering	As per Yummy Food Inc.,: 70 x Main Unit breakfast @ 10:00 at Unit base, 70 x Lunch @ 16:00, Running tea & coffee all day please
Rushes	To go to Windmill studios on wrap. Film rushes to go to production

ADVANCED SCHEDULE Tuesday 4th OCTOBER
UNIT CALL: 10:00 AM

Sc	SET/DESCRIPTION	DAY	CAST	PG'S	NOTES/LOCATION
734	INT DAVID & ROSIE'S FLAT Rosie kicks David out	D4	5, 6	1	Bruise; Sam Pirate latest wrap 10.45
243	INT DAVID & ROSIE'S FLAT Helen arrives with champagne	D1	6, 14	5/8	Bruise; Ram Sparrow latest wrap 1645
404	INT DAVID & ROSIE'S FLAT Rosie kicks David out	N3	5, 6	1 3/8	Bruise
612	INT DAVID & ROSIE'S FLAT A horrible silence	N5	5, 6	1/8	
614	INT DAVID & ROSIE'S FLAT David dreams about Red	N6	5, 6	1 6/8	

TRANSPORT Eamonn Target (555 6019700)

Pass Van	Standby at Main Unit base
Ken Ford 555 287 3665	08:45 P/up Diva Queen from home & convey to unit base
John Bentley 555 258 3987	10:00 P/up Hunk E. Guy from home & convey to unit base
Brendan Daewoo 555 2020781	11:30 P/up Moustache Man from hotel & convey to unit base
Brendan Daewoo 555 2020781	12:30 S/By to P/up Bertie Davis & chaperone from hotel & convey to unit base

CREW LIST

Title	Name	Number	Props		
Director			Props		
Assistant Director			Dog Handler		
2nd A/D			Costume		
2nd 2nd A/D			Costume		
DoP / Operator			Make up		
Focus Puller			Make up		
Clapper Loader			Hair		
Camera Trainee			Hair		
Grip			Locations		
Video Assist			Catering		
Script Supervisor			Catering		
Sound			Transport		
VFX			Minibus Driver		
Rigger			Camera Truck Driver		
Carpenter			Props Truck Driver		

Figure 2.24 *A UK call sheet, the back page*

available, and this may be adjusted earlier if there is a pre-light or rig happening before the standard shooting day. Your lunch will be as per the crew deal, for example between five or six hours after unit call. You never put the wrap time on the call sheet, unless you are doing an extended day (that is, planned overtime), and even then it's a judgment call as to whether you declare it on the sheet.

If there is to be some unusual circumstance such as an extended day (planned overtime), unique conditions (shooting on a boat, for example) or any other special requirement (from workboots to be worn by all crew, to someone's birthday), you might put it in bold across the top of the call sheet as a **banner** advertisement for everyone to see. This will not replace your telling the crew this information, and the way to do that is on wrap of the previous day, by broadcasting it over the walkie and aloud as you announce the unit call for the next day.

Secondly, you'll look at the **weather**, which is right below the unit call. Unless there is a weather catastrophe approaching, most lower-budget productions shoot through whatever the weather happens to be. It's a fact of life that for rain to be visible on camera it has to be backlit or falling in front of a dark surface, so you can quite feasibly shoot a scene where people are sitting poolside in the rain, as long as you can't see the drops hitting the pool. (Typically, you'll also be shooting this scene in the freezing cold, which is fine until you can actually see the goosebumps or the actors' lips turning blue. We once had a problem shooting in the cold when the lead actress' lines were becoming increasingly indistinct—we were worried that she might be secretly drinking, but discovered that it was simply that her mouth was so cold she could hardly form words with her lips. There are health and safety implications to this, of course, and you need to be able to distinguish between discomfort and abuse.)

On the top left of the call sheet are the **names** of at least the director and producer. Beware of the producers' names on the call sheet—the Second will inquire diplomatically in prep whose name goes on, and whether they can go in alphabetical order. Even though the politics involved are not the Second's responsibility, it is s/he who will receive a torrent of abuse if they're incorrect—and the more producers there are, the more insecure many of them will be about their position. On some shows, the writer(s) may sometimes also be listed on the sheet.

Across from these names is listed the name of the **location**, which lists the set and the unit base (if different). The next column you'll look at is the scheduled **scene order**. Unless otherwise instructed, the Second will have transposed the scenes straight from the shoot schedule. On Day 1, that probably stands, but as the shoot progresses you will potentially be rearranging the order of these scenes for every call sheet.

When you have the scenes in the right order, look down through the **story days**. What you want to avoid is costume changes, and these can be easily spotted if you have your story day incorporated into your DAY/ NIGHT column: having a leading lady change from day 1 to day 3 is time-consuming, and changing her back to day 1 again will lead to high-volume squawking from many directions. This can only be done if you really have no other choice (a time of day issue, or major location/equipment/effects requirements, etc). If so, you must advise everyone in advance (hopefully at the production meeting) why this has to happen, and make sure that the Second explains it to the cast before they see the call sheet at the end of the day. Even then, there will be grumbles but you won't waste time explaining it in the rain.

The times you tell the Second that you will need the **actors on set** will be what s/he bases the actors' call times on. What I like to do is give estimated timings for when you will start each scene; for the first few days, the Second will err on the side of caution in terms of getting the cast ready ahead of time; as s/he gets to know the makeup/hair/wardrobe team and the rhythm of the production, s/he will know how much of a buffer to leave. It is a very contentious issue for some actors being made to hang around; we try to keep this time to a minimum, and most actors will be professional about the time they inevitably have to wait. If you have a real moaner and you're certain that you are doing everything in your power to facilitate their time, you may want to mention it to the producer that the actor seems unhappy: it's better that they hear it from you rather than the actor's agent.

As a First, you will probably have sketched in rough timings on your own copy of the strips to be sure you're hitting the right call times based on daylight and other requirements. As with everything, these will evolve as you go, especially as you learn more about the director's shooting style, but you want to always have a sense of roughly where you want to be.

The next section covers the cast: their character names and numbers, real names, pickup times, wardrobe/makeup/hair time, and their on set time. (If you're dealing with big stars, you may replace their real names with code names.) Here you can see why the actors' agents sometimes get shirty in prep about their clients' cast numbers: on the call sheet all the actors look at their numbers and compare them to everyone else's, and everyone wants to be number 1! Deciding these call times is a sophisticated science that separates great Seconds from bad; if you have a bad Second you will get the actors complaining to you about how long they're hanging around, or, worse yet, you'll be on set waiting for them.

What I tend to do is give the Second my timings for the actors to be required on set, then they work back by talking to makeup, hair and wardrobe about how much time they need, adding in time for breakfast, and checking with transport how they will travel and how long it will take. It's important to keep the Second informed all through the shooting day as to how things are going, in case someone needs to be rushed to set, or in case their call time might slide a little later. If you can delay picking them up, do—better they should be hanging around at home than in their trailer, no matter how kitted-out it may be…

Stunt performers will often be listed in the cast category, and if they are doubling for a cast member will be given the same number as that actor with an X—1X, 3X, etc. Although they are often team players and often behave like crew members, stunt performers are cast members and should be treated as such.

The first time the actors are being given their call times, or the "first work" calls, it will come from the casting director or production office. After this, the Second is solely responsible for informing the actors directly as to their pickup and call time, either before they wrap or by phone. Times listed on the call sheet are still provisional, with the Second having the final say. A useful technique when calling or messaging actors, extras or crew is to ask them for a return text message to confirm that they have received the communication.

Background actors will be the next category, particularly if you have special or featured extras, with on-set times listed in the same way as the cast, but grouped, rather than individually.

Beside or below this you will see the **requirements**: all of these elements will be taken straight from the shooting schedule, and listed as per department. (On a US call sheet, only the departments with special requirements will be listed; in the UK, every HOD goes on the list, and this is where contact numbers are provided.) Before the call sheet is issued, the Second will check with each department that these requirements are still accurate before running them past the PM—it can happen that a crew member might try the "back-door" approach of trying to add something to the call sheet through the Second, without going to the PM first, and so if the PM sees anything they weren't expecting, they can iron it out before it's required. Early calls should also be double-checked with the PM. No detail is too small for the requirements section, and you and the Second should also look through the scenes in the script to make sure that there isn't anything in new script pages you might have missed. Although you might not have added all the props to the shooting schedule, they need to be here, otherwise if they don't turn up it's your fault.

The **advance schedule** is also crucial, and for now will also be a straight transposition of the information on the one-line schedule.

Finally, **transport** will all be listed at the bottom. This is the most sensitive area in relation to protecting the cast from any security concerns—generally, if you're dealing with stars you will not list their address during the shoot, but say simply "from hotel" or "from home." The Second, the drivers and the office have these addresses, and no one else really needs to know.

It's important that the second AD's phone number is clearly visible, as the second AD's phone is the main point of contact for all off-site crew members, along with the location manager's—they need to be contactable, even though their second-in-command will most likely be covering the set if the manager themselves isn't there. And at the end of the page—your name. You're standing over it, so you want it all to be right. I hate typos on the call sheet; I think it indicates that other aspects of the department might be messy, too, so I always correct them when I see them.

The **format** of a call sheet is variable—all Firsts and Seconds have their own preferences, not to mention PMs and local variations. What matters most is that it be clear, intelligible, and contain all of the above information.

The call sheet will often be accompanied by a movement order (Figure 2.25) and map (from the locations department), and/or a risk assessment (from production) (Figures 2.19, 2.20). A movement order contains written directions to the locations. Often people will also list the location's latitude and longitude, so that it can be plugged into a GPS system. The written directions should be written as bullet points, with a new point at every turn or junction—imagine you're trying to read it in the dark while driving—you don't want a big block of text to try to navigate at every stop sign.

A risk assessment is a document you will have generated in prep, which is attached here so everyone can refresh their memories or see it for the first time. There are numerous templates that are used and you will probably be provided with the format by the POC, unless you prefer your own. Essentially, what it lists is the Subject—the action; the Hazard—what harm or hurt could be done; the Persons at Risk; Details; Control Measures—very important: every possible step you took to ensure that the hazards were reduced to an acceptable level of risk; Significant Aspects of the Risk—the bottom line as to what could possibly happen in a worst-case scenario; and Risk Level—from low to high; the higher the risk, the more paperwork you will need, to be able to prove, if necessary, that you did everything in your power to ensure the safety of

<u>Movement Order</u>

<u>FAB SERIES</u>
From Production Office, Happy Studios, A Town to
Location 4: 13, Moonlight Crescent, A Town
Monday, Oct. 4 2011

- Leave Production Office and take an immediate **RIGHT TURN** onto Happy Street, continue **STRAIGHT**

- At the **THIRD RIGHT** take Dumpster Street

- After 2 miles, **MERGE** with Route 66 and continue **STRAIGHT**.

- Pass all of the exits for Eldorado until you reach the **LAST EXIT** signposted **ELDORADO/PARADISO**.

- **EXIT HERE** and with the Exxon station in front of you take the **RIGHT TURN** onto Hellfire Lane.

- **CONTINUE** past the Druid's Chair Country Club on the Left for 3.3 miles

- At the next intersection, take the **LEFT TURN**

- You are now on Moonlight Crescent – **CONTINUE 1.5m** and Eddie Muppet's house is on the **LHS**.

- Standbys and essential vehicles only to park at the house. All other vehicles park in the parking lot just past the house on the LHS.

- Please park as directed

Fire:	911
Eldorado Police Station:	(555) 666 5750
ER Our Lady of Misery Hospital:	(555) 221 4000

Location Manager:
Don O'Malley (555) 832 4220

Figure 2.25 *A very basic movement order, but easy to read in the dark!*

all those at risk; Who Will Take Action—this is usually the first AD, sometimes the key grip (if they are the designated safety officer) and the stunt coordinator (if the risk involves a stunt). Naturally, depending on the situation, the special effects supervisor might also be involved in this capacity.

Diligent productions may issue risk assessments for every shooting day or a general one on the first day to cover the usual daily hazards: cables that could lead to trips and falls, sharp objects, heavy equipment, moving vehicles, etc. However, only the RAs that involve unusual activity or significant risk will be attached to the call sheet. One other note that's useful to add at the end of the sheet is the breakdown of department on the walkie channels.

Walkies

Walkie-talkies, or radios, are the AD's main tool. Generally, Channel 1 is the main set channel and the voice of the First. The only time anyone else speaks on Channel 1 is to find someone else and ask them to go to another channel—"Mike on Channel 4, please." "Linda go to 6, please." And the only time the First should be talking on Channel 1 is when imparting information that is relevant to the entire company: "Rolling, Action, Cut, Checking the Gate, Moving On, Last shot of the scene, etc."

As soon as I put on my earpiece in the morning I say "walkie check," and someone will say back "good check." This is just standard to make sure all the equipment is working fine. Channel 2 is usually the AD's overflow channel—to talk to anyone on my team, I would say "Go to 2" on Channel 1 and have the conversation on 2. However, when I say conversation, I don't mean that in any traditional sense. Walkie talk needs to be brief and to the point, otherwise it should happen on the phone. If you're on a big movie with 13 channels going, even more people need Channel 1, and there is nothing more annoying than not being able to roll because some PA is yapping on Channel 1; it won't get you fired, but it's a first strike.

To get someone on walkie, I say "Name, come in please," and expect to hear back, "Go for Name." Not "yep," "what" or any other variation on a theme, especially if it's a big crew. Walkie communication should always be in very short sentences, preferably yes/no questions, and end with "Back to 1," indicating that the conversation is over and reminding you both not to forget to switch back. This is why expressions like "roger," "check" and "copy" work well—they're brief! Some people like to say "over" and other lingo from CB radios and war movies, but I find normal English does just fine. Swearing of any description is verboten, however— it's rude in Europe and illegal in America as it is legally defined as broadcasting, for which they have very strict obscenity laws! Walkie speech must be brief, and leave gaps for the other to reply. If two people both talk simultaneously, they get "stepped on," which means no one hears either and results in a nasty sound in everyone else's ear. If someone steps on the First calling "rolling," it can lead to obvious problems.

The other channels are divided among the other departments: for example, electricians on 3, camera on 4, locations on 5, transport on 6, etc. Whatever channels are decided on at the beginning of the job should be maintained.

You may find, if you're shooting in a city, that you and another production are "bleeding" onto each other's channels. Manners would dictate that whoever was there first keeps the channels, but this is best resolved in a phone conversation between the two Seconds. Typically, the larger production will ignore the smaller one; either way you need to find some channel that is totally clear to become your new "Channel 1" equivalent, and designate other channels accordingly, announcing this to all crew. For example, you can switch to the other end of the dial and make Channel 18 your Channel 1, 17 your Channel 2, and so forth. The actual numbers don't matter, but the protocol does.

Every PA should have a fully charged battery on their walkie, and a spare or two on their belt to be used themselves or to be given to the First. They should also have a phone in their pocket, switched off, until they need to make or receive a call for production. During the takes, walkies' volume needs to be turned down— even if you're wearing an earpiece, the sound can leak out, and you don't want to be the one ruining the take—and, of course, turned back up at "cut."

Walkies should only be handed out to those crew who sign for them on a walkie sign-out sheet; this also avoids the excruciating conversations at the end of the day trying to remember and recover who might not have handed theirs back in. Accessories must also be signed for, and waterproof bags should be provided and used if there's a chance of inclement weather or humidity and dust, which can also jam up walkies.

The most important thing for any AD to be wearing is your own walkie head-set (or earpiece and mic). These can be obtained from any decent electronics communications store or website for less than 40 dollars. As you might expect from the price, they are prone to breakdown and do need to be replaced every so often, but that's your single most important tool so it needs to be working.

Week Four Checklist

These are some of the things you want to be sure happen, if they haven't already:

- Final production meeting
- Day one call sheet prepared, including map, movement order and risk assessment (if required)
- Tech scouts
- Camera, makeup, wardrobe tests
- Rehearsals
- Cast read-through
- Fittings
- Pre-lights or pre-rigs
- Set walk-throughs
- Props show and tell
- Walkies received and charging

Chapter 3

Production

Leadership is the art of getting someone else to do something you want done because he wants to do it.

General Dwight D. Eisenhower

Whether you're shooting film or capturing media, the military analogy with a film production is justified. On any shoot there is a clear-cut goal as specific as any military target (it's on the call sheet with your name on it), and the first AD is the lieutenant in charge of logistics to ensure that the goal is achieved in the most efficient manner and with minimal casualties to your troops. The general/director is often in a tent at a remove from the battlefield, while you call the charge and lead the battalion into the breach, again and again and again.

As in any military operation, there is a hierarchy, not because anyone is power-mad (although they sometimes are) but because this is simply the most efficient system. On set, as in war, there simply isn't time for democracy: if everyone knows their job, and especially if you have done your job in organizing the campaign properly, there won't be the need for discussion or disagreement. Talk is very, very, very expensive. That very loud meter ticking is the constant sound in the First's ear, and while you do need to appear relaxed and confident, inside you need to be running like hell. Not just because it's your job, or out of loyalty to the producer, or because you love the script, but in my view because waste, in a world full of hungry people, is simply immoral, and I like to try to keep waste—be it of time, money or food—to a minimum.

One of the beauties of this job is that no two days are ever the same—if they were, it would make for a very boring movie! There is always an element of discovery and surprise, which makes it one of the more interesting jobs on the planet. That being said, certain objectives and requirements are eternal, regardless of the media being used or the personalities involved in the production. These universal elements are what we will discuss here. While appreciating that local context will impact hugely on the detail, these are the basic structures I feel are important on any set.

Every First has a different style, so I'm just going to describe how I approach a shooting day and you can find your own way as you go. A First's "manner" can be a big part of why someone hires them, and can influence hugely the atmosphere of the set and the happiness of the crew. I don't like being shouted at, myself, and I like to be asked "please" and told "thank you," so I would naturally behave that way with the cast and crew. I don't think it's acceptable to be impatient or rude to people just because they might happen to be at this point in time lower in rank than I am, and I try to avoid wherever possible having an argument or conflict in public: this is often a waste of shooting time, not to mention the ambience. It's my view that people work better when they are relaxed and encouraged, rather than stressed out, and while I don't do a lot of shouting, I find that my sets run as least as well as those where the First has a boot camp approach. It's a question of personal taste; some directors like to hire screamers, so they look nice by comparison. I've had directors get annoyed with me because I didn't publicly humiliate someone who messed up; I believe in karma, and I also like to try to enjoy my job. To me, the set is an opportunity to be like the famous duck on the pond—floating serenely along while underwater paddling like hell!

RUNNING THE SHOOT

It's not the time it takes to take the takes that takes the time; it's the time it takes between the takes that takes the time.
Anonymous

Starting the Day

Call time, or unit call, is the single most important piece of information on the call sheet. However, what call time actually means varies from set to set. One of the most important elements of the crew deal is what is expected to be ready for unit call, and this needs to be reiterated gently at every production meeting so there can be no doubt. On US shoots, there is unit call (when the majority of the crew report) and a shooting call (when they expect to be rolling). On a UK shoot, I aim for unit call to be the time when the director and the actors demonstrate the action for the first scene of the day to the crew. For either scenario to happen, a certain amount of work needs to go on beforehand.

Step 1—Locations, Facilities, Second AD and PA, Hair, Makeup, Wardrobe Departments

In a studio situation, parking and catering will probably be adjacent to the set, bathrooms and dressing rooms will be equally accessible, and so the whole start-up and wrap process is much more straightforward. On location, the location will dictate how close to the set parking, catering and the actors' facilities will be. Let's assume that on our production we have a unit base, generally a parking lot as close to the set as possible. The work trucks (camera, electrical, props, etc.) will be parked immediately outside the set, and everyone else needs to park up at the unit base and travel, either by foot or production transport, to the set. Hopefully, on the tech scout you saw the unit base, or at least have a very clear picture of how long exactly it takes to travel from base to set, and have factored this into the call times for the cast. Even on a contemporary low-budget project, the lead actress usually requires an hour in the morning, even if that's just to have breakfast and put on some mascara.

While unit call is important to the entire crew, **cast call times** dictate call times for locations (access), facilities and transport (catering, toilets, trailers, Winnebagos, etc.), unit drivers (collecting the cast), hair, makeup and wardrobe. The call sheet will announce the times that each cast member will report to hair, makeup, wardrobe, etc., and these departments need to be set up and waiting before this time. The person on the ground who is making sure all this is happening is your trusty second A.D., who will always be there before anyone else, making sure the cast trailer or dressing room is clean, warm or cool (depending on the season) and contains whatever special needs the cast member demands. (In theory, the facilities crew should ensure these things, but as it's the second AD who will get the complaints if there is something wrong, it's best for him or her to double-check. If there is a DVD player, they might need to make sure it doesn't have a driver's DVD in it! It has happened, and the DVD wasn't PG-13.) The Second will generally put signs on the dressing-room doors to show which area is for which cast member; these are always posted with the name of the character, rather than the actor. Even if your cast are unknowns, it's the right habit to get into.

Step 2—First AD, Second Second AD Report to Unit Base

I always report to location or studio at least an hour before unit call. Some Firsts may consider this excessive, but if there's something going wrong I like to know about it as early as possible. I can't tell you how many mornings I have been through a massive adrenaline rush and possibly a huge drama before 6 a.m. I generally also ring the Second on my way in, just to touch base and find out the mood at that stage and any possible delays, and because often I will have some thought relating to the day's shoot that might have occurred to me too late to pass on the night before (it's an occupational hazard to suddenly remember something important at 2 a.m., although these things are often less of an emergency in the light of day!). If you want to have time to park, eat, talk to the Second and get to set, you need an hour not to be under pressure.

You will know immediately, or pretty soon thereafter, which actors show up on time and which don't. It is standard practice (for good reason) for actors to be collected and driven to set by a professional driver. Not only is it usually in their contract and a good insurance policy, but at least you can get a handle on where they are when. (Exceptions to this are soap operas, where actors generally drive themselves, and low-budget US productions when PAs drive the cast.) Many are the mornings that a driver has spent long minutes buzzing a doorbell or knocking on a door, but at least s/he can then tell you how late they are and you can react accordingly. If you notice a pattern, such as when a particular actor is often late, you can give them earlier call times, as well as informing the producer of what you're doing. In fact, as soon as an actor is late you should inform the producer, as they need to be able to keep an eye on it in case it develops into a problem. They don't want to hear about it two weeks later. If an actor is consistently late, the producer will talk to them, then to their agent, and if the problem persists will consider whether they can be re-cast. An actor who is moody, abusive or even drunk is less dangerous to a production than one who is late, and producers can't tolerate the negative impact a threat to the schedule has on the entire project.

I generally park up and go straight to the second AD—ideally housed in a mobile production office at unit base. **Checking in with the Second** means ensuring that all of the cast are present and on time as per the call sheet, getting your walkie, and having any last-minute conversations about any of the day's elements. The Second will usually have "**sides**" to distribute to everyone as well: reduced-size copies of the day's scenes in call sheet order, with the call sheet as the cover sheet. One of your team—generally the Second Second—will distribute these to the crew who require them, typically the director, DP, focus puller/first AC, sound department, and the cast. The Second Second should also be in at least 45 minutes before call time so they can distribute the walkies as people arrive for breakfast.

I like to greet my crew every morning to talk them through the particular challenges, if any, of the day ahead. At best, only the Second and Second Second will have had any prep, so the others are facing a brand-new set (or several) every day. It's worth the few minutes as you're having coffee to spell out your approach for any company moves, big crowd scenes, vehicle work, etc., and invite them to ask questions if they have them. When you're working with a good AD team, they will help you by thinking ahead as well. During the day, they may ask you whether they should move some extras ahead, or warn you if the cast are late. They may advise you that the art department is still dressing or that someone is in tears in the bathroom—any bit of information that might impact on the schedule is your business.

Depending on the size of the shoot, if the Second is getting a large number of actors or stunt performers through "the works," that is, wardrobe/makeup/hair, they may have an assistant, or additional Second or Second Second. This assistant may be a daily (as in, they only work on designated days) or fully fledged member of the AD department. There may also be an additional PA, sometimes known as the "base bunny," bringing breakfasts to the actors, escorting them to makeup or hair, knocking on their trailer door to call them, etc. As you can see, this person needs to be personable but professional. Managing actors at ungodly hours of the morning is an art form unto itself and I have the utmost respect for good Seconds who can both soothe and motivate…!

Step 3—Walk the Set

By at least half an hour before call I will have touched base with the Second to ensure that all the cast are on time (and what moods they're in, if any of them are emotional), gotten my walkie from the Second Second and walked the set with the Second Second so you can both be sure there aren't any location issues. You and the Second Second need to know where the bathrooms are, where extras holding is (if there are to be extras) and the locations of fire exits and fire extinguishers. There should always be a first-aid kit and fire extinguisher on the set, if not a medic or nurse standing by. If any of these things aren't in place, you need to talk to locations. Everything needs to be properly sorted at least a half an hour before call time. If there is a serious problem, as in the location owner is nowhere to be seen and not answering their phone, or the location has become a crime scene overnight (it does happen), you need to inform the PM immediately and discuss the options. The set should also be dressed. You may find art department frantically putting in last-minute touches, particularly if they have only recently gained access, but they need to be finished at least 15 minutes before unit call.

Step 4—Call Time

If the location has any potential hazards, or if there is to be any stunt or safety work, the First is obliged, at call time, to call a **safety meeting** with the crew and actors present. This may be only 5 minutes long—to outline what the risks are and how they can be minimized—but if you don't do it you can be held accountable later.

My preferred method of beginning a day is to try to get the director and actors to the set about 15 minutes before shooting call time so they can **rehearse** "privately." This achieves a number of things: firstly, it can mean that the director/actor chat is happening off-the-clock, so to speak, without a grumpy, impatient crew standing around (ka-ching, ka-ching) while they puzzle out the nuances of the scene. It also draws the key crew members onto the set so you don't have to go around chasing everybody, and ideally it means that on the stroke of call time the crew can watch the rehearsed scene and begin the process of shooting it. This is my personal preference, but on any set this walk-through rehearsal should begin no later than call time.

The actors will then need to return to the chair to be finished off in hair and makeup, but it's important that they come to set in wardrobe, as the colors and texture of what they're wearing will have a bearing on the lighting. It's also important that the cast stand-ins watch this rehearsal, as they will need to repeat as exactly as possible what the actors did in the scene.

Once the actors have run the scene, I would check whether the DP has any comments that might affect the blocking (as in don't play the whole thing in front of the window, for example), and then get the actors off the set, back to makeup/hair, as fast as possible. You don't want them listening to the conversation between the DP and director for a number of reasons. One is that they should have the illusion that the director is in total control, the other is that you don't want them getting involved in how the scene is to be shot. This can happen, and it's not pretty. Clear the set of the actors, and then the work can begin.

In an efficient scenario, the director might have an idea of how s/he wants to cover it; s/he may have spoken to the DP about it before, or the DP might agree with the general idea and offer a few thoughts on the detail of the coverage. In an inefficient scenario, the director and DP need to have a fully fledged discussion of what the shots will be, and a disagreement—often a disguise for the DP not being happy to adjust his shots to the actors, rather than vice versa. In any case, the First must ensure that no matter how long it takes, the total number of shots required to shoot the scene are agreed upon before the first shot is set up, never mind shot. (If there are more than two characters in a scene you wouldn't believe how easy it is to paint yourself into a corner between eyelines, crossing the line and moving the camera.) You should be able to write down (I use the back of my sides) a **shotlist**, and the script supervisor should be eavesdropping on this conversation to ensure that the shots planned will cut together elegantly.

It's a very high-risk strategy to light the scene in such a way that the actors have their blocking decided for them in advance; some actors, when they sense that this is what's happening, will resist the direction as a matter of principle. It depends on the context: TV actors are usually professional enough that they'll find a way to make it work for themselves no matter where the director needs them to be; but on a film, some actors will adamantly resist the idea that the lighting dictates the blocking, and the director will be caught in the middle, trying to sell the actor an idea that s/he may not entirely believe in. If this happens, you as the First need to find a way for the actor and the director to discuss or even block the scene before the lighting happens, even if that's the night before.

If you're using prime lenses, the director and DP might be able to look at the action with a lens mounted on a pentafinder (a kind of handle for a lens that lets you see in advance how it would look in the camera). If you're shooting digital video on a small camera, the DP might use the actual camera to show the director various sizes or positions, always using the stand-ins for these discussion purposes.

I would always do a quick **timing** on my sides to be sure that the number of shots fits into the time allocated. If you're shooting traditional 35 mm with lighting, you need to allow at least half an hour per static shot. If you're shooting digital video with available light, it's still never going to be less than 20 minutes per setup. If I had a dollar for every time something was supposed to take 5 minutes, I'd be rich. Nothing takes 5 minutes and no shot is "grabbed." You need to be realistic about what's achievable and if you get ahead, then great, you can get extra shots. If the timings don't seem to fit, talk to the DP and director before you begin filming; if they want to press on with the plan that's too long, they need to decide in advance what in the day they're going to compromise.

Once you know what the shots are, it's best to start with either the widest shot (widest in terms of lens size, the frame where you see the most of the set) or the master, which is the longest in terms of time, and might cover the whole scene. The wide shot and the master are often the same thing. There are occasions where the director might want to start with a close-up, if it's a particularly emotional scene and s/he doesn't want to use up the actor's energy on the wides, but for any other reason you should argue for the wide master first. It commits everyone to their continuity and has many additional side benefits.

When you know the shots, you should **communicate** on Channel 1 of your walkie how many shots there are and what you're starting with. This information is relevant to everyone; for example, if it's a wide, makeup has less work to do than if it's a close-up, but you'll need to have all the extras in the shot and background traffic held. The second AD needs to understand exactly what the shots are and which one you're doing, so they can report this information back to the PM, producers and anyone else who isn't physically standing on the set. There is nothing worse for a producer than to ask the Second "where are we now?" and the Second not to know. It doesn't just make them look bad, it makes you look like you're not communicating the information properly, or the set is out of control. Either way, it's vital that everyone on and off set knows where you are exactly in the scene. If you should forget to announce it, or after three shots not announce that this fourth shot is, for example, the medium close reverse, the Second or Second Second should ask for the information. It's their responsibility to know it as much as your responsibility to share it, and this is part of their being active members of the team. It's standard practice on some shoots for the Second to set up a group text or email system, where at every important juncture (completing a scene, breaking for lunch, etc.) a message goes out to all concerned parties. It's a method I like to use as it's fast and thorough.

If the first scene involves more than a few **extras**, I have a slightly different approach. I would call all of the extras in for a half-hour before call time and get them on set rehearsing (if it's a period film, of course this will be much longer). Of course, you may not know what the principal cast's action may be, but that's okay. If you have upwards of 10 people, each will need to be given specific action, and if it's a bar, street, supermarket, etc., you can put a shape on the crowd without even knowing where the camera is looking. It's a thousand times easier to adjust background action than to start from scratch once you have the frame, because you won't have the space (dressing and lighting will be going on) and you won't have the time (as a first, I find it unacceptable if the shoot has to wait for me). In theory, the second second AD blocks the extras, but in practice s/he works to general instruction from you—e.g., let's have three shoppers in this aisle, use five crosses BG (in the background) and three wipes (that is, people crossing so close to camera that they are more a dark shape than a clear person—these can be re-used frequently within the shot). You will know from the length of the scene how long your background action needs to hold.

You should be able to block the extras and rehearse them twice or three times in the half hour before the cast and director arrive for their rehearsal. You then send all the extras away to continue getting ready or have breakfast (typically, the Second will have a system where half have eaten and the other half dressed) during the rehearsal, and once the cast have left and the lighting and dressing is complete, you will bring them back in and run another background rehearsal with the stand-ins. You can watch this rehearsal on the monitor to identify any adjustments you need to make, under the instruction of the director.

This practice is invaluable in terms of the time it saves in the working day. There will again be potential resistance from hair/makeup/wardrobe in terms of how early their people will need to come in, and possibly also from the PM in terms of the length of the extras' day, but both of these costs are still cheaper than the expense of an entire crew standing around for half an hour while you block the extras on the clock (that is, during that precious time between call and wrap). It's cheaper, more efficient and provides the momentum that a production desperately requires to keep moving forward, so I would really fight for this process, even if only once—once people see it in action they can only accept its value.

As soon as the first setup or shot of the scene is ready in terms of lighting and camera, you'll bring the cast back onto set. I always check with the DP before calling them back; some DPs will say they're ready, then just as the cast are walking in start making some adjustment to the lighting. The relationship with the DP can be delicate and the DP can make your day or break your heart. The DP who wants to be the center of attention is the most challenging kind, both for you and the director.

The Rhythm of the Set

There is a very simple, repeated cycle on an efficient set, pointed out to me by a very experienced, kindly old grip on my first big job: block, light, rehearse, shoot; block, light, rehearse, shoot; block, light, rehearse, shoot.

It sounds so simple, but in fact with all of the multiple elements and personalities combining on a film set it's very easy for things to descend into chaos. Block, light, rehearse, shoot. It's really straightforward, in the same way that riding a unicycle or surfing is really straightforward in a book. When the waves start pounding, this mantra will become more valuable and you will understand why I am repeating it so often: block, light, rehearse, shoot—it can be like a tow-line to a drowning first.

We've already discussed the blocking; when the actors leave the set to the stand-ins and the shots have been determined, the camera will be put in position (track laid, if necessary), lighting will take place and as soon as the lamps are safe you can bring in your extras. If lighting is taking more than 20 minutes, you have a problem. Even if you don't have any lights, you will probably need a few minutes to move the camera, adjust the props or dressing, or any other preparations that need to occur.

After 20 minutes or so, you should be able to welcome the actors, now fully ready, back onto set. You would normally then do a camera rehearsal, or "mechanical" rehearsal, not for performance but simply for technical issues. There will often need to be a couple of adjustments made, either for lighting, camera or sound, to accommodate what are now the final elements. These should be quick, and hopefully don't require another mechanical rehearsal to confirm. If the sound mixer wants the cast to wear radio microphones s/he should generally be sure to get them on before the cast come back to set, although this can sometimes happen on the edge of the set, particularly if it's not a historical picture with more complicated costume, or if it's a male actor. At this point, you're ready to shoot.

The First will announce on the walkie's Channel 1 that this next take is "for picture" or "shooting next time" (or whatever their personal preference of vocabulary is) and to "lock it up" to let everyone know you're going to roll. If there is a bell and red light system, such as in a studio, the PA responsible will ring the bell (often once for shooting and twice for cut) and turn on the red light, meaning no-one should enter or exit until cut. Alan Parker, from what I understand, doesn't allow hair, makeup and wardrobe checks on set, but on every other set this is the time when these departments step in to have "last looks" (also known as "fluff and buff" or any other number of expressions) at the cast and extras and make sure everyone looks correct.

I have my own lingo for communicating the next beats; every First will have their own. Typically you might hear something like this (I put an asterisk beside things I would say both aloud and on the walkie.):

First: Lock it up, this is for picture, places please.*

Second Second AD (and any other ADs either on the set or at base): Quiet please, shooting this time, lock it up (or a variation thereof).

First: Stand-by.*

Second Second: Standing by.

First: Camera ready?

Camera Operator: Ready

First: Roll sound, please.*

Second Second (et al.): Rolling!

Sound Mixer: Speed.

First AC/Focus Puller: Mark it.

Second AC: 101A, take 1. (claps the board)

Camera Operator: Set.

First: Background action...And action.*

The action happens...

Director: Cut.

First AD & Second Second AD, et al: Cut, thank you! Reset to go again.*

There are slight variations to the above depending on nationality and whether you have synch sound and extras, but the basic structure of this is the same all over the world. There are some directors who prefer to call action themselves, but generally after forgetting to do it on a few takes they are happy to let the First take over. It makes more sense for the First to do it because s/he is watching a number of elements to be sure they're ready before calling action—the camera operator, focus puller and grip, the extras, or other crew members who might be leaping out of shot at the last minute. I say "And, action" to give people a count-down—sometimes the dolly grip will use this as a run-up to speed, for example, or, alternatively on stunts or effects shots I might give a "3, 2, 1, action" to help with synchronization. The First is also beside the camera, while the director might be at the monitor at some remove from the set, or sometimes even the next room. It's simply more practical for the director to be able to focus on what's on the screen in front of them rather than the various activities on the floor.

You'll have noticed that the second second AD was echoing some of what the First says. Every First has their own lingo, their equivalent to "On your marks, get set, go!" In my case, I prefer to call for "Places, please," "Stand-by" and "Roll sound," before calling "Action," but any words will do. After the First day, the crew will understand what your rhythm is and act accordingly. The Second Second doesn't echo you because you're an egomaniac, but so that the whole crew can hear what's going on. Some Firsts love to shout—I don't. I prefer the tone around the camera to be quiet and calm, and if I'm screaming "Stand-by!" loud enough for the whole set to hear, it's a little disconcerting for the cast and director. I say these things loud enough for the people immediately around the camera to hear, and on the walkie—the Second Second covers everybody else. This also goes, crucially, for "Cut!" I echo the director, the Second Second echoes me, simply with the objective to make sure everyone in the vicinity is aware that they can continue working between takes.

Hopefully, after the take, the director will speak first to the cast, then the DP, then advise as to whether you will go again. You will notice that in the above dialogue I automatically reset the action to be ready to go again, whether or not the director has called it. This is because if you only reset when you get word from the director, you can lose a minute or two waiting to hear. It's best to explain to the director before you start shooting that this is how you'd like to work, so that (insecure creatures as they can sometimes be) they under-stand you are not usurping their position but simply trying to give them more time for the important stuff.

Hopefully, the director will come to talk to the actors in person quietly about what s/he wants in the next take. Some directors will yell from the monitor, which actors hate. (Some even do it during the take, which actors hate even more.) Others will ask you to pass on a note, particularly if you're on a very long lens and the direc-tor is at a distance. What I do in this situation is ask the Second Second to switch to Channel 2 and give their walkie to the director, switch to Channel 2 myself, unplug my earpiece and let the cast hear the director's exact words over the walkie. It's much clearer for the actor and quicker for this exchange to happen directly between the two of them, rather than repeating the director's notes yourself, which has two problems: a) repeating some-thing by rote can take the meaning out of it, and b) if the actor then has a question about the note it's much quicker for them to ask it directly. The cliché of a bad First is one who interprets the director's notes for the cast, who then play the First's notes instead of the director's. Directors hate this and there's no need to take the risk of getting in the way like that. Even though it's a little cumbersome to switch channels and share the walk-ies, it's the most efficient way to facilitate communication, which is the main objective of the first AD role.

In all likelihood, you will do at least three takes of the first setup; if you do more than six there is something not working, and if you do more than six consistently you need to rehearse more. What's acceptable to the producer (who will have a view) depends a lot on their personality and what format you're shooting on. On

35 mm shoots, directors are always getting pressured not to shoot too much film. Nowadays, the film stock and processing are much cheaper, and with digital media some people seem to feel it's unlimited, but the discipline is still important; takes take time and a huge amount of storage space at the post-production facility, not to mention the poor editor or assistant who has to sit through it all. Sidney Lumet wrote in his autobiography how he liked to be sure on the first day to do only one take of an important shot—a close-up of a lead actor, say—to keep everyone on their toes. If you're regularly doing 8–10 takes, the actors and the cast and crew start to get disgruntled and/or casual; they know they'll get another few goes, so they relax about getting it perfect on the first one. There are also some actors who are much better in the first couple of takes, and as time goes on they start to lose it, while others improve as they go on. It's important for the director to identify which is which and not end up "printing" or selecting takes that aren't great for the early bird actor. If you're working with an inexperienced director, you can help him/her identify these issues. If you continue to do 8–12 takes per setup, it may require a conversation with the producer and the director to examine what you can do to help—either the director needs to have a clearer idea of exactly what they want, so they know when they've got it, or you need to rehearse more. The director may also be trying to do too much in each shot, particularly if they're long tracking shots with elaborate blocking and background action. Is the style of the shoot consistent with the schedule? These are creative discussions the First needs to be a part of, ideally before shooting, but the shoot is often when these issues arise.

When the director is happy, if shooting on film, you "check the gate"; on other media, you might play back or check the time codes—whatever it may be, you announce to the floor that that's what you're doing, so they know you're about to move on. Once you've completed your first setup, you announce it over the walkie and describe the shot you're moving on to (while reminding everyone that this will be the second shot of four, for example). As soon as you're clear to move on, release the actors and swap them with the stand-ins for the director and DP to choose the next camera position. You'll know from your list roughly where it will be, but the two should look through the pentafinder before choosing the exact position. The grip will mark this spot, the focus puller will put the lens on the camera (if needs be) and then the grip will bring the camera into position. The DP may ask the gaffer to tweak a couple of lights or flags, and the art department might make a couple of quick adjustments. You will then bring the cast back in, do a mechanical rehearsal for this new setup, call for makeup and hair "checks," and then shoot it. Block, light, rehearse, shoot.

I can't tell you how important this sequence is. While all about you are losing their heads, if you're focusing on this rhythm you will get through the day, no matter what else is going on.

Right of Way—or, How to Keep the Crew from Killing Each Other

A large part of the First's role is directing traffic—that is, keeping operations moving on the set without gaps or people bumping into each other. If you get a traffic jam, people will quickly get annoyed with each other and especially you, as you are there to manage the flow. There is a simple order of operations, as basic as block, light, rehearse, shoot, that will keep things moving in an orderly fashion and is as logical as it is simple. Naturally enough, locations are the first into a set, to be followed by art department, then lighting. Depending on the situation, camera will come in at some stage in this process, then the extras, then the cast. This is very easy when you're dealing with the first set of the day, or where people like dressing props or the electricians or riggers have had a chance to get in before the shooting crew. However, what is typical on lower-budgets is that you all arrive together, and everyone wants to work at the same time. In this case, you have to enforce the order.

Once the director has rehearsed with the cast and the shots have been decided, if there is any furniture to be moved or other dressing needs, art department goes first. This is logical in the sense that there's no point in lighting an empty set, or one that is going to change. But as everyone is under a time pressure, lighting and art department are often trying to work at the same time. This is messy and dangerous, as lamps are loaded with high voltages and very heavy if dropped. The safest, and ultimately quickest, solution is to give the art department an allocated time frame (10 minutes, unless something major needs to happen, in which case you should be considering what else you might be able to shoot in the interim), and hold them to it.

Then the electricians (or sparks, as they're known in Europe) can have the set to themselves for their allotted time. You will announce that this is happening by saying something like "clear the set for lighting, please." To determine how much time is needed, you should ask the DP, and if s/he or the gaffer can tell you what needs to happen, you can see for yourself how close or far away they are from being ready. For example, if you know they're putting up a 10 K and two 1 Ks, you won't be asking them if they're ready until you see these lights go up. DPs are sometimes jumpy about revealing this information, I suspect because they often want to see the effect of the first few lights before tweaking them, but a gaffer will generally be willing to privately say what they have left to do. When you're given an estimate, write it down, so you can justifiably come back to them when the time has expired and expect them to be ready. You will learn after a couple of days (or less) how accurate (or not) the DP's estimates are, and plan around this accordingly.

Anywhere lighting is happening needs to be clear of crew and especially cast or background artistes. When you're almost ready to shoot and there is a small lighting adjustment it is tempting to leave everyone in position while this occurs; however, even the most experienced electrician can drop a lamp, and it's your responsibility if someone gets hurt. You need to clear the immediate area for as long as the work is happening.

Once the lighting is complete, then the set is free for extras and cast, and you may proceed. Sometimes the DP needs the camera in position to evaluate how the lighting is going. Anytime there is someone carrying a camera—generally the first AC—you need to protect and clear a path for them. This is especially important when the AC is carrying a very heavy 35 mm or HD camera, but is just as relevant when it's a little Canon 7D, as people tend to be less cautious around it. The camera is probably the single most expensive piece of equipment on the set, and you need to be as careful that no one knocks coffee over it or bumps into it as you would a newborn baby. The ubiquitous AD phrase "watch your backs" is often followed by the phrase "camera coming through" to help the AC navigate the often crowded and dark area surrounding the set.

When you are finally ready to roll, it is customary to allow hair, makeup and wardrobe in for a "last look" or "checks" for picture. The actors usually welcome someone reassuring them right before we roll that they look okay. This reassurance is often more emotional than physical: I have seen hairdressers simply pat the head of an actor a few times over the course of the day and take home a fat paycheck. But it's not just about the hair: it's comforting the actor at the very scary moment before they bare their soul in front of the camera. Okay, not every actor gets emotionally naked for every shot, but it's still a very lonely place once the cameras roll, and this moment with the "fluff-and-buff" team is like the boxer's man in the corner, pumping them up before the bell rings.

Occasionally, there will be an effect that requires the makeup, hair or costume person to wait until you have actually rolled before they clear frame: tear stick, for example (to give the actors eyes tears), sweat, or in the case of nudity (which we will discuss more later) a dressing-gown may only be added or removed after you have marked the slate and before you call action. In this case, you are the one announcing the various steps in this process, and as always you want to be calm, clear and in control.

To recap, here is a standard sequence of events:

- Locations
- Art Department
- ADs (at the latest)
- Camera
- Lighting
- Sound & Continuity
- Extras
- Director (at the latest)
- Cast
- Hair, Makeup, Wardrobe

Aside from block, light, rehearse, shoot, the most important focus for a good first AD is the future. You should always be thinking ahead, to the next shot, the next scene, the next day: there is almost always something you can be doing to get ahead, even while the camera is rolling.

While the block, light, rehearse, shoot is going on, I'm constantly looking back at my timings on my sides. If I have allocated a half-hour per setup, where are we in relation to that now? What is the impact that will have on the next scene? Are there cast, extras, equipment, vehicles or crew that need to be advised or amended? Are all the required action props in position? Are the extras all present and rehearsed? Does sound need to put on a wireless mic? Is the set for the next scene open, dressed, and lit? Can anything be done in advance to prepare it better? Does the next scene require extras, in which case the second second AD can go to the next set with the extras and rehearse them, leaving a PA with me on the set? Are there vehicles in the next scene, are they dressed into position on the next location? Can the DP release any of his electricians to pre-light the next set? What about the next location—is it ready from an art department point of view? How is everyone else traveling? Do you have a convoy list or a head count for the lunch break or the unit move? Do locations have maps to hand out as soon as you break? Will you break for lunch on time? Would the director like a cup of coffee? The list of possible things to check and double-check is endless, and you need to be on top of all of them.

Whatever the next scene is, you want to walk onto it with the director and DP to find a lit, dressed, extras-blocked set that requires only the final touches to be shootable. On really big Hollywood productions, they might have an entire camera crew, with a camera on a crane, ready for the director and DP to arrive and shoot within minutes of stepping onto the floor. The opposite extreme, of micro-budget shooting, requires exactly the same degree of preparation, as it's on these shoots where the most potential for disaster can occur. The location owner overslept, the car broke down, the information never got through, and so on. The measure of a good First is not just how well the floor is run, but, like a good director, in the transitions—the changes from one scene or set or location to another, because that's where it can get ugly. A crucial transition is the break for lunch.

Lunch

Assuming you've spent the morning blocking, lighting, rehearsing and shooting, you'll be thinking mid-morning about lunch—but not just because you're hungry!

In the US, there are generally two kinds of lunch break: the catered lunch, which officially begins **half-an-hour** from "last one through" the lunch line, and the **walkaway**, in which people leave the base to get their own, and are given an hour plus walking time before they're due "back in."

You will also need to factor in **travel time**: if you call "lunch" at 1 p.m., but everyone has to clear out of the location and travel to the unit base for catering, they might not get there until 1:30, which is when lunch officially starts. If the deal was to break at 1 p.m., they will charge for the half-hour overage. You will discover how pedantic people can be around the time of lunch break, but in their defense, the moment you call lunch is not the moment people walk away—the camera has to be made safe, actors sometimes have to remove accessories, the lights have to power off, etc.—so they are already working a few minutes into lunch generally. After the length of the shooting day, the second most important element of the crew deal is the lunch hour, as if it's badly run it can cost time, money and morale.

The solution is to break in enough time to get to catering at the right time. In the above scenario, you would break at 12:30 to allow the move and travel so people begin lunch at 1 p.m. You have to then give them their allocated time before you can ask them to travel to the next set. This is part of the reason why you want the unit base, which is where catering generally happens, to be as close to the set as possible, as every minute traveling is a minute less shooting.

In the UK system, lunch is almost always an hour plus travel time. On guerrilla productions with small crews you might eat in a nearby restaurant or café, which is great as it allows everyone the chance to sit down and be served, which is always a treat! However, the food needs to hit the table as you sit, so ordering in advance is crucial. Even more crucial is ensuring that the restaurant staff understand this, and have the meals prepared and on the table at exactly the time you have given them, which rarely happens. The restaurant staff often just can't get their heads around the notion of preparing the food before the crew arrive, but that's what has to happen or it will cost you time.

A **"rolling" lunch** is a fantastic invention where the crew agree to be broken sometime within a 1.5 hour range—for example, between 12:30 and 2 p.m.—and you ensure that the camera actually stops for a half hour at some point during this time period. The beauty of this is that you can stagger the cast and crew meal breaks: not only do you avoid the inefficiency of a lunch queue of people all trying to get fed at once, it also means if you manage it cleverly you can have departments working in advance. If you break makeup before camera, they can get the actress ready for the next scene while you're eating, and when you return from lunch the set is lit, the cast are ready and, if you're working with two cameras, one of them might already be in position. Inexperienced Firsts might struggle to capitalize on the opportunities this kind of strategic break pattern can afford, but if you have the mind of a baseball manager you'll love the complexities of managing a big crew's lunch shifts and the maximizing of efficiency that results when you're doing it well, as well as an earlier wrap time (you can shave up to half an hour off your day, which also helps with cast turnaround). In fact, once you've gone this route, the standard lunch break feels prehistoric.

You really don't want to interrupt a scene with a lunch break. The actors and director hate it, and generally the quality suffers. If you're shooting exterior it's particularly problematic because the ambient light is invariably going to change. You want to schedule your day so that you can complete whatever scene you're on before you break. If you get delayed, and need an extra half hour to complete the scene, or if it would make more sense to break for lunch early, it will depend on the nature of your crew deal as to what you can do. In some cases, you can ask the crew nicely if they will stay on to complete the scene as a favor (in the US, you can generally ask the HODs and let them answer for their department; in Europe, you often need to ask each individual member of crew). Some people, such as electricians, may agree, but that doesn't mean they're doing it for free. In all likelihood they will be getting lucrative penalties, which they're more than happy to incur. This is why before you make anything official you need to run it past the PM—if they're on set or at the unit base you can have this conversation in person; if they're off site, the Second can get them on the phone and explain the circumstances. They may still need to talk to you directly, in which case you get the second second AD to cover the floor at an opportune moment while you have a brief phone call with the PM. This is often brief because the answer is simply a flat no! If that's the case, it's a little tricky as you will have to report this to the director and DP. The PM may need to talk to them in person, or, as is more likely, will want you to do it.

If the answer is yes to breaking for **lunch late**, it's important not to start asking people at the exact moment when they're supposed to be breaking for lunch. You should be able to tell at least half an hour in advance as to whether you're going to need the time. This is also crucial to relay to the caterers, which your Second should automatically do. They're usually racing to provide the meal on time under pressure, and would appreciate the extra minutes; conversely, no one wants to eat something that has been sitting under a heat lamp for half an hour.

The alternative, **breaking early**, has its own complications, as in every deal there is a finite amount of time after lunch in which the crew can work before they accrue suppertime meal penalties. For example, let's say your day is normally a 7 a.m. call, 8 p.m. wrap. If you're working on a 6-hour to lunch, 6-hour after lunch deal, you would break at 1 p.m. for lunch, might be back in at 2, and wrapping at 8 p.m. means you avoid any late breaks or penalties. If you break at 12:30 for an hour until 1:30, you're going to owe another meal break at 7:30, which is really messy as there's no point stopping at 7:30 to eat when you wrap at 8! So scheduling your lunch breaks properly is one of the most important decisions a First makes, as there are serious financial implications for getting it wrong.

There is a fifteen-minute **grace** period, in which you are allowed to break late for lunch to complete a setup without incurring penalties. In the UK system, this is called "**calling a Quarter**," but the First has to announce and ask, at least 10 minutes before the scheduled lunchtime, that lunch break is going to be pushed by 15 minutes (a quarter of an hour) to *complete the current setup*. In any case, both grace and a quarter cannot be used to "grab" another setup—it is only to avoid a situation where you need another take and don't want to have to break for lunch to come back and get it.

When you call lunch, say it loudly and clearly and over the walkie, along the lines of "That's One-Hour Lunch, Lunch One Hour, back in at 2 p.m." When you give the time you're back in, you will often get a few voices of opinion—"should be 2.05" kind of thing. After a couple of days you will work out a system with these individuals. And it does need to be worked out. If you ignore them, it'll show up on their invoices and you'll get blamed for costing the company money.

The script supervisor will record the exact time at which you called lunch, and you want to be sure you're synchronized. His/her notes go on the production report, and if it looks like you're calling lunch 5 minutes late every day it won't impress the producers or investors. S/he also records the time the first setup is complete, wrap time and all other points of interest, most of which you're responsible for, so you want to be very clear about all of these points before they're published and the bond company are raising eyebrows for some reason. Your professional reputation is going on record and you could make yourself look bad without even realizing it, simply because your watch is 2 minutes different from the script supervisor's.

Unless you have security, you will need someone to stay on set through lunch to guard the set and equipment ("setwatch"), usually a PA, locations PA, or both. Two people can share the job in shifts, or someone will bring lunch to the person doing the setwatch. Either way, a First should never leave the set until they see the person who will be covering, in the correct position. Setwatch can actually be a really pleasant job, as it's a moment of calm in the storm.

To sum up, if you are working to a fixed lunch rather than a rolling lunch, you want to schedule your day so lunch falls at a natural break. If you run into trouble, inform the PM immediately as to your options:

a)   Swapping scenes so you do a shorter scene before lunch to still guarantee breaking on time.

b)   If you can "go over" (that is, work past the official lunch break time) deals range from penalties counted in intervals ranging from 15-minute blocks to full hours (for example, as with overtime, if you go 5 minutes over, for some departments this may count as a half-hour, so you may as well work the time you're paying for). The PM will have final say on the ability to do this.

c)   If you can't go over and don't have grace, you may be able to break early and suffer the consequences at the end of the day.

d)   The worst-case scenario creatively: interrupt the scene for lunch break.

Generally, the director and cast will be asked what they would like for lunch by the "base bunny" or second AD's PA and it will be brought to them in their dressing rooms. It's politically wise to also ask the producer(s) if they would like lunch brought to them. Depending on the budget of the project, there may be a producers' trailer on a par with the cast's; sometimes they share the director's—it really depends on financial scale. Some directors eat with the crew, but ideally they should be somewhere totally quiet to recover from the intense social barrage of the shoot, and to prepare for the afternoon.

The lunch queue also needs to be managed, with shooting crew (camera, sparks, props, sound, continuity) as priority, followed by dressing crew and other crew (art department, drivers, etc.) followed by extras. I'm sorry to say that lunch is a time when extras often get the short straw, sometimes having to wait half an hour to get their food and then being told to hurry up and eat as they're needed on set. SAG has rules about this type of thing, but otherwise the extras can be the bottom of the heap when it comes to lunch. In any case, on big days it's worth assigning a PA to patrol the lunch line to be sure the critical crew are fed first. People are often too shy to jump the queue, but will later complain that they were stuck behind a crowd of extras and didn't get their full lunch break. Much of what we ADs do involves the prevention of whining.

The Call Sheet (Part 2)

The first AD's lunch is not a break but an opportunity to meet with the second AD to go through the call sheet for the next day. The Second will typically already have eaten or will eat after the crew return to work, and will have spent the morning preparing a **draft call sheet** for the next day. In my dream scenario, I will have been handed this draft mid-morning, so I can make my notes on set to discuss with the Second at lunch. Either way, while you eat you will be reading the call sheet and making notes as you go. (Because you're working through lunch, a PA may bring you a plate to the "office.")

In the last chapter, we covered the general intentions of the call sheet, but preparing it in prep can be slightly different from in the heat of the battle, so I'm going to go into a little more detail here about working through the call sheet at lunchtime.

The most important information on the call sheet is call time or unit call—you'll need to check that you're still on target to meet that call time, determined by cast turnaround. The second most important thing is the location; there may be a new location, or you'll want to double-check the base and that the cars or vans to ferry cast and crew, and their drivers, are planned for.

Weather, sunrise and sunset time are also useful for obvious reasons and will be filled in before you see the sheet so you can refer to them when examining the scene order.

The **scheduled scenes** are where the planning comes in; unless otherwise instructed, the Second will have transposed the scenes from the strips order you created in prep: Scene Number, Set/Synopsis, Day/Night, Story Day (so you see at a glance if it's D1, D2, etc., and whether there's a costume change), Page Count, Cast Required, and which location it takes place in. The logical scene order may need to be amended, as you may know more now about location or cast issues than you did when the last schedule was issued.

Generally, you schedule the day the way you schedule the shoot: exterior day scenes first, interior night scenes last. The weather forecast may also play a part in the order you choose, as well as the sunrise/sunset times. Finally, cast requirements will dictate. All else being equal, if you have a leading lady who takes over an hour in "the chair" (makeup and hair), then if you can avoid having her in the first scene all the better. However, the golden rule trumps even this convenience: wherever possible, start with the biggest, most difficult, most emotionally challenging or most important scene for the story. This scene deserves the attention that the first scene of the day often gets, compared to the last scene of the day, which often has to be rushed. There is one caveat to this rule: if you have a scene that is tiny and easy and can be completed quickly—an insert, say—it's sometimes good to start with that, as shooting soon after call time can get a momentum going for the day (it also looks good on the production report).

Basically, you always put the most important or most difficult scene first, and the least important, or easiest to rush (or, in the worst-case scenario, to drop) last. Likewise, if there is any amount of rigging or prep, you start with the hardest thing first as it's quicker to remove: the beard and wig, for example, or the blackouts that can be pulled down. In an interior that has been blacked, you start with the night scenes. And whatever you do, keep them together—you can't go back and forth, any more than you would on an actor's change. As mentioned before, you don't want to interrupt a scene with lunch. Make sure you can complete whatever is before lunch, or move it until after lunch.

You don't want actors waiting around any more than necessary between scenes, and so, as you did with the schedule, you always try to consolidate their work. If there is a major gap and the actor is emotionally adult and able to use a mobile phone, you can sometimes release them for a couple of hours on the proviso that they are "standing by from 1300," for example. It's much nicer for all concerned to have them out shopping than hanging around unit base getting stir crazy. And even if they decide not to leave the base, they won't be resenting you for their boredom.

I write **timings** beside each scene number (see Figure 3.1) to ensure that the day "fits," and to give the Second the estimated times you will want the actors for those scenes ready on set. The Second will then work backwards to ascertain the timings for wardrobe, makeup, hair, breakfast, and transport, and liaise with the various departments when you go back to set, to be sure everyone is on board with these timings. I also factor in any "private" rehearsal time before unit call to ensure this happens smoothly. These estimates are also useful for locations and other departments who are working in advance of the shooting crew—set dressing, pre-lighting, rigging, etc.—and for potential fittings and/or casting of day players who have been booked subsequent to the start of the shoot and need to be fitted in around filming.

PLEASE NOTE STUNT REHEARSAL SC. 103 (2/5) TO BE HELD AT 10AM ON L(

	SET/DESCRIPTION	SCENE	CAST	DAY	P/gs	LOCATIO
11	EXT. PRECINCT Jack chases Jill	103 (1/5)	23, 24	9	1/8	Loc 1: Studic Standbys trucks only to
11.30	EXT. PRECINCT Jill narrowly avoids being hit by a car	103 (2/5)	23, 24, 24x	9	1/8	Loc. 2: Smith
1.15	EXT. PRECINCT Jill pulls out into traffic	103 (4/5)	23, 24	9	1/8	Loc. 2: Smith
2.15	EXT. PRECINCT Jack's POV of Jill's car	104 (2/4)	12, 23	9	1/8	Loc. 2: Smith
2.45	EXT. PRECINCT Jack nearly trips over a peeing dog's leash	104 (3/4)	23, 23x	9	1/8	Loc. 2: Smith
3.30	INT. JILL'S CAR Jill sees that she's not being followed	104 (4/4)	24	9	1/8	Loc. 3: Jones
	16:00 – LUNCH					
5	EXT. PRECINCT Jack hails a cab	103 (5/5)	12, 23	9	1/8	Loc. 2: Smith
5.45	INT. TAXI Jack argues with the taxi driver	104 (1,3,/4)	12, 23	9	1/8	Loc. 2: Smith
6.45	COMPANY MOVE TO BRIDGE STREET					
7.45	EXT. DAVID & ROSIE'S FLAT Rosie has on new knickers	131	5, 6	N1	1	Loc. 4: New
	TOTAL PAGE COUNT				1 5/8	

#	CAST	CHARACTER	STATUS	LEAVE	REPORT	REH	SET	NOTES
12	Moustache Mann	Taxi Driver	WF	11:30	12PM	12:30	1PM	Van

Figure 3.1 *My handwritten timings against the draft call sheet scenes—this can also be done on the one-line schedule*

When you have the scenes in what you think is the right order, look down through the story days to make sure you're not creating costume changes. Then GO BACK TO THE **SCRIPT**. It's the easiest thing in the world to omit this step, and if you're embarrassed the next day it will be nobody else's fault. Look at the script pages first to double-check that you have all the cast on the call sheet who could be needed (even though your Second checked the script against the schedule in prep, new pages might have been issued since then and need to be checked as well), and there might be new or different props, costume, makeup or other needs that slipped through the cracks until now. It's incredibly useful to read it through with the Second, as you will both have thoughts and reactions that are more informed now than they were in prep. This gets more important as the shoot gets on, and forgetting or not bothering to do this is a recipe for disaster. Particularly on episodic TV, where there is simply more information than any one brain can hold simultaneously, the script is the key to a solid call sheet. You'd be amazed how easily major elements can become confused—a scene may be changed from DAY to NIGHT, for example, with no indication beyond an easily missed asterisk on the right-hand side of the new page, and you don't want to discover your mistake standing on set with the director and DP.

New information may arise from this double-check, and there is a general dividing line for how to **pass on the information**. If it relates to someone who is part of the shooting crew on the set (that is, someone who can see the camera) then the First will pass it on. If it relates to the backstage crew—that is, either someone who works mainly at the unit base, off-site or anywhere else—the Second will inform them, either at the base or on the phone. It's so important to create and maintain these lines of communication. As I've said before, the dissemination of information is the most important responsibility of the AD department, and while there may be individual differences in style, once the crew knows how your team works, they can work with you comfortably. The most damning phrase an AD can hear is "Well, no one told me." It reflects badly on the AD team. Better something should be repeated than omitted.

If there is a **company move**, you will want to reflect this with a banner on the call sheet in the position it will occur (between the last scene in one location and the first scene in the next location). You do not need to add a banner for lunch, as this will be reflected under the unit call.

The cast names and character names will be listed in their numerical order, which makes the call sheet a confidential document for crew and cast only—not for extras, or any member of the public.

If there is to be a body **double** or stunt double, they will also be listed as cast, with the same cast number as their replacement with an "X" added beside it to indicate that this is a double. Any other, non-doubling stunt performers are given their own cast numbers and listed as such. Remember that stunt performers are for all intents and purposes cast members, and even though they are generally less precious than actors about their changing rooms and conditions, and often behave socially like crew members, they should be treated with the same respect and courtesy.

Below this is listed the number of extras and their call time. It is useful to indicate here which scenes they are being used for, and whether they are to be changed to work on more than one scene. Wardrobe, hair and makeup should be advised in advance that this is the plan, and it needs to also be reflected on paper.

The Requirements section is critical: if it's not on the sheet, it's not on the set. It is sometimes called Departmental or Special **Notes**, but its purpose is the same on every call sheet: to identify the elements each department is expected to provide. There is huge variation in people's attention to these elements. Many departments have their own breakdowns and often ignore the call sheet detail, but this is your only way to cover yourself if there is something missing: if it's on the sheet and not on the set, you are in the right, end of story. (I can't tell you how many times I have been grateful for the proof I have been able to provide when someone is trying to pin their mistake on me. It's not all about blame, but it's nice to have a clear conscience.) These requirements are transposed by the Second from your master shooting schedule (as distinct from the strips) and so once again this is why it's important to go back to the script to ensure that everything indicated in the script is on the call sheet. Sometimes if the prep period is short, details about costume, props, hair or makeup may not make it into the shooting schedule, and this is the time to rectify that. If there is genuinely nothing specific for a department, the Second will simply write "as per" the head of department's name, meaning that they are responsible for their own requirements. In the interest of teamwork, you would never simply add something to the call sheet and expect the relevant department to spot it and provide it: as with any information, the First shares it with the shooting crew, and the Second with everyone else. The Second, during the course of the afternoon, will also solicit the other departments to be sure there's nothing else they want to add. There are often elements that have been discussed privately by the director and an HOD, and this is the time to obtain that information and publish it.

A note on information: never try to second-guess what is relevant to whom. Having considered it carefully, it seems to me that the only two departments who have no professional interaction are the grip and the hairdresser—but I'm sure now that I've written this, on my next job such a circumstance will arise. The only information that should be guarded is personal or political—everything else needs to be shared as widely as possible. A good Second, like a good POC, will know who needs to get what most urgently, but I'll repeat again: the ADs are there to communicate—verbally, on paper and electronically. No one ever complained about getting too much information, but missing out on even a tiny detail can have grave results. The one thing an AD will get battered for, and rightly so, is not communicating information. It's not easy—the larger the crew, the more difficult it is to spread the facts fast and clearly—but anyone who is complaining should remember the days before emails, mobile phones, walkies, and even photocopiers, and somehow they made movies then. Surely today in the era of personal hotspots and webtexts we can keep the flow going?

In the departmental breakdown should also be the phone number of every HOD. If they don't wish to have their phone number listed, they should delegate this task to someone in their department who will be answerable. In the US, the **call time** of each individual is also listed on the back. This is important to determine when they report and the length of their working day for their timesheets, and is sometimes required for their union.

One of the most important elements for the PM is the **catering** breakdown, especially the figures for lunch. It can be a constant bone of contention between the caterer and the PM as to how many people actually eat, or what's known as the "plate count." The odd caterer will do their best to inflate these figures, and PMs are vigilant about making sure the numbers don't creep up. It's the responsibility of the Second to count as accurately as possible in advance how many people will need to eat, including all cast, crew, extras and any others. Some productions actually station someone beside the catering truck to count the plates, if the distrust has gotten really bad. Hopefully things won't come to that, but it's very important for the Second not to just casually guess the numbers but to be able to stand over the exact head count as every plate is costly.

The **Advance Schedule** is also a crucial part of the call sheet—again, it will be transposed from the strips, including the company move banners. It's worth looking at the scene order here, too, as other departments will be taking it as the plan, rather than just the transfer of the strips. There may again be new information that might impact on these scenes and they can be adjusted accordingly, especially new page counts if script changes have come in. I do a brief timing against those scenes as a guideline as to whether there is a problem with time, lunch, travel, or any other issue, and I recommend putting the proposed call time on the advance schedule so everyone knows what you're aiming for. As always, it spares you the time it takes someone to ask the question and get an answer. Every second counts!

Transport is the Second's area of expertise. Based on the on-set times you have given her/him for the cast, s/he will liaise with the transport captain to ensure that all of the cast arrive on time, and that their special stipulations are met (some cast might have a clause in their deal memo guaranteeing them sole ground transport, meaning they don't have to share the car with any other cast). It's important that the collections are scheduled correctly, and that no confidential information is revealed—this is the place where the greatest mistake can be made in terms of protecting the actors' privacy. As mentioned earlier, depending on the degree of protection required, sometimes only character names are used, and if collecting from home the call sheet will simply say "home," if from the hotel simply "from hotel." The driver will be informed personally as to the address of either location, and the driver's name and phone number will be listed on the sheet so if the actor needs to contact them, they can. The director is often also transported to and from set, sometimes with their personal assistant or the producer, and the DP sometimes also gets a lift. Any and all "talent" transport the second AD is coordinating will be reflected in this section of the call sheet; other transport, such as flights, that is being coordinated by the production office, will be reflected in movement orders (Figure 2.24) that are distributed to relevant parties, the first and second AD among these. (In some places, such as Prague, the entire crew is also collected from hotels or accommodation and driven to set in vans or minibuses. In this case, these pickup times would also be reflected on the call sheet.)

If you are aware of an impending **visit** of a photographer or other visitors on set you should at the very least be informed in advance, and try to get permission from the PM or producer to reflect this on the call sheet. For various reasons, they sometimes prefer not to advertise such visits. However, if a stills photographer, EPK crew or other media are planning to visit, the producer should be the one to inform the cast personally before the visit occurs, preferably at lunch or wrap the day before. Cast are often a little nervy around these people and on occasion refuse to work in their presence, so if there is going to be a snit, better it should happen before the guest arrives.

There are also sometimes visits from executive producers, investors, studio executives or other people who may be very important to the production but are complete strangers to the cast and crew. It's important that the producer warn the First they are visiting, and hopefully introduce them so the First can ensure they are treated courteously: tea, coffee, a chair by the monitor etc., and so the First and Second can answer the cast and crew when they ask who this person is.

A note on set etiquette in relation to visitors: if you have a friend or family member who wishes to visit the set, the first port of call is to the production manager or producer. If they okay it, you then need to clear it with the First and introduce them at an opportune moment as soon as possible after they arrive. Inviting someone for lunch is a bad idea as it costs the production money. Whoever the person is, they should not hang out beside the director at the monitor and should be as silent and as unobtrusive as possible. Even then, a temperamental actor may notice them and ask why they are there, in which case they will probably be asked to vanish—embarrassing for all concerned! Despite the fact that a film set sometimes resembles a cocktail party without the drinks, it's actually a very strictly policed environment, where anyone who doesn't have a very clear and important role is generally unwelcome. The best way to watch how a set works is to be an extra rather than a guest.

If there is any weather cover planned for the week, you should reflect this on the advance schedule so the various departments won't be taken by surprise. A general rule is that the more elements required for a scene, the earlier the decision to call weather cover needs to be made.

At the bottom of every call sheet is an important name: Yours. Even though every department has contributed to the information being published, your name at the bottom means that you are ultimately responsible. If your Second made a typo, if you forgot a prop, if the extras are called too late—it's your fault. Once you start shooting, the call sheet is the bible and it's critical that you train yourself to read it carefully and thoroughly. That sounds easy when you're not in the midst of a crisis, but it is actually very challenging to focus when a million other things are swirling around your mind with great urgency. Signing your name isn't just an ego trip, it's a commitment, and it's also proof that you took responsibility for these elements. If you want to join the DGA, you will need to prove your hours served by providing the call sheets you delivered, much as a pilot has to provide a log book of their air miles to get their wings. It describes who's running the show.

On some jobs, the POC might literally type the call sheet to the Second's instructions, but I have never found this to be a reliable method and don't recommend it. With the technology we have today, a call sheet can be written and sent from the top of a mountain—however, no matter how sophisticated the method, the crew need hard copies at the end of the day. Sometimes the biggest logistical challenge comes from finding a place somewhere nearby that can photocopy the call sheet! The Second may be able to print out enough sheets for the whole crew, but it's something that needs to be figured out well in advance of wrap.

Once you've trawled through all these details the draft call sheet will probably be covered in notes. If you have time before you're "back in" to work, the Second might get to make the changes before you return to set, but typically you will go back to work and be sent a revised draft as soon as possible after lunch. If this looks correct, I always try to get the director to look over the scenes when they're waiting for something else—not to spot mistakes, but so they can get their head around it a little bit, and share with you any ideas they've had that they haven't had a chance to express (finding the right time to do this is delicate, as if they're not able to focus on it, it's no good to you). You'd be amazed the important details a director might announce just in the nick of time, which could potentially require a complete re-think of the day. If they don't see the sheet until wrap, accommodating these changes is far more difficult. Many directors will wave it away, saying they can't even think about it right now, which is fair enough. In this case, at least try to have a very brief chat—between scenes or when there is a proper time gap for lighting or something else—in which you talk her or him through the scenes for the next day, so at least it's not a complete surprise. If the director has no additional comments, I would also try to get the DP to glance at it to be sure s/he doesn't have something up his/her sleeve that they've neglected to mention. The more conversation about the next day that can happen during the course of the shooting day, the better, as there is still time to adapt.

If you, the director and the DP are happy with the sheet, it's time to show it to the PM for final approval (if they weren't in the production cabin with you at lunch). The PM will make whatever comments or notes they wish, and these will be reported back to you. You will also attach any risk assessment or health and safety notices, as well as the directions to the location and a map, provided by the locations department. If there are any new script pages, or even a new copy of the one-line schedule strips, these may also be attached.

Once all of these elements are in place, you will "run" the call sheet. This simply means that the production office, or your team (if you are too far away from the office), will generate the copies to be distributed. You will be given a clean, official copy sometime in the afternoon. You may let others look over your shoulder (the gaffer might have a question about call time, or wardrobe about extras), but you never, NEVER, hand out the call sheet until wrap. There are many reasons for this, the most simple being that it might all change.

A number of factors may dictate amendments to a "final" call sheet, but the most common of these is **pushing the call**. Depending on cast or crew turnaround, you may need to "push" the call a half-hour or an hour later to accommodate a problem that has arisen or a delay. The old-fashioned way to reflect a pushed call, especially if you're not near a copy machine, is to get all the ADs to write in red Sharpie across the top of every sheet "All Calls Pushed Half Hour," for example. You do this rather than simply changing the call time, because while everyone's calls may be slightly different, they all relate to the overall unit call. If you have the technology to change the call sheet electronically and the time to print or copy enough versions to distribute to the crew, then great, but typically the decision to push the call is made at the last possible second. If a new call sheet has to be issued after the original was distributed, the call sheet might be issued on a pink page.

To sum up, here are the main points a First under time pressure will check on the call sheet:

- unit call
- weather
- scene order and cast changes
- requirements as per the script and shooting schedule
- unit base
- cast on set times and turnaround
- extras numbers
- stunt or body doubles
- additional crew or equipment
- unit moves
- advance schedule

Once you've done the call sheet with the Second, lunch still isn't over. There might be a wardrobe fitting for an actor who wasn't cast during prep, which the director needs to see. There might be an animal, special effect or prop that s/he needs to approve, or even a location scout. Lunch isn't a great time to do a tech recce, but sometimes it just works out that way, and you end up with the DP and the director having wolfed down some food on a hair-raising high-speed drive to see a location and then speed back to set. People generally prefer to eat first and then scout, but if at all possible I would grab a snack in the hand and eat when they come back or else the lunch break vanishes and you end up coming back to set late, never a good thing.

Back In

After lunch, whichever kind you've had, you'll sometimes want to give a five-minute warning over the walkie, and then announce that you're "back in." This is equivalent to a second call time, except now everyone is sleepy from the carbs, and it can be harder to get a momentum going at this time than at seven in the morning. It helps to get everything possible into position before you break for lunch, so you can do your best to hit the ground running.

Company Moves

Company moves, also known as unit moves, are anytime the whole circus needs to travel from one location to another—including the base. (Sometimes a few locations may still be serviced from the same base, which is a camera move.) I always allow an hour for this, unless the two locations are really far away, as even if they're close by, the process of loading and unloading the trucks always takes at least half an hour. There are, of course, ways to manage this process to reduce the amount of time required. If you can schedule your move for straight after lunch, you can get a jump on things as people generally don't want to hang around the lovely environs of whatever parking lot or waste ground your unit base might be in. Often, people start moving before they're officially "back in," which is always a bonus for a First. If it happens that your lunch has to come after your move, then you're under real pressure to be sure to break and move on time, as it's annoying to incur meal penalties for people sitting in traffic.

It's crucial to ensure that everybody understands when the move is happening, where to and how they're traveling (own transport, crew van, etc.), which must be coordinated by the ADs. Most people won't still have their call sheets from the night before, so you and your team should have a stack of maps and directions from the locations department to distribute when the move happens.

Generally, the trucks are slow to move and cars are faster. You want to organize the transport so everyone knows exactly how they're traveling before you call the move. If the crew parking has to transfer to the next location then people drive themselves. If the unit base stays in the same place, but the set is in a different location (further than a walk away carrying gear—which is anything over 100 feet) then you would ideally have a minibus or van to ferry the crew. If there is a unit driver available, you might jump in with the director, DP and even, hopefully, the first AC who is carrying the camera him/herself rather than breaking it down and putting it back on the truck. Circumstances will dictate whether this can work, but the ideal scenario is for you four to arrive to a set that is pre-lit, where your Second Second has already blocked the extras and the cast are ready and traveling to be there 5 minutes after you arrive. In this case, the director can go straight into a rehearsal, and by the time the trucks and the rest of the crew arrive you're ready to go back into block, light, rehearse, shoot.

Sometimes a unit is moving somewhere that isn't a simple street address. I find that the more time I put into the specifics of who travels in what vehicle, and sometimes even the order of these vehicles, the smoother the move will be. It's a case where micro-managing is useful. Any plan is better than no plan, and you can ensure that your team are totally up-to-speed with the plan and able to corral any stragglers or the confused. An AD department can be judged on how effortlessly a company move happens. Generally, a member of the AD team and someone from locations wait to ensure that the "last man out" isn't abandoned, and the first AD must be among the first people arriving to the new set. The Second will make sure the cast are all minded and moved, while his/her assistant will be supervising any extras' travel. This all sounds simple until you see the unmitigated chaos a badly executed move can descend into, and the commensurate loss of shooting time.

Wrap

Wrap is a critical time, just like call time. Due to its impact on turnaround, it can determine when you can make the call for the following day, as well as affording the opportunity to make the next day run smoother. I always check with the director that we are definitely wrapped before I call it. Once I'm certain, I call it over the walkie and on set loudly and clearly, such as, "That's a wrap. Call time tomorrow is 7 a.m. Unit Call, 8 a.m. Shooting Call, on location in Westchester (for example), maps are on the call sheets. Thanks everybody." It is important to say thank you, as if you mean it, and especially more so when it has been a particularly challenging day. You may also have insider information on who may have really been heroic, and it's worth seeking them out and letting them know their effort was recognized and appreciated. Everyone wants to be acknowledged and it costs nothing. Hopefully, the director will express gratitude as well. This makes an even bigger impression than yours, sometimes, and people really notice when s/he doesn't say thanks.

When you call wrap all the lights go out, and, if you're shooting a night exterior in a field, it can suddenly be very dangerous for the crew wrapping out. You will hopefully have ensured beforehand that there will be "work lights," either from the sparks or from locations, on the path from the set to the unit base and, if necessary, to the car park. It's no fun slogging through a muddy field in the dark with a heavy case trying to find your car, and you can prevent the whole crew from having a good day turn bad at the end by checking with locations and the PM what the plan is in advance.

I always catch the director and DP to have a brief chat about any outstanding issues for the first scene the next day, generally as they're walking to the car. Your second second AD, meanwhile, should be facilitating the crew "get-out" of the location as safely and quickly as possible—not letting people stand in doorways, clearing the way for camera (first ACs can be a little shy about saying "get the hell out of the way," but they are thinking it, and an AD can be a godsend if s/he does it more politely for them), making sure there's enough light to work and walk safely, and making sure everyone knows where they're going. S/he will also be getting back the walkies, sometimes a little too eagerly, as until most of the crew are cleared out there may still be some communication requirements. I ask them to leave it for 10 minutes after wrap unless there's more derigging going on.

The First can officially leave at wrap; the DGA gives the Second and Second Second a half-hour "wrap allowance," to acknowledge whoever is staying on to see out the last crew. I generally leave when the camera is back on the truck. The Second will generally still be wrapping out the cast when you return to unit base—getting them to sign their "Exhibit Gs" (timesheets—see Figure 2.11), and seeing them into their cars. When the Second Second arrives to replace the walkies it's worth seizing the moment to very quickly (and I mean less than 5 minutes or you'll be hated) describe any challenges or issues relating to the following day. It's also sometimes a chance to have a catch-up about anything that went on during the day—any disagreements or difficulties, any issues with cast, crew, logistics, production—sometimes it sounds like gossip but is actually important information and should absolutely go no further, unless you feel it's something the producer needs to know about. Most nights, though, it's simply a chance to return your walkie, say "thank you and well done" to your team and wish them goodnight.

The Second will ensure that all the paperwork ("the football") gets back to the office, and the Second, Second Second or DGA trainee, if there is one, will wait until the last of the crew are wrapped and the trucks pull away, to record the "out time" of every crew member. There is an allocated time of 30 minutes after official wrap time for all equipment to get back on the truck (if the camera wraps early, the packing-up time starts from the projected wrap time—six hours after lunch—so the crew have more time to wrap). If the gear isn't wrapped within this half-hour period, the relevant crew is entitled to meal penalties, calculated in 6-minute increments. All of this information will then be added to the production report the next day.

Overtime (OT)

Producers will often say "there is no overtime." This may be the case, as in there is no budget for it. However, you need to know when overtime would kick in if the unspeakable were to happen. You really don't want to be having that conversation anytime later than your first day of work, especially when the director isn't completing the day or the actor is getting on a plane. In such a scenario, the producer is the only person who can authorize overtime—or not. Under SAG rules, overtime starts after 12 working hours and costs time-and-a-half for the next 4 hours, with double time after that (not to mention the turnaround headaches). The rest of a US union crew are paid OT in 6-minute increments (in the UK system it can be 15-minute or half-hour blocks, depending on the union and the deal). You may get up to 15 minutes "grace," but if that happens more than once a week it will probably be reflected on the invoices as overtime.

If you pass midnight, a whole new raft of penalties can kick in. The best thing is to be informed on what the deal is, and don't wait until 5 minutes before wrap to inform the producer. They should know before you start the scene if you don't think you're going to complete it on time, and won't appreciate a frantic phone call when it's too late. If overtime is approved, it is customary not to assume that the crew will automatically work longer. I prefer the PM ask people to stay on a) because I usually don't have time to do it; and b) because I don't have the authority or information necessary to negotiate if there is some kind of dispute. If there is no one from production available and we're under time pressure, as a last resort I will announce that we are asking everyone to stay on for the specific amount of time, for what purpose, and that anyone who has a difficulty with this to please see me right away.

Dailies

It seems a long time ago now that the HODs would gather in a screening room to watch selected takes from the previous day's work. A great example of this is in Michael Winterbottom's *Tristram Shandy*, as everyone in the room focuses exclusively on their own department and the wardrobe woman silently weeps, ignored, in the back. Nowadays, rushes (or dailies) are typically issued on DVD or uploaded to a secure website where everyone who needs to can watch them, and it may be all of the raw footage rather than selected takes. None of this really affects the First (as you're not expected to watch rushes) beyond the scheduling implications of the director's transport and/or sleep requirements.

RUNNING THE SET

> *It's easy to get good players. Getting them to play together, that's the hard part.*
> Casey Stengel, Baseball Manager

A set is an infinite combination of tiny details, that add up to a kaleidoscopic whole. As the First, you're like the nucleus in an atom, holding the space and trying to speed all the electrons on their way. Every set has its own vocabulary, but if you're familiar with some of the universal tricks and techniques, you can facilitate what needs to happen that much more quickly.

Some Common Phrases and Practices

"**Locking it up**" and "**holding traffic**" are two of the most common jobs for PAs on a film set. Locking it up means securing the set to the degree that no one talks or moves during the take. Of course, this has completely different implications depending on whether you're shooting in a studio, a private location or a busy street. In a studio, there is typically a red-light system. In a controlled location, the Second Second or PA serves the function of a human red light, ensuring that no one passes once sound is rolling. On a busy street, you will need a lot of bodies to manage the public, and your lock-up crew will consist of a mix of PAs, locations crew, and sometimes security, depending on the neighborhood. No matter how well you lock it off, even, occasionally, with barricades, you will get the odd resident who insists on walking through the set, generally muttering bad-tempered opinions! It's best not to resist this too much, or to abuse the person who might have let him or her through, as sometimes resistance can just escalate the problem. If they're in your face and after a few seconds aren't responding to your charm in asking them to step aside (I sometimes invite them to watch, but from a specific nearby area—often near a monitor—rather than in front of the camera, and they generally get bored very quickly and leave), then it's the responsibility of the locations department, who employ security and will call them in if need be. What you don't want is anyone from the AD department to get bogged down dealing with this person, as you all have other responsibilities, and locations are there to deal with this kind of issue. Ultimately, you must never be rude and NEVER, EVER touch the person, while asking them to leave, as there are loonies around who will welcome the chance to sue. Equally, you may sometimes encounter people who decide to play their stereo at high volume when you arrive, hoping for the locations department to pay them to stop. Again, this is a locations issue, which you don't want to get dragged into, no matter how simple it may seem to ask them to stop—leave it to locations.

Here's one way to get rid of nosy **onlookers**:

CURIOUS PERSON: Making a movie? Cool! What's it called? Who's in it?

ME: It's a mayonnaise commercial.

Gets 'em every time. With due respect to Hellmann's, no one you have ever wanted to see has appeared in a mayonnaise commercial. Can you even remember ever seeing a mayonnaise commercial? For this reason, no matter how thrilling the car crash that you're about to stage looks, the person will generally say "ah…" with a tinge of disappointment and disdain for you, and after a couple of last looks drift away. By the time they find out that it's *Mission Impossible 6*, hopefully you'll be gone.

If you're shooting in a small town, this strategy won't work, as they'll know more about the production than you will. In this case, I find it helpful to involve them as part of the team. Especially in rougher areas, where teenage boys, for example, may want to interrupt or disrupt filming, being confrontational or authoritative will only lead to resistance and intensify the situation. I can't tell you how many times, even when dealing with potential thugs, explaining what you're doing (that is, what the shot is) and asking them to help by helping keep it quiet during the take and letting things go afterwards has worked beautifully. If it's possible for them to see a monitor without disturbing anyone, I invite them to "see it on TV" at a discreet distance from whatever crew need to see it. Generally, after a few takes, they get bored and drift off, but as with any human being if you treat them with courtesy and respect they respond in kind. Making them part of the team removes the conflict.

Of course this has its limits. Shooting in areas controlled by gangs or paramilitaries has its own behavioral responsibilities, which you'll need to research extensively. I also recommend having a clearly communicated evacuation plan in place if trouble breaks out—hopefully, you'll never need to use it. Preparing to film in an area of Belfast that was prone to riots, I prepared an extensive evacuation operation, complete with a "code red" signal to clear the area instantly. It did feel a little like overkill when the location manager showed me photos of the potential rioters—children under 12, smiling sweetly at the camera—but I still needed to have a plan in place. It doesn't matter who throws a rock for it to hurt.

Holding traffic can refer to people or vehicles; if it's the latter, in most places it must be implemented by the police. While it is the locations or production department who organizes the police to be there on the day, typically you as the First will deal with them directly on the shoot. You will respectfully describe where your frame ends and allow them to choose the best position to stop traffic, out of shot. There will normally be at least two police, who will need to be issued with production walkies and to be instructed when you are rolling and cut. This communication can be done directly with the police or through the location manager, depending on personalities and requirements. I don't consider traffic held until I get confirmation from each person holding it, and have seen myself the last car they let through pass me personally. Cars passing through a set can travel quickly and working crew assume they're protected, so you and your team will spend a lot of time telling people when cars are coming and to step back or "watch their backs." All crew working on public roads should be wearing high-visibility jackets and use reflective cones for protection.

As a First, you have to appreciate that people in their cars, and especially truck drivers, get impatient very quickly when forced to wait, and in a residential neighbourhood or small town you don't want to incur the hatred of the local inhabitants. If you can release traffic between every take, this is ideal, though the director and DP will rarely allow this to happen. Depending on the length of the take, you might get two or three before you have to clear the traffic, that is, release it and wait for all of the waiting vehicles to pass through. When in this situation, I would wait until the very last second to hold traffic before rolling, and when we cut, unless the director says immediately that they would like to go again, I would clear it, to avoid resentment and also a buildup that is going to take longer to clear the next time. If, after cut, the director says "let me see that one back," I immediately release traffic and clear the backup. If the director wants to go again before clearing, I will say on the walkie, "We're cut, but we want to go again straightaway, can we keep it held, please?" Generally, the police will be okay about this, but when you start getting the messages that they really need to clear it you need to respect their commands. Sometimes a cop will just decide on their own to clear traffic, or not to hold, and this is both annoying and dangerous, as if you think traffic is held you might have people working on the road. If this happens, you need to advise them of the health and safety risk that has been created.

If you are shooting on a road and need a complete road closure, this needs to be requested and organized a long time in advance, as it requires permissions from local government bodies. Even with permission, you still can't make the road totally impassable, as an ambulance or other emergency vehicle may need to pass. This is a process of negotiation, as almost always the desire is to lay track across the whole road. You can stand a crowd in the road, but track is tricky, no matter how much the grip says he can "whip it away" in a matter of seconds. If you were suffering a heart attack, would it be quick enough? This is the kind of responsibility you are taking on. Sometimes, there may be an alternative route that eliminates the need to have emergency access, but it's your job to evaluate all the possibilities and know before you arrive what you can allow the camera crew to do. Even if it sometimes means being the "bad guy," that's better than blocking someone from medical attention…isn't it?

The phrase "**release traffic**" refers to both cars and pedestrians—even, in a private location, to crew. It's the book-end command to "lock it up," and can also be used to indicate that, for whatever reason, you may no longer be standing by (a cloud covers the sun, a lamp has blown, or an actor needs a moment, whatever it might be).

There are other technical issues, or tricks of the trade, and expressions commonly employed on film sets that are handy to know. For example, let's say you've rolled sound, but someone asks you to wait or something else prevents you from rolling camera. You would say "**hold the roll**" if sound is rolling but camera hasn't. If camera has rolled, then you will need to cut, but despite the cost of film, tape or digital media I would still ask the director, "Is it okay to cut?" and get their permission first. With many directors, this won't be necessary, and you will quickly learn which type you're dealing with. But some are more insecure, or more obsessed with being in control, and they won't want you to be the one to call cut under any circumstances.

If you did roll camera, but cut before you called action, the board will be marked with AFS: "**after false start**," to let the editor know that there is a second, complete, take to follow the first one.

You may also sometimes wish to do several takes "**on a roll**"—for example, if the shot is a close-up of someone flicking a switch, or doing some kind of action that requires a specific position in the frame, sometimes it's easier to do the action a few times within the same take, rather than cutting, resetting, and going again. This can also save on film stock and time.

Sometimes, you may also wish to do a **silent roll**, that is, roll sound and camera without advertising it or saying it out loud. For example, if you are working with a child and they happen to be doing what's required, you'll want to shoot that without distracting them with all the build-up of a normal take. In this case, you would quietly tell sound and camera that you're doing a silent roll and communicate this to the Second Second and the world by whispering it over the walkie. The Second Second will be able to alert anyone relevant as you proceed.

When doing a silent roll, you will often want to use an "**end board**" or "**tail slate.**" This means clapping the board at the end of the take, rather than the beginning, in which case the clapper is held upside down for the clap, then righted so the editor can read it. This is useful in silent rolls and when the opening frame makes it almost impossible to get the slate into shot, or even sometimes when the second AC has their hands in a film-loading bag or on the truck and they haven't handed over the clapper to someone else in time! Either way, when the director says "cut" you will say "tail slate" or "end board" to remind the first AC not to cut camera before getting the clap. Once camera cuts, you will then call a general "Cut!" to the cast and crew.

Overlapping can refer to either action or dialogue. The time-honored tradition is that edits happen on action—that is, as someone sits or stands, for example; the continuity of action can disguise the cut from one shot to another. For this reason, even if the shot is designed only to cover a particular section of a scene, you will typically "overlap" the action by running it from a little earlier than required to a little past what's required, to give the actors momentum and the editor cutting options. In this case, it's a good thing. To sound mixers, overlapping means actors speaking over each other's lines, which is a nightmare for sound editors. However, sometimes performances with no overlaps feel staged and awkward, simply because in real life people rarely wait for someone to finish a sentence entirely before speaking themselves. It's an ongoing debate as to which is preferable, and the director decides whether to get the actors to overlap for performance, or not to, for sound.

Insert shots are similar to cutaways, in that they are often very tight close-ups of inanimate objects or a hand doing something (like the light switch referred to above). Generally, if you know there will be one or two in a scene, they're handy to shoot while you're waiting for some other element, such as cast, to get ready. However, what you don't want is the cast hanging around while you do an insert. If it's something extremely straightforward then you can probably "knock it off" in 15 minutes, but don't leave yourself any less time, as sometimes with these shots the lighting and focus become critical, or a discussion breaks out as to which angle it should be from, and the time starts draining away. Generally, they're the part of the scene you shoot last, unless there is a big delay at the start or in the middle.

Pickups are shots taken to cut into a scene that has already been shot—either because they were dropped on the shoot, or because the editor wants to change something in the scene. Whatever the reason, they obviously have strict continuity demands. You'll need the script supervisor's notes from the original shoot to be able to match the original scene perfectly.

A **banana**, aside from being a fruit, is a term for when an actor needs to take a curved path rather than a straight line between two points, due to the impact of a particular lens. Just an aside: time flies like a bird, fruit flies like a banana.

Eyelines are an integral part of the technique of film production and the word has several meanings. The first is literally what the actor is physically looking at; if you're trying to do a love scene and behind Actor Y is a grip snoring, it doesn't help Actor X's concentration. Any eye contact can be particularly disturbing, as it takes actors out of the scene. While of course the crew want to watch, one of the most common things you will say as a First before a take is "Clear the eyelines, please." I prefer not to mention anyone by name, even if there is only one person, typically a junior member of crew, staring at the actors. People learn fast and

Figure 3.2 *Correct eyelines*

Figure 3.3 *Incorrect eyelines*

generally won't repeat the mistake, but even the most experienced crew members can sometimes unconsciously drift into position an actor's eyeline. Actors appreciate the First being aware of this, as some of them feel like divas if they have to ask for it themselves.

Eyelines also refer to the direction the actor is looking in the frame. Correct, or matching, eyelines create in the viewer the impression that two people are having a realistic conversation, even if they are in different countries at different times. The most basic of these is that Actor X looks camera (or frame) right, Actor Y looks camera (or frame) left (Figure 3.2). When these are cut together, it looks like they're talking to each other. However, If Actor X looks a little bit higher, then Actor Y will need to look a little bit lower. What you're hoping for is that their gaze meets in the middle and they feel connected. If you're off by even an inch or two, the audience will sense something wrong and be slightly disturbed by it, even if they can't identify what the problem is (Figure 3.3). Likewise, if the eyelines are too wide (that is to the right or left of the camera) there will also be a disconcerting effect. Some directors deliberately employ this effect to make the audience uncomfortable, but in all other cases the eyelines, and often the size of the shot, want to be exactly matched.

It is also generally desirable to have the eyeline as close to the camera as possible; for this reason you will often have Actor X, in front of the camera, looking at Actor Y sitting on an apple box, squeezed in as tight as can be to the lens. Sometimes, even this isn't enough, and Actor X will be delivering their lines to a white tape mark on the lens' matt box, even when Actor Y is beside the camera. This is a judgment call—it can make a prettier picture, but if your actors aren't that experienced, performance can suffer.

It is the holy grail of multi-camera directors to see both of the actors' eyes (as opposed to profile), and one of the main arguments for shooting single camera is often that it allows tighter eyelines. (In multi-camera, if you

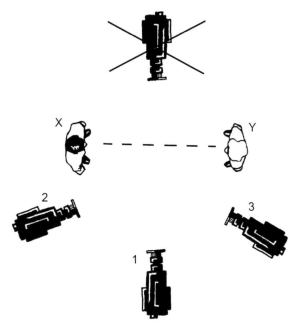

Figure 3.4 *The "line," drawn between two characters*

get too tight you start seeing the other camera.) This is a distinction that I suspect audiences don't appreciate, but DPs are adamant about.

It's not the First's responsibility to be good on eyelines, but it helps. And if you have more than two characters in a scene, even if they're sitting static at a table, the most experienced directors can very quickly paint themselves into a corner. This is when it's important to be familiar with the essence of blocking for camera: **crossing the line**.

There are a million different ways to understand crossing the line, and all communicate the same basic concept. Let's begin with a scene with two people. Some DPs prefer to think of the images and how they cut together, but this is a little too abstract for me. My preferred method is to take a bird's-eye view and literally draw a line between the two (Figure 3.4)—this is the famous line, and as long as you always stay on the same side, no matter where you put the camera, the scene will cut. If you cross the line, you get bad eyelines—both actors looking left, for example. Another way of imagining it is to picture a football match; the cameras are always on the same side of the line, and if they use a reverse angle they tell you, otherwise you'd be confused about which direction the ball is traveling. It's that simple. And that complicated, once you get into a space with walls that don't move and actors who do!

Of course, when an actor moves, the line moves with them (Figure 3.5), which is relatively simple, even when the actors swap position. However, once you add another character into the scene, things get complicated: you now have a triangle, rather than just a straight line, and you need to be on the correct side of the line depending on the actor's eyeline. If Actor X is looking at Actor Y, they will have a different eyeline, and line, when

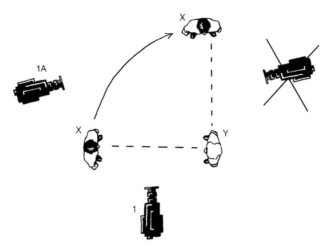

Figure 3.5 *When the actors move, so does the "line"*

they look at Actor Z. You can commonly require two angles on any given actor, one for each eyeline, in every scene, dictating that with your wide shot you could have a minimum of seven setups for the scene. If one of the actors moves, depending on where they go you could have just added another three shots—if you need a single on each actor for every line. It's not your job to decide where to put the camera, but it is your problem when, halfway into a scene, the director and DP and script supervisor are in a long discussion about which shots will cut together and how many more they need. Your best way to prevent this is to practice the method described earlier: after running a rehearsal of the entire scene, you clear the actors from the set and record the result of the conversation the DP, the director and the script supervisor have about what shots are required to cover the scene. (If you have a camera operator, you probably won't be having this discussion, as they are typically the most proficient at these issues. A first-time director can go into meltdown.)

The script supervisor, or, in the old days, continuity, is the editor's representative on the floor, and determined to ensure that the scene will cut elegantly. Sometimes this person is ignored or omitted from the preliminary shotlist discussion, and that's a big mistake. Too many times I've heard the script supervisor pipe up as we set up the fourth shot of seven, pointing out that the shot won't cut, and suddenly the whole plan falls apart. If you map out (and I literally map out on a makeshift floor plan, as an illustration) the camera positions for the whole scene, you will see immediately whether you're crossing the line or getting into a situation where the camera needs to be somewhere it can't physically access. Even if this takes a few minutes (and of course you're desperate to start shooting), these minutes could save you hours later. As I said, you're not responsible for the solution, but you need to be able to identify a problem before you get there, and if you can quietly whisper to the DP that you will be crossing the line, thus allowing him/her to save face and make a quick adjustment, you will be a valuable asset to the team both from a timekeeping and creative point of view.

Screen direction can also create the illusion of continuous action, and like eyelines and crossing the line will sometimes be deliberately misused to create discomfort in the audience. Generally, however, screen direction is maintained, the classic example being in any kind of chase—both the chaser and the chasee would move left to right, or right to left, in every shot. A director might, at some point during the chase, alter the direction, but the simplest method is to maintain continuity. It's something for a First to be aware of as early as possible, so that when you're doing the tech scouts you'll already have an idea of which way you should be looking, and be able to quietly remind the director if a shot is being planned to accidentally change the screen direction.

"Quiet, please!" If you've spent any time on a set, you'll have heard this phrase repeated more than once. Obviously, if you're recording sound, it's important that it should be as clean as possible—that is, with no extraneous sound whatsoever. However, even when you're shooting MOS (which allegedly originates from a German director intending to say "without sound" and producing MitOut Sund), it's still important that the set be as quiet as possible, to allow the cast and the technicians to focus.

It's not just during the takes that you need a quiet set, however. Between shots, there is always at least one important conversation happening—the director might be talking to the cast, the DP to the gaffer, the First to the Second Second, and this is already noisy. Add to that any casual chat and the work conversations have to come up in volume to be heard, and when everyone starts talking over each other you very quickly have complete bedlam. A phrase I would love to never have to say again is "Take the chat off the set!" In other words, if you're on set you should be silent, unless your talk involves purely professional purposes that are directly related to the scene at hand—advance work can be done elsewhere. Even then, there's no need to shout; the more quietly you can communicate, the better, unless everyone really needs to hear your information.

Sometimes you will hear the First say "**Settle**" after "turning over," or rolling. It often refers to a member of crew who is still getting into their position for the take, and in this case I find it a little obnoxious. It can also refer to an inanimate object that is literally settling—a lightbulb's cord, or a floorboard that springs back into place. Some Firsts use it as a follow-up to "quiet, please," if things still aren't silent enough for their liking. Where I personally use the phrase is in the time between the slate being clapped and calling action. Sometimes you need to wait for someone or something, and if there's a big silence while this happens people think you have forgotten to call action and get distracted. Saying "settle," or "stand-by," indicates that there is something happening and that you haven't simply fallen asleep. Like radio silence, people get nervous about dead air, so it's a way of reassuring them that the process is still moving.

Finally, you should treat the camera like a loaded gun: never stand in front of it, unless you're standing in for an actor. If you have to cross in front of the lens, especially while someone is looking through it (and they may be only doing so on a monitor, so the rule applies even when no one is at the eyepiece), you say "**crossing**" to acknowledge that you're disturbing the view. If someone has to take a flash photo, it is a courtesy to announce it by saying "**flashing**" before doing it, so the electricians don't think a bulb may have blown.

Poor **Abby Singer**—for whatever reason, his name has become synonymous with the second-last shot. One version has it that he was a first AD who allegedly wrapped all the extras, thinking it was the last shot, only to discover that it was the second last... As a First, I have only sympathy for the man, and would bet a fiver that the director told him it was the last shot, only to change his mind afterwards! In any case, if you tell the crew "It's the Abby," they know what you mean.

The **Martini** (or the Guinness, as it's called in Ireland) is the last shot of the day. When you know for certain you're on the last shot it's useful to let everybody know, not by shouting it across the set, but rather by announcing it on the walkie and saying it quietly to the HODs. You don't shout it, because the actors can get disconcerted and distracted, and you let everybody know that it's the last shot so they can start wrapping any gear that isn't being used. Be cautious about calling the martini until you're sure your director isn't the kind who likes to "just grab one little thing" after your last shot. You don't want to be responsible for the grips carrying the dolly back up the stairs. But if you know it's the last you can start wrapping extras, equipment, even some crew, which makes for a quicker and more efficient overall wrap.

Smoke & Mirrors

Needless to say, there is no smoking anywhere on a set at any time. The only exception to this is when a character needs to smoke on camera, and there are regulations governing the type of least-harmful herbal cigarette they can use. Some actors who are smokers (and so many of them are! If they don't smoke, have a look at their fingernails, often bitten to the quick) will suggest that they smoke real cigarettes, as they prefer it. However, it's not up to them: it's a health and safety issue for the welfare of the crew, who have the right to a smoke-free workplace. Most American directors have a horror of smoking, and even outdoors will object to anyone smoking within a 50-foot radius, as they have a right to. Occasionally, you will encounter a director who loves to smoke, and insists on doing it beside the monitor, exterior and interior. This is a delicate situation; what you can do is privately advise him or her that you have received complaints from the crew (even if this isn't true); if they ask for names, you will never reveal them (especially if it isn't true!). I once saw Liza Minnelli asked not to smoke by a security guard in Lincoln Center, and rather than losing her head in a "don't you know who I am" scenario, she was so gracious and apologetic that I was very impressed by her humility. If your director isn't this type, and their attitude is more "fuck 'em" than "excuse me," you will need to speak to the producer about it. The producer is the only one with the power to make the director do anything. As mentioned earlier, all you can do is advise; the producer, especially in TV, has usually hired the director, and if anyone has any control, they should. If you have a weak producer, poor you. If the smoking continues, you will have to tell the director that you're in danger of a strike or mutiny, and that s/he will have to step outside when they want to smoke. If they flip out, it's an indicator of how much they care about the welfare of the people they're working with, and a sign that you'll need to be particularly vigilant when and if there's any stunt work involved.

Sometimes, of course, you will require smoke as an ambient effect, either for lighting or story reasons. There are now smoke machines that are allegedly perfectly safe, employing a water-based system rather than the cracked oil that was visually stunning and held in the air well, but was more than certainly bad for one's health. (On a student film, I once saw a budgie that was near a smoke machine keel over and die at the end of the day—I'm not proud to have been on a project that resulted in the death of any animal. As the crew gathered in shock and horror, the gaffer cradling the tiny bird in his hand, the art director entered and, taking in the scene, got a shock and then exclaimed, "What happened? Oh, it's the bird? They're only $5.99 at Woolworth's! I thought it was the lamp!" While the lamp, worth two grand, would have been a tragic loss for the art department, her candid reaction nearly got her lynched.)

When dealing with interior smoke in a relatively small area, this can often be managed by the stand-by prop person with a small smoke machine. However, if dealing with a large space or exterior smoke, you will need a special effects person to supervise it. And you will always need to advise the locations department beforehand of what you're doing, so they can liaise with the location owner. It's very disconcerting for someone who owns a family home to hear some crew member ask another "So where are we doing the fire?" Anything unusual, including smoke, needs to be flagged in advance, to avoid the owner simply throwing you out.

Any reflective surface can become a mirror, and you will often need to corral everyone to a particular side of camera, or well away from the action altogether, while the camera crew are draped in black duveteen to avoid reflections. Pictures on walls are ideally de-glassed, to avoid reflections, or need to be carefully angled. On tech scouts beware any rooms with large mirrors, especially in gyms, or any store windows that are going to be dark, as they also lead to embarrassing shots of the crew. Finally, cars, teapots, eyeglasses, even a teaspoon if the shot is close enough, will all need to be carefully checked before rolling. "Anti-flare" is a spray that camera departments often carry to address this problem, but it can't be sprayed on every surface.

Don't Touch My Stuff

As mentioned in prep, the most well-intentioned "help" can actually result in serious disruption. The electricians will say that only they touch anything with a plug—although props will get a "feed" from the sparks if they need to work a toaster, likewise the hairdresser for a blow-dryer. You may be standing closest to a prop that needs to move, but if you move it, prepare to incur the wrath of the person whose job it is. Not only is it impolite (how would you like it if they started calling "action"?), it is impractical—a prop person might want to mark the prop's position before moving it, or need to photograph it, or may have sprayed it with anti-flare, or any number of other possibilities. The simple solution is to ask the person before touching it; if their hands are full, they'll thank you, and if they can do it themselves they'll still appreciate the courtesy. This protocol extends to all departments: no matter how much quicker or easier it may seem for you to do something, don't just wade in. The only thing an AD should touch is their notebook and their walkie—everything else is someone else's department. The odd exception to this is when you're shooting in the rain or cold and a costume person simply doesn't have enough hands to remove the actors' keep-warm coats and umbrellas. In this case, you might help by holding something, particularly as a PA or Second Second, but as quickly as possible you return the item in question to costume and certainly don't put it down anywhere. Makeup may also appreciate a helping hand bringing their gear onto the makeup bus or dressing room, and very occasionally at the end of a long day even the grip might let you help fold down or stack C-stands. But you never, EVER touch a light, a dolly or a camera case unless requested. It's just not worth the danger, be it from injury or abuse!

Blacking Out

Not to be confused with drinking too much at the wrap party, blacking out is necessary when you are shooting a night scene in daylight hours in a location with windows, doors or skylights. It involves literally draping black fabric over the areas that let in natural light. It's crucial that this be requested in advance, at the very latest at the tech scout, as it's inevitably a time-consuming process and can require additional manpower in advance to achieve it, depending on the size of the blackout. Almost any black material can be used, from the proper electrical department blacks or duveteen, to garbage bags, as long as they're opaque enough to seal the light out.

A crucial aspect of a black-out is whether there is a door that has to play during the scene, and whether the DP wants to light through the windows. If so, it's not good enough to simply fix the blacks directly to the door or window frame, but rather they need to be "**tented**," meaning a little extension needs to be created to allow space for the actor or the light to fit between the black and the aperture (door, window, etc.). This is a bigger job again, and always needs to be done as a pre-rig, before the shooting crew arrive. It is up to the PM to negotiate how many people are required and for how long, and when the work is to be done, but it is up to you to have this on the shooting schedule, thus the call sheet, and to mention it when talking through the schedule at every production meeting.

What to Wear

They say there's no such thing as bad weather, just inappropriate clothing, and that's certainly true on a film set. Some locations will have a list of requirements for people working there, such as steel-toe boots and safety helmets on a construction site. Even if that's not a legal requirement, nowhere is it appropriate or safe to wear flip-flops, sandals, or any open-toed shoes, unless you're shooting on a beach. If your location doesn't demand boots, you can wear sneakers, but don't be tempted to have any part of your foot showing – it will get stepped on, banged off or dropped on, and if it hurts in sneakers it will bleed in sandals.

There are different standards expected of the different departments—people might be disappointed if the hair and makeup departments weren't often as brightly decorated as Christmas trees—but ADs, generally, are expected to dress functionally. There is a wonderful moment in *Living in Oblivion* when the director takes aim at the First for wearing the most distracting, brightly colored shirt she could find! Which might not occur to most people when getting up at 5 a.m., but you're beside the camera, and your Hawaiian number may be just a little dazzling in a prison cell set. The main determining factor in what you're wearing should be climate and comfort; generally layers that you can remove, given that you might be moving from a freezing street to an overheated office in the same morning. I'm going to give you my personal recommendations, gleaned from years of suffering.

If it's hot, you want very thin layers, not acres of skin. Hot pants and belly tops are not appropriate, no matter how fit you are. T-shirts with sleeves and light trousers are about as skimpy as you can get away with.

If it's cold, my perfect scenario is silk long johns, then knee-high wool socks, followed by fleece sweatpants, topped off by waterproof leggings. It's not flattering, but this is the lightest, warmest combination I have ever found, and it has gotten me through extreme temperatures. On top, first a t-shirt, then a thermal long sleeve top (the t-shirt underneath means you can wear the thermal for much longer—ideally it's silk, which you don't want to have to wash every day—and the layer underneath really holds the heat), then another long sleeve, possibly cotton, before a layer of fleece, then the outer jacket (which ideally has a warm, removable lining). This whole ensemble is lightweight, snug, and easily ventilated if you find yourself running or otherwise heating up in cold weather. You need well-supported, waterproof ankle boots; a good pair of thin, waterproof gloves (although I often find myself only wearing one, Michael Jackson-style, as I need my fingers on one hand free to change walkie channels and write notes); a fleece cowl is better than a scarf, as it's smaller and lighter and has no space for air leaks; and the piece de resistance, a hat. This is your one opportunity to express yourself, but function still dictates form: it needs to cover your ears and keep your head warm. I once worked with a director who had an Arctic coat, complete with little burners you could light and put in specially designed pockets in the back lining at his kidneys, to ensure that they keep functioning when his other organs start to shut down, but if you're in that kind of cold you'll be having trouble keeping the cameras working anyway. The only problem with this ensemble (besides the fact that you'll have the physique of a yeti) is that there is still no good way to protect your face. The cowl is great when you're not speaking, as you can raise it right up to your eyes and lower it again with ease, but eventually you may find it hard to speak, when your face starts to freeze. Balaclavas, in certain contexts, can have unfortunate associations. Whoever finds the solution to this problem, wins.

Your Kit

Besides a perfectly functioning headset, I also have in my stash sun block, lip stuff, tissues, wipes, a bag of nuts and raisins, and water—all available elsewhere on set, but handy to have with you if you or someone beside you wants one quickly. I recommend the aluminum case clipboard camera departments use; it's solid, and you can tape a smaller notebook to it if you need more paperwork with you. You may also want to have in your set bag a Leatherman or Swiss Army Knife, painkillers, mints, and a small flashlight.

Slowpokes

We have all been (or will be) on sets where things are just moving really, really slowly, for no obvious reason. Sometimes, at the end of a very long, tough job, the crew is just so exhausted that they're moving in slow motion, and no amount of hustling by the First is going to improve things. Other times, in spite of your best efforts, you're falling behind. As it's the First who people are going to question, in these cases my estimated timings (beside each scene number on my sides) are even more important for knowing how we're doing. Producers and PMs expect you to be able to tell them how behind or ahead you are, and if you know you wanted to be on the second scene at 10 a.m. and it's now 10:30, you can tell them instantly.

If it's a particularly slow shoot, I record exactly where the time is going, for example:

10:05	Rehearsal
10:15	Shots discussed
10:20	Track laid, lighting
10:30	Rehearsal to camera
10:40	Discussion between director and DP
11 a.m.	SHOT CHANGED—track moved
11:10	Rehearsal to camera
11:15	Take 1

And so forth. This is, as we say, an ass-covering exercise. Remember 50¢ a second? Producers will want to know where their time is going, if things are behind, and if you can't tell them you will quickly come to be seen as the problem. Timekeeping is your job, and I have found in difficult situations that being able to present very clearly how the time is being spent can allow the correct steps to be taken rather than simply firing you! Even if no one else ever sees it, it can be very useful to you to know where the time is going. Is it that you're doing 6-minute takes? Are you doing 10 takes a setup? Is the director spending ages talking to the actors? Is it the lighting? Too many rehearsals? Sometimes in the thick of it you're so focused on keeping the train moving that you're not taking in the scenery, and this can be a handy method of understanding where a problem may lie so you can take steps to fix it.

Knowing Your Place

A certain amount of skill in being in the right place at the right time is instinctive, but there are some general rules of thumb you can practice until it is. Every First will have their own way of working and positioning preferences. There are no hard and fast rules, but this is what works for me.

I want to be close enough to the camera to be able to hear the first AC or operator say "Set" when you roll, but not so close that everything I say is right in their ear, or that they feel crowded when they need to change a lens or a magazine. (This is especially true if you're using a loudhailer—many first ACs have been near-deafened by an overzealous First shouting "Action!" in their ear.) If the DP is operating the camera, this position is even more reliable, as, strangely, it's often the DP who has the most requirements when you're setting up the shot. Once the director has approved the frame, it's basically up to you and the DP to get it ready to shoot. So being beside the DP and making sure they have all the elements they need is a big part of your job.

If there is a camera operator and the DP is beside the director at the monitor, you will need to be beside them throughout the setting-up process so as to relay instructions to your Second Second and other members of crew. If you're at a distance, the Second Second will take your place beside the camera, working to your direction. Once you're ready to roll, you'll swap places—the Second Second will hover behind or beside the director so they can echo when you're rolling and advise you when the director calls "cut." You will typically be back beside the camera to call action and echo cut to the camera and cast.

Very often, you will find yourself in truly tiny spaces and it's more important than ever to give people as much physical space as you can. If the camera is in a small bathroom where you physically cannot fit, you can be on the other side of the door and ask the first AC to give you a very loud "Set!" so you can call action accordingly. Sometimes, you may even need them to call it on the walkie; on one occasion I actually clapped the board and held the boom mic, the space was so tight—every situation will have its own solutions, the trick is to work out a plan in advance. If people want to amend the plan, that's fine, but you don't want to be figuring it out for the first time when you're ready to roll.

Ideally, I like to stand beside the camera in the director's eyeline. Wherever you're positioned, you want to be able to see and hear the director. It's uncanny how you will become attuned to the director's voice to the point where you can hear them say "um…" through a crowded room.

I like the Second Second to stand a far enough distance from me for me to have some space, but to maintain constant eye contact, the way a good waiter is constantly scanning the room to see if the customers need anything. (In fact, a talent for waiting tables or bartending is actually good practice for working on a film set, where you need to be able to think about six things at once, and maintain cordial relations with a large group of people while working under pressure.) A lot can be communicated simply through sign language once you're used to working together. The Second Second will potentially also be beside the main access, so as to be able to "**lock up**" the set (that is, make sure no one goes in or out) during the takes, although on bigger sets this will require a PA so you and the Second Second can still see each other. On a smaller set, particularly on location, the Second Second may not even be in the room; certainly, they don't need to echo if everyone on the set can already hear you.

Listening is just as important for the Second Second as watching. There are times when the First will turn down their walkie, particularly if taking instruction from the director, and a First rarely needs to hear the ongoing chatter on Channel 1—some Firsts will only turn up the walkie when trying to communicate with someone. But it's crucial that the Second Second have their walkie on and in their ear all the time. If someone is trying to reach the First, the Second Second can tell them, and the Second Second will also get a good picture of what's going on off-set by the walkie chatter and can thus inform the First if need be. But most importantly, the Second Second is listening for the instruction from the First. I once had a PA who had an inability to listen to his walkie, and after three different occasions trying to reach him, I fired him. That probably sounds harsh, but if you've experienced the frustration of a medical emergency on set, with a dozy Second Second visibly chatting off in the distance out of earshot, you'll understand. It's a basic job requirement and if they're not listening, they're no use to me.

The PA will maintain a parallel relationship with the Second Second, trying to anticipate the Second Second's commands and generally keeping an alert eye on them from a distance. If I need to leave the set for any reason, the Second Second covers and the PA Second seconds, and so forth. Most of my communication will be directly to the Second Second, rather than the PA, mainly so there is a clear channel of communication and we aren't asking the PA to do three things at once. This chain of command may seem militaristic, but it is simply the most efficient. It's not an ego trip unless you make it one.

Set Politics

This section could form an entire book. My basic rule of thumb is simply that no one needs to be publicly humiliated; when in doubt, ask the person above you what to do, and any sensitive information goes to the First; if you're the First, to the producer.

There are two potentially horrible dynamics, and both involve someone trying to usurp the position of the director. Either the DP tries to assume the spotlight on the floor, or the producer quietly drips poison and doubt into the director's ear at the monitor. With the DP, you can make it clear, if you have to, that you answer to the director, and when the DP starts directing you can redirect people's attention and requests back to the director (this is particularly common, unfortunately, when the director is a woman). Some DPs think the whole shoot is about the camera, which is understandable, but in fact that's only the little picture compared to the director's overview of the entire project: development, script, editing, marketing, etc. There has to be a hierarchy or else the whole thing falls apart. Even if the director isn't inspiring, experienced or even competent, when the lines of command are blurred you can get anarchy in 60 seconds.

With the producer, it's more complicated, as s/he is also your boss, and you can't intercept these conversations. If the producer is second-guessing the director, however, it will start costing you time, and this is when you can step in with a request—not on the floor, but at the end of the day you can have a chat with the two of them and explain that doing things various ways, or changing the shots, is costing a lot of time. You can also privately have a word with the director so they know you're behind them. And, in an extreme example, you might ask the producer directly if they're having doubts about the director. You can in all honesty say that it appears as if the producer is overruling the director, and that's starting to create anxiety and concern throughout the cast and crew. The producer won't necessarily tell you the truth, but you will have sent the message that his/her behavior isn't helping the project. I suppose this is where, when push comes to shove, a First is either a director's or a producer's First. I believe that a First should be both, but I also believe that once a director is hired, they need to be supported and facilitated to do their best work, and if a producer doesn't believe in a director they should either fire him/her or let them get on with it. Sowing seeds of doubt is one guarantee that the project will be terrible, and I'm speaking from experience. As with so many things, confidence is half the battle, and a director who has any trace of insecurity (and who doesn't?) can be totally subverted by bad management from above, below and beside.

A word here about being mistreated—it may happen that you are spoken to by the DP or director in a disrespectful manner, or otherwise treated in a way you don't like. The time to address this is not on the set with the clock ticking; the professional approach is to continue doing your best work to complete the day, and after work have a conversation with the person in question, if they haven't already apologized. Again, I find a nonconfrontational approach works best: you don't want to have problems between you, so if there was a real issue to address earlier you can discuss that. If it was something minor you can simply move on, but at least they will understand that such behavior will have consequences, even if it's gentle, after hours and in private, and that can be enough to make them hesitate before doing it again. Unless you're dealing with serious sexual harassment or verbal abuse, it's your problem to address, not the producer's, although if it's serious or repeated the producer should be informed calmly by you so they don't hear about it first from someone else.

If you believe that a member of the cast or crew is being unfairly treated, you have to make delicate judgment calls about how to handle it. Some directors are simply bullies and can be confronted. If it touches on sexual harassment or safety, then you have a duty to intervene—again, I recommend a constructive conversation rather than a challenge, to elicit the director's feelings on the issue and their possible idea of a solution. If it's a crew member doing the bullying, a firm private word should put an immediate stop to it, and it should be reported to the PM.

As you advance in your career, very often the people get nicer as you go along, but sometimes you just have to work with assholes. I consider it a spiritual practice and get on with the job. It won't last forever.

The most political zone on the whole project, however, is the cast.

Loving the Cast

I tend to view cast as I would children—not in a patronizing way (I don't speak baby talk to them), but in the same way that I would protect, consider and be patient with any child who happened to be working. Some Firsts look on actors with sufferance, or as simply another member of the crew, and to each his own. I like to combine personal kindness and sympathy with a professional distance, and this is the balance I'm always aiming for.

The cast are generally nervous, however well they conceal it, and creating an environment in which they feel safe is important. A set that is professional, quiet and polite is a good first step. I would always make sure that when the cast are on set the banter ceases and the focus is entirely on the rehearsal or take. Many cast members will have their little idiosyncrasies, and if these can be easily addressed then by all means do whatever it takes to facilitate their security blanket (and be equally kind and courteous to their assistant). What you never want to do is become friends, and you will hopefully never engage with them in any social situation; that's the director's area, and the less contact you have with them off the set the better.

At the risk of repeating myself, I will reiterate—never give the cast the schedule. If they see it, they go making plans, and when things change, they get irritated. They should be informed as to which scenes they should be preparing for the next week, at the most.

The timing of bringing the cast to set, particularly if the unit base is at a distance, is one of the trickiest aspects of a First's job. You need to have a good working relationship with the DP so that once the cast are traveling, s/he doesn't add in some extra element that means the cast have to wait around on set for tweaks. It also depends a lot on what the cast are like themselves. Some prefer to be on set rather than in their trailer, and don't mind if they're a couple of minutes early. Others start complaining to the producer if they have to wait for 30 seconds. Some actors, as soon as they're called to set, suddenly need to pee. Others want one more makeup check. It's something you have to balance on an individual basis, every day.

I genuinely like actors, and admire the work they do, and I try to facilitate their mango smoothies or assistants' requests as I would for any other department, without making judgments or rolling my eyes. But it's the Second who really has to live with all their tempers and tantrums, and you want to be sure that the Second you hire will be in synch with your approach. On one overseas job I inherited a Second who spent her time complaining to the lead actress, who would come to set in a sulky strop; it was obvious who was the source of this negativity when the Second was sick and the actress' attitude immediately improved!

If you're in a situation where the director doesn't like actors or know how to deal with them, I think it's acceptable to offer the occasional word of encouragement after a particularly challenging take. Especially with younger actors, I think it's fine to say "well done" when they've pulled something off, even though this is normally the remit of the director. However, if the director is in a tent, not encouraging the actors or even responding to them, s/he is unlikely to care what you do. However, the rest of the crew know the protocol, so it should only be very occasionally that you respond to the actors' work. Less is more in relation to this; you don't want to usurp the director's position. Anytime an actor asks you anything beyond a time or schedule question, you defer immediately to the director—whether or not you know the answer. Even an idiot director is the director, and if the role isn't respected—at least by you—the wheels will come off.

The famous situation, that mercifully happens only rarely, is when the actor, for whatever reason, is refusing to come to set. You'll hear about this first from the Second, when they feel that they have done all they can. At this stage, you might advise the director (and producer, if present), and go have a word yourself. This probably won't make any difference, but it is an opportunity to find out a little more about what the problem may be; 99% of the time the issue is not what the actor says it is, but is simply good old terror. There's only so much a First can do about this, and it's usually the remit of the director, and then the producer, to entice the actor back to work. A standard approach is the "this picture is bigger than all of us" method, and in fact in my opinion the best depiction of this producer–star situation is in the film *I Could Go On Singing* (1963), both educational and a treat if you like Dirk Bogarde or Judy Garland! One piece of advice I can offer is to shoot something—anything—while you're waiting, even if it's just a cutaway of a prop. The fact that the show is rolling without them can remove the pressure from or add incentive for an actor to go back to work.

When an actor is "picture-wrapped," meaning they have finished all of their work on the shoot, it is customary for the First to announce this, and for the other cast and the crew to give them a round of applause.

Enormous Changes at the Last Minute

It is often the case, particularly on TV shows, that there can be extensive rewrites going on while the unit is shooting. It's a real test of the AD department how well these changes are managed and incorporated seamlessly into the production flow, and sometimes this can be a little like trying to crochet on a whitewater raft.

Let's imagine a scenario where a ream of new script changes come in, relating to work planned for the following day, shortly before the call sheet needs to be run. My suggested scenario is that the second AD comb through them quickly with a view to determining the difference in page counts, cast, extras, and the big elements like animals, effects, stunts, etc. S/he might then come to see me (and the Second Second) on the floor with the pages, and tell us about the changes. Depending on the circumstances, s/he might return to the unit office and amend the call sheet accordingly, while I find an opportune moment to have the same conversation with the director (if the director can be involved in the first conversation, so much the better). It's important to flag these changes to the director before issuing the call sheet because s/he may not be happy with the loss or addition of certain elements and need to advise you (and thus, production) about their views, and it can result in serious upset if the director only discovers on set the next day that their donkeys and chickens have been cut from the scene. If the director approves all the changes, the revised call sheet can be drafted and looked over—the revised page counts are very important here, as the scheduled day might have become too light or too heavy—and hopefully issued on time.

The First will verbally inform any of the on-set HODs about changes, and will announce at wrap that there are new pages that affect the following day's work.

It's crucial that the Second very clearly informs the actors, when they're being wrapped, that the new pages relate to the work for the next day—if the pages are given to the driver or left in the car, an actor who is still half-in-character, exhausted and in the dark may not be sufficiently aware of them and will be blaming the ADs the next day when they don't know their lines. The Second should also be informing all of the backstage crew at unit base as to what the main effects of the changes are while distributing the new pages. Late pages can be the cause of significant grief and woe, and it's critical that the ADs communicate the information swiftly and clearly to all concerned.

THE DEPARTMENTS

Regard your soldiers as your children, and they will follow you into the deepest valleys. Look on them as your own beloved sons, and they will stand by you even unto death!
Sun Tzu, the Art of War

One of the most important parts of an AD's job is understanding who does what. As a First, you will be exposed to a barrage of requests coming at you incessantly. The important fact to remember is that you're not supposed to satisfy every request yourself, but to know who the right person to ask to do it is. The First is the hub of all the information and requirements flying around the set, and by understanding the intricacies of each crew member's role, the better you'll be able to judge who is the most appropriate and efficient person for the job. You don't need to ask the art director about a prop, or a prop person about the set dressing turnaround, if you understand the distinction between their roles. The next section is designed to give you some understanding of these roles so you can be an efficient conduit, communicating effectively between all the departments. It improves with practice to the point where it becomes automatic, but in the early days it's worth considering in advance.

We've talked a little bit about the locations and art departments, since they are such an integral part of your prep. The following is going to address the main departments of the shooting crew, with whom you are in close physical contact every day. While the personalities of those crew members are different on every job, their responsibilities and requirements for you are remarkably similar, across all budgets and formats. I think it was Brecht who pointed out that a German butcher has more in common with a Spanish butcher than with a German judge, and while there may not be a class system in film production, there are certainly roles that are pretty much universal.

Directing the Director (Part 2)

If you are working with a top director who is organized, clear and gifted with the cast and crew, then that's great, and your life will be comparatively easy as you simply work ahead with all the information you have. Often, however, you will find yourself in the less than ideal world of having to guide, cajole, discipline, and otherwise manage the person who is in titular command but just as often needs help. The role of the First is to execute the director's vision within the time and budget allocated; to prevent mutinies and create the impression that the captain is in perfect control and leading the ship to the promised land. Sometimes creating this impression demands a performance at least as inspired as the actors'.

The first requirement is getting the director to set, at the time you think s/he should be. I have worked with directors who want to walk onto a set that is dressed and lit, and the extras and even the main cast have rehearsed. (Whether the main cast are willing to rehearse without the director is another question, but in this case they were quite young and he was an Oscar-winner so they went along with it.) This generally resulted in his arriving anywhere from half an hour to 45 minutes after call time. That is, in my experience, an exception. In my perfect world, the director is there 45 minutes before call: long enough to have breakfast, look at the set, refresh his/her mind as to the scene, and to have a private rehearsal with the cast, so as to present the scene on the dot of shooting call time. Directors are all different, but this is what I aim for. In the morning, I like the director and DP to have a chance to have a brief chat about the scene before unit call, if possible, so they can avoid disagreement later. On locations with shared transport, I would try to travel with the director and DP and gently float a question or two that they then might discuss while I eavesdrop.

The second most important thing is that they have prepared, or at the very least re-read the scene before the cast arrive. I've had directors ask me "What's this scene about again?" before the cast step on set, which is a little terrifying, but generally that isn't the case. If they're a first-timer, there's every chance they have been up in a cold sweat since 5 a.m., running through it all in their head incessantly, or lamenting what they got wrong the day before. It's important to remember that almost all directors (at least, on feature films) are working in a thinly masked state of terror, with all of their inner demons dancing on their head, and the producers breathing hotly down their necks. If they appear casual or relaxed, they're often either entirely clueless or amazing actors. While you don't have to love them, it's helpful to be kind; if that means indulging them a little, so be it—kindness is a great spiritual practice, and if all they need is their coffee a certain way and the semblance of support that's not too much to ask. Besides, it's in your interest that they be working to the best of their ability and making the best possible show.

The third crucial element is that they make decisions: any decision is better than no decision. If a director has done their prep well and knows what the theme of the story is and the visual metaphors that will reflect that, it takes a lot of the terror out of the process and many of the questions have already been answered.

Being a director is a very lonely place—there really isn't the camaraderie that everyone else enjoys, and you're the closest thing to a department they have (unless they actually like actors). Everyone else has a dedicated team, and you're theirs. While acting like their friend and confidante, however, I am very careful that this is a one-way street. Most information, particularly bad news, I will only relay on a need-to-know basis. If there is a problem, I will be sure we have done absolutely everything we possibly can to fix it, and created a list of possible solutions, before I trouble the director with it. I once worked with a line producer who seemed to delight in presenting the director with intractable problems, which the director would do her best to try to solve cheaply or easily. Eventually, she'd give up, the line producer would say, "Yes, there really isn't a good solution. I didn't want you to fix it, I just wanted you to know." Wanted you to know? Like the director doesn't have enough problems already? To me, that's the opposite of good producing. No matter what you think of their personality, you're there to protect, honor and serve the director, and a lot of protecting involves not sharing information that isn't going to help or inspire them.

In keeping with this, if it comes to it and the director has to be informed about some piece of bad news, I'm always sure to present a few options for possible reactions to the situation, and what their consequences might be. If it's a director who's good at logistics, they may have their own original idea for a solution, but many directors come from a writing, visual effects or editing background, and the prospect of 70 people standing around while s/he tries to resolve a practical issue can be intimidating, if not paralyzing. As always, if the director insists on pursuing a course of action that you think is unwise, all you can do is offer your advice, and then inform the PM. No matter what you think of it, you must embrace it and try to make it work every bit as well as the alternative you might have preferred. A set is no place for "I told you so."

One other thing to remember, not just for the First but for the entire crew, is to leave the director some head space to think. It may look like s/he is just staring into space, but s/he might be visualizing the edit of the upcoming scene or trying to remember a note for one of the actors. It's particularly important to hold fire on any opinions or questions immediately after a take, when the director may have a number of things in his/her head that they're trying to remember long enough to pass on. When I need to speak to the director about something, I tend to lurk until they look my way, and then ask whether it's an ok time to discuss whatever it might be. If it's an urgent question then I might not ask, but if it's relating to the next scene or day

I wait until they can actually take the time to think about it, rather than getting scrambled and giving me some information that will ultimately change on reflection anyway.

At lunch, you want to be sure that s/he eats and rests as much as possible. The director should be treated like cast when it comes to meals, privacy and special requests, and if they don't have a personal assistant, one of your team will have to look after them. This includes spouses, children, friends, agents and miscellaneous other visitors they may have, who will also need to be fed and watered and who will respond quite extremely—positively or negatively—depending on how they are treated. Warnings of these visitors should come from the POC to the Second so they don't arrive unannounced and get treated like intruders. Likewise, any investors or producers' friends should also get VIP treatment. It will rebound on you via the director, either well or badly.

One general rule I live by—and get really annoyed when it's broken!—is that almost any information the crew need from the director I will have, so they should ask me first. As mentioned at the final production meeting, I don't like hearing crew ask the director something I could have answered, because I want all of the director's brain to be focused on relaxed creativity, not repeating him/herself. If the cast have a character question, I immediately defer to the director, but nine times out of ten if crew have a question I can answer it, and if I can't I'll find the best possible time to ask. In this way, the First is also a director's mental bodyguard, trying to ensure that his/her energy is maximized and not ground down by a thousand tiny questions.

The other area in which a director might need encouragement is in engaging with the cast. S/he needs to keep them on-side and onboard, and there's only so much anyone else can do to help this relationship. I once worked with a first-time director on a very long shoot who completely lost the cast early on, to the point where toward the end of the shoot they were actually humiliating him on set. I had to have a quiet word with the main instigator, who was then abusive toward me, but she still had to recognize that, love him or hate him, he was the director and it was unprofessional and unpleasant for everybody to see him being publicly embarrassed. It didn't matter that I may have agreed with her criticisms—there are clear lines of command and loyalty that must be sustained, especially under pressure. If the producer had been capable, this would have been his job, but unfortunately it fell to me to remind the actress of the protocol. If the situation was reversed, and the director was being abusive, I would speak to the producer, and if it continued, to the director him or herself.

Video Village

Trying to imagine the days before monitors were connected to the camera is as difficult as trying to imagine operating without walkies or cell phones. How did they shoot anything then? The video tap has become a ubiquitous production tool, with mostly positive consequences. Gone are the days when the director had to rely entirely on the camera operator's word and his naked eyes to judge how a shot worked. Nowadays, publicity photos of directors looking through the lens are generally staged—there is rarely a practical reason why the director would ever mount the dolly, unless they are really worried about the color quality of the monitor and need to reassure themselves of how the image looks. (In fact, even this is not accurate, as the exposure and the format will impact significantly on the final "look" of the shot.)

My personal opinion is that the monitor is brilliant for rehearsals, but that the director should watch the actors from beside the camera so s/he can see the subtleties of their performances (few monitors other than

HD are clear enough to grasp delicacy of performance) and it also gives the cast a powerful audience to play for, and a great feeling of trust and support. Now that every take can be replayed, there's no reason for the director not to be on set—s/he can always look back at the shot if s/he has any doubts.

Yet most directors never leave their little TV set, clinging to it as their port in the storm. It's a haven and a bunker, where they can stage their various possessions and sit comfortably in most weather. It's one thing to be at the monitor when there is space to have it in the same room as the camera, but very often the director will be in the next room, listening through headphones and interacting less and less with the cast. Depending on the distance, the director might even ask the First to relay notes to the actors.

If you watch rushes for any show, the moment the director calls "cut" you will see the actors' faces turn quickly and hopefully toward the director, like children looking for approval. Typically getting no response, they look away and a veil closes down; look at the director and s/he will often be frowning at the monitor screen, murmuring to the script supervisor or calling out to the DP. The cast are often the last people the director speaks to, and they feel suitably unimportant in the pecking order. Even if the director has to be at a distance, this can still be addressed. As s/he calls "cut," s/he can add "lovely work, X," or "great performances" or "very nice, X and Y" or whatever it may be, just to indicate that they were actually watching the cast and not the boom shadow or the framing or a million other things. It's incredible what even just this minute amount of communication can do for their relationship.

Typically, directors either love the actors, having come from a theater background themselves, or hate them, viewing them as cattle who question their authority. Many times, this hate is simply a basic fear; they may not speak "actorese," and find the more specific they are ("we're shooting this on a 75 to cut in with the 50") the less the actors understand. Judith Weston writes brilliant advice for directors working with actors on film, and her books are invaluable for those who wish to improve their skills. Sometimes even the most experienced directors create a power struggle, which they can only lose. Even if they win the battle, they will lose the war. The reality is, most actors welcome direction, and only resist when they don't understand why they are being asked to do something. The short answer is to put it in character terms—not to say, "I need you to hit the mark closer to Actor Y," but to suggest that they play the scene more intimately. The director has the big picture view and the actors will accept his/her direction if they trust him/her.

The reason the director's monitor is sometimes referred to as "Video Village" is because it is rarely the case that the director is alone. Even when there is a second monitor in position for everybody else (usually, hair, makeup, wardrobe, costume, props and possibly the Second Second, depending on whether there are extras involved), the director will be joined by the script supervisor, and often the producer. If there is more than one producer, it can get a little crowded, but this is where they like to sit, beside the director, spouting their opinions in his ear, sometimes even during the take. As a First, if there are extras in the scene I will generally watch the monitor from a discreet distance. If not, I'm watching the action (if there's anything physical going on) or the director, especially during the few moments when you're expecting him/her to call cut.

Responsibility for the operation of Video Village falls to the video assist, which is generally the most thankless job on the crew. (Props generally manage the chairs, while the grips or art department look after any tenting that has to be done. Sometimes, rather than a tent, a "courtesy flag" will be raised on a c-stand to cut the glare and help the director see the screen.) The only perk of the video assist job is that s/he gets to see the monitor, and sometimes sit down; otherwise, it's potentially constant stress. Every time the camera moves, the video cable needs to be unplugged from the camera, and plugged back in the second the camera lands in its new position. It's a lonely road, as s/he's not really part of the camera, nor a part of the director's team. The technical expertise required is immense: understanding how the video tap on the camera works (and this can vary widely depending on formats), understanding how to operate the computer and machinery required to record and playback every rehearsal and take, correctly labeled, and sometimes at varying speeds. Sometimes the sparks don't have time to provide an electrical feed, requiring heavy batteries, which need to be charged and lose power very quickly, and on top of this sometimes the cables or their connectors randomly stop working, so a passion for tinkering with hardware and soldering under extreme time pressure is also a plus. People just don't seem to accept that it requires any time to do well, and I've seen a very good video assist technician develop nosebleeds from the stress of being constantly used as a whipping boy for the director's various frustrations. Add to this the chance that there might be two or more cameras, and you get some sense of the job description.

If you're lucky, there will be two monitors—one for the director, script supervisor and producer(s), and one for the rest of the crew (hair, makeup, wardrobe, etc.). If there's only one, you can help the director by keeping him or her from being crowded, and also ensuring that there isn't chat or unnecessary goings-on around or during the takes.

The Producer, Line Producer, and Production Manager

Once you're shooting, your relationship with these three individuals shifts slightly from what it was during prep. Your engagement with the producer will typically be exclusively big-picture and/or creative—anything relating to the director, cast or crew from a story or artistic context, or if it involves serious cost or main cast. Depending on the producer, you may have very little contact. You will, however, be in a continuous ongoing conversation with the line producer or PM (if there are both, then probably the PM) about almost any decision you're making about the schedule or the shooting day. Anything out of the ordinary costs money, and it's your responsibility to ask the PM's permission for anything you haven't already discussed. Even the smallest details can have a knock-on effect on the budget, and the earlier the PM is aware of these issues the better it is for everyone. I've never had a PM complain that I was giving them too much information.

A good PM will be present at the set or unit base at Breakfast, Lunch and Wrap, whenever possible. If the location is miles from the production office, if there is a second unit shooting or if there is some emergency happening, they may not be physically present but will most likely be available via phone. It's handy to touch base with them, even for 5 minutes, at all of these times, either to pass on any new information, receive any from them, and, ideally, to share some decision-making. The PM is the person closest to you in both rank and experience, and the more you collaborate the better the relationship and the shoot will be. Not only will you benefit from their imagination and expertise, it's also comforting to know that you're not out on your own on the high seas. Many PMs have previously worked as first ADs, and even those who haven't should have enough familiarity with your job to be able to help make the best decisions for the production. If you see the PM on the set, get over to him or her as quickly as possible, as they generally aren't hanging around for the glamour. And as soon as you have any concerns about getting behind or making the day, get a message to them. Even if there's nothing you actually want them to do, they will prefer to be aware of what's happening on the set, and depend on you to keep them informed.

As described earlier, a call sheet always needs to be approved by the PM before it's issued, as would any schedule or other published information. Sometimes unscrupulous crew members will ask the Second to add equipment or personnel to the call sheet without going correctly to the PM first, and these should always be double-checked, as the PM needs to have given permission for any special requirements on the sheet. There will almost always be something to talk about at wrap relating to the next day or the next week. Typically, each project will have at least one big sequence or set piece that creates ongoing conversations in the build-up. Wrap is a great time to update and get updated, when you don't have the pressure of the unit's ticking clock weighing you down.

The bottom line is that the PM deals with pennies and dollars, while the First's currency is time—seconds, minutes, setups, scenes, days and weeks. Time equals money, literally, and as the PM tries to save every possible cent, the First is trying to save every possible second. Sometimes this relationship is harmonious, and both are singing from the same hymn sheet. Sometimes a PM focuses exclusively on the finance and ends up costing more time because they cut too deep and went too cheap. It's your job to advise the PM when you think a "saving" is actually a costing, because it will take longer to do it the "inexpensive" way. A good PM doesn't lose sight of the ultimate creative vision—you shouldn't come in under budget, any more than you should wrap early (as popular as that may be). You want to manage your time and money in such a way that you are maximizing the creative vision of the director, and the experience for the audience. That's the ultimate purpose, not to save time or money for the sake of it.

Schedule Changes and Holding the Schedule

Inevitably, as the shoot proceeds the schedule will need to change—whether due to cast availability, weather, locations or any other number of issues, the schedule you begin with on day one will be quite different by the time you wrap the shoot. Technically, the schedule remains under the auspices of the first AD throughout production. If the changes are relatively light, you as the First will implement them to the master shooting schedule either over lunch, after wrap or at the weekend. (If you are going to have to work over the weekend, you need to discuss this with the PM and agree as to what your payment will be. If it's less than an hour's work, I would personally tend to throw this in for free. If it's any more than that, you should agree on an hourly rate and stick to the estimated amount of hours.)

Sometimes, however, the changes are occurring fast and furious, and there simply isn't time for you to amend the schedule and do your job on the floor. In this case the First, depending on the nature of the scenes currently being shot, might ask their Second Second to cover the floor while they work on the schedule. Under certain conditions (for example, if the work on set is too complicated to delegate and the changes need to be made immediately), the PM will "hold" the schedule and make the necessary changes, working to your suggestions. S/he will then show you this revised schedule for your comments or approval before the new draft is issued.

There can also be a situation in which you can dictate the necessary changes to your Second, who will implement them according to your instructions for you to review at lunch or on wrap. Every situation will depend on the nature of the changes and the particular circumstances of the shoot, which you will need to judge. However, even if the PM has assumed temporary control of the schedule, it immediately reverts to your responsibility once the revised version has been issued, and the master document will once again be held on your computer. There is no time in which the first AD is not responsible for delivering what's in the schedule, and if you don't think it's achievable you need to raise that with the relevant parties before it is issued.

The Camera Department

The head of the camera department is the **director of photography**, and you will know quickly which kind of DP you're dealing with; normally, the first, DP and director form a kind of triangle, in which the first listens in to the DP and director's conversations, implements their conclusions and liaises with both individually about respective elements—lighting, grip and camera for the DP, actors and extras with the director (often these elements overlap). But sometimes you'll come up against a DP who isn't a good communicator or team player, or who will use up all the available time lighting, or constantly questions the director's decisions, or flirts with the leading lady, or berates his focus puller or operator, or any number of other unpleasant types of behavior. If you feel that his or her behavior is costing you time, or undermining the director's confidence or respect among the crew, you need to talk to him/her privately about it and then, depending on the outcome, advise the producer. I have actually experienced DPs who treat my interest in their conversations with the director as if I'm simply nosy. In fact, I don't care about the artistic references they're discussing (I'd like to, but that's just not my personal taste), but I really do need to hear everything they say. It's through me, as the First, that their ambitions are going to be achieved. So even if you're encountering resistance, you need to be gracefully and relentlessly part of the conversation—mostly observing and listening, but fully armed with all the practical and logistical information about the implications and requirements involved.

If none of the above are happening, but after the first week there is tension arising between you, it's important to have a private conversation. I find it quite effective to take a conciliatory approach, in which you find out from him or her how they think things could improve or if there's anything you can do to make his or her life easier. You might also pose a question around the problem you see developing. What you want to do is engage them in a solution, rather than creating an adversarial relationship, which won't benefit either of you or the project.

Most camera departments shooting with one camera typically consist of a **first assistant camera** (focus puller, in Europe), **second assistant camera** (clapper/loader) and a **trainee**. Nowadays with less and less film being shot, the loader is often a data wrangler or digital imaging technician, downloading the media from cards onto a laptop, but the same principles apply. On bigger-budget shows, there will be a **camera operator**, a highly skilled technician who is as much involved in framing and designing the shot as simply operating the camera. Nowadays, more and more DPs operate themselves, although of course if there's more than one camera that's impossible.

The first AC does more than pull focus—they are considered a head of department, and your contact with them would reflect that. They would usually have at least a week's prep, to check all the camera gear and be a part of any tests or pre-shoots. If there is a problem with any of the numerous pieces of equipment that make up the camera package, they have to identify it and get it replaced by the rental company before the shoot starts (in conjunction with the PM). Likewise, if anything goes wrong mechanically during the shoot, the PM is the first person you call, as they are ultimately responsible for all of the gear and will facilitate any repairs or exchanges. Sometimes, the equipment is owned by the DP and rented to the production, which makes such issues more problematic, as there is no rental house you can call and expect to immediately service the problem. Many shoots, especially if on a location at any distance from the rental house, will carry two camera bodies at all times, in case one fails. The cost of the second body is inevitably less than the cost of the crew doing nothing waiting for a camera to be repaired.

You will have worked out before the shoot starts what you expect to be ready at call time—in the UK system a good first AC will have the camera built, while in the US they will at least have had breakfast and be opening the truck. The first AC, when **pulling focus**, will use a tape measure or an electronic equivalent to record the distance of the subject from the camera's "gate" (the aperture where the light hits the medium). A good first AC won't stick his/her tape in the actor's face just before every take, and will certainly not ask a top female actor exactly what they're going to do just before rolling a shot of her having an emotional breakdown (you know who you are…!). The first AC's pain threshold is determined by how much light the DP is allowing into the lens—many DPs will shoot at as low an f-stop as they possibly can; this gives a visually beautiful look by deliberately reducing the depth of field, meaning there is very little room for error on the focus. A first AC nightmare is a night exterior, shooting "wide open" (the lens at its lowest aperture) trying to follow a subject moving toward camera. Any movement, even by day, is more difficult if it's toward or away from camera, as opposed to laterally, when it remains on the same plane in relation to the lens.

This book isn't designed to teach you about photography, but a certain amount of familiarity with the camera equipment and practices is required as it will impact on your job. A **"long" lens** is, in terms of 35 mm lenses (which are still a standard reference point, even if not shooting on 35 mm film), anything from a 75 mm up. The longer the lens, the greater the distance the camera can be from the subject—for example, you can shoot a close-up of a face from 5 feet on a 25 mm lens, and from 30 feet on a 75 mm lens; on a 125 mm, you can get roughly the same size frame from 50 feet, and on a 200 mm lens, from 65 feet. (I say roughly the same size because technically there is a difference—the perspective will be different on each, the space will be more "compressed" and the depth of field will be less.) Naturally, once you get more than 20 feet from the actor you are out of earshot, unless you like shouting at actors (although usually they don't enjoy it!). In this case, you will station your Second Second or PA as close as they can get to the cast while still staying out of frame, as you will, as always, be beside the camera. You may need another PA on walkie beside the director, to pass on any notes.

This system works fine until you get into really long lenses, such as 300 mm upwards. In this case, the camera may be on the other side of the valley from the action. The basic principle is the same, but depending on the terrain you may need to use mobile phones instead of walkies to communicate, and this will need to be tested in advance. Lenses over 150 mm are not usually part of your standard camera package, and will have been requested specially by the DP and so will be on the call sheet. When you see these kinds of lenses being planned for, you will need to double-check with locations that they are aware of the distances you're covering, and you may need an additional PA or two for the day, depending on the nature of the shot.

As the lens gets longer, so, too, the focus puller's job becomes more challenging. For the first and second AC to lay marks takes longer and is more complicated, and you may need to give each of them a walkie (if they're not already on walkies normally), so they can communicate when dropping the marks. During the take itself, the second AC will often call the marker numbers to the first AC, from a position where they can judge the movement of the actor or subject on a more visually advantageous plane—parallel, rather than perpendicular.

A first AC will also need to be good at mental arithmetic. The DP will usually give the AC the "basic" **stop**—that is, the *f*-stop exposure level without correction for filters or other internal elements like back focus or shutter speed—and expect the first AC to calculate the correct stop. Exposure has always been critical to photography, and despite the advances in post-production technology and format sensitivity, it's still crucial, and a big artistic decision, to get the stop right. The rushes that everyone sees every day will typically be ungraded—that is, not color-corrected—and most DPs would prefer that these be as close to the final product as possible. It's now uncommon to grade "in camera," that is, to commit to a look while capturing the images themselves; rather, most people try to shoot completely "clean," knowing what they will do later to adjust the colors. Some very famous DPs can choose a look in advance and more or less lock the film into that, but most studio executives get spooked by seeing anything different and will be more comfortable seeing something recognizable and "commercial." Naturally, these choices depend hugely on the nature of the material. Shooting a dark children's story isn't a great bet: no one wanted to see *Babe: Pig in the City*.

Most ACs will have their own, "on-board" **monitor** attached to the camera, so they can see exactly what the frame is at all times. This is an extremely handy tool for you to use as well, but you need to be sure that you're not invading their space to view it. It is often their own personal piece of equipment, and don't appreciate it when directors grab it and turn it so they can see the frame while they're talking to the cast—the arm connecting it to the video tap is often delicate and can be broken if treated roughly. There are also times when the director wants to be in the same room as the actor, and if the set is small, you may ask if they can share the on-board with the first AC. This is usually fine as long as it's only under certain circumstances, and doesn't become the modus operandi.

Besides the technical elements, the first AC will also be the one who complains to you if you're going late for lunch or wrap. If you respect their experience, they can often help you out of a hole, particularly on unit moves, when they can suggest ways to move some of the gear—like the camera and lenses—in a different vehicle than the camera truck, which can be much slower in transit. First ACs often also have a good sense of humor, and can be the person you can share a look with when something bizarre is occurring but you have to keep a straight face. Whenever possible, if you can get a stand-in to show them the action and positions rather than the main cast this is preferable. Any time an actor stops, it's advisable to "**drop a mark**"; even if the actor is incapable of hitting it, it gives the first AC a reference.

The second AC will be the one to drop this mark—if you're not seeing the floor, and depending on its surface, this will typically be with tape, a different color for each character. If it's on concrete, sometimes it will be in chalk. If an actor needs help, sometimes they might use a "sausage" or a small sandbag that the actor can feel with their toe without looking down. In any case, the actor wants their toes to be lined up along the mark if they can manage it (one explanation for where the expression "toe the line" came from). If you're seeing the floor, a prop or bit of dressing might do the same job.

Not just actors get marked—generally, props and cars do too, although this is often shared between the second AC and the stand-by props person. Sometimes the camera crew will use a grease pencil to mark a filter to match a frame with another shot. But the most important marker is the slate, or **clapper board**, which is the second AC's responsibility. As ancient as this tool is, it is still used everywhere and on most shoots. There are variations—if you are recording your sound straight into the camera, you don't need to clap the board to give the editing room a synch mark, but you still want to identify the scene, shot and take and give any other relevant information to the editor. Sometimes, for music videos or other uses of playback, you may have what is called a "smart slate," an electronic board where the time code runs from the audio playback onto the board, locking in the synch for later. Even if you have only a piece of paper and your hands to clap, the basic principle is the same: identification to avoid an editor facing a mountain of footage with no idea what order it's to go in.

There is a different identification system between North America and Europe—in the former, the shot is designated according to the scene number and the chronological sequence in which this setup occurs. For example, the setups in scene 26 would be 26, 26A, 26B, 26C, etc., traditionally using the NATO phonetic alphabet: "Alpha, Bravo, Charlie…" (and any amusing variations thereof, as long as the editor can understand what the letter should be), returning, if necessary, to "AA" and so on. In the UK system, the first shot of the shoot is slate number 1, the second is number 2, and so forth. There is often some kind of celebration, or at least acknowledgment, when you hit number 100, 500, etc., and sometimes a crew bet to guess the final number of slates.

Either way, it's not the First's problem to care about the system, but you do have to understand it enough to read the slate, as you may sometimes be asked to mark it for the second AC if they're extremely busy dealing with rushes or loading, or they just have to go to the bathroom, when they may ask you to cover for them. In a normal situation, you figure out where to hold the board so it's in the center of frame (it will depend on the length of the lens), and when the first AC says "mark it," read the scene number, slate number (if different) and take number, then clap and clear frame as fast as possible (do not go the long way 'round—if you can find somewhere you can drop to a crouch, out of shot and with your back to the actors, this is best. Occasionally, the frame will be tight enough to require you to read the slate, then rotate it so the actual clap is in frame, but this is getting fancy.

If it's an end-of-scene ident, wait until the director says "cut," call out "end board!" or "tail slate!" and wait for the first AC to cue you. Then clap the board upside down, turn it right side up and read out the same information. At the end of the take, you immediately write the number for the next take in the correct place so you're ready to go again, and be prepared to tell the second AC, when they return, whether you have rolled on that take. (Occasionally, you will be asked to record the footage count on the back of the board, but this is only on film and rarely required these days.)

Protecting the Camera

There are various situations in which the action or an effect requires steps to be taken to protect the safety of the camera and its crew. The simplest of these is an **optical flat**, which is simply a clear filter placed in front of the lens to prevent any spray or debris touching the highly sensitive lens surface. As a First you won't even necessarily need to be aware of this element, still less call for it to be used. However, you do need to warn the first AC before any spraying or spritzing goes on near the camera, as they may need to temporarily protect the lens. The next step up is if there is the likelihood that any kind of substance will potentially splash over the camera or crew, or nearby. **Plexi** is simply a sheet of plexiglass placed in front of the camera, typically rigged by the grip, which shouldn't affect the image quality. The crew may also need to be issued protective clothing or eye gear, particularly if dealing with Fuller's earth dust or other such substances. The camera does have rain-protection gear, but if a bucket of blood is being hurled near the lens you'll want more than that to keep it safe.

Towers

Scaffolding towers can be used either for the positioning of lamps or for a camera and reduced crew, and must only be built by qualified riggers. Working at any height above ground level is a hazard, and you should ensure that safety rails are built around the edges of the tower at the top. If they need to be removed this should only be done "to camera," that is, only cleared out of shot, and replaced as soon as the shot is over. On towers, I prefer that everyone wear harnesses—it's awkward and time-consuming, but it's too easy for someone to slip and break their neck, so it's a discussion worth having. If there is serious resistance, a simple mountaineering clip onto a belt that is attached to a rail is enough for me. Many towers have wheels and can be moved easily enough; it just means they have to be carefully leveled and the brakes locked on before anyone tries to climb them. Obviously, no person or any equipment can ever be on top of them when they're being moved.

Formats

The film format, that is, the media onto which the images are recorded, has changed faster in the past 10 years than in the previous 100 years combined. Since 1996, when film was still standard and the choices were 35mm, 16mm or Super-16, we have moved through DigiBeta, DVCAM and miniDV, but the real game-changer was HD. Even those DPs who were the most snooty about shooting on film had to admire the clarity, resolution and flexibility of the new digital formats—the RED, Panavision's Genesis and the Arri ALEXA. More and more lower-budget productions are using the Canon 7D and 5D, which are basically SLR still cameras that record digital video. Even 3D is now becoming commonplace (although as long as it's difficult to shoot in rain or wind, it may have a slow take-up in some places). One thing that has become clear throughout all these shifting formats is that whether it's HD or Super-8, the lenses are often more critical to the ultimate look of the picture than the format, and beyond all this is still the talent and skill of the human being.

Without going into the technical details of the various formats and cameras, the elements you will need to know about are reloading and how long it takes; whether it takes prime or zoom lenses; if the camera can shoot slow-mo or fast-mo without additional gear; how heavy it is and whether handheld camerawork is possible; whether the shutter and other menus can be altered quickly; whether the material can be played back safely (on film, obviously, you can't play takes back from the camera, and most people resist doing that on tape for fear of damaging the tape in the process, whereas media files can be replayed at the press of a button—generally, all playback will come from video assist, but you need to understand the options and time involved); if and how it needs to be used for visual or other effects; and whether this is the first time the first AC is working with this format. You will also want to know whether there is a second body on the truck, and if rented, how far away the rental house is from the set in case of disaster. (We'll talk later about working underwater and at height.)

Single Camera and Beyond

Most films and TV are traditionally filmed "single camera," even if they use more than one camera, to distinguish them from "multi-camera," that is, typically, studio-based and vision-mixed, like a sitcom, soap or talk show. Single-camera is what most civilians imagine when they think of filming and is a relatively straightforward way to work: you point the camera in one direction, shoot all the shots looking that way, then turn around and shoot "reverses," that is, all the shots looking the other way. (This demands a knowledge of the elements we covered earlier such as eyelines and screen direction.) As shooting methods go, this is certainly the slowest, as well as being more challenging for the actors, as they have to match their performances in numerous setups that can stretch across a couple of hours. It also requires adjusting the lighting to appear to match, which isn't always as simple as it sounds, particularly if it's exterior or the set has windows that let in the outside fluctuations.

Projects that have a little more money will often bring in a second camera to reduce the demands of all of these elements. This, however, creates its own work practices. The most immediate of these is simply the clapper board and calling the roll—the First will still roll sound in the same way, but the "A" camera and "B" camera will either both have separate markers, which you will need to be sure are both completed and both cameras are set before you call action, or they will have a "common marker," meaning they will both point at the same slate before repositioning to their correct opening frame.

Most DPs will resist the impulse to "cross-shoot," despite its obvious attractions for various departments. Cross-shooting is when you have, for example, two actors sitting at a table and you put "A" camera pointing at Actor X and "B" camera pointing at Actor "Y" (Figure 3.6). This makes life easy for a) the actors, who both get to act with the same intensity, knowing they're both being filmed; b) continuity and the editor, who don't have to worry about the action and performances matching; and c) sound, who can boom both simultaneously from the same distance. DPs, however, have a traditional resistance to this approach, many of whom say that it will impact negatively on the lighting. Whatever your opinion on this issue, it's not for you to decide the merits of the argument, but simply to execute it.

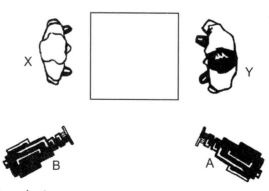

Figure 3.6 *An overhead view of cross-shooting*

What many DPs prefer is cameras side-by-side as close as they can get, shooting two different sizes simultaneously. Obviously, this reverts to the original downsides for the actors and continuity, and creates an additional problem for sound: the boom will only be able to get as close as the wider of the two frames allows, which, they complain, isn't close enough for the closer shot. When it comes to a battle between picture and sound, camera almost always wins. Again, ours is not to reason why, but this is the background to the issue. Before you start filming you will want to work out privately with the director and DP which approach they're taking, so you can warn the affected parties and plan for it accordingly.

When you are doing a larger scene with more actors and more cameras, the same principles apply, even down to staying on the correct side of the line; it just takes a little bit longer to put the marker on, and you may need someone with a walkie beside the cameras that are out of your earshot to give you a "set" and to pass on when you're cut. You will want to use a loudhailer to give "action" in this case, because you won't want there to be a delay as that command is relayed—everyone on the set needs to hear "action" at the same time. As the First, you will stay beside "A" camera at all times, even if it's moving and handheld, unless you will truly be in the way. In that case, you drop back to the director to await "cut," unless there's anything potentially risky happening, when you will cover that area.

Each camera will require at the very least an operator and an assistant; it's common for two cameras to share one second assistant, but if a third camera is added they will need another full camera crew. Second camera is a First's dream if you're shooting lots of dialogue scenes on sets or stages where there is room to operate— you can fly through long scenes in half the time. If, however, you're in cramped locations or your director isn't very *au fait* with how to get the most out of the second camera, it can slow the process and cost money shooting unnecessarily. Second camera crews really like to shoot something, anything at all, and even if you're shooting on digital all that material still needs to be logged, digitized, and viewed by somebody, so it's not free. It's more economical to bring in a second camera crew on designated days when you have large scenes with a number of extras, horses, or other material that you would otherwise struggle to complete in a day, and under such circumstances, as a First I would occasionally ask the question in prep as to whether it might be worth considering. Having a second camera body on the truck is not an invitation to use a second camera, however, as even though the first AC might enjoy operating a few shots, you quickly run out of personnel to manage the rushes and carry the gear, putting the whole department under much more pressure. There may also not be a second head, additional lenses, etc. Ultimately, if you're using a second camera you want the director to have a plan for how it's going to be used and where it's going to be placed—directors with a multi-camera experience might give you a floor plan reflecting camera positions, which is a First's delight, or the First might draw up a diagram to distribute. Often, however, they will just show up and figure it out on the day.

Multi-camera Filming

Multi-camera shoots—soap operas, sitcoms or other shows filmed before a live audience, and live broadcasts, among others—are a completely different beast, despite some obvious similarities to single-camera shooting. Multi-camera shows tend to have three to four cameras mounted on pedestals (rolling platforms), and at least three sound boom platforms, also wheeled. Much of the editing happens "live" in a gallery, where the vision-mixer cuts the shots as the action flows, usually entire scenes at a time. The first AD's equivalent is a floor manager, who, before the shoot, will be presented with the director's floor plans, designating where the actors are going to stand and move and where each camera will be. The cameras are all equipped with shooting cards, which indicate what size shot they need to be framed up on and when. They'll know they're recording as they're warned by the script supervisor (also in the gallery) and when the red light on their camera comes on. The director can be either on the floor or the gallery watching a "quad" monitor, so called because it is divided into four pictures: one for each camera, and the "mix," or the edit, as the vision-mixer is laying it down. I don't know of any features shot in this fashion, although I welcome correction on that.

On multi-camera shoots you generally do about three takes unless something is going very wrong, and then move on. This rate of speed means you can shoot about 20 pages of material in a single shooting day—an entire feature film in a week—which explains the quality you sometimes see on these shows. You would often also have two or three units shooting simultaneously, meaning that an actor might start the day with unit A, then go to unit B, back to unit A and then possibly over to unit C. Each unit will require them to have their parts of the 80-odd pages for that week memorized perfectly—there is no tolerance for not knowing your lines on these shows, there simply isn't time. Actors who can't memorize that much dialogue will be quickly let go—and, of course, they need to keep the baroque twists of their storylines clear in their heads (does she know I murdered our baby yet?). When they leave the studio, they often have to pass fans reacting to what was broadcast two months previously (and for some reason, soap opera viewers seem to have a harder time than most appreciating that the characters are played by actors and are not real people) before going home to try to memorize the 80 + pages that are coming down the track next week. It is a truly grueling schedule that some actors sustain for years at a time, and they deserve enormous admiration simply for saying the words and not bumping into the furniture, never mind giving great performances at 60 miles per hour for directors whose degree of enthusiasm can be, let's say, mixed. That said, these kinds of shows often develop tremendous community spirit (the pressure does help with bonding), and as they go on for years at a time can evolve into a family-style environment that some people really enjoy. In these cases, cross-shooting is the name of the game.

Final Thoughts on the Camera Department

If you're shooting on the top of a mountain, ask the camera crew if they need any help getting the gear back down the hill. They will appreciate it, when you're on the move, if you call "everyone grab something to carry—no one empty-handed" and they will have in mind cases or batteries that people can carry if they have a free hand. One caveat—don't be over-ambitious when it comes to gear; a case that seems okay when you first pick it up can be impossible to carry 50 yards down the road. If you twist your ankle when you're carrying something heavy it will sprain, and it's really hard to first with a bad ankle. And you generally need one hand free to change walkie channels when you're on the move. A battery, filter case or apple box is generally my speed; it's not just about you personally carrying stuff, but also advertising the fact that they may need help.

Checking the gate: when shooting film, the "gate" is the rectangular opening where the film goes through and is exposed to light. It's possible that dust, hair or other foreign bodies can make their way into the gate and potentially ruin the image by creating a line or mark across the frame. Before moving on from a setup, the first AC checks the gate to be sure it's clear, and in some cases, when finding a bit of debris, will show it to the DP to ascertain whether it intrudes on the image and whether another take is required. (Sometimes, a small imperfection in the magazine might scratch the surface of the film slightly, resulting in a buildup of emulsion from the negative, which might create the same problem.) The DP will make the judgment as to whether the offending particle is "in safety" (or in the safety zone of the film, that is, outside the image), but the safest bet is always to do one more take, just in case, since no one can know how long the debris has been there, or whether it might have traveled across the frame during the take.

Although now we rarely shoot on film, there are still sometimes checks that need to be done to be sure the data is recorded or the tape is safe, and while there may no longer be a gate, everyone on the crew will know what you mean if you say "checking the gate" or "gate's good, moving on." Checking the gate is a signal for everyone to be ready to move to the next setup or scene and is still a useful bit of lingo, no matter the format.

Both the first and second AC have the opportunity to completely destroy the work of everyone else on the crew with a simple error. If the lens isn't sitting in the bay properly or there's a hair in the gate, nothing else matters—so they're working under intense pressure, even when they look calm, and good ones deserve the utmost respect.

Grips and Gear

Depending on the territory you're working in, grips are generally part of the camera department. In North America, you tend to have a key grip and a dolly grip (but they may be the same person). The key grip is the head of department who supervises all of the other grips with responsibility for rigging and laying track. On North American productions, grips also look after the flags, nets, gels, cookies, and all the other various bits and pieces that are required to shape or alter the lighting, as well as hanging any blacks—it has been said that they deal with anything that goes on a c-stand. The dolly grip, as it sounds, looks after the dolly, should you be using one, and if not, whatever else the camera is mounted on, be it a tripod, monopod, slider, crane, high-hat, e-z rig, etc. While the first AC is responsible for making sure all the bits and pieces are mounted safely on the camera, the grip is responsible for making sure the camera is securely mounted to whatever it's sitting on.

The key grip can sometimes be designated the health and safety officer, and if this is the case you'll need to have a chat in prep about the responsibilities and expectations involved.

The most basic piece of camera gear is the **tripod**, which requires a separate "**head**," or mount for the camera. This head is what the operator uses to move the camera in a "pan" (left and right) or "tilt" (up and down), and can be either a pan-handle head with a single lever attached for the operator to handle, or a geared head, which has rotating cogs that allow the operator to use his/her right hand for the pan and left hand for the tilt.

A "**Dutch Head**" is a head that allows you to do a Dutch tilt, which is tilted on the diagonal one way or the other and is so named due to its popularity in German Expressionist cinema, or "Deutsch" film. A Dutch head will allow you to move from one diagonal to another, which in some cases can be achieved by mounting the camera at an offset to its normal position. This isn't possible with all cameras and heads, however, so if a Dutch tilt is required it needs to be planned for, and a head ordered, in advance. This is rarely something carried as standard on the truck. There are other heads I won't go into here, but the other bit of gear you will inevitably need at some point is an extension or a "eubange," which allows the grip to mount the camera overhanging a banister, say, or under a table—places the tripod or dolly can't reach.

A **dolly**, be it pee-wee, western, Fisher, hybrid, or any one of the numerous variations, adds two important functions to the camera movement: the jib or boom, meaning movement on a vertical axis, and whether on track or wheels, tracking, meaning moving on a horizontal axis. A dolly, if not tracking, typically makes positioning the camera quicker, certainly when selecting a height, as the back lever raises and lowers the head at the turn of a knob. (A dolly should never be touched by anyone other than a dolly grip. On one set, the camera suddenly smashed down onto a table, narrowly missing crushing the actor's hand and banging her shoulder. It turned out that the director, a first-timer, had given the jib arm a jaunty little twirl as he was passing. He learned a valuable lesson and gave the rest of us a heart attack.)

Naturally, a dolly takes up more space than a tripod, and needs a more secure base to rest on. If you're shooting in a field, to prepare the ground for a dolly might require building a temporary platform, whereas a tripod can simply be stuck into the ground. If you're tracking, then of course only a dolly will do, and if there is any kind of slope or soft ground it will require the grip and his assistants some time to be certain their rig can hold the dolly (500 pounds), the camera (another 30 pounds), the operator and the focus puller—a pretty heavy load. If a floor is very smooth, you might have the option of going on "soft wheels" and roll the dolly without a track, although this introduces potential slight variations in the dolly's path, when it's not locked onto a straight or curved track. Naturally, the longer the track, the more time it takes to set up. Sometimes the shot will require a variable path for the dolly to move, and if the floor can't be driven on directly the grips will need to build a "dance floor"—a surface smooth enough, typically made with sheets of plywood, to be able to roll the dolly freely. All of these elements should be discussed and planned for in advance. You don't want to be waiting around while the grips build a 30-foot track on a beach, and if the director has that bright idea on the day you will need to shoot something else in the meantime. I have heard stories of directors buying themselves time to think by asking for a track to be laid, but none of them tried it with me!

A wonderful piece of kit I love is a **slider**, the most common ranging from 2–6 feet long. It resembles a steel plank sitting between the head and the camera and can be mounted on a tripod or dolly, allowing the operator to slide the camera back and forth along its rail. This is particularly helpful for making adjustments if you're shooting over-the-shoulders and one actor is being masked by another, for example; or if the director wants a short tracking shot and there simply isn't space to get a dolly and track into position. On some shoots they use ultra-long sliders with a motorized control to be able to match the speed for a composite shot, but that won't be on your typical mid-budget movie or TV drama.

Steadicam isn't really a grip item, but as we're discussing camera accessories I'll mention it here. Most civilians know what it is and would recognize the kind of shot it provides; from an AD point of view, the question is whether you have a second camera body you can use on the Steadicam rig, as it can be time-consuming to mount and balance the camera. You certainly don't want to be going on and off the Steadicam unless you have two bodies. Older models also require being set in either low-mode or high-mode, which also requires time for a switch-over. As always, all of the pedantic questions need to be asked in advance. Steadicam allows for fluid, long shots, up and down stairs, in elevators and through complex sequences that could only otherwise be achieved handheld. Both handheld and Steadicam are sometimes offered up as time-saving solutions, but in fact they are just as demanding as other shots and shouldn't be under-budgeted for on the daily schedule.

Another piece of gear that is usually an extra addition is a **jib arm**. This is effectively a short crane that attaches onto the existing camera mount and gives total freedom in terms of camera movement up, down and around. The difficulty is generally in being able to operate the camera, as there is a limit to how high the operator can reach! A jib will give you a nice sweep, and is even sometimes useful when outside simply to cut down on repositioning time—I have seen one cameraman take all his static shots with a jib arm. It's very quick to choose the camera position if you're on a track and a jib arm, and the arm can be pretty much locked into position once you've chosen it.

But the bit of kit that everyone wants is a **crane**, and the longer and bigger the better. This is the time when you see the boys-with-toys at play, as every DP and director will ask for the longest, biggest, fanciest, most telescopic crane imaginable, and the PM then has to negotiate them down to something the production can afford. The real difference, from a first AD point of view, is whether it's a "ride-on," that is, with the operator and first AC mounted on the crane, or whether it's a remote, or "hot" head—that is, operated from the ground with a geared head by the operator watching a video feed from the camera. Cranes are always time-consuming, even when you have them rigged up in advance, but if the DP and first AC are riding on, the grip can't add the final weights to the back of the crane until these two humans and the camera are physically in position. There are seat belts on the crane seats, which you will ensure they use, and cranes always expose the cast and crew to more danger than a camera on the ground. There is the possibility of being struck by the crane itself or something the first AC might drop, as well as the operator and first AC potentially falling, in spite of the safety belts. It's crucial to keep all cast and crew away from the crane, not only under or in the path of the arm but especially the back, where all the weights are, and which could cause serious injury. If the camera is to be at any point above an actor, animal, etc., I will ask the grip to rig a safety cord between the camera and the crane arm. I have never seen a camera suddenly snap off its plate and fall, but if there is to be a first time I would prefer to be prepared. Cranes are sometimes used for direct overhead shots, perhaps of an actor in a bed, for example, and it certainly makes the actors more comfortable if they know you have taken all possible precautions.

If the crane is on a track, the danger increases again, as there are more people now involved with moving tons of steel in perfect synchronicity. If someone stumbles or catches their foot on the track, there might be no way to stop the crane in time to avert an accident. There are also very strict limits as to how close a crane can come to electrical overhead cables, which needs to be addressed in advance with the chief electrician on the tech scout.

When working with cranes, you will probably begin the take standing beside the camera operator—either at the camera or the crane monitor—and during the take make your way to a position where you can hear the director call cut. If you need to see the monitor—for example, if there are lots of extras—stay beside the operator and have a PA listen for the director's "cut" before going to get any director's notes. The First's priority is the safety of the cast and crew, then what's in the shot. For this reason, I sometimes ask the Second Second to watch the background action while I watch the set.

The very poor man's crane is a **ladder pod**. This is basically a tripod made from three ladders joined together at the top. It will give you height and not much else—if you look down and try to pan you will quickly start to see the pod legs. However, it's cheaper and quicker than building a scaffolding tower, and is often carried on the truck for the whole job. As long as you have the floor space required for the area (the legs demand quite a spread), a solid, level base and are conscious, again, of any overhead power cables, you can get quite good production value from this height. You do need to keep an eye on safety as the first AC and operator are climbing up and down, particularly when one of them, or the grip, is carrying a very heavy camera. And, of course, no one should ever be walking below or between the legs. The legs should also be linked and secured by steel cable.

More and more movies are using **motion capture** nowadays, although usually only the most expensive shoots can afford them. Its purpose is to record movement so it can be translated on to a digital model, as in Steven Spielberg's *The Adventures of Tintin*, for example. These shoots take place in specially designed chambers equipped with multiple LED cameras, where the props are transparent, real-life wireframes and the actors are wearing capture suits, tailor-made to fit them exactly, and capture helmets. The camera itself (or steering wheel) that the director or DP holds is not a recording device, simply a means of transmitting data to the computers, and the need for all of the physical devices that we've been discussing—dollies, jibs, cranes, etc.—are surplus to requirements. But they still need someone to create and manage a schedule, and look after the actors on a daily basis, so they still have a first and second AD, however high-tech things may get!

There are, of course, innumerable other kinds of equipment, I'm just covering the most common here—I have been on many jobs where the director requested a **hovercam** (just like it sounds, basically a camera mounted on a small propeller that can be controlled remotely), but I've never seen one actually make it to set. Likewise, with the amazing quality possible on a **GoPro** mini HD camera, shots can be taken from toy helicopters, underwater, thrown from buildings and over cliffs, not to mention inside planes, trains and automobiles. They even record sound! The quality isn't yet on a par with other formats, but it's only a matter of time.

The Script Supervisor

In North America, the script supervisor is part of the production department, and in the UK system, the camera department, even though they don't carry any cases or hang around the back of the camera truck. A good script supervisor can save your life, and a bad one can make you want to take it.

The script supervisor will have about a week's prep, although they won't often spend it in the office. Their initial work, as it affects you, are the **story days**, **script timings** and **scene length calculations**. A script supervisor will sit with the script and a stopwatch, reading the dialogue and leaving enough space for the action described in the stage directions to happen (the famous line "chaos ensues" is an example of a deceptively short stage direction—you can make up your own examples!). S/he will thus calculate the **estimated screen time** for each scene, as well as the movie or episode overall. This is a black art and a gift, and a lot of responsibility is involved with these estimates—if a producer discovers that the project is 15 minutes over, s/he is going to push strongly for script cuts, as there is no point shooting material that can't be used. Equally, if an episode is coming up short (and in TV there is no latitude in relation to timings: a 26-minute episode needs to be exactly 26 minutes) there will be a minor panic, as the creative team try to figure out how to extend the story without padding it. This will, of course, have implications for the schedule. If after writing new scenes and shooting them the episode turns out to be running long, you can guess where they'll point the finger.

Of course, these initial timings are simply estimates, and as the shoot progresses the script supervisor will be able to tell very quickly what kind of pace the director is moving at and whether the actual screen time—s/he times from when you call action until when the director calls cut, so there's always a little extra than will be used—is working out longer or shorter than the estimates. An experienced TV director will always be keeping an eye on these timings, as it's preferable to adjust them in the shoot than to have to lose or try to add a scene in the edit.

Less fluid and more mathematical are the script supervisor's **page counts**, which you will add to the master schedule as soon as you get them. It's a dull task to amend each breakdown sheet to reflect the correct count, and if this happens late in the day it is something you can ask someone else on your team to do, providing they have some familiarity with the software. These page counts do matter, as that total at the end of each shooting day, even in the schedule, will generally indicate if you're in the right ballpark. The completed pages and screen time, as well as their averages to date, will also be reflected later on the production report.

Once you're shooting, the script supervisor will generally be beside the director at the monitor. On some UK TV shows, this person also gets involved in production duties, but everywhere else s/he is looking at the **continuity** of a million things in the frame: Is the actor delivering the lines word-perfectly? Where are they moving and when? Are there props involved and at what point? What is the actor wearing? What are the extras doing? What is the camera doing (moving/static) and when? Are the actors' eyelines correct and are we on the right side of the line? And, the million-dollar question, will the scene cut? The subset of this question is, is the action covered? This is more than any one human being should have to worry about, and I don't know what kind of brain it takes to be good at this job but I know I don't have one. Playback affords the chance to check details if there is a difference of opinion, but good script supervisors rarely ask for something to be played back—they watch it, they note it and they know it.

The script supervisor can be of enormous help to you in relation to **extras**—even though they shouldn't have to be—and they often fulfill the same helpful role to wardrobe, makeup, hair, props and the actors themselves, who can almost never remember which hand they used to lift the glass or open the door. Continuity is crucial to maintaining the illusion that a number of shots, potentially filmed at different times in different locations, are a real-time depiction of something that actually happened. It's the foundation of the suspension of disbelief, without which drama doesn't function. Every time an audience member notices a continuity gap, they're taken out of the emotion of the story and the film fails, if only for an instant. I say all this because sometimes the person supervising continuity is treated like a pest, instead of the lynchpin of the storytelling process.

Everyone whose work is onscreen—wardrobe, hair, makeup, props, art department, and the ADs in relation to extras—has to be constantly watching continuity. Millions of dollars were spent on Polaroid film before the welcome advent of digital photography, recording every detail of the actors and set for every scene. This isn't just in the case of one scene leading to the next and shooting out of story chronology, but also because no one ever knows when a scene may need a pickup shot because it wasn't done on the original shoot day, or a shot may need to be re-done because of a technical problem or a new idea in post. All of this documentation is kept until the film is delivered (and sometimes beyond), as no one could possibly ever remember how every detail was on the day.

Occasionally, you will have to break for lunch (or, worse still, overnight) in the middle of a scene. In this case, the set is taped off, and is known as a "**Hot Set**." This means NOTHING should be touched from the way it currently is; everything has been "established" in continuity, and must not change. The First will announce, as the crew breaks, that this is a Hot Set and reiterate that nothing can be touched until they return.

The frustrating part for a first AD is that it's sometimes not until you're just about to roll that a script supervisor speaks up about something being incorrect—hopefully, it's simply a prop position or hair check, but sometimes they will advise that they believe that the camera is in the wrong place altogether. To avoid this, it's very important to include the script supervisor in the initial decision-making process regarding the scene's **shotlist** so if there is any discussion to be had, it can happen then. You really don't want an argument about eyelines with the cast standing there, as the more of an audience s/he has, the less the DP or operator is going to want to admit a mistake. If there needs to be a conversation, I would try to get the concerned parties away from the camera (and the cast) and over to the director's monitor, where, if need be, video assist can replay any takes that might have an implication for the current situation.

What you, as the First, really want to avoid is the so-called solution, "we'll do it both ways," often followed by, "that way we're covered." If you're on an unlimited schedule and budget, then you can do it every way you like; but if, as is usually the case even on big jobs, you're not, the director needs to commit, otherwise you can end up doing two shots for every setup, so you have it "both ways." Except in highly unusual circumstances, that really isn't plausible. If the director is too inexperienced or weak to make the decision, I would have a quiet chat with the script supervisor and, if you respect his or her judgment, take this to be the official line and subtly push for that choice. Even experienced operators and DPs can make mistakes when it comes to areas like eyelines and screen direction, and the script supervisor's job is to be the editor's eyes and ears on set.

After every setup, the script supervisor will record the director's preferred takes, or "**selects**" (on film, the printed takes) and then go to the first AC to record the **technical information** for the notes: lens size, height, focal distance, any filters or mattes involved and the *f*-stop. This information is critical when you need to re-shoot a shot, or shoot a shot to cut into the scene. Five minutes into the next setup and it will be very hard to remember, never mind weeks later when shooting pickups halfway through the edit. If there are two cameras, the script supervisor needs to get the information about each, as well as recording what each was doing during the take. Once you get into three cameras it's cruel to expect any one brain to be able to take in what's going on and there should be a second script supervisor, or an assistant, hired to supervise the overflow, although there often isn't.

The script supervisor's day continues after wrap, when s/he writes up his or her notes. This is a compilation of all the camera information, the "tram-line" or marked-up script pages, as well as the information that matters to and reflects on you: the unit call time; the time the first setup was complete after call; the time you broke for lunch; the time you came back from lunch; the time the first setup was complete after lunch; and the time you wrapped (in the US, the Second may be recording some or all of this information).

These notes go to the POC, who uses them to create the **production report** and sends a copy to the editing room, so they have a reference for the rushes. At a glance, any of the investors will be able to see if it took two hours to get the first shot, and there will be questions in your direction, aimed via the PM or producer. If anything unusual happens that causes a delay, the script supervisor will make note of this also, and I would always ensure that you speak to him or her directly about what was involved: an accident, medical issue (no matter how tiny—anytime someone receives medical attention, it needs to go in the notes—it could be crucial for insurance purposes later if the problem develops), technical failure, or weather delays or other difficulties. I would also, on occasion, ask the script supervisor to note if a particular actor was late in reporting to set, if it was happening frequently or causing a delay. The PM can decide whether to include that on the production report later, but meanwhile at least they have an explanation of why the first shot took 3 hours to complete.

Script supervisor can be a truly thankless job, as no one ever praises a film for good continuity or eyelines being correct, while people seem to love spotting mistakes in movies and have whole websites about it. In defense of most script supervisors, the number of times they get overruled when they're actually correct is phenomenal. Maybe because so many of them are women, or their role is simply misunderstood, but I have heard numerous directors dismissing their points with phrases such as "they'll never notice" (meaning the audience) or the best one, "we'll fix it in post." At least once a project, a script supervisor will watch something being done wrong, know that their name is on it, and have to just accept it and move on. Their only consolation is the note they can write to the editor: "I know this is wrong! They went ahead anyway!" For a script supervisor, that might not be a bad epitaph.

Lighting and Electrical

Around the world, the sparks often have the toughest union and the best deals. I have worked on many jobs where an electrician is getting paid more than the director, and that won't change anytime soon. The electricians' deal is one of the most important points you'll cover with the PM in prep, and you'll need to stick to it or very quickly cost the company huge sums of money.

On an average low-budget job, you'll have the gaffer (chief electrician), best boy (the gaffer's second), an electrician and the genny op. (Outside of North America, this person actually drives the generator to and from the location, and his/her hours and turnaround time are included in the length of the shooting day. This is how a genny op can earn more than anyone else on the crew, aside from the other electricians!) If you have the resources, you may have a secondary electrical crew who pre-light and strike your sets, and additional help on specific days, or "dailies."

One major difference between the USA and elsewhere is that in the States, lighting work is split into two groups: electricians and grips. The electricians only deal with equipment that has a plug: all the flags, gels, cookies and other lighting accessories are operated and rigged by grips. A US electrician might set up a light, plug it in and turn it on, but a grip has to supply and place the sandbag to weight it down. In Europe, Asia and Africa, the electricians deal with anything relating to lighting (from silks to sandbags), and the grips are concerned exclusively with the camera and its related equipment.

I'm not going to describe every bit of kit that relates to lighting, or the extensive slang that goes on around the world in relation to this gear (where else but on a set would you hear someone asking to "kill the baby," "axe the redhead" or "save the blonde")—the only need-to-know in all of this is what's involved and how long it's going to take. You'll start picking up the lingo from your first day on the set, and once you've identified who are the sparks and who are the grips you'll be fine. In any case, most of your dealings will be with the key grip, who will probably be right beside you and the camera, and the gaffer, or chief electrician, and you won't need to worry about all the accessories.

As mentioned before, I'll get a time estimate from the DP as to how long s/he needs to light the scene, but if these estimates are at all inaccurate it's worth quietly asking the gaffer what has to be done. This way, I can see for myself how close or far away they are from being ready. A point of interest is whether the light is a 5 K (5 kilowatts) or below. If it's below, one man can lift it into position and operate it. If it's over 5 K, it may need a special stand, two men and a very solid surface underfoot, which will take longer.

Ground-floor locations are not only preferable in terms of carrying gear up and down stairs or in an elevator, they also mean an easier job for lighting, as the lamps can stand on the ground outside and shine through the windows pretty easily. Every floor you go up increases the height the lamps need to rise; if you're two stories up, you're going to need at least one cherry picker. Alternatively, you'll have all of the lights on the floor inside, which will cut down the amount of space the director and actors have to work with, and will also be a major headache if you need to see that part of the room at any time. Generally, location managers shouldn't be showing directors places that cannot realistically be serviced without lots of time and expense, and the PM should have already had this conversation in prep. Even at the tech scout, it's not too late to re-think. An inexperienced director will choose a location for the view, not realizing that the first thing the DP is going to say is that the windows will have to be gelled or avoided. So in the early days, find out what the director likes about the location—especially interiors—as there may be implications they're not aware of. The DP isn't going to say they don't like the location—they'll just ask for the tools they need to service it, making it the PM's problem, who then has to talk to the director and seems like a killjoy. You can intercept this conversation if you make the director aware of the requirements for a particular location. They may not care what floor the apartment is on, and would be happy to change if only someone had told them.

Parking the generator is not your responsibility, happily, but you should be aware that there is sometimes a tussle between the sparks, who would like to park the genny right beside the set, and sound, who can hear its engine from a good distance away. Sometimes, if locations are busy, the genny operator might come up to you and check where he's parking, and you may see that it's out of frame and think it's okay—but sound is a crucial part of this equation and the genny op will know how far away s/he has to be, and may simply be trying to save the bother of laying cables any further than they think they have to.

Cherry pickers, condors, scaffolding towers, or other types of equipment for working at height need to be prepared in advance. It is slow and noisy getting a lamp on a condor into position, and you don't want to be waiting for it. Typically used on night shoots (or interiors such as the one mentioned above, where you're lighting through windows), whoever is mounting the light and going up with it needs to be getting ready at least an hour before the DP expects to see it. This kind of work can't be safely rushed, so you need to leave lots of time for it to happen. One of the few fatal accidents to occur on a BBC shoot was when a cherry-picker tipped over because it was parked on soft ground. Naturally, it's not your job to examine the ground where the cherry-picker parks, but you would still be feeling very bad if you were on that shoot and had been hassling the guys to hurry up. The gaffer will ensure that the cab isn't going to be raised near any electrical cables or other hazards, and in the case of rain will alert you if there is any danger from water, lightning or wind. In this case, whatever they say goes and there is no arguing the toss or overruling them.

If you're pre-lighting on the day of the shoot, you'll need to work out the timings carefully with the gaffer and then the PM. Let's say your unit call is 8 a.m. and you need the pre-light to happen before then. Your gaffer says he and his men need an hour's pre-light. You might call the electricians for 6:30 a.m., let them work till 7:30 and then have breakfast, so they're on the same meal schedule as the rest of the crew. If you don't give them breakfast, you might be hitting expensive penalties six hours after their call time; similarly, you need to be careful if you're breaking the crew early for lunch, as once again six hours (or whatever your deal is) after they're back in from lunch, you're owing another meal break. It's not complicated, it just needs to be specified in advance. If your gaffer is a little tricky, you will be sure to formally announce that they are broken for breakfast at 7:30 so there is no confusion later. If there are to be any early calls for pre-lights, they need to be on the call sheet so the accountants aren't surprised when the timesheets come in.

Sparks, like camera and grip, will also have half-an-hour's wrap time, unless they say that it is going to be longer, which again should be discussed with the PM in advance. Generally they can wrap pretty quickly, so unless there's miles of cable to be wrapped in the rain or snow it shouldn't take more than half an hour. This is also why it's important for you to keep the crew informed as to how many shots remain at the end of the day, as the more they can wrap in advance the cheaper it can be for production.

The electrical department deals with the most dangerous equipment on the set and this is part of the reason why they are—correctly—twitchy about anyone going near their stuff. As you respect the safety standards they maintain, you must also ensure that everyone on the team is also respecting those standards. It used to be common practice for electricians to have a few beers at lunch; happily, this practice is now completely gone in North America and very rare in Europe (although France still has its unique relationship with wine, even in this regard). I would argue that any drinking during the working day is completely unacceptable by anyone on the crew, and I would expect any producer to back that up. If you see anything you think is unsafe, or are unsure about it, it's your job to report it to the PM as soon as possible. It's an area in which it's best to be over-cautious—fire and electrocution are no joke.

On a different note, there are, of course, different working practices all over the world. One DP I know who was going to shoot a commercial in India was talking to the lighting rental company and he was asked if he would like stands with those lamps. Yes, answered the DP, what else would he use? Oh, replied the man, it's just that a man to hold the lamp is cheaper than a stand. Leaving aside what that might do for your lighting (how long can someone hold a 2K over their head without wiggling?), those men certainly aren't on union minimums.

Sound

It's been said that picture tells you what's happening and sound tells you how to feel about it. Be that as it may, sound is certainly underappreciated on a film set and often treated like second fiddle to the all-important camera. But the reality is that while audiences will watch a scratchy old print of *Casablanca*, they won't tolerate muddy or distorted sound for a second. It's a more subconscious element, and a sense that we rely on perhaps more than we realize. I used to think that seeing the actor's eyes was all-important—but when you watch animation or puppetry, even Barbie dolls can create an emotional reaction, and this all happens through the actor's voice. In fact, we may not recognize someone visually but hearing them speak can instantly transport us across decades. I'm just reminding us all of the powerful cinematic tool that sound is, because mixers can be a really annoying lot!

A good sound mixer will be invisible; a bad one will drive you insane. If they're not waiting until the last second to put a radio mike on an actor, they're complaining about a lawnmower four states away or shaking their head in disgust during a take because a fly went near the boom. I have heard a sound mixer lobbying to fire the caterer "as a matter of principle—you always have to fire the first caterer," and been lectured as to the minutiae of the penalties regarding a rest day during a national holiday. I'd like to think these are the exception, and perhaps the same obsessive qualities are what lead to them being masters of their craft. I have worked with too many good mixers, however, to be fooled into thinking that being annoying is a job requirement, and some of the best mixers I've worked with have also been a delight on the floor.

There are typically at least three people in the sound department—the mixer, the boom op and the cable basher or sound trainee. This trainee also will sometimes operate a second boom, if required. If you're running a rehearsal at call time, sound will be there to observe; sometimes, they may wish to hide a wireless mic in a prop on the set and at least they can watch the movement of the actors with a view to booming it. The mixer's cart will be somewhere adjacent to the set and most of them will have their own monitor running the live picture from the camera. Boom ops in Europe don't wear headphones, but in North America they generally do, to hear the sound they're capturing. The mixer will also supply headphones to the director and script supervisor, and whichever producers are on set. (If you're expecting producers' visits, it's kind to inform the sound mixer as s/he may need to bring extra headphones—producers can get very put out if they don't have a pair.)

If the mixer wants to get radio mics onto the actors I would prefer that they do this when the actors are changing into their costumes. It's more private, especially for the women, as the cable generally has to run up their front under their clothes. I will often ask if this is the case, but I also expect them to make me aware, rather than waiting until we're ready to go for the final rehearsal and then piping up. If this happens, I would just privately ask them to let me know next time in advance so we can give them the time they need off-set.

During the rehearsal, the boom op will get into position and practice getting the mic into the best position while not casting any shadows. These boom shadows are the bane of the boom op's life, and some DPs make it easier than others. If there is one general source, augmented by smaller lights, that is easier for a boom op than a situation where there are lights pointing in various directions, which may look nice on camera but can make his or her job almost impossible. Many times, the issue can be addressed by flagging part of the lamp, and eventually some compromise will be reached, but it can become a flashpoint if either one's temperament lends itself to argument. Despite the time pressure, what you don't want to do is exacerbate the situation by making it public or wading in to hurry it up; if need be, you can first ask the boom op if they're ok, when generally they will say they're fine and they'll work with it; if not, you can have a quiet word with the DP, suggesting that the boom op is struggling and is there anything s/he can do to help? Then, if they move the lamp they are a savior and a hero. This is obviously preferable to saying something like "come on, guys, sort this out, we need to move" loud enough for everyone on the set to hear.

As a First, your job is to create an environment in which everyone can do their best work, and that includes sound. Tech scouts need to investigate the proximity of any airports or flight paths (*Lost in La Mancha* illustrates this point well), as you'll need to hold the roll for any planes. You hold traffic for sound and picture, as well as keeping the crew still and quiet during the takes, not just for sound but for everyone's concentration. If there is a lawnmower, baby crying, music, alarm, or some other unwanted sound effects, you will ask locations to address it, and have to wait until they do. While waiting, if there are any cutaways or inserts that don't require sound, you can consider shooting these then, but it will depend on how long you think it will take to address the sound issue. Breaking up a setup is a worst-case scenario, and to be avoided unless the delay is at least 10 minutes. These are actually great times to look at the next day's call sheet and talk it through with the director, DP or anyone else on the floor you need to discuss it with.

There will be the occasional time the noise just isn't going to go away (some house alarms, for example, can go on for hours). You will have to discuss it with the director, but it is always better to shoot something or move on. You can shoot the entire scene as originally planned, understanding that it will have to be dubbed in post; you can shoot it all in such tight close-ups that you get the best possible sound on the day; or you can try to swap the scene with one that is less sound-dependent in the hope that the offending noise will be gone by that point. Whatever decision you make, make sure your Second informs the POC or PM so no one gets a surprise later. If you think the decision made is the incorrect one, make sure the PM gets your opinion immediately, probably via the second AD.

The decision will be impacted somewhat by the ultimate destination of the media—if it's for TV, it's obviously different than if it's something that's going to be played on Dolby systems in huge cinemas. That said, however, there are still limitations—if you're working on a period piece, there really is no way you can live with that engine noise, so your choice of locations will be even more critical. People sometimes think that the look is everything, and I have even had a camera person say to me that the film rushes are the most important thing because without the visuals, there is no story. I would argue that no one wants to see a silent movie—and, in fact, people listen to the radio but they don't watch TV without the sound…!

Wherever you're shooting, you'll want to get a minute or so of **room tone** or **atmos** once the scene is complete. This feels like a strange waste of time until you have had to be the person in the editing room splicing frames together to create the sound of silence. Basically, every space has some sound—a hum that is imperceptible until you take it away. If you want to add a pause to a scene in the edit, you can't simply throw in a slug—you'll instantly hear the dead air. So a minute of room tone saves the editor (or assistant) hours of tedious work later and sounds much better. Besides this, I think room tone is actually one of my favorite moments on a film set. It's like a minute of meditation, a holy silence in the middle of the onrushing roar. No one can move or speak, which sometimes leads to vicious fits of giggles if people make eye contact; but I find it such a relief to close my eyes and rest for 45 seconds—it really is restorative! Of course, I've never actually told any sound people—or producers—that! Room tone is especially precious if you have been shooting in a location that isn't totally silent. Whatever background noise there is can be manipulated into a smoother soundscape if you have a long enough piece of it "clean."

The other sound element distinct from the camera is **wild tracks**. These are lines of dialogue or sound effects (a door opening, footsteps) that are recorded when the camera isn't rolling. There can be various reasons for this. Sometimes the boom op can't physically get the boom in the best place for sound during the take itself; perhaps it's a steadicam shot, where the sound of the camera crew walking on gravel is encroaching on the actor's lines; maybe a line has been changed in the edit and the actor needs to say the new line; any number of reasons dictate why a wild track may be needed. While the sound crew will have a list of what needs to be done, it's up to you to decide the best time to do it. I generally try to get them done as soon as they come in, as if it's left until the last day, the actor might have been wrapped or is on a different location. I keep the list in my notebook and every day check if there's something I can write onto my copy of the call sheet. If it involves cast, I'll ask the Second to mention it to them at the start of the day, so they're not surprised later (especially if they have to do it just before they wrap).

Music **playback** is sometimes required to set a scene, or, in the case of music videos, run throughout the take. The normal order in which you would call the shots in this case is to roll sound, wait for speed, roll camera, mark the slate, then set, playback, and action (or run playback at a low volume first, and bring it up after "set."). On a music video you will generally work with a "smart slate," with an electronic display that matches the time code on the music track. On a drama shoot, you may wish to start the music playing at the correct volume to give the actors a reference so they will speak loudly enough to be realistic, or to give dancers a beat they will then continue moving to. In both of these cases you would drop the playback out at a pre-decided moment, before the dialogue begins. (You would never record dialogue over music, as it can't be edited later—music is always laid in afterwards.)

I find maintaining eye contact with the playback operator (frequently the sound mixer) and using the old faithful cut-throat hand gesture works fine, and I then don't have to shout over the music. Equally, the easiest way to call cut if you are playing music throughout a take is to stop the music, then call cut, or you'll find yourself hoarse by the end of the day.

If you are to have playback, it needs, as always, to be discussed in advance as to who is providing it and operating it; is the media that will be played back currently in the correct format (sounds obvious, but is it a CD/drive/etc.—the POC will make sure it gets converted, if need be, but you should ask the obvious questions); and, of course, it should be on the call sheet. Finally, on the day, the operator and gear should be on the designated location, set up and tested an hour before the playback is required.

Video Playback

While we're on the subject of playback, **video playback** that will be seen on camera—a TV, say, or a film on screen—works in much the same way, although it has nothing to do with the sound department. Responsibility for video playback is one of those things that easily slips between the departments, especially on smaller crews, as art department, camera and video assist generally want nothing to do with it, while you and the PM will need to be constantly following up to ensure that everything works as it should. It starts in prep, when you are doing your initial breakdown—anywhere in the script where there is a reference to playback, be it on a TV, computer monitor, cinema screen, etc., you'll need to discuss with the POC. S/he will already have begun the process of "clearing," that is, getting legal permission, to use the clips, and s/he can update you as to how this is going. With this information, your next meeting with the director should talk through the playback, as there may be something specified in the script that h/she doesn't actually want, but no one may have asked him or her about it. If s/he has a change in mind, advise the producer before going any further (it may not be the director's sole choice)! If something is proving either difficult to access or ridiculously expensive, thinking about alternatives needs to start early.

Assuming that all the clips required are copyright cleared, they need to be converted into whatever format they will be played back on. Again, the POC will coordinate this with the editor and the playback operator, but you need to ask the question at least once a week, as these things can get pushed down the list of people's priorities. Once you know what equipment is being used, that goes onto the shooting schedule, and thus onto the call sheets when the time comes. I would advise ALWAYS testing the playback during prep to be sure it all works perfectly, and inform the camera and sound departments that the test is happening, so they can prepare any unusual bits of gear that may be required. It's all perfectly straightforward if all the planning has been done correctly, and testing is everything, as sometimes it's one tiny little adapter that the sound mixer has at home that could make all the difference, if they'd only known…! If the first AC and mixer are at the test, then they're involved and more responsible than if they're seeing it for the first time on the set. At the very least, you should have a conversation with them no less than a week beforehand about the technical specs and what advice or requirements they may have.

When you're shooting the scene, you'll probably film it normally, with the sound on the playback material muted; you will then shoot the playback footage, or at the very least a wild-track of the entire audio track, so the editor has a clean pass to use as they wish. The live sound from whatever device the footage is being played back on will almost always sound better than a "clean" recording from the original material, which then has to be amended in the mix to approximate the set's inherent characteristics. There is also the scenario in which the screen (TV, cinema, etc.) is covered in green or blue screen, for the image to be dropped in later in post.

Finally, the issue of **roll bars** applies only if you're shooting on film, as film and video have out-of-synch film speeds. There are numerous ways to get rid of the black bar that scrolls across a TV screen if you're shooting on film; the simplest I have seen is the addition of a "synch box," a little piece of gear that attaches to the camera and magically addresses the issue. You can also have your video footage converted to the speed your camera is running at. The issue is less pronounced in Europe, where cameras run at 25 fps as opposed to the North American 24. Ultimately, the technology isn't your problem, the logistics are—you want to ask the question as to how the roll bar will be eliminated on your production, and how long it's going to take. Computer screens now don't seem to offer as many problems as once upon a time, but as always, the answer is to test, especially if it's a period piece. Movies, if they're projected from a film print, won't have any such problems.

Hair and Makeup

It's not fair to group these two departments together, as they do completely different work, but with all due respect to their distinct skills, from a first AD point of view they operate in parallel. It's possible to add costume to this mix, and from a psychological point of view they are in this area, but they may have their own truck and their own agenda.

The most straightforward kind of shoot you can have from the hair and makeup point of view is contemporary and mid-range—basically, trying to make people look their best in "normal" life, as in most TV shows, especially comedies and soaps. In this case, the Second will get their time estimates for the following day, depending on who the cast are and how many there will be. In fact, even if you're shooting sci-fi, horror, or something with elaborate prosthetics and wigs, it doesn't really matter much to me what they're doing as long as they stick to the amount of time allowed.

Of course, the difference between good and bad hair and makeup can be seen clearly on screen: audiences are generally watching the actors' faces, and this is where these designers' work appears. But the real difference between artists and craftspeople is in the work the audience never sees, the alchemical interplay that prepares an actor for their imaginative leap. A good makeup or hair chief is expert with brushes, and with the fragile ego of an actor, particularly women of a certain age. The actors can form a co-dependent relationship with the person stroking their cheeks and smoothing their hair and telling them they look beautiful and they're going to be great. Conversely, if you were in the chair and someone was yakking on about their lousy boyfriend and their flat tire with pop music blaring, you wouldn't arrive on set in the most positive condition. Add to this the fact that actors may have been collected from home (or from the pub) at 5 a.m. and are almost always nervous about the scene they're about to do. It's a powerful potential Molotov cocktail that a really good makeup or hair person knows how to defuse.

The makeup and hair people typically earn their money before unit call, when the actors are arriving for the day (these arrivals may, of course, be staggered throughout the day, but the intensity level often subsides the later the actor has to arrive). It might appear to the casual onlooker that all they do on the set is sit around, chat, and give the odd puff of powder onto someone's nose. But in fact, they are supporting the cast, who are trusting them to spot it if they have a hair out of place, and sometimes a lot more.

If you have a cast member who has a substance abuse problem, romantic difficulties or struggles with parenthood, the makeup and hair people will know all about it, and won't breathe a word. There's a good reason why stars who can request it bring their personal hair and makeup people with them wherever they go. Daniel Craig generally doesn't need a huge amount of hair checks, but he likes and trusts his hairdresser, and why take the risk of having to work with someone you don't like, if you can afford to bring a friend? Of course, they're qualified and talented—as in most departments, skill and ability are a given or you wouldn't be invited to this party in the first place. So all else being equal, why not spend your many hours waiting around with someone whose company you enjoy, instead of being at the mercy of a stranger?

Happily (for me, at least) almost all of the drama in the dressing rooms is under the auspices of the second AD, who is also a psychologist and a gifted diplomat. It is often the chief makeup or hair artist who can console, cajole and entice the cast member to feel good enough about themselves to go to work.

As a First, the only thing you really have to look out for on set is giving makeup and hair a chance to have a look before you roll the first take of a setup, known as "last looks," "checks" and an infinite number of variations. Other than that, your relationship will typically be pleasant and full of laughter—and they often wear cheerful colors, which can brighten up the mood! Both hair and makeup will need time anytime there is an actor's "change," particularly changing from one story day to another. A big mistake in a script is to have a character get a dramatic **hair change**—I understand the storytelling reasons, but ask any director who has done it whether they would do it again and I think you'll get a negative reply. What happens is that the hairstyle starts to dictate the schedule—if the character is female, you can assume at least a half-hour changeover, just for hair, and there will probably be a commensurate makeup change, too. That's manageable if you're shooting in a studio with sets standing for the duration of the shoot, or if you're able to film everything before the haircut in one block, and the post-haircut afterwards, but both of these are unlikely scenarios. Due to locations, weather or other actors' availability, you may find yourself literally waiting on hair, which is a really boring place to be (no offense to hairdressers, it just feels horrible to have a whole crew standing around a set doing nothing—and boy, is it expensive.). If there's no other way to depict the character's turning point, then at least encourage the director and the hairdresser—in prep—to devise a simple enough maneuver that can tell this story without costing an hour of shooting time (and, especially, not a real haircut!). In prep, you can even shoot tests to see how it reads on camera and experiment with different versions. No sane hair designer is going to want to do something so elaborate that s/he will have the entire production department bearing down on him or her every time there's a change, so if the director can sign off on something beforehand that is achievable quickly, then that's the best of both worlds.

I once worked on a job where the lead actress, who was in every scene, got a perm halfway through the film. And yes, it was a real perm. So much for pickups or re-shoots, and the entire schedule was built around this perm date—was it worth it? Who knows. The same can apply if you have a character with a beard, who shaves, or vice versa. Although it involves hair, because it is **facial hair**, *it is now part of the makeup department*—the hair department covers only hair on the head. If you have a fake beard, it takes a significant amount of time to apply believably, but less to remove. If your actor starts with a beard, or stubble, then shaves, it will grow back but probably sometime after you wrap. Again, it's worth teasing out with the producer and the director how necessary these transformations are, and if there's an alternative way of conveying the same information about the character's inner world. It certainly tells a visual story, but can compromise the shooting time enormously so it's a choice with real consequences that you need to make them aware of (otherwise, it will be you they're giving out to when it's taking too long). I once had a hairdresser tell me with great gravitas "you can't rush hair." But I still try.

Hair designers, besides dealing with the aforementioned changeover issue, will be responsible for **wigs** and **extensions**, **coloring**, **styling** and will collaborate with makeup to minimize the look of **balding** (sometimes an actor's scalp will be spray-painted a color closest to his hair). I don't know why, but I often find male actors more difficult about their hair than women—and women more difficult about their makeup. Men seem to have a particular horror of balding, and can channel all of their vanity and insecurity into strong feelings about their hair. Some male actors that I know to be lovely people have reduced hairdressers to tears. I'll let you speculate as to why that is!

Blood, Sweat, and Tears

Blood is an area of overlap between makeup and props. A rule of thumb is that if it's on the actor, it's makeup, if it's elsewhere (on the floor, weapon, etc.) it's props. Good stage blood is often highly staining, so you need to be sure you have repeats of any costume or prop that is porous enough to get damaged. Blood is often accompanied by some kind of prosthetic wound, which, with a good makeup artist, can be surprisingly quick to apply, and then dress with blood and possibly glycerin and/or other potions. Any blood effects will need to be on the schedule and call sheet in advance, be it makeup or props.

Glycerin is also used to create the appearance of **sweat**, and is totally lighting-dependent. Just as you won't see rain unless it's backlit, so, too, you won't see sweat unless there's light shining on it at the right angle—I have seen an actor literally drenched in the stuff and it still didn't read on camera. Sweat is usually applied at the very last second, when you call for makeup "checks" or "last looks," just before rolling. The overall effect often needs to be enhanced by the wardrobe department to show moisture on the costume.

Tears, when not produced by the actors themselves, are often created by the makeup artist's tear stick, which is like a tube from which s/he blows a chemical vapor into the actor's eyes, creating a safe but tearful reaction. Actors are often a little embarrassed that they're using tear stick, so you don't have to declaim it around the set that that's what they're doing. Tears, however, need to go on at the very last second, even later than sweat, so you might actually roll camera, mark it, tear stick up and then when the makeup artist has cleared frame, call action. You should also check that the makeup artist has tested this particular tear stick on the actor in advance, in case it causes some kind of freak allergic reaction. At least that way the actor, too, is familiar with the process and won't be distracted by the tears on the set.

Makeup artists get to do all sorts of other fun stuff, too—when an actor's skin anywhere on their body is showing, it usually needs a dab of makeup, if only for the actor's comfort. Tattoos, rashes, cold sores, spots—a lot of the makeup artist's bag of tricks involves concealment as much as highlighting (but anyone who uses makeup at all could tell you that!). Makeup artists get more familiar than they might wish with the cast's personal hygiene, but that's all part of the job. They might need to clip toenails, trim nose hair and pin back ears—all in a day's work. And this is before they get into any exotic horror, science fiction or fantasy creations.

Some makeup **effects** will require an entire team creating masks, prosthetics and other tools for the characters. Any fittings or tests for these elements will be done in prep, as with any standard makeup, hair and wardrobe sessions. You'll need to know exactly how long these variations take to apply, and if there are any health and safety concerns in relation to allergies. A combination of chemicals against an actor's skin under hot lights may have a certain exposure limit, and you'll need to have an idea of what that is before the actor starts blistering! There will also be some de-rig time for these elements, which will count as part of the actor's day, as s/he won't be officially wrapped until s/he is returned to their previous condition.

The Costume Department

Okay, I'm going to say it: if you're wondering who the worst-dressed people on the set are, 10 to 1 it'll be wardrobe. Now keep that to yourself. And never tell anyone that they're all crazy, either. Because they're not as crazy as food stylists, so stop it. They are crazy though. That's why we love them. Because there's good crazy and bad crazy. Let's face it, you'd have to be crazy to want to get up at 4 a.m. every morning to report to some parking lot where you'll spend the day in the back of a windowless truck trying to get even more crazy actors in and out of costumes that were the right size in the fitting before the actor gained or lost 5 pounds and then poured hot chocolate down the front of and by the way they haven't used deodorant so you're going to have to get their pungent b.o. out of a beautiful period silk shirt while not getting creeped out by the fact that the other actor isn't wearing underwear (you can provide some, thank you) and after a very long day in which you are expected to suddenly provide, oh, maybe a 18th-century hankie or a complete change for a costume that was not only approved but already shot on, after all that and dressing a hundred freezing extras who keep sneaking their watches and eyeglasses onto set you don't get to leave when everybody else does but no you have to wait around until the last actor gets off the phone and gets out of the damn costume that they have spilled tea all over and which needs to be cleaned by 7 a.m. the next morning!!! You'd go crazy too!!!!

Okay, that's not the costume designer. The designer, depending on their predilections, can avoid the set most of the time if they so desire, because it's rarely the designer who people are looking for when something is required, damaged, soaked or just wrong… It's the wardrobe assistant on the set who is on the front line, and it's the wardrobe supervisor who may be the lucky duck to work off the back of the truck as the designer's second in command. If there's a collar sticking out in the rushes, it'll be the wardrobe supervisor who will hear the complaints. If there's a box of shoes missing in the delivery from the costume rental house, the wardrobe supervisor has to track it down. If the ADs screwed up the fittings schedule, it's the wardrobe supervisor who is going to have to work on Sunday. You see where I'm going with this? It's really not their fault they're crazy.

If they're good crazy, you might only know it by the manic glint in their eye or the sharp occasional cackle. If they're bad crazy, they can be like a black hole, sucking all around them into their orbit of bitterness, misery and despair. It's not great for the cast or the second AD, and there will be tears at some point, hopefully not yours.

None of this should really be your problem, and theoretically you need never know about any of the hysteria or meltdowns going on behind the curtain. The Second manages the backstage area, and the actors will arrive on set for rehearsal in the correct costumes as per the plan. Most of your dealings with wardrobe will involve situations where you need **repeats**. These range from situations when an actor gets wet or otherwise covered in goo, or a costume has to rip in a particular way, or when there is a body double or stunt double. When it's a case of wet or ripping, I always ask for six repeats and I usually get four. (If you can get more, do—it's always a budget thing, and if you think you don't have enough you can speak to the PM about it and get special permission for the costume department.) I ask early, and I repeat the amount of repeats we have at every production meeting, so that everyone, especially the director and DP, are in no doubt as to how many takes we have to get this. Occasionally, you'll get two takes with the same item of clothing, but you should assume that after every take the actor is going to have to return to their dressing room to change.

If it's for a **body/stunt double**, I would request that this double have their own entire costume. You don't want the actor and the double sharing, for reasons ranging from logistics to hygiene. If it's a period shoot and there exists only one of some particular item of clothing, this should not be part of the costume choice for the particular stunt or sequence. The most obvious reason being that if it gets seriously damaged, continuity is blown, never mind everything else. Again, if these conversations happen in prep, and you point out at the production meetings that you will need doubles of particular costumes, there should be no problem arranging this.

The stunt double will also need to be brought in for a fitting, and, if possible, shot on in a test or at least shown to the director and DP so they don't get any surprises on the day. There are certain elements that don't work well on film and no experienced costume designer should be offering them up, but white, black, thin stripes and herringbone can all cause problems on camera and should be avoided (this is the case for extras as well as main cast, of course).

There is one other important rule of thumb relating to watches, jewelry and other items, particularly those specified in the script and which seem to sometimes overlap between wardrobe and props: if the actor wears it, it's costume; if the actor carries it, it's props. A crown, for example, may an important prop throughout the story, but if it goes on an actor's head, costume must provide it. To really split hairs, props might provide a sword and costume the sheath, but ideally, in a case like this, props will provide both. If you're in any doubt, you'll clarify this privately in prep and reiterate it at the production meeting—it should then always be in the shooting schedule, so it will be visible at the production meeting and on the call sheet.

The costume department are also supposed to provide keepwarms—coats the actors can wear between takes if the weather is chilly (the stars will have their own, with their names on the back, and there will be some for general use) as well as thermals if they can disguise them underneath a costume. If the actor is going in the water, the wardrobe department will make sure the costume can fit over a wetsuit, but production, in coordination with wardrobe, will probably source the wetsuit itself. If it's raining or snowing, wardrobe will provide umbrellas, and the ADs should help with the task of sheltering the actors, as the costume department will probably not have enough hands on deck. Wardrobe should also have hand-warmers, hot water bottles, safety blankets and anything else the actor might conceivably wear.

Cast will often wear tissues around their collars to prevent makeup from rubbing onto them, and it's important to cover the costume if the cast have to eat or drink while wearing it. The wardrobe assistant will tell you and/or the second AD if there is an item, such as a corset or boots, that needs a little extra time to put on and a warning given before they travel to set (no one, besides masochists, wants to sit around in a corset all day).

No one, but no one, goes home in their costume, even if it belongs to them. Wardrobe is one continuity issue that even the most myopic viewers will spot, and the risk of an actor losing, damaging or just forgetting the item isn't worth any possible benefit. Along these lines, costumes that are priceless or extremely precious and cannot be damaged shouldn't ever be on the set, as Murphy's law dictates that this will be the thing that gets coffee spilt on it.

If you're working on a historical film, there will be an army of tailors, dyers, assistants and other wardrobe crew beavering away behind the scenes, and your team will need to organize and facilitate the fittings for all the extras, as well as the main cast. (We cover more about the AD teams' responsibilities in relation to this in Chapter 2.) Depending on the size of the project, this can happen anywhere from the wardrobe truck to a warehouse. Besides scheduling, booking and running these fittings (aside from the actual costuming itself), the ADs also need to keep an eye on the extras on set, making sure they haven't smuggled their glasses, watches, books, hearing aids or other personal contemporary possessions onto the set. There simply aren't enough wardrobe people, no matter the size of the crew, to police this entirely themselves, and they'll be grateful for any help you can give them in this regard.

Finally, despite what I said earlier, I have enormous respect for what the wardrobe team do: telling the story in an immediate and significant way, expressing the character in a vocabulary everyone understands, and doing it under significant time and budgetary pressures. Laurence Olivier said that the key to a character is in his shoes, and the best costume designers are truly artists in all senses of the word (and artists are all a little bit crazy, aren't they?).

Props and Art Department

Props function both as a subset of the art department and as a separate department, and it's important to understand the subtle differences. Art department, as described earlier, will have designed and supervised the construction of all of the sets, when on a stage, and approved and dressed all of the locations. The head of the art department is the **production designer**, who supervises the art director, set dresser and all auxiliary crew members. The head of the props department is the prop master, who ultimately reports to the production designer, but supervises a team of their own: the prop buyer(s), dressing props and the stand-by prop team, which generally comprises at least two people. The prop master will almost never be on set, as s/he will be supervising the elements required in advance and after their usage, and often has a lot of paperwork to address. During prep, the prop master will be present at every show-and-tell with the director and designer, and will generally get all props approved by the designer before offering them up to the director. As a First, you can't assume that information you give the art director or designer will be passed on to the prop master—communication is your department, and you'll need to inform props directly yourself.

Most of what the art department does, once you start shooting, shouldn't be part of your reality unless you need to adjust the advance schedule as a result of some change to location or construction time. If a set is still being dressed when you arrive, there is a problem, and if it happens more than once or twice then you need to have a word with the designer. If s/he says that the schedule isn't permitting them to complete their work on time, you need to involve the producer and see whether additional personnel might solve the problem, or whether the schedule needs to change. It can sometimes be a question of resources; if it's bad management that's a bigger problem and up to the producer to resolve.

On the set, the designer, art director or **stand-by art director** may be present to watch the frame, seeing what is included in the shots and ensuring that everything is as desired. They will speak up if the camera is including an ugly plug socket, or ask props to move or re-arrange objects or furniture to their requirements. I once heard an art director choosing which cow we would use for the close-up, as "she's the prettiest." Needless to say, he heard that phrase repeated a few more times by the end of the shoot, but choosing the prettiest cow was his job!

The stand-by **props** people (or props assistants) look after every physical thing in the frame, aside from the cast or animals. Smoking, drinking, papers, briefcases, tables and chairs, you name it, if it needs to be moved or adjusted, it's props who will do it. Often mirrors or picture frames need to be angled for lighting or reflections—props. The door needs to open only to an exact angle—props. An actor is packing a suitcase—props (supplemented by cast clothing they will have sourced from wardrobe). Props will also generally look after small amounts of ambient smoke, steam, water or spray, and up to a few buckets of blood. Breakaway glass, fizzing "champagne," fake beer, wine or spirits are all the props department, and they need to have an ability to handle minor DIY skills and have an engineer's brain. A good prop assistant will know how to use fishing line to make anything move, and will moisten a paper bag to stop it making too much noise. The best props people have a genius for inventive solutions; the worst can't stop telling you how they did it on the last job.

If a prop has a mechanical or other effect, or is beyond a small scale (of smoke, steam etc.), then it may cross the line into **special effects**, and this is, as always, something you need to determine in prep. As with costume, you will sometimes need **repeats**—if a page is to be ripped, for example—and you will need to work out in advance how many they can provide, and what the reset time will be. It is usually quicker to wait for the props to be reset than to try to shoot something else in the interim, as a split in focus can lead to additional time taken for both. After every take, props should re-set automatically, without waiting to be told, even though you will, of course call it.

Any **weapon** is care of an armorer, not props. This is one area where savings cannot be made (see "Weapons" later in this chapter). Outside of a toy or water pistol, all other weapons need to be supervised by a qualified weapons specialist, and if you as the First allow any deviation from this practice then you deserve whatever guilt, and legal action, is attached to you in consequence of an accident. This is not a fluid area, this is how people get hurt and killed. Brandon Lee, the son of legendary martial artist Bruce Lee, died while shooting *The Crow* from a gunshot on set, from a gun that was handled by a prop man, not an armorer. There's simply no excuse for deviating from best practice in this regard.

Locations

We have covered the AD's relations with locations in prep, and once you move to shooting you will continue a similar relationship. Even on the smallest job there are usually at least two locations people, as any company move will require one at each location. Very often, the location manager will be working ahead, while the locations assistant stands by at the set or unit base. It's rare to be on a job where all of the locations are confirmed before the start of shooting, so the location manager may be still photographing potential locations, finalizing paperwork or wrapping up locations that have already been shot on.

Many locations will have specific limitations or requests that should be in the notes section of the shooting schedule and as a banner across the top of the call sheet: no high heels on the parquet floor, for example, or all crew must wear safety helmets or life jackets. If shooting in a private home, there will often be floor coverings laid down, which should be respected and replaced wherever they are out of frame.

If anything on the location needs to be moved or changed, from a tree branch to a table lamp, it is a courtesy to locations, not to say standard practice, to advise them and ask permission before proceeding. It may seem like a delay, but if a location owner gets annoyed they can at any moment demand that we all leave (no matter what it says in the contract), so it's worth always checking with locations before moving furniture, cutting a twig or going into any room. Ideally, locations will have hung signs saying which rooms are private and which are to be used as sets. Needless to say, no one should be using gaffer tape on any walls or other painted areas, when paper tape was designed for this purpose, and no tea, coffee, food or smoking, other than as part of the scene, should be brought onto the set. If this rule is violated, it will be to you that the locations and/or art department direct their displeasure, and they're relying on you and your team to police this when they can't be there. When it's necessary to bring water to set, people should have their own marked cups, and the assistant bringing the water should collect every cup as soon as it is finished with.

In a situation where the locations department are understaffed, it is the duty of the ADs to fill in the gaps: we were once shooting in a cemetery where the set was some distance from the entrance, and one of the ADs was annoyed that she had to take up a position at the gates to direct the crew—she felt that that was the locations department's responsibility, not hers. I was not impressed; my view is that wherever there is a gap, it is up to the ADs to fill in, until such time that it can be addressed. We're responsible for communicating all the information we can, and directions to set are, to me, the most basic of this information. ADs should always be willing to help locations, as we would expect help in return. The two departments often work together when locking off a street or other area to pedestrians—almost always, a combination of locations assistants, ADs and possibly security will work together to keep the set clear and quiet. I suggest a brief chat with those involved beforehand (even if only on the walkie) reminding them that you are effectively in people's homes (even when you're on the street) and you should at all times remain friendly and polite, no matter how rude a member of the public may be. If it gets really bad, you call security. When holding traffic, you will be in direct communication with the responsible locations assistant (or, preferably, manager), and if the ADs are understaffed, the locations assistant will often pitch in, if they can.

This can happen during company moves where the unit are moving from one set and unit base to another unit base at some distance from the new set, on the same day. Ideally, you need four people manning this: one to see out the last of the crew at the first set, another to do the same at the first unit base and provide directions to the next unit base; another at the second unit base to park up and direct crew to set, and a fourth at the second set to facilitate parking up the stand-by trucks and direct the crew to the set. Evidently, in such a case locations and ADs will work together, and if the same people take the same roles at every move it should be relatively painless.

I'm sure it never happens with Teamsters, but often drivers, especially those driving passenger vans or other cars, need constant reminding as to where they're going and what the best route is to get there—BEFORE the director or crew get into the vehicle. The movement orders that were attached to the call sheet should be in every car (even in the era of GPS systems and sat-navs), and the driver should have read them beforehand (Figure 2.24).

Whenever possible, you don't want the location owner present when you're shooting, as it can be quite traumatic for them to see the army of people taking over their house, the heavy black cables snaking through their hallways, and crew treating them like they're in the way. If someone insists on being present, I recommend treating them like they're a producer. Get them a seat near the monitor (if you have two monitors, the crew one is best), offer them coffee and let the director know that they're there. I would quietly suggest in as diplomatic a fashion as possible that they not distract the director, and if there is a producer there, they're generally great at entertaining location owners, who are often so overwhelmed by the whole experience that they sit very quietly minding their manners like a small child on the first day of school. This is how you want them!

If there are any pets in the home, they need to be removed before you shoot. It's not just distracting, it's also dangerous for the animal (you remember my story about the budgie and the smoke machine? No? It's not pretty.) A dog can escape from wherever it's being kept and run into the road, and can be very disturbed by all these strangers intruding on its territory and get scared or threatened. It's best to have the whole family out of town, if not the neighborhood, as long as you're going to be there.

If something does get damaged, you need to inform locations immediately. And at the end of the day, locations get the unenviable job of making sure all traces of the shoot are gone (including garbage), and staying until the art department have restored the set to the way it was before the crew arrived. This can often go late, which is another reason why there should be at least two people in the locations department: someone needs to see out the location, while someone else needs to park up the facilities anytime from 4 a.m. the next morning.

Some very good production managers start out in locations, and if you have a unit manager then lucky you. In any case, the Filmmaker's Code of Professional Responsibility describes the 20 commandments of location filming (see Appendix 2). This lays out in black and white what you should instinctively be practicing, and what you will be responsible for enforcing if others aren't.

Stills

Most shoots can't afford to have stills photographers as full-time crew members, and will employ them on a daily basis, choosing the most visual locations and certain key cast. Stills are crucial to the marketing of the film, and deserve more respect than they commonly get. They are often seen as an intrusion and delay to the business of making the film, but if it can't be publicized, no one's work is ever going to be seen!

Weirdly, some actors have a real problem with stills being shot, and so you should make sure it's on the call sheet, and get the Second to point it out to the actor the night before, so you can discover whether the producer needs to have a chat with them to allay any misgivings they may have.

Stills photographers should always have "blimps" on their cameras to muffle any sound, although with digital formats this is less and less of a problem. The best time to shoot stills is during rehearsals, from as close to the actual camera position as they can get. If this isn't possible, they'll ask for about a minute after the last take of a setup with the lighting exactly as it was on the take; sometimes, they will ask the actors to run the scene, alternatively they may ask for a few posed snaps. There is no sound rolling throughout this time, of course, so you can allow the crew to work quietly in preparation for the next setup insofar as they can.

If stills need an actual dedicated shoot, as in a specific arrangement for a poster or other marketing materials, this should be treated in the same way as you would a scene, on the call sheet and on the working schedule of your day.

Photographers are so used to being resented that they are almost always extremely quick and grateful for any time you can give them. On the photographer's last day, you will often want to arrange a "crew photo," generally at the end of lunch break, and this, too, will need to be announced on the call sheet. It's important to specifically point it out to the POC, so s/he can make sure the production team and off-set crew can attend, as well as informing any other producers who may not read the call sheet in detail but who will be very put out if they're not included. If your stills person is on the crew full-time, you should try to take the photo when the greatest number of principal cast are working. And if you want to be in the photo, make sure you can see the camera!

Transport

Your transport captain can make your day or break your heart. It's one of those jobs the audience will never know about, but whose skills and talents can massively affect how smoothly your shoot goes, how many setups you complete and therefore the final edit of the film. In the US, most drivers belong to the legendary Teamsters union, while in the UK and elsewhere they are simply professional drivers.

On lower-budget projects, the Teamsters will generally take care of any vehicle over 16′ long: trucks, Winnebagos, etc. Ideally, your show will have unit drivers for the cast. Sometimes you might rely on a car service or taxi, but these are, of course, less reliable than drivers employed by the company specifically for this purpose. Moreover, a unit driver will have the experience and savvy to be able to get an actor out of bed (or the bar) and will listen selectively to what the actor tells him or says on the phone in the car, and know which bits of information to pass on. (In the US, PAs can drive cast and crew, while in the UK this isn't standard practice.)

Drivers who transport cast, the director and DP can overhear a multitude, and it always amazes me how some people, especially executive producers, behave as if the person behind the wheel is deaf. I have sometimes asked a driver to listen out if I'm concerned about something, and they have always reported back to me with discretion and valuable information.

The Second will work closely with the transport captain in coordinating the timings and collections of the various actors, the director and any other crew (producer, DP, etc.). Some cast will have the right to sole transport, that is, no sharing, while other more unfortunates will be the first collection and have to sit in the car as however many others are collected. Of course, this is minimized wherever possible, and their time reduced, but depending on the budget and the intelligence of those coordinating the pickups, it can be a long morning before they even get to the base.

In the UK, the truck drivers will help with loading and unloading the gear, and will often grab an apple box for the set or fulfill other requests that may arise. Not so with the Teamsters—they are paid to drive, and this is what they do. That said, they will be expert drivers, and rarely need to be closely supervised. Generally, they will know where they're going and the best way to get there. When you're organizing a unit move, of course the transport department should be involved in any planning, and communicated with as early as possible to get the benefit of their experience and prevent any surprises. In my experience, Teamsters will save your life when you need them, and equally you don't want to make enemies of them.

No unit driver, no matter how expert, should ever be used for stunt work: this is solely the provision of trained precision drivers, and is an inviolable rule no matter what the budget of the shoot. As with armorers or stunt performers, if the production can't afford the driver, it can't afford the stunt.

Visual Effects

Generally, an effect that happens on the set "in camera" is a special effect, and if it happens in post-production it's a visual effect. Of course, the two areas often overlap, and it's important to keep lines of communication open, with the first as a central hub: if you don't know about it, you can't plan for it and it won't happen as it should.

Figure 3.7 *Shooting off greenscreen—as long as the subject is completely surrounded by the key color, it doesn't matter what else you see*

There are volumes written about visual effects, so I'm not going to go into too much detail here. The most common is blue- or green-screen, which is, as it sounds, a quantity of blue or green backdrop of a particular color that makes it relatively easy to "key in" or replace in post. The subject needs to be surrounded on all sides by the key color; however, if you shoot off the color itself that's not an issue, as it is all being replaced (Figure 3.7). The green or blue backdrop needs to be evenly lit, which requires a bit of time or a pre-light.

Shooting static against blue/green is easy to match later; if you're moving the camera, the new background the image will be dropped into will need to match the speed and direction, as well as angle, of the subject being filmed. This is when motion-capture and other elaborate mechanisms come into play.

You, personally, must understand the physical requirements to make the shot work, and it's important to ask all the dumb questions that the director or DP might not want to ask for fear of looking uncool. The First doesn't really need to understand what's going to happen in the computer later, but you must have a very clear idea of how it's going to get there. Sometimes, even experienced VFX supervisors will be vague or dazzle you with tech talk; you must have the nerve to be pedantic to the point of downright annoying, because you won't be able to be fuzzy when communicating to the various departments what the requirements are. Besides, it shouldn't be so impossible to explain. I have worked with VFX supervisors who are geniuses in their own right but find social interaction almost impossible; it's still my job to be patient and insist that they be the same in describing to me what it is they need. Even an effect that seems standard and that you have shot before needs to be talked through step-by-step, as technology advances at such a rapid pace that you don't want to make incorrect assumptions. Better to sound dumb in advance than look dumb on the day.

The single most important thing I can tell you about visual effects is to ensure that the person responsible for creating the effect in post, most commonly the visual effects supervisor, is involved in all of the planning relating to the effect, and is on the set at the time the effect is being filmed. I repeat, the VFX supervisor (or their delegate) MUST be present on the set when the effect is being shot, to ensure that the effect is going to work properly. If not, if there is any problem with it blame will fly in all directions, including yours (especially since in post you're long gone). It can be a little intimidating to step onto a set when you're not there every day, so it's important to make the VFX person feel as comfortable as possible when they arrive, and make sure they find their way to the director's monitor. Also ensure that they know that if there's anything that needs to be adjusted, they come to you. And before you consider the setup complete, double-check with them, as it may be important to do a variation at a different speed or angle to guarantee that it will work. Generally, despite the expense of a film crew, it's cheaper and faster to do as much as possible in-camera, and it often looks better as well.

Catering

"An army marches on its stomach," said Napoleon, and Michael Caine is alleged to have said that when offered a part, his three questions were: "Where is it shooting?", "What's the money?" and "Who's the caterer?" This sounds more flippant than it actually is, for the standard of the catering is symbolic of an overall approach the producer is taking. If the caterers are good, you may trust that you will be treated with a certain amount of respect and consideration. If the caterers are bad—and by bad, I don't mean that they are simply unimaginative or boring, but that you can feel that the food was cooked with hate—you will need to watch your back and double-check that things are being done properly.

This sounds a little extreme, I appreciate, but can I tell you how I have suffered? Ok, I won't, but suffice to say I did one job that we nicknamed "Knife in the Mayo." Say no more. There is a certain amount no caterer can help—if you're shooting in New York in January, bagelcicles are a tasty treat, if you have a chisel to chip some cream cheese off the frozen block. In seriousness, it's worth insisting on decent food, if for no other reason than from a health and safety point of view. It's important that your crew doesn't get hypothermia, and having hot soup to hand can help with that. It also helps with fatigue, which is the main cause of most accidents, not to mention morale. If the food is good, tell the caterer—they'll be grateful for any positive feedback, and many of them are artists in their own right, who like to get a response from the audience.

If you're hearing continuous complaints, you should let the PM know, as they will deal with the caterers themselves. If the director and cast like certain treats, why not pass this on? Anything that can cheer people up is productive, and it's incredible how primally encouraging good food, or a special treat, can be. What you don't want is heavy, rich food that makes everyone want to fall asleep after lunch—turkey isn't a good choice, and even if the crew aren't into salads, the caterers can help by providing fresh, seasonal ingredients that will help with energy levels.

It's always amazing to me how quickly perfectly mature adults become like children in relation to food, and particularly the road to hell known as craft service, or crafty. European crews are always amazed by this element, as they're accustomed to the availability of tea, coffee, and, if they're lucky, some cookies on the side; in North America, I have seen crews behaving like spoiled children at a party, whining about how they don't like crunchy peanut butter. My advice to any ADs, especially on commercials, is stay away from craft services unless you're getting it for someone else.

However bad the food is, it has to be on time. Lunch being late has major time and cost implications, so unless it's a bona fide emergency I would have a very limited tolerance for any lateness caused by the caterers—it's simply unacceptable. The First, however, can torture the caterer intolerably, and expect them to roll with it; it happens sometimes that you think you'll break early, sending the caterers into panic mode; then it becomes clear that you will actually not break early or even on time, but that you'll be going a little late, at which point they try to slam on the brakes so all the food won't be an overcooked mess by the time the crew show up, and then, hey—guess what! We're going to break for lunch in 10 minutes! Can you be ready? "Like hell I can," may well be the understandable (unsaid) response, but its follow-up, "we'll do our best" is what will come back to you (via the Second), when you will probably say "okay, we can break as soon as you're ready" and the pressure is back on the caterers to get it all ready NOW!!!!!

Part of your deal with the crew will also reflect when you may owe a "late break" or second meal. For example, if you plan to continue shooting for more than six hours after you're back in from lunch, production needs to offer a second meal and a half-hour break in which to eat it, or pay cast and crew meal penalties. Many productions address this issue by ordering in pizza or other takeaway delights, as if it's unplanned-for the caterers will be long gone, preparing for their early start in the morning. A line I like from the Canadian actors' guild, ACTRA, specifies "It is understood that 'snacks' (e.g., soft drinks and hot dogs, etc.) do not constitute a proper meal."

It's the PM's responsibility to inform the caterers if there's a change to the call time and what the plate count is, although the caterers will also talk to the Second about these issues informally.

As described in the section on "Lunch" earlier in this chapter, the plate count is a highly controversial issue that you don't want your department to get sucked into, if you can help it. It's simply a total of people who were fed, and for whom the caterer can charge. Even bad food is expensive, at least $20 per person, and so it can easily mount up. If the caterer is accidentally adding five people a day, that's $500 the PM has to find in a week. The PM will often monitor closely how many people the Second has listed be fed on the call sheet, and if things get really bad either the PM or a PA will actually count the number of people going through the line. Either way, a good caterer can be one of your most crucial crew members, and they should be adored accordingly.

ADDITIONAL ELEMENTS

The pessimist complains about the wind; the optimist expects it to change; the realist adjusts the sails.
William A. Ward

As if making the day, managing the departments and running the set weren't enough to be getting on with, there are some additional elements that might be factors across the whole shoot, or sometimes only on one day or even scene.

Sex Scenes and Nudity (Part 2)

Even the most beautiful movie stars have hang-ups and insecurities about their bodies, and I have yet to meet the actor who was entirely comfortable about doing sex scenes. They're an occupational hazard and part of the job, but if you really enjoyed them you'd be working in porn. Because of this, they generally need to be managed with the same preparation and attention to detail you would bring to a stunt, so there are no unwelcome surprises and the actors can put their energy into acting instead of flinching.

The foundations of a good sex scene are in prep, when you will make sure the director has rehearsed (fully clothed) or at the very least had a detailed discussion about the physical action involved. It should be mapped out like a dance: you'll kiss, then he'll put his hand on your breast, you'll run your hand down his back, etc., etc. Ideally, there will even be storyboards, not for distribution but so the directors and actors have a point of reference.

Nudity is almost always an issue. Every female actor will have specific parameters as to what they're comfortable with, and it can sometimes be a little late in the day when the final say on what these limits are is revealed. It's crucial that this is all ironed out before the day of filming. A typical scenario is that the actor's contract doesn't come in until the week before the sex scene shoots; there is an issue with nudity; the producer talks to the agent, who won't budge; then the director talks to the actor, to find out what exactly is possible, discovers the actor won't do the scene as envisaged, and has to re-think the scene!

If you are shooting any sex scene, it's best practice to operate a **closed set**, which should be advertised as a banner on the call sheet. This means any crew who don't physically have to be present when the camera is rolling leave the room before you roll and remain outside until the actors are decent. Generally, there will be a wardrobe assistant with bathrobes for the actors to wear between takes. The First might do the clapper board during the take, letting the second AC go, and if the shot isn't tracking the grip will leave, too. A professional crew shouldn't have to be told twice that it's a closed set, and if you notice any lurkers you need to banish them in no uncertain terms.

There are different forms of protective non-clothing the actors can wear to either mask their privates from camera or prevent contact with the other actor. Commonly known as "modesty patches," among other things, they're as small as is physically possible and often made from latex or some other skin-colored substance. Female actors may also sometimes wear little nipple covers, or "pasties."

If an actor's nudity restrictions are very limited, or for various other reasons, there may be a body double for sex scenes. This is entirely different from the body double who might replace them as a passenger in a car or other nondescript action. Actors often have the right to approve their body double and what physical action the double can do in their stead. These doubles are often sourced by the extras coordinator or another AD, unless the actor has a preferred double that has worked for them in the past. I would recommend shooting as much of the scene as possible with the actors, before shooting whatever pickups or inserts are required to complete the scene with the body doubles. Remember, body doubles get approved by the director, cast member (and possibly DP) in prep, not on the set.

If the director isn't gifted, the First has to assume the role of making sure the actors are comfortable, and the set is warm enough, quiet, professional but not tomb-like. It's sometimes better to have a laugh while doing these scenes than for everyone to get so quiet it becomes tense. If there is no need for tongue, the director should actually say that to the cast, as again they will be more relaxed the more ground rules there are. Occasionally, an actor will have a shot of alcohol before doing a scene like this, which you don't need to know about.

Children, Animals, and the Elderly

As detailed in Chapter 2, children's welfare is legislated for extensively both under federal and local law as well as union rules. Because there are legal variations from state to state, and country to country, the only way to ensure that you are following the law is to have a thorough talk with your PM and second AD. There is further information about US state labor laws in the *Websites and Other Resources* section of this book, but either way you will need to double-check current legislation, union and legal, before every project. If there are any areas of confusion, the second AD needs to follow up directly with SAG (or the relevant union in whatever jurisdiction you are working).

The age of the child dictates the number of hours they may work in a day, the time of day they may be called in in the morning and kept until in the evening, and the number of breaks and supervised study they may have to do throughout the day. In any case, every actor under the age of 18 requires a teacher or chaperone, who can either be the child's parent or a designated minder. Sometimes, one chaperone will look after a number of children.

A certain amount of leeway depends on the chaperone and their view of how the child is doing; they do have the power to withdraw the child if they feel they are being mistreated or are unhappy. SAG also performs spot checks to ensure their standards are being complied with, and the child's times of work will be carefully examined on the production report. It's one area where the First and Second have to go strictly by the book, as a production can be closed down if SAG feels that inappropriate or unsafe actions are being taken.

It's often up to you as a First to evaluate how the child is doing and whether they are being pushed too far, either physically or emotionally. You will need to protect them, in the sometimes overwhelming environment of a film set, and make sure the crew aren't too loud or scary and they watch their language. They shouldn't be plied with sugar or any other kind of substance to raise their energy levels, and if a child cries they need a break, if not to be sent home. Sometimes perfectly decent human beings, when they're directing, become so entirely focused on what they need for the shot that they temporarily lose their compassion, and it can be up to you as the First to intervene if you feel the child is being pushed too far. The shot is important, but the child has to come first.

It is sometimes the sad case that the greatest danger to a child's well-being is their parent, who may be overly willing for the minor to work longer hours or do more than is legally permitted or wise. It will come down to you to make the judgment call, and I think we can all agree that there is no excuse for mistreating children, no matter how important the shot. I know of a toy commercial where the children were kept waiting around so long that by the time they were brought to the set to play with the toys they were all in tears. The agency insisted on shooting them, even in this state, hoping that it would look like they were actually laughing. I never saw the ad on TV.

Animals must ALWAYS be accompanied by a handler, or "wrangler," and the production office will ensure that the handler has all the necessary paperwork to prove the animal is medically sound and legally owned. Dogs are the easiest animals to work with, followed by horses, but even a dog should be rehearsed in the location in which the action is to take place well before the cameras roll. They should also "meet" any cast members with whom they will be interacting, ideally in prep, especially if they have an important story link. It's best not to have any animal on the set other than when they are rehearsing or performing, as it can be a stressful environment (even for humans!). All animals, like children, will have limits to what they can do, and the handler, like the chaperone, will inform you when they feel you're approaching your last takes. Their word is final.

Cats are particularly awkward (as the expression "herding cats" testifies) and any young animal—puppies, for example—may want to please but just be too young to get it. Creatures like rodents and insects will all have their own requirements, which you need to be aware of before the shoot. Snakes can die if the room is below a certain temperature, and wild animals, no matter how contained, are still wild, and no crew members or cast should be in a proximity that might be considered dangerous if the animal were to attack. Even a cow can lose its temper, and a cow can do serious damage to a person or set. Rats and mice create particular safety risks as they leave trails of highly dangerous droppings wherever they go (Weil's disease, from rat urine, can lead to blindness and death); the area they move around should be limited and contained, and anyone who has to touch anything within that area should be wearing protective gloves and be sure not to touch their face or anyone else before washing their hands. As a First, you will always make an announcement about the safety procedures and practices to be followed before the animal is brought to set.

You will also need to know (from production or locations) the contact details of the nearest vet, in case of an accident. It is not good practice to drug an animal to make them more "relaxed" in the case of filming, and there are legal issues pertaining to this that you will need to ascertain from the PM and impart at the production meeting. In some cases, such as working with horses and stunts, a vet will be required to stand by on set, and any time you think there is a risk to an animal you should request this presence. There is no excuse for injuring or killing an animal in the course of filming, any more than there is a human being, and there are very strict laws around animal welfare that are enforced (never mind the bad publicity for the film, and your own guilty conscience). Even if it's an accident, it's your responsibility, and you will be answerable for it if anything goes wrong.

Unlike children and animals, there are no restrictions on the type of abuse you can mete out to **elderly people**, which seems a little unfair. On one very big-budget film in Europe, the extras, children and elderly among them, spent the morning in heavy period costumes standing under a rain machine. At lunchtime, they were told they could either dry off or eat—there wasn't time for both—before they were sent back out into the heavy rain. Needless to say, that violates basic ethics, but that's what can happen when the money clock is ticking.

There may not be laws saying that you can't work an 80-year-old woman for a 12-hour day, but do you really need laws to guide you on this? If in doubt, the rule of thumb might be "Would I make my granny do this?" Chances are, the person in question is someone's granny or granddad and just because they're extras is no excuse to ignore their age. Letting them sit down, offering them tea or coffee or water, and making sure they get bathroom breaks are perks that the other extras, if they have souls at all, aren't going to object to, and the people concerned will be grateful for your consideration. No one needs to suffer or get hurt; it's only a movie.

Background Action

Extras are people, too. I can't tell you how many times I've heard ADs refer to extras "swarming" over the craft service table, or "stampeding" the catering truck as if they're a crowd of wildebeest rather than, simply, hungry people. Yes, of course, there are those who want to set a new world record for dessert consumption, but that's sometimes the case with crew members as well, and we don't treat them with a combination of disdain and disgust. I've worked on war films where the extras playing displaced refugees were unintentionally experiencing method acting—standing for long hours in the heat and cold and being shouted at by the local ADs in a tone I can only describe as abusive. Some of them may have had it easier during the war. This is no way to treat people! Let's imagine the extras as background artistes, actors in their own right, who deserve the same respect as your cast and crew.

The only part of an AD's job that is actually seen on screen is the **background action**, and if you mess it up you won't be in the editing room hearing the curses, but you will hear the silence of the phones. The editor will look at the shot a hundred times more than you will, and will spot any extras' continuity errors, or if the extras are looking down the lens (at the camera). The one thing a producer will go nuts about is if they paid for 50 extras and it feels like 10. I have heard producers say "Where are all my goddam extras!?!" So if you call them out, you need to make sure they earn their fitting fee, lunch, overtime and mileage. You and your team are the only ones responsible for this, and there's nowhere else to share the blame.

When the extras arrive, they will be checked in by the assistant extras coordinator or a designated PA, who keeps a constant flow moving through the processes of breakfast, hair, makeup and wardrobe, with a view to having the entire crowd ready by the time the First has asked for them. Often, as a First, if every last extra isn't ready I'll work with the ones who are to put a shape on the background action; dressing in the stragglers later is easy enough. It's crucial to keep track of how many actually show up, as this will be reflected in the almighty plate count, as well as the actualized budget.

Throughout the day, it will be only the ADs who address the extras; if the director speaks to them directly, it raises their daily rate, which you should make sure the director understands. If they are "featured," that is, have to perform some highly specific action or have an emotional reaction, distinct from the rest of the crowd, they may also be eligible for added fees (see the section on SAG in Chapter 2).

Firsts are generally required to **fill a space** with less people than may be ideal, and there are a number of common techniques to do this. The height of the camera is hugely important in this regard. If the camera is at eye level or lower, you could have a hundred people there and only the first few rows will be seen. Conversely, if you raise the camera above eye level, you will quickly reveal the crowd of extras (or lack thereof). The focal length also has a major impact—the longer the lens, the easier it is to make it seem crowded—not just because the shot is closer. You might have a 50 mm lens at a far enough distance to give you the equivalent of a 25 mm, for example, but the way it compresses the space automatically makes it feel more crowded. My own personal theory is that what creates the impression of crowding is the edge of frame. If you always ensure that the edges are messy, it will give the subconscious impression that there is lots more happening outside the frame. Of course, you'll be making sure that every possible person is actually in frame. Sometimes we lay tape marks on the floor, or even rope off a section, to indicate the area the camera can actually see, so if you have people moving and crossing, in a nightclub, for example, they don't go wandering way out of frame.

Crosses and **wipes** are another way of creating the illusion of busy action. A "wipe" is literally a black shape that passes in front of the camera—usually an extra, but if the wipe is close enough to the lens it really won't matter who it is. It creates the impression of movement and gives an editor a nice cut point. The amount of wipes within a given time depends on how busy the scene needs to feel, and it can be overdone so needs to be used carefully. You also don't want the wipe to pass at the exact moment the actor is reacting to something, so you do have to judge the action of the scene.

Crosses are simply extras moving from one part of the room to another (to continue the nightclub example, people are moving to get drinks or to meet someone across the room). The way to get the most mileage out of a cross is to have the line of action move along a diagonal (see Figure 3.8). This way, they stay in frame for the longest possible amount of time. Equally, if you're shooting a street scene, try to send as many of your extras as possible along the diagonal, even if it means crossing the street (which is a nice excuse for keeping them in frame even longer, and adding to their screen time). These can be repeated only sparingly, unless the lighting or focus is so shallow that you won't recognize the same guy going backwards and forwards like a moron.

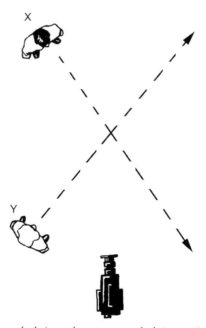

Figure 3.8 *Blocking extras along the diagonal relative to the camera extends their screentime*

One particular bugbear of mine is the common sight of two people talking at each other simultaneously and over-enthusiastically nodding and agreeing all the time—only extras talk like this. The more you give them mini scenes and motivation, even the subject matter they are discussing, the more natural their behavior will appear. Another strategy is to do "**rhubarb**"—that is, to ask them to simply repeat the word "rhubarb" a few times back and forth to each other. Some bright spark decided that this combination of sounds gives a plausible facial movement to background actors, and it stuck. "Peas and carrots" and "watermelon" are also sometimes used in the US.

These words are also often used to record "walla" for sound. If there is a crowd scene of any size, at the end the sound mixer will probably request a wild track of the indistinct but recognizable sound of a crowd of people talking. It's always best for the show to get this in the location with the number of people you have. If they're decent performers, you can ask them to do rhubarb or just talk, and if, as is commonly the case, the very chatty people who you have been asking all day to be quiet suddenly clam up, you can give them a theme to discuss. I would let the nature of the scene provide a suggestion—if there's a break-up, or a secret, or whatever, just ask the extras to improvise on this subject.

Kids as extras are easily mistreated, and should be a priority: used early, preferably as a cutaway not linked to any main action, and sent home quickly. The rule about seeing them applies even more here, as there's no point bringing out a child and not using them. The same age brackets that dictate the requirements for cast children in relation to breaks, work hours, supervision and study apply, and again this is not at the discretion of the ADs but is the law of the land and must be obeyed.

As regards extras' **continuity**, your Second Second should do it automatically, but I always draw a very rough map of who is where, so I can spot it instantly if they have changed position and have their names to hand so I can address them quickly and directly. If someone is talkative or odd I move them right to the back, and the more intelligent and reliable ones go beside the main cast. One of the worst things an extra can do is ruin a take by looking at the camera—professional extras shouldn't need to be told, but sometimes they just can't resist. In North America, many extras are interested in acting and may have some talent. At least, they often take it seriously as a career and behave like professionals. In Europe, it can be something people do part-time, for a little "fun." It's not uncommon to ask someone in the extras crowd to do something specific and to see their hands trembling with fear. My favorite was the piano player who was missing a finger, but that was really the agency's fault—they should have asked him if he was missing any digits before they booked him. Live and learn.

Stunts (Part 2)

I'll admit it: I don't like stunts. Yes, they're often spectacular, but what I don't like is that there is always the very real chance that someone will get hurt. No matter how meticulous you are in preparation, how many times you've rehearsed and how skillful the stunt coordinator and performers may be, there is always the possibility of human error, and you can't ever prevent that entirely. It is my prayer that I reach the end of my career with no one ever getting hurt on a stunt on my watch, and may the same go for you!

A certain amount of the advance work for stunts has been covered in prep, and this is where the vast amount of the work should be done. The defining word here is ILLUSION: the performers are creating an effect, leading the audience to believe something is happening. If you're shooting something that is really happening, it's a documentary or a snuff film, neither of which is the purpose here. Nothing on a film set should be "for real"—not alcohol, sex, or, especially, stunts.

It's extremely useful to have **storyboards** for any stunt sequence—they don't require a professional storyboard artist, if there aren't the resources for one, but it's crucial for the director to think through what they need from each shot before the shoot, so you can set up the stunt for maximum effect. Directors and editors nowadays can't resist cutting, sometimes the faster the better, to create the impression of heightened action, when often, like dance, the narrative of the sequence is clearer in one wide, continuous take (like a good old-fashioned Errol Flynn swordfight, when you could see clearly exactly where everyone was and what was happening—some of the fight scenes in films today are so heavily cut that it's challenging to keep track of who is where, and the effect is ultimately alienating). But this is just my personal opinion. It's likely that you're going to cover the action from multiple angles, and preferably with more than one camera.

Many action sequences are broken into numerous shots, which may often happen at different locations. This is why storyboards are so important; from them, you can generate a shotlist and from this a schedule. It's worthwhile to remember when shooting, and if necessary, remind the director, that the whole stunt is not going to play in one shot, and not to tire out or risk the stunt performers unnecessarily. If a director is digressing from the storyboards, which will have been approved by all the producers and potentially even the investors, you will need to let the producer know immediately, as this has potential political implications, as well as health and safety aspects. Sometimes you may also need to remind less experienced directors as to which piece of the action exactly is required from the shot, as it's easy to drift into the condition of wanting the entirety of the action to work on one angle, when it will never be cut that way later. Each setup has its own particular purpose, which needs to be remembered.

I like to walk through the action several times on set when everyone is in position—at least once at half-speed, so that the camera crew and stunt performers know exactly where each other are going to be all the time. Stunts often work in tandem with special effects (from a glass breaking to an explosion), and as in prep, where all of these departments will be at the rehearsals and the tests, so, too, the SFX coordinator will be calling out during these half-speed rehearsals when the effects will happen. It's not really possible to over-rehearse these sequences and it is far more likely that you will shoot it too early, as everyone is so impatient to do it "for real." It's your decision when you actually feel that everyone is as clear as can be as to what's involved, including the cast and any extras who may also be involved. In all aspects of the stunt, the first AD's word is final. It doesn't matter how much a DP or even the stunt coordinator insists that something is ready or safe; you, personally, have to be satisfied before you proceed. I would recommend that when requesting an adjustment to a maneuver, you preface your request to the driver or performer by saying "If it is safe to do so, please...." This is a habit that reinforces the priority of safety over the coolest-looking shot. If you need to make something quicker, it's worth using the phrase "as fast as you can safely, could you please...." Again, this just keeps safety in the forefront of everyone's minds.

Fights are, in my experience, the most common kind of stunt work; any time a punch or a slap is to be thrown, it needs to be arranged and supervised by the stunt coordinator, who may never be doubling up as a performer. There are simple, effective and well-practiced techniques for making stage combat look real, and people have been using them since the dawn of theater. The basic principle is that it is always the person on the receiving end of the blow who controls the action. Imagine Actor A has Actor B by the hair and is throwing them around: the mechanism for this is that Actor A holds a loose handful of Actor B's hair; Actor B holds Actor A's hand tightly against their head, and Actor B throws their own head around the place, creating the illusion that it is Actor A causing the movement. It's the same with a slap or a punch, where the recipient sells the action in the way they move their head and body.

Anyone operating a weapon or performing a stunt needs to be a qualified stunt performer, cast by the stunt coordinator. Equally, anyone driving a car in an action sequence must be a qualified precision driver, and if they're on horseback have been vetted by the horsemaster. If they have to do anything on a horse other than ride on level terrain, they need to be a stunt performer. Almost anything a character has to do, especially "small" stuff like jumping off a low wall, galloping on a horse or running at height, has to be covered by a stunt double. Some actors say they want to "do their own stunts," and this is a decision that can only be made by the producer. As a First, I would oppose this on principle, no matter how "minor" the stunt or how athletic the actor. The actor may well be capable of doing whatever it is once, but consider 10 takes from multiple angles and the risks increase exponentially. The bottom line is, they're not stunt performers, and the actors should consider how they would feel about stunt performers deciding to "do all their own lines." There should be mutual respect for the variegated skills, which do not automatically overlap.

Stunt **doubles** should, of course, resemble as much as possible the height and coloring of the actor being doubled, and where possible, should be approved in advance by the director. If a stunt involves a particular kind of skill such as rock-climbing or parachuting, the stunt coordinator may choose to hire an expert in this discipline who may or may not have stunt experience but who is correct casting for the particular skill involved.

Anytime any kind of **fall** is involved, you must insure the use of "crash mats," or other pads or mattresses; the performer may also need additional knee, elbow or body armor to cushion the fall, to be provided by the stunt coordinator. High falls are a particularly specific kind of stunt work, that need careful planning and liaison with the stunt coordinator and the operators of any cranes or other special equipment required. The performer will typically have a walkie with a hand mike concealed in their costume so they can give the word when they are ready for action. Performers for high falls get paid per fall and you may be asked to verify how many times the action was performed.

Stunt work involving **vehicles** is often the most dangerous, as they may require the greatest number of different technicians working together and thus the greatest chance of miscommunication. Everyone involved in the stunt must be on walkie on the same channel, and you will announce at the start to "keep the channel clear," which means any communication not relating to this matter take place on other channels (this shouldn't be a problem as the other departments have their own channels, should they need to communicate, but really all the focus should be on the stunt for as long as it takes to achieve). After sufficient rehearsals and before you roll camera, you will need to double-check that every driver, performer and person holding or controlling traffic is on walkie and able to both hear and respond to you. From a vantage point where you can see as much of the action as possible (generally, but not always beside "A" camera), you will get "set" from the drivers, call the roll and then get "set" from each camera. You will also, commonly, on stunts, give a countdown rather than just a simple "and action," typically a "3, 2, 1, action" so anyone who needs a lead-in for speed or positioning has it.

During stunt work is the one time that someone other than the director has the right to call cut; as a First I would always make sure that all of the performers, drivers and cast and crew are reminded of this before the take, so that anyone, at any time, can call cut if they know that something unplanned-for is occurring or something is unsafe.

There should always be a **paramedic** and ambulance standing by during stunt work. This gives anyone injured the best medical attention as quickly as possible, and can protect the company from an insurance point of view. I would always request these elements, no matter the budget of the project, and would consider this medical support an integral part of doing any stunt work that involves a moderate scale of special effects or precision driving work. My ideal scenario is an ambulance crew who have nothing to do. You also need to always know the location of the nearest medical emergency facility, and this should be on the call sheet.

Ultimately, the final call on whether something is safe enough for a stunt person to achieve has to be made by the stunt coordinator, to whom even the producer and director must defer in this judgment. The single most dangerous element on the set is the director trying to change the shot or the action from what was planned for. Because everyone wants to facilitate the director's vision, and generally make the shot as spectacular as possible, as the First you may occasionally find yourself in the lonely position of resisting the director's requests. You have to protect the cast and crew from their desire to make it bigger, better, faster. The BBC have a very informative short film that they show everyone who works for them, and one section demonstrates perfectly how moving a camera position only two feet from its original position leads to a car crashing into the camera and crew. Luckily, in this case, no one was killed, but the footage is harrowing. Some stunt performers are too eager to achieve an effect; I once had to talk down a performer who was insisting on doing a stunt, despite the fact that the dummy had been burst violently during the test; his words were "it's my body." Equally, the stunt coordinator may be willing to try something, but is only responsible for his or her team: you are ultimately responsible for the safety of the entire cast and crew, and have to make decisions with the ultimate welfare of the entire company as the guiding principle, not whether the shot, or you, will ultimately look "cool."

Morally and legally, you need to err on the safe side. Sometimes, you will have to say no, and these are some of the hardest moments you will face in your career. If the director doesn't accept this and insists on continuing, do you stay and try to make the situation as safe as you can, or do you walk away and face potentially damaging effects on your career? The producer is your only hope: they can say no, and have the power to stop the shoot if they feel the situation is unsafe. If they choose to continue, on their head be it; don't let it be on yours.

Weapons

Any kind of weapon, from a sword to a club to a machine gun, is the responsibility of the armorer. If the production is extremely low-budget they may not have an armorer, in which case there can simply be no props on set that could under any circumstances injure anybody: no guns that were once guns, swords with a tip, real glass bottles, etc. If the production can't afford an armorer, then they can't afford weapons. This, like stunts, is not the area for shortcuts.

If an armorer is to be used, they and the actor using the weapon are the ONLY two people to ever touch that weapon. No exceptions: no prop men, other actors, ADs, anyone; and the only time the actor holds the weapon is in the last 60 seconds before the take. Before giving a gun to an actor, the armorer will offer it to the first AD to show them that the chamber, should it have one, is clean and empty. Some guns will be decommissioned by having their chambers blocked with melted steel; in this case, the armorer should demonstrate, pointing at the floor, what happens when the trigger is pulled—hopefully, nothing.

Firstly, no live ammo should ever be used anywhere near a set—that's PAGE ONE. Secondly, props don't handle weapons, only armorers do. Finally, **blanks** are explosives and should never be fired at actors; there is always the chance that some debris might dislodge or cause even minor injury. The skill of filmmaking is creating an illusion, and it's very basic skill to be able to place the camera in such a position as to create an angle in which it appears that one actor is firing directly at another. There is simply no need to do it for real.

As regards blanks, they can be very loud, and crew required to be within ten feet should be offered protective earmuffs. When blanks are fired, gunpowder gas can be vented forward and sideways through the front of the cylinder, not just from the muzzle. This gas is hot, and may contain small particles of powder debris. At arm's length it dissipates harmlessly into the air, but if hands, face or other parts of the body are in close proximity to the vent hole it can cause burns, cuts or abrasions. Anyone using the gun should keep their face and hands well away from the vent hole in the top of the barrel when loading, handling or firing the pistol, and they should only be fired with the arm fully extended and at least six feet from any other person. No loaded weapon should be pointed at another person, even during the shot, and never, ever point blank. There is a story of an actor with a blanks pistol doing a *Deer Hunter* imitation, putting the muzzle to his temple and pulling the trigger and killing himself, which I hope is just an urban myth. Either way, blanks can be as dangerous as live ammo, and need to be suitably respected.

It's a strange trick of the film camera shutter that, when shooting on film, if you see the flame blast on the video monitor it won't be on the film, and vice versa. So when playing back, you're watching to ensure that you *don't* see the blast!

Before any firing of guns or other explosions it is common practice for the First to shout "**Fire in the hole!**" just before rolling camera—the result of this is that no one gets a fright during the take, as they're expecting to hear a bang. (The phrase originated in mines, where miners needed to be warned of an imminent detonation, and was also used by soldiers operating cannons and more recently when throwing grenades into small spaces. We just can't shake the military analogy!) You should also, of course, have alerted the locations department so they can warn anyone in the neighborhood that there will be blanks firing—in some areas, it's illegal without proper permits.

It's amazing how quickly guys with guns or swords become children—swinging them, pointing them, play-fighting. It's understandable; after all, a love of this kind of play may be one of the factors that got them into this business—and completely unacceptable. Actors' and extras' weapons must be handed back to the armorer between takes and especially setups; it's boring and time-consuming, but no one should risk someone getting injured. Sometimes, being a First means being no fun, but it's less fun when somebody loses an eye!

Cameras and Cars

Working with cars in any way is always time-consuming, but as always, planning can minimize the time required and maximize efficiency. The simplest car shot is a **drive-by**, which is, as it sounds, the camera outside the car, typically on the side of a road, and the car drives by. This is frequently shot on a tripod and the camera either pans with or against the movement of the car. Depending on the light and the size of the shot, whichever cast are supposed to be in the car can frequently be doubled; the actor or driver needs to be qualified and insured, though not a precision or stunt driver, and the passenger can be any extra in the right costume and general shape of hair. The term *drive-by* can cover horses galloping past camera, bicycles or any other setup of this type.

The next step up is when the camera is inside the car; with smaller, lighter cameras this can be done hand-held, but it's generally preferable for both safety and operating to have it mounted on "baby legs" (a small tripod) or bazooka (a columnar support), or if the angle doesn't allow for either of these, then the grip may rig the high-hat (a base for the head to sit into, also used in extremely low-angles) on an apple box or two to get into position. Either way, as it sounds, it may require pre-rigging and sometimes the removal of seats.

Whatever the nature of the shot, anytime you're using an onscreen vehicle—a **picture car** or **action vehicle**—you want to make sure the grip has seen it in advance, so he can bring the correct gear. (Without inspecting the car, not only will it take more time, but the grip may also need to damage the interior or paintwork.) Sound will also generally want to rig a microphone, which can only be done after the camera is in position and also takes a little time. What you want is for the car to be parked adjacent to the set while you're shooting something else, so the grip and sound team can have all this rigging done in advance of your arrival.

Shooting with the camera mounted outside the car has an almost infinite number of possibilities. The most convenient, and also the most expensive, is a low-loader or tracking vehicle (also known as an **insert car** or **process trailer**), which is a low-lying trailer that the picture car can be driven onto and towed. This allows the gaffer to rig lights from the attached generator without too much bother, and offers a number of possible camera positions from the towing vehicle. This rig is generally what is being used when you see actors in scenes very obviously not driving the car, as they can sometimes become too relaxed with the steering wheel. It's the simplest rig from which to shoot frontally, although the route choice is critical because it becomes a very long vehicle with restricted turning options. If you are using any kind of towing vehicle you generally need to get police permission, if not an escort, and you still can't mount any light or camera tray protruding any wider than the width of the low-loader itself without closing down the lane of traffic it intrudes into (if it's on the curb side, you still need to close the lane to prevent any knocking into parked cars or signage). The route will need to be scouted in advance with the actual driver of the rig before the day of the shoot, and the route map photocopied to be distributed with the call sheet.

Camera trays (or "**hostess trays**") are typically small platforms that can be mounted on the side doors of a car for a two-shot or single of the actor(s) inside at a profile or ¾ angle. A **hood mount** is, as it sounds, a mount on the hood of the car shooting either toward the actors, or, if the car is not being towed, facing the road for a POV. Wider lenses are generally used when shooting in cars, both because the camera is usually relatively close to the actors, and because they show less shaking than a longer lens.

The alternative to a low-loader is an **A-frame** or **tow rig**, with which the picture car is towed with its wheels on the ground. Both low-loaders and A-frames can be rigged only by qualified and experienced grips, not simply mechanics or any other person who is "good with cars." This is a potentially life-threatening situation for both the cast and crew and the public, so care must be taken. The A-frame is less comfortable and less controllable for shooting, but as with the low-loader, the skeleton crew will usually be in the back of the towing vehicle: director, DP, first AD, first AC, video assist, one props person, the script supervisor and the gaffer, if you can all fit. (If not, props and video assist will travel separately, with the director being given a small monitor or "clamshell" to view the shot.) The sound mixer typically sits in the front seat of the tow rig, or in the trunk of the action vehicle. The rest of the crew who come on the road will be in a "follow" vehicle, normally a van that can fit a crowd that includes hair, makeup, wardrobe, props, the second AC and anyone else, as well as all the additional camera and lighting equipment. An AD will be in this van to communicate with the crew members on board, and the driver. Naturally, if the camera is seeing out the back window of the car, the follow van will actually lead instead. This van will also be carrying any camera cases, props, wardrobe and other bits and pieces that need to be accessible along the way, as well as water, tea, coffee and whatever bits of craft service someone felt like throwing in. (If an actor asks for a coffee during driving scenes you have my permission to pour it on them.) It's useful to have an on-camera follow car (a second picture car) so you can control who follows in shot—the public love to flash their lights, honk or make obscene gestures, aren't they cute?

There is an ongoing debate regarding to harness or not to harness? Some people make the argument that the crew in the tow vehicle—essentially the back of a pickup truck—would be safer if they were harnessed to the vehicle. The opposing view is that this is actually more dangerous, as someone could be dragged behind the vehicle rather than falling free. I have spoken to a cameraman who says he nearly died because his harness became entangled and almost crushed his diaphragm, so I can understand both sides of the story. The best you can do, I think, is to ask those crew involved beforehand whether they would prefer to be harnessed; ensure that there are enough harnesses available on the day should people choose to do so; confer with the grip involved and get his/her perspective on what the safest method is; and inform the PM as to how you intend to proceed. In reality, no one should ever fall out of a towing vehicle—ever. When you pull away, everyone should be seated in a secure position, and by its very nature the rig isn't going to be making high-speed turns. As long as you keep everyone in their secure positions when the vehicles are moving, the harness issue should be a moot point.

The director will probably be given their own walkie, to communicate with the actors in the car when moving, all on their own channel (which you will go onto to give them action and cut, if the director doesn't do that themselves). Some directors prefer a hand mike for this purpose. Even on a beautiful sunny day, it's cold on the back of a tracking vehicle, so you will need to be sure that you and the director are adequately dressed (everyone else should know this, but if you're a real mother hen you can remind them). Also, there won't be any bathroom stops along the way—the actors will need to be reminded of this!

Before you pull away, you will call it and be echoed by the Second Second, so if there's anyone you haven't seen still working in or around the car they can let you know. If you're certain you have the all-clear, you will radio to the driver to pull away. S/he will generally beep the horn twice, then very slowly start moving until you're certain the vehicle is completely clear. You may be carrying two walkies—one on the director/actor channel, and one on the location/driver channel—or using one and flipping between the channels as you go. (That's less possible if it's cold; on the back of the truck your fingers will become less nimble).

No matter how well you have rigged everything in the safety of your controlled parking lot, as soon as you pull out onto the road the DP will want to stop and check everything before you roll, so you will need to have a plan for where this can happen between your base and the chosen filming area.

If you're closing a road it's rare that you will get to actually shut it down for the duration of your filming requirements. It's more likely that the police will agree to hold traffic for you during the takes. (I don't know of any territory where it is legal for film crew to do this themselves.) Depending on the road involved, you will need at least two police, one to stop traffic coming in either direction, and you will also need at least one person stationed on every intersection along the way. The most dangerous roads are those with driveways or lots of houses—it's almost impossible to control every single one, and if a dog, child or car comes out of one of these without looking it can be very dangerous. Locations will have done a mail-drop in advance, warning residents that the road will be controlled on that day at that time, but you still need to be highly alert to any possible public interference.

Likewise, if you have to stop at the side of a road where traffic is not held, crew forget entirely about the danger from moving cars, as they are focused on their jobs. You and locations will want to immediately drop traffic cones to protect the necessary area, and be wearing high-visibility vests to indicate to approaching motorists to slow down. The police should be able to help you in securing the shoulder area safely as well, ideally with some flashing lights.

As discussed in the section on holding traffic, when holding a road for filming, it's useful to have the officer on each end tell you the make and color of the last car they are letting pass, so you can be sure these cars have passed you before you pull out and roll. As always, you need to balance the requirements of the set with those of the police and public and try to avoid a massive buildup or delay for people trying to use the road. If you're shooting at rush hour the police will tell you when you need to release and clear traffic. Often, I will say something like "cut, thank you, please release and clear and let me know when we're held again." There is almost always some little lighting tweak that needs to happen, or a chat between the actors and director, that can take place while we're clearing whatever traffic has built up. If the director wants to go again straightaway, I will say "we're cut but keep it held please, going again straightaway," or occasionally not call the cut at all. If the director is happy to keep going without a long talk, I would encourage him/her, depending on the format, to do several takes within one roll, because the minute you cut someone wants to jump in and tweak a light, a mike, the makeup, what have you. Unless there's actually a technical fault, you're better off just keeping it rolling and going again from the top.

You will want to keep announcing everything that's happening over the main walkie channel, to keep the Second Second on the follow van informed of what's happening, particularly if the producer is in the van.

If a car forms any significant part of a story, by far the most efficient system is to get two cars exactly the same. It's often the case that you will need drive-bys to intercut with the scene for which you're shooting the car interiors, and you don't want to be waiting around while they de-rig the car to do these—it takes some time and it's just a waste. It's also the case that while you're doing the interiors, a second camera could be shooting the drive-bys, in which case the light and the locations are all going to match. There are a number of situations in which having a car **double** is going to save you hours, especially if there's any stunt driving required, and I would request early on from the art department that they only offer the director cars they can repeat.

Vintage cars are a sound nightmare. The owners, even if they're professional movie people, are often proud of the fact that it's the original engine. But these engines, particularly on military vehicles, will completely drown out the dialogue if you try to have one drive past when two characters are talking. Besides this, they are temperamental and often break down at just the wrong moment. In my dreams, the action vehicle companies would replace all of the original engines with electric engines, and we could dub in the authentic sound afterwards and have nice action both outside and inside the cars without tears. (Or hysterical laughter, in my case. On one film we had numerous scenes involving 60's and 70's English army vehicles, and one night at about 2 a.m. when I was looking for a Jeep and saw the vehicle man under its hood for the millionth time I finally lost it and just couldn't stop laughing. The director was slightly concerned for my mental health, but the scale of delays caused by antique "authentic" engines had become comical—at least to me. Sometimes it's laugh or cry.)

Finally, the **process** shot—we've all seen old movies where rear-projection was used to create the impression that the actors, in a stationary car with fans blowing at them, were "driving" down a road in France, for example. This was a staple of 50's cinema, and has also been employed ironically by filmmakers in the '90s. It simply involves a large screen, onto which is projected footage of the desired location, and the actors in a car in front of it (it's actually not that simple, as the projector has to be positioned carefully for the spill light not to affect the car lighting, and yet straight on enough that the image being projected isn't distorting, and of course the angle and lighting of the footage and the actors has to match perfectly). It was effectively a primitive green-screen, done in camera. This is rarely used any more as it just looks, well, cheesy! What is still commonly done is a **"poor-man's process"** for night car scenes. This can be done either exterior at night or in any kind of blacked-out space; the electricians move lights across the stationary car to create the impression of movement, and a few props people or PAs lean on or bounce the car to create the effect of movement. Despite this configuration looking slightly ridiculous on the set, it's extremely effective onscreen and makes a night interior car scene far more controllable—it's even easy enough to add rain, snow, etc. It takes a bit of time to set up, but much less than actually driving around at night.

Tanks, Pools, and Water Work

If a scene or sequence in your project involves underwater photography, or an actor going in the water, you'll need to involve special experts and equipment. Purpose-built **tanks** in studio sets are generally the most film-friendly, as you would expect. Anytime an actor or crew member goes in the water, you'll need a safety diver as a lifeguard, employed to intervene if anyone gets into trouble, with a knowledge of water safety and resuscitation techniques. Even if your camera operator and actor are both PADI-certified divers, when working underwater they're concentrating on other things and can quite easily get into trouble.

The production is responsible for providing suitable waterproof gear for the equipment and personnel required to go in the water, and the number of people going in must be kept to a minimum. You must be satisfied that the water is clean enough and warm enough (but not too warm, especially in bathtubs) for the actor to enter safely, and rehearsals will be carried out on dry land before anyone enters the water. There are underwater walkie systems, but I've never seen them work properly; it's usually easier for everyone to surface and discuss the take before going down again. Most cameras have some kind of viewfinder that the operator can use to frame up, but some don't, in which case s/he is shooting "blind," and it's all the more important for the actor to hit whatever marks are given. Typically, I will hold a long pole at the point on the surface of the water where we want the action to happen, to give both the actor and the operator a place to aim for.

It's important to provide adequate facilities, as close to the tank as possible, for the actor(s) to be dried off warmly and privately. It's also important to have safety blankets and first-aid kits standing by, and on occasion we have even rented portable hot-tubs to keep the actors warm. However, I've been told by safety experts that it's more dangerous to place an actor from cold water to warm water and back to cold again, rather than letting them remain at a constant temperature, even if that's low. This makes the hot-tub idea only plausible at the very end of filming. It's important to get advice from your own water safety expert, as it will be their expertise informed by your specific situation that will form the company policy.

Often, a tank is unavailable or unaffordable, and the decision is made to shoot in a **swimming pool** instead. This has its limitations, as often they may not be deep enough to achieve the effect the director has in mind, and there can also be issues with lighting and color. Pools often have a combination of skylights and fluorescents, and the DP may need the skylights blacked out to control the color temperature of the lighting. The ceiling of the room may need to be dressed, and it's common to have to lay black or green cloth along the floor of the pool to cut out the color of the tiles and create the impression of a lake, pond or whatever the pool is standing in for in the story. Of course, this work must all be done in advance. (For this to be done, the pool owners have to be willing to drain and replace the water after you've left, as you'll be making it dirty, but this is a locations/production issue.) Swimming pools are quite unpleasant to work in, I find, mainly because of the sound—it's very difficult to maintain good lines of communication when it's all so echoey. You also have the added hazard of electricity around water.

The gaffer will ensure that the lights are kept at what he considers a safe distance from the edge of the pool, but you can ask him or her to pull them further back if you're uncomfortable. Theoretically, a film lamp would short and die immediately upon hitting the water, rather than electrocute everybody, but you don't want to test that kind of theory. There are also cables running from the camera to the video monitor that have a potential electrical current, and there shouldn't be any other kind of electrical equipment—including hair dryers and phone chargers—being used in the pool room. Because of the heat, echo, and risk involved, I would try to keep everybody possible out of the actual pool area until required. It'll be faster and safer that way.

Shooting in bodies of water such as **canals, rivers and lakes** pose their own challenges. Shooting on a **beach** is in some ways the easiest of these scenarios, as while you may have the hazards of riptides and currents, the presence of your safety boat and diver will eliminate all but the most freakish of possible accidents. Lakes, too, are comparatively controllable, the main concern being the cold. While shooting in pools or tanks I wouldn't get into the water, whereas in the sea or a lake, given the potential distances between the camera and the director, I would often don a drysuit and go in. (This also allows me to monitor just how cold the crew and cast might be getting, and know when reheating needs to occur.) It's worth having a medic standing by, as in any outdoor body of water actors' and stunt performers' core temperatures can get danger-ously low without their realizing it.

When shooting at a river or canal, for insurance purposes, a sample of the water should be tested to evalu-ate the presence of the dreaded Weil's disease, but it can take two weeks to get the results and, with a river, the water composition will inevitably have changed by this time. Nonetheless, if the water tests positive for the disease, you will need to either re-think the location, or take comprehensive steps to protect the actors and crew. The playing area in a lake must be scouted in advance, on the same day as the shoot, to ensure the removal of any broken glass, garbage or anything else that could cause injury if someone stood or kneeled on it. This rule is even more serious when shooting in a canal or river. By their nature, these waters carry all sorts of foreign bodies along with them, and are constantly bringing new bits of debris in their flow. If an actor has to walk across or touch bottom, the safety diver should stand in for them during all the rehearsals to make sure there is nothing potentially hazardous, and I would encourage shooting any time the actor does the action.

Whenever possible, the actor should be wearing a wetsuit under their costume, and certainly wetsuit booties. If the camera needs to go in or around the water, but wetsuits are excessive, you will ask production to pro-vide waders for the DP, camera operator, first AC, first AD and anyone else who may need them depending on the context. These come in shoe-sizes that will need to be requested in advance.

Even if there isn't Weil's disease in the water, there are more than likely rats living alongside it, so everyone on the crew, especially those carrying gear, like camera, sound and lighting, should wear gloves and be sure to clean their hands and faces thoroughly before touching anything else or eating. You should announce this before filming, and at your request production will supply adequate supplies of disinfectant wipes, that can be easily and safely discarded.

If there is a significant amount of action in and around water it's worth engaging a marine coordinator, who can provide all of the expertise and knowledge to advise the production on relevant equipment, personnel, and timings. Either way, you'll have a water safety meeting with everyone involved well before shooting, and at any production meetings reiterate the protocol and the plan for working in this area, in detail (you may be repeating it at every production meeting as new crew come on board every week, so much the better). At the production meetings you should also ask anyone who can't swim or is uncomfortable around water (or heights) to make themselves known to you privately.

Food Styling

As anyone who has tried to take a photo of a delicious meal knows, making food look edible or attractive on camera takes a lot of work; as Oscar Wilde said, "there is nothing more artificial than appearing natural." From painting peas to blue "milk," every food stylist has a bag of tricks as elaborate as any makeup artist for making something that has been sitting under hot lights for an hour look delicious.

There are two main types of food: that which has to be eaten, and that which doesn't. That which doesn't can be prepared in advance and may not even be food, but some combination of plastic and organic matter that will hold its shape and shine for hours. Food that has to be eaten is of a different category altogether, and overlaps into the zone of health and safety. If at all possible, it's best to avoid chicken, eggs, rice, shellfish, and any dairy—the obvious things that can cause serious health problems very soon after spending any time in a warm room. In prep, you'll want to check what the script or director has in mind for any of the actors to eat, and see if you can guide them into safer territory, if need be. Once you know what they're eating, you'll have to check that none of the cast has any food allergies to whatever it might be, or even phobias (I knew one actress with such a fear of spiders that she couldn't stand spaghetti—I'm not saying it's logical, but we had to deal with it).

When you're shooting a scene that requires food preparation, you'll need to check with locations and possibly the electricians to make sure the food stylist can set up in an area as close as possible to the actual set. (Lots of food shots require steam or other manifestations of heat, and if your stylist is running up a flight of stairs the steam will be gone by the time s/he arrives. Adding the steam on the set never quite looks right, although I have seen turkey breast injected with water quite effectively to produce a juicy flow when sliced. Sounds pretty yucky right now.) The food stylist should be given a call time two hours before their products are required. It takes a long time to load in all the supplies, get set up and prep, besides the actual cooking time. It's worth you or the Second talking it through with the stylist to be sure that even two hours are enough.

Even if a food stylist has an assistant, the props team will work closely with them, as their jobs overlap. The knife that "Dad" will use to carve the ham will be provided by props, but if there are any slices to be already carved, the stylist will do that. Spritzing, spraying, plumping, painting—these are some of the actions the food stylist will perform. The trick to making everything run as smoothly as it can is to have as many repeats prepared as far along the process as possible. So if "Dad" is going to carve a ham, you have three more hams already cooked and ready to be oiled up and brought to set.

Because so much chemistry is often involved in making food look edible, it's generally the case that it shouldn't be eaten—and this includes the crew. When the scene is completed, there is typically a plate of something edible that the stylist is happy to let people eat, and smelling food being prepared for a couple of hours will make anyone hungry. But the firm rule is that no crew member, ever, touches or eats any food or drink before or during the filming. Besides the health risks, it can badly affect the supplies the stylist may have to get through the scene, not to mention continuity.

When food has to be eaten on camera it's both a courtesy and a necessity to provide a spittoon, or bucket, for the actors to immediately spit out whatever they're eating in the take. Some may be shy, others inexperienced, but it's a health and safety issue and you have to insist that they not swallow anything if it's not being filmed—after many angles and takes they can easily be physically sick. At first they think it's gross, then they're grateful.

Unusual Locations: Underwater, Mountaineering, Extreme Weather

As with every other element in filmmaking, preparation is everything. In unusual locations, it can save your life, literally. Every case is different, but the important thing is to find and listen to experts in whatever situation you may be working. In some cases, you will need two kinds of expert: the local, who, for example, will know the tides, the weather patterns and the behavior of the local wildlife; and the authority, who may have a knowledge of the equipment, the governing laws and guidelines for the location and/or the safety and legal regulations.

The basic process of setting up a shot is the same wherever you are. You're trying to arrange the elements in such a way that they can be filmed: block, light, rehearse, shoot. Whether you're on top of a mountain or at the bottom of the ocean, the process is largely the same. The variables are what you investigate, in depth, and envision every possible thing that might go wrong, and how to prevent it.

Helicopter Filming

Filming with helicopters also follows the same basic principles, the difference being that the camera is simply on a higher mount (that, yes, can kill you if you're not careful). As with any additional requirement, you will have a meeting in prep with the director, the PM, possibly the producer, the DP, the camera operator (if not the same person) and the helicopter pilot. It's useful to have a few visual references at this meeting, to discuss the specifics of what the director wants to see in the shot, and thus the helicopter height and lenses. At this meeting you will go through the local safety regulations (every city and state have their own laws as regards how low the helicopter can go and during which hours), and these must be rigorously obeyed. It is often the case that the DP and director will want the helicopter to go as low as it possibly can, and the PM should be able to provide the height restrictions that everyone will sign up to. You will also discuss the logistics of the operation itself: the time of day required and length of shooting time; the gear, that is, the type of camera and mount, lenses and video assist monitor to play back the material to the director and DP; the nature of ground-to-air communication and procedure; and the logistics of setting up in the morning and de-rigging in the evening.

Two kinds of terrain are particularly dangerous for helicopter filming: cliffs by the sea, and mountainous areas with sudden changes in wind flow. I witnessed a crash by a very experienced helicopter pilot who had flown for years in Vietnam. Even he was caught by a sudden freak wave when flying over the sea approaching cliffs in the west of Ireland, and the chopper went into the water. Thank God he and his co-pilot were rescued and survived, but your best chance for a fatal accident in filmmaking is when using a helicopter. Of the 26 fatalities that occurred on film sets from 1980–89, 10 of these were helicopter accidents, making it by far the most common fatal accident on film production for that decade. This is all just to remind you not to underestimate the risks involved, as some helicopter pilots are macho types who like to appear quite casual about the whole business.

Helicopters can land pretty much anywhere there is a wide, open space with level ground and no electrical cables nearby. If you're going to request a landing somewhere other than an approved helipad, the pilot himself will need to see the place—on the ground—in advance of it being used, and you will need to confirm with the PM that it meets all the applicable safety regulations and local ordinances. Locations will also want to inform local residents if it is in a residential area. Anyone moving around the helicopter should follow without fail some basic safety procedures, which you will make clear: always walk around the front of the aircraft and never walk under the rear propeller, even when the rotors are stationary, as a gust of wind can blow them down below head height. When the rotors are turning, you should only approach the aircraft after getting a signal from the pilot or ground staff.

There are at least two ways of filming from a helicopter: from a gyro-rig fitted to the helicopter itself, with the camera operator on the equivalent of a geared head inside the cabin, or with a door open and the camera operator filming out the door. You can guess which of these I prefer. If it is not to be a mounted camera, you need to ensure that the operator has experience in this kind of filming, not just for their own safety but also for the quality of the shot: you don't want them practicing on your picture. Naturally, if this is the case, everything needs to be locked down and harnessed. You do not want to lose anybody or anything from the cabin, and you can't have gear falling to the ground, where it could kill somebody.

The big question is whether the helicopter is filming general views, in which case the director and DP will probably be based at the helipad, or whether they're filming action that you set up on the ground, often simultaneously with other cameras. If it's the latter, the helicopter takeoff and landing position will often be at some remove from the set, and you and the PM will probably need to arrange it so the camera crew can report to this location. Depending on the shot, you and the director may also report to the helipad, then watch back a pass by the helicopter crew to ensure that the general idea is correct. If the helipad is some distance from the set, and the camera needs to be returned to the main unit, I would ask the DP and the PM whether it may be worth employing a second camera crew—first and second AC—for the day so main unit aren't delayed waiting for them to return after the helicopter footage is completed.

The First will probably be at the set, with the director, directing the action (typically lots of vehicles and extras), with one of your team at the helipad (on a mobile phone if the walkies don't reach the distance. Don't forget to arrange to get the helicopter's ground-to-air walkie from the helipad to you!). If this is going to be the case, it's even more important that the action the director wants to cover, and the nature of the shot, has been communicated very clearly to the camera operator before the day of filming. Communication will be much more difficult at a remove.

The action should be rehearsed before the helicopter goes up; and knowing how long it will take to fly into position, you should be ready to roll when it arrives. You will have two radios at this stage—your set walkie and your ground-to-air radio—and you'll call all of the commands the way you normally do, in this case waiting for your "set" from the helicopter crew before calling action. You will get notes from the director and the camera operator before running the take again. As with any stunt, you'll preface your requests to the pilot with "if it is safe to do so, please…"

Some wireless transmitters can send the picture from the helicopter to a director's monitor, but as with any wireless technology, they can suffer interference from other signals, especially in built-up areas. In some cases, when both the director and camera operator feel that they have the shot, they may both travel to the helipad to review the footage, while everyone else waits for the word (ideally, the crew could break for lunch while this is happening, but you'll probably be shooting helicopter footage in either the morning or late afternoon, as the light is better). If the director travels, I would go with him/her so you can see clearly what, if any, adjustments need to be made, before doing another take.

When everyone is satisfied that you have the shot, the helicopter will return to base and you will move on. If the camera assistants need to de-rig and bring the footage or gear back to set, they can meet you at the next location, along with the PA who was standing by at the helipad.

Even when following all of these procedures, there is still always danger involved with aerial filming, the greatest of which is wind. No matter how much it has cost to arrange all of the elements, if there is a forecast for high winds, the pilot should never be pressured into taking off regardless. As with any member of cast or crew before a risky activity, you should have a private chat ensuring that they are not feeling uncomfortable with any aspect of the action.

Second Units and Splinter Units

Helicopter filming is commonly one of the elements that is delegated to a "second unit," typically either a smaller unit operating out of the main unit base, shooting any shots that do not require main cast, or a completely distinct unit shooting some time after main unit has wrapped. Shots with doubles, stunt doubles, landscapes, drive-bys, passage of time, establishing shots, inserts and cutaways, elements for visual effects—anything that can be taken off the main unit schedule can be added to the second unit. There is a big difference between second camera and second unit: second camera, or "B" camera, is part of the main unit, shooting the same material as the "A" camera. If the "B" camera is sent out to get additional material, it becomes a second unit (or, if it is simply a camera crew with no additional crew members, a splinter unit).

While the second unit is generally supposed to be smaller than the main unit, it does require proper crewing levels to be effective, and sometimes main cast do have to join second unit for certain shots—for example, if a set is about to be struck, or an actor or a location wrapped. If this is the case, the main unit director will endeavor to join the second unit for these shots, but often will have to instruct the second unit director in his/her stead.

The second unit can be directed by another director (in TV, it may commonly be a director from another block of the series, who already has a relationship with the cast and crew), a stunt coordinator (if the action involves stunts), the producer, the visual effects supervisor, or even a first AD who is trusted by the production. It depends entirely on the nature of the material being shot and the makeup of the production.

It's ideal to have a second unit shooting as late in the main unit schedule as possible, as things may consistently fall off the main unit schedule and can thus be mopped up all at once. Sometimes this isn't possible, due to location or cast restrictions, and second unit happens in the middle of the shoot. It's quite a thankless job, working on second unit, as the main unit crew often feel put-upon that they have to service both units, and you are very much second fiddle when it comes to requests for gear, costumes and personnel. The second unit call sheet will be attached to the main unit call sheet, often in a different color to distinguish it, and may have later or earlier call times than main unit so everyone isn't trying to prepare or eat at the same time. It's rarely the case that the main unit director or DP is thrilled with the material that second unit shoot; it's inevitably slightly different than they imagined, and having to get shots approved before moving on can be a frustrating and time-consuming experience for all involved. It's much quicker and more pleasant the further from main unit the second unit is, and the more independently it can operate.

Another kind of second unit is the "beauty unit," a camera crew that are sent off to get the sunrises and sunsets, scenery and other beauty shots that the main unit could never spend the time on. As simple as these shots may seem, if you are required to have even a single extra, and you will often have a double or two, you're immediately into a situation of requiring ADs, wardrobe, makeup and hair. It's also crucial to have a script supervisor on the second unit, who can keep track of where these shots are designed to fit in and label them correctly for the editor, even more so if you're shooting a cutaway that has to drop seamlessly into a scene that has already been assembled: the original script supervisor's notes on lighting, filters, lenses and continuity are all going to be crucial. Special effects may be required as part of an action sequence, and it's your job to ensure that costs aren't cut so deep that you're operating unsafely: stunts and special effects cost money.

If you're firsting a main unit with a director who knows that a second unit will be shooting, you need to guard against the tendency to over-delegate to second unit. It can be more expensive to re-create a set and lighting to match the scene than to take the 20 minutes to shoot the cutaway there and then. I would advise against considering second unit as a cure-all for not completing scenes, because when the second unit schedule is budgeted for, the producer might cut some of the shots out for purely cost purposes, and the scene won't cut elegantly without them. It's also not uncommon, when shooting second unit, to be suddenly summoned to main unit to pick up whatever shots may remain of a crowd scene or other sequence, while main unit move on. In this case, the second unit shotlist falls off the schedule, meaning certain shots may never get done. If you feel that your director is getting too comfortable with the sense of backup that second unit provides, you may need to talk to the producer about it.

As a main unit First, you should be generous and supportive toward the second unit crew. I find it shocking sometimes how main unit First ignore the needs of the second unit, as if it's not their problem. They can be stingy with time and personnel, and apart from the selfish attitude this reveals, it's just plain old bad karma, as the roles may so easily be reversed on the next job. Everyone on the project is on the same team and it's in everyone's interests that the show be good. So if you're firsting the main unit, you need to make the time to have a proper meeting with the second unit first about everything that's being shot, and if you're firsting the second unit you need to be skillful about getting the information you need from every department without getting in their way. If you hang out on the main unit set for a day and choose your moments carefully, everyone will have a few moments when they can and will want to talk to you about the upcoming shoot.

Union Rules and the Shop Steward

Only the one who isn't rowing has time to rock the boat.
Jean-Paul Sartre

Once your crew deal (Figure 2.12) is solid, there's generally not much else people are going to fight over. Given the various unions and their differences and the speed at which amendments are made and adjusted within varying contexts, I'm only going to touch on the shop steward here. Originating in the early days of the labor movement, a shop steward was, and still is, the representative of the workers' interests in dealing with the employers. On a film crew, despite the different departments' entitlements, they may still unite behind a single shop steward if there is an issue they are feeling strongly about. The shop steward can be from any department, and will typically approach you to broach the issue.

Whatever it is, you need to listen carefully and be sure that you actually understand what the issue is. Once you do, it's important to then ascertain the shop steward's view on what the possible solutions may be. As in any negotiation, you won't commit to a solution at that time (unless it's something that is completely within your control and is easily addressed), but will pass on to the production manager exactly what was said in this conversation. Labor relations are ultimately not your responsibility, and by assuming too much involvement in the discussion you can actually badly mess things up. Many's the time something that sounded perfectly innocent to me turned out to have major implications behind the scenes, which I had no way of knowing. So pass it all on to the PM as soon as possible after the conversation, and let them direct you as to what the next step is. They may suggest a course of action for you to follow, or they may wish to have a direct conversation with the shop steward themselves: it's their decision, not yours. (Thank God! You have enough politics to deal with on the set!)

The only time I've seen crews getting really disgruntled is when they feel like they're being treated with disrespect—and I have heard some producers say "fuck the crew!" So there can be legitimate grievances, and there can be whining. Your opinion as to which it is is irrelevant and should be kept to yourself. The one thing, as a first AD, that you must never do is rabble-rouse or become an advocate for either cause. You are a member of the production department, and a member of the crew; you are there to fairly represent the interests of both parties, and remain exactly ON the line, not crossing it in either direction.

International Variations

The process of filmmaking is universal—the same things always need to happen—but there are, of course, cultural differences. An entire book could be written about the various ways in which film productions differ, but for the purposes of brevity I will give a brief overview of my own experience, and welcome readers to add detail of their own.

We have, so far, dealt mostly with the North American system, in which strong unions operate and in which nonunion productions imitate, to varying degrees, the common union practices employed. The UK and Ireland operate on a similar system to North America, and it's very easy for crew to work between the two. There are a few main differences, as outlined here:

Unit call in the US means the time the crew open the trucks; shooting call is when the camera and cast are expected to be completely ready. In the UK system, it's possible for the camera to be built and ready on set at unit call. The standard shooting day is five to five and a half hours until lunch, an hour's lunch break (plus travel time to and from), and five to five and a half hours after lunch. Calls are rarely pushed, as turnaround encroachments can be paid for. The second AD doesn't do the production report, but the Second Second keeps track of on-set elements and provides this information to the POC in the form of an AD report. Despite the fact that the on-camera time in the UK system seems to be an hour shorter than in the US, the fact that more happens before unit call makes them almost equivalent in terms of shooting time, and the UK version less punishing: a 10- or 11-hour day instead of 12 to 13. The variation on this is the increasingly common practice of 10-hour continuous days, especially on features.

Lunch is also handled differently—as described earlier, the US system is either a half-hour break after "last one through" the lunch line, or a "walkaway" that allocates an hour plus walking time, whereas in the UK if there is a break it's one hour from when it's called (plus travel time to the unit base, if necessary).

One major difference is in the grip and electrical departments. In the UK system, electricians set up the lamps and handle all of the accessories that go with them: scrims, nets, flags, trace, gels, etc. The grip belongs entirely to the camera department, and is supported commonly by four stand-bys: a painter, rigger, carpenter and stagehand (sometimes a plasterer replaces one of these trades). These four have dual roles as assistants to the grip—laying track, lifting the dolly, helping with cranes, etc.—and in their own trade, should something need to be rigged, painted, hammered, etc. This system works well if you are shooting primarily on stages with constructed sets that may require these skills; if you're shooting handheld on location with no constructed sets, having four stand-bys hanging around is unnecessary, and there have been disputes and labor relations issues relating to this for some time.

On the continent, German crews operate roughly similarly to the North American style, particularly when it comes to turnaround. In the UK and Ireland you can pay a penalty for encroaching on someone's turnaround (within reason). In Germany, you have no option but to push the call. They also have some practices that may seem strange to English-speaking countries, such as the location manager and the first AD often being the same person, and I have heard of other doubling-up such as the caterer and the production manager being one individual. I hope that's a myth.

French crews, in spite of the term "French hours," don't always work continuous days, but only on late calls, when they start at lunchtime, then work a 9-hour day straight through. The peculiarity of the French system, to outside observers, is that they take very seriously European legislation relating to the 39-hour week. French workers cannot legally work longer hours, and timesheets are provided to the authorities, so it's a challenge for French producers to achieve what they need to while maintaining this length of shooting week. I'm told that if a French producer decides to stand down a crew for weather or some other issue, if they cancel the day the night before they don't have to pay the crew for the lost day.

An assistant director, in the French context, is much more of a creative collaborator than a logistics expert. Locations and production fulfill many of the duties a first AD would on an English-speaking set, and while the AD runs the set, they do so entirely from the director's perspective, rather than trying to accommodate the needs of the producer or PM. This reflects the elevated status of the director as auteur and artist, rather than technician, that is prevalent in French culture.

Many productions now choose to shoot in Eastern Europe, particularly in Budapest (Hungary), or Prague (Czech Republic). Unless you're working as a local, you will probably be on a production that brings HODs, if not entire departments, from overseas, and retains the habitual work structures of the place of origin: UK productions work the UK system, and so forth. The biggest differences are largely social: fewer crew may own cars, for example, which might impact on the transport requirements, and often more crew—particularly in construction—may be employed. Not to mention the difference in the food!

When **working abroad**, it's always best to adapt to the local practice rather than trying to change the habits of an entire crew. Your initial conversation with the local PM will be even more crucial than usual, and it's also worth trying to talk to a First from the area to get their advice, as they will have the front line information. As long as the requirements are on the call sheet and you're able to communicate effectively enough to get the shots, that's all that matters. And you may even find that there are some elements of their system you might want to incorporate at home.

If you're coming from an English-language context and working in a non-English-speaking location, in some places the crew will have enough English to understand you; in others, they won't, and you may have a translator to interpret for you. This can lead to some "lost in translation" moments, when you can clearly see that the translator is putting their own spin on the information, which is particularly possible when s/he is also a First in their own right. I would suggest that instead of another First, you hire the equivalent of a local second second AD, so there is no opportunity for a power struggle. I would also be sure to hold your position in terms of literally calling the shots— "places, stand-by, rolling, action," and so on, as most of these terms are comprehensible no matter how little English people speak, and if you stick to them, by day 2 they will all understand what you mean. Unfortunately, perceptions can sometimes be important, particularly if, say, you're a female First in a patriarchal culture: you must be seen to be running the show, and calling the roll is a simple and clear demonstration of who's in charge.

When working abroad or entertaining foreign crews as visitors, it's polite to remember that they think you're as weird as you do them, but it's a collaborative medium so the objective is to find the common ground. It's worth also remembering that at the end of the job when they fly back home, you have to continue to work with the local cast and crew. Sometimes foreigners of any description (including us abroad) can be a little casual when it comes to the treatment of location owners or crew members. But no matter who's shouting at you or threatening you, you can't lose sight of the fact that you live in this town and want to work again—at home.

Coping with Disasters

> *Only two sailors, in my experience, never ran aground. One never left port and the other was an atrocious liar.*
> Don Bamford

All happy shoots are alike; each unhappy shoot is unhappy in its own way. There isn't a one-size-fits-all solution to a horrible shoot, and unfortunately sometimes all you can focus on is doing your job to the best of your ability and maintaining your integrity—and one of the best things about this business is that every job, eventually, ends. (There is a hoary old phrase that hopefully you'll never feel the urge to repeat: "who do I have to fuck to get off this picture?") When the problem is a **personality** issue, you generally just have to get on with it as best you can. Things happen; mistakes will be made; we're all only human. If you screw up, the best thing is to take responsibility quickly and do your best to fix it—as in all walks of life, the cover-up is usually worse than the crime. However, if you get a fully fledged disaster, there are some steps you can take.

Firstly, is **medical attention** required? Anyone who suffers any kind of injury must be advised to get medical attention, and if it's a bang on the head they have no choice: you must insist that they leave the set, right then and there, to be examined by a doctor. This is non-negotiable, no matter how much people want to be brave, you don't want to be the person in the story afterwards when it all goes wrong.

Secondly, **inform the PM** and producer immediately—probably via the second AD who has the production phone. Even if whatever has gone wrong may not seem like that big a deal to you, there may be insurance implications you're not aware of. If an actor vomits or the director trips on a cable—you have to pass it on, even if there's no apparent consequence. If it turns out to be something serious, delaying the information could create legal and financial complications.

Thirdly, you may have to **adjust the schedule**, and this needs to be done as soon as possible, either at lunch or wrap, whichever is soonest, ideally in a meeting with the PM. As soon as there are potential changes, alert the location manager and make sure the second AD knows, so they can highlight any potential difficulties you may not know about. You'll also need to alert the other departments about the change.

Finally, you are going to want to be sure that every course of action is recorded and **documented**, so you could, if necessary, prove in court how you acted in the interest of the cast and crew welfare. The best way to do this is through the script supervisor, and subsequently the POC, to make sure the events are recorded on the notes and subsequently in the production report.

The Bond Company (Part 2)

If your disaster is really serious—let's say your lead actor breaks his leg, or the set is washed away—there will be an insurance claim. You will need to be sure you have a copy of the schedule as it was at the time of the disaster (the office will probably have one, but you should save a copy separately, dated, of your own), so you can then compare the pre-disaster schedule with the new one. The production company will need to prove to the last detail exactly what the effects of the disaster were on the schedule and all of the associated cost implications, and this can take some time and a lot of paperwork. In theory, the company will be compensated for the costs involved, but no insurance company hands over money without a fight, so it's a laborious process to demonstrate and receive payment. Hopefully this happens during the main block of principal photography, when everything and everyone are still together, even if a few extra days need to be added on.

If your disaster is bigger still—let's say a producer completely fails to control a director, the rushes don't resemble the script and the budget is going to be gone before the end of filming—the Bond Company may step in. I've never been on a job where it has actually happened, but I've been on a few where there were murmurings about the Bond Company, in the manner one might quietly discuss the visit of Charles Manson or Jaws. This is the all-time worst thing that can happen (from a production point of view and obviously not including injury or death). It simply means that the Bond Company assert their ownership of the film and can proceed to complete it in any manner they see fit. This generally involves firing either the producer, the director, the cameraman, the First, or all of the above—and that's if they choose to continue filming. They may simply pull the plug, hire an editor to make a film with the footage acquired thus far, and sell it to whoever might buy it.

Although most bond company production supervisors come from a production background —and thus know how to read call sheets and production reports—they are not paid to care about the story or quality of the film beyond its purely commercial value. You really don't want to see or hear from a bond executive during the shoot, and if you do it's the first foot in the grave of the production. Most TV shows are not bonded, and more and more features are shooting without bonds; but if you see them coming, your shoot days are numbered.

Paperwork

One could argue that what separates fly-by-night productions from the big time is paperwork. Put another way, you could have an Oscar-winning movie, but if you don't have the paperwork to prove that you can sell it, the film will be buried forever (*Tomorrow La Scala* is a case in point—a brilliant movie, whose distribution was scuppered by music clearance issues). As a First, you'll be responsible for shooting and one-line schedules, DOODs, and the call sheet. Your Second Second may provide an AD report, and your extras coordinator will be managing your extras chits or vouchers. After these, the most important paperwork in your life will be the **production report** (see Figure 3.9), called the progress report in the UK.

In the US, the second AD creates the production report, while in the UK system it forms one of the main elements of the POC's job. It's compiled from the pile of script supervisor notes, camera sheets, sound notes, AD report, and any and all other documentation crossing his or her desk. It's the after to the call sheet's before—and, all going well, it simply translates what was planned for on the call sheet into what actually happened on the production report.

The production report is delivered to every producer, investor and, generally, distributor, as well as the Bond Company if there is one. Firsts have the right to be copied on these, and you can ask the POC to include you as it may not happen automatically. There are a couple of numbers you will immediately look at on this form: the setups completed (as distinct from the slates or boards), the first setup after call completed, the first setup after lunch, and the times of lunch and wrap. This is, effectively, your report card, and if these times aren't consistently reasonable, questions will begin to be asked in the offices that receive this report. You may well be asked why it's taking an hour-and-a-half every morning to get the first shot, and if you see it yourself in black and white you may be able to either take steps to improve that, or go to the PM or producer to discuss the reasons with them before they come to you.

Also recorded on this document are the cast's working hours, the number of extras, the all-important plate count, and, of particular interest to all concerned, the amount of screen time being shot each day. If this is for TV it will be broken into episodes, and in any case estimated timings will be in a column beside the actual timings. It will be relatively clear at a glance whether the project is running long or short, and conversations will start to occur about what might be done to address either issue.

The most interesting section of the report is the Notes, where anything unusual will be described, and where your comments to the script supervisor relating to any delays, accidents or other events will go. Occasionally, your note will not be on the report, and you should check with the PM whether they chose, for their own reasons, to discard it, or whether it simply didn't make it through the notes process. If there is anything entered into the section "scenes scheduled and not shot," you may want to have an explanation in the notes section. If there is anything entered into the "scenes shot but not scheduled," all the better for you!

Finally, the red-letter section is whether the production is any amount of time behind; you won't need to wait to see it on the production report, but it's good to know what the investors know about (or don't)!

There are many different names for **release forms**, but their purpose, for both people and locations, is to give the company permission to record their image and sound and use it for whatever purposes it may choose (See Figure 3.9). The extras' release form is usually included in their voucher, so they don't get paid without it, and for cast or day players these permissions will be in their contract; for crew, in the deal memo. The only time you'll need to get a release form from someone is if a member of the public walks into your shot, for example, but you should always have a few in your bag just in case someone "off the street" ends up on your

"Fab Series"
DAILY PRODUCTION REPORT NO.   2

Producers: Joe Soap, Jane Doe, Guy Fawkes   **Director:**   John Doe   **Date:** Monday, 3 October 2011

Schedule Start Date:	10/02/11	**Location of Work**		**Scene Numbers**	
Schedule Finish Date:	11/07/11	**Location** Studio 5, Smith Street		**Scheduled:** 903 (1-5/5), 904 (1-4/4), 131	
Estimated Days:	24			**Completed:** As above	
Days to Date:	2			**Pt. Completed:**	
Remaining Days:	22	**Unit Bas** Studio 5 Backlot		**Sch. Not Shot:** 904(3/4) pickup	
Days Over (Under):				**Shot Not Sch:**	

DIARY / SCRIPT SCENE INFORMATION / SLATE NO.S

DIARY		SCRIPT SCENE INFORMATION	Scenes	Pages	SLATE NO.S	
Unit Call	11.00		Scenes	Pages	Prev:	218
Turnover	1125	Completed today	3	1 5/8	Today:	33
Lunch Start	1600	Previous	7	4 5/8		
Lunch Finish	17.00	Total to date	10	6 1/8	To Date:	251
Unit Wrap	2210	Script total	96	86 7/8		
Total Hours on Set	9.52	Remaining	86	80 6/8		

		Estimated Time	Floor Time		
	Completed today	06.15	08.30	Daily Average Setups	19
	Previous	46.55	01.00.14	Daily Average Screen Time	05.17
	Total to date	53.10	01.08.44	Daily Average Pages	3 1/8
	Script total	01.57.37	Difference between estimated time & floor time to date	Daily Average Scenes	5
	Remaining	01.04.27	+15.34	Daily Average Gigs	273

ARTIST	ROLE	PICK UP	CALL	ON SET from	to	DAYS WORKED	EXTRAS
12. Moustache Man	Taxi Driver	1130	13.00	1330	18.52	2	20 c/o Movie Extras
23. Diva Queen	Jill	845	10.45	11.30	17.15	1	5 drivers
24. Hunk E. Guy	Jack	10.00	10.45	11.00	17.50	1	
23x. Daree Deville	Jill Stunt Double	O/T	10.00	10.00	14.00	1	
24x. Butch Fella	Jack Stunt Double	O/T	12.00	13.00	17.50	1	
						*Work Finished / Role Completed	

CAMERA GIG	A CAM	B CAM	SOUND CARDS		CATERING	
	A CAM	B CAM	Previously	2	Crew Meals	30
Previous	356	0	Today	1	Cast Meals	9
Today	198	0			Extras Meals	4
To Date	554	0	To Date	3	TOTAL	43

ADDITIONAL EQUIPMENT / FACILITIES/ANIMALS	CAST & CREW TRAVEL	ACTION VEHICLES	ADDITIONAL CREW
Giraffe Crane		Jill car	1 x Wardrobe Trainee (Coz McGrath)
Tow Rig		Jill car double	1 x Add Grip (J. Geranium)
Dog		Stunt car	1 x Stunt Driver (Sam Bam)
Police Escort			1 x Paramedic (Chancer Mullen)
Arri 435, Split Diopters, Iconix			Stunt Coordinator Bill Fallover

COMMENTS

Shooting was briefly delayed when Ms. Queen trapped her hair in the car door, resulting in some anxiety but no injury

Ima Goodboss
Line Producer

C.C Producers, Director, Line Producer, Broadcast Executives, Investors,Producers Assistants,
Accountants, APOC, Script Supervisor, First AD, Editor, Insurance Company, Bond Company

Figure 3.9 *The Production Report: your report card*

set. (In the US, of course, this is more serious, as you would need to "Taft–Hartley" the person, but in many other territories a simple release form will do.) This is especially common if you have a mock-documentary element to your project, where "real" people may, wittingly or otherwise, be involved in the action.

There are also local (to the territory) regulations on how much you can see of people in a crowd; typically, you can shoot a general crowd, as at a football match or on a street, as long as none of their faces are so particularly identifiable as to become "featured." Likewise, sometimes you may be shooting in a location such as a bar or restaurant that is open to the public. In this case, some crews post notices with wording to the effect that "shooting is taking place in this location today, and your presence here indicates your permission to be filmed." This doesn't legally absolve you from any responsibility to get release forms, but it certainly reduces the potential for someone later seeing the picture and deciding to sue.

Location permits are required for many public amenities, including roads and streets, depending on the locale. It's not your job to secure the permit, but you need to know that you have one. Copies of these should be in the mobile production office, or, if there isn't one, in the possession of whomever from the locations department is supervising the shoot. These are different from the **location contracts**, created for any privately owned location.

If there is a question mark around the permit, I advise you to keep filming while the discussion is happening, if at all possible. The best strategy is to introduce the person asking whether you have permission to the location manager or their assistant, who will get them at some distance from the set to have the conversation. If the questioner is stubborn or savvy to film sets, they may position themselves in front of the camera, in which case you will have to evaluate whether there are any cutaways or other material that may be captured in spite of the disruption. If it transpires that there is no permit, you may quite easily be evicted from wherever you are, causing serious expense to the production. Part of the blame will stick to you if blame is flying around, which is why you want to be sure everywhere is properly cleared.

Schedule Drafts

Once you start shooting, every time you make a change to the schedule you need to re-name it (in Stripboard Manager) with the date amended. This will become an important paper trail in the event of an insurance claim, which may happen after you wrap on the project. All of these drafts will be distributed, as a matter of course, by the production office, but as a courtesy at the end of the picture it's convenient for them if you give them an electronic copy of the master schedule file, in which they can access all the incarnations of the schedules over the course of the prep and shoot.

Rushes Clearance

Originally a crucial part of filming—when shooting on film—rushes clearance was a message from the lab that the dailies were intact, with no physical or chemical problems in the processing system. It usually came from the POC to the first AC, who would inform the DP. As a First, you would only hear about it if there was a problem: a scratch, a focus issue, or sometimes the negative simply gets mangled in the lab. Depending on the nature of the problem, you may need to re-shoot, which is why you'll hear about it from the PM.

Shooting on film still involves these lab reports to reassure everybody that nothing is going wrong—this can also be useful on location, when shooting in a remote place where viewing the dailies can be difficult and often delayed until days after the relevant shooting day. On digital, there may be no lab but simply an ok from the post house to confirm that all is well. Either way, rushes clearance is the signal to the art department that a set can be struck or undressed.

Chapter 4

Wrap

Talent wins games, but teamwork and intelligence win championships.
Michael Jordan

The Wrap Party

It's often the case that the longer and more painful the job has been, the wilder and more decadent the wrap party is. As much as you deserve to go completely wild, the embarrassing stories from office Christmas parties are no less applicable and worth remembering here. Because the job is over, it may feel like you may never see any of these people again, and that can have romantic possibilities, as well as the temptation to let people know what you really think of them, both good and bad. But even in major cities like LA and New York, I can tell you from experience that the film community is small and you are more than likely going to come into contact with everyone on the cast and crew again, whether on the next job or in 20 years' time. I would advise anyone to treat the wrap party like another part of the job. If you need to go berserk, do it with the friends you had before the job started. It may make the wrap party less fun to treat it as a part of your professional life, but it means you'll still have a profession in the morning.

Getting Paid

Since firsts rarely have agents, it's up to you to make sure that you have a deal memo (if not a contract) and a paycheck. The paycheck should come at the end of every shooting week. In prep, the producer might beg for a week or two of grace, as the last couple of weeks before filming can be crunch time in terms of closing various deals, and on independently financed films this is a plausible request if you trust the integrity of the producer. But once you start shooting, checks are issued by the end of the week. If they're not, you need to quietly find out who else isn't getting paid, and call a meeting with the PM, producer, and a few relevant HODs to find out exactly what's going on.

Unfortunately, occasionally a show will go into production without the money to pay the crew, and disreputable producers will try to finish the shoot without paying everybody all they're due. This is not only annoying, it's illegal. But more important than that, the crew has the right to refuse to work until they get paid. If the Teamsters or SAG haven't gotten their money, then the show will automatically close. If it's just the nonunion crew who are getting stiffed, it's still a huge threat to walk away, as the producer will be hard pushed to replace everyone at such short notice, especially once word gets out that people aren't getting paid. I was on a show once where halfway through, people had to decide whether to stay on for free or walk away, and most of the crew actually felt sorry enough for the producer that they stayed on. Whatever the deal you arrange, it needs to be made up front and adhered to.

In your original deal, you should discuss overtime, phone bills, petrol, mileage, per diems, hotel rooms or any other possible payments you may be entitled to. Any conversations after the job are too late, and many producers will simply not pay up. If you're seriously getting ripped off, you may need legal advice.

Getting Fired

> *The absent are never without fault. Nor the present without excuse.*
>
> Michael Caine

Unfortunately, this will probably happen to everyone at some stage, and is often no reflection on your skill or ability. If a movie is going down the Swanee, even if it's because the director has a drug habit, the first step the producers or the bond company can take is to fire the first. (The next is to fire the DP, and if the message still isn't getting through, only then will they fire the director—this is the worst-case scenario for all concerned, as the actors' contracts may be linked to hers/his and even if not, unless he's a monster they don't want a new director once they've started shooting.)

You may, of course, be fired for something you did or didn't do. I had a PA once who was incapable of answering his walkie, and when I berated him for it told me to fuck off. That was an easy decision for me, but the production had to keep him on for another two weeks in the office and the PM informed me that he was the only person with the power to fire anyone! (The PA in question then tried to corner me at the wrap party to explain that his behavior was all because of issues with his mother. Ah, the glamour.)

Or maybe you're just in over your head—the time I got fired I was on a horrible film in New York acting for the first time as a second AD. I was spending the night in the office and still not getting through my work (I now know that the POC was taking advantage of me by getting me to do her job). When the first told me she didn't think things were working out, I agreed, thanked her for her time and offered to stay on until they found someone else. She was shocked by my response, and I was thrilled to get off that picture. It didn't ruin my career; I just wasn't ready to upgrade to second and especially not on a show that size, with an Oscar-winning young actor, a first-time director, and a first who was famous for blowing out walkies screaming so loud at her crew.

Either way, when and if it happens, my strategy would be to make as clean and graceful an exit as possible, and people will quickly forget about it. Quitting, in its own way, can actually be more dangerous.

On one 18-week TV series on location, we never once during the whole shoot completed the call sheet. It was obvious why this was happening: the director would report to set at call time, spend hours rehearsing the first scene while the crew sat around bored to tears, and at least one scene would fall off the end of every day.

I tried everything in my power to fix the problem, but the producers were indulgent and as it continued I started to despair. It violated every bit of my training and objectives as a first, and I felt that I couldn't bear it any more. I discussed leaving with the camera operator, who had, among other projects, been a staple of the Bond films. He gave me some very good advice: "If you leave now, they'll blame you." Even though nothing would change, the disaster that this project's schedule had become would be linked with my name, and the way gossip works, who knows what story would be repeated around the industry. I stayed, we eventually wrapped (missing, I kid you not, a third of the scripted scenes) and the series went on to win the extraordinary title of the "Best TV Series in the World" at a prestigious TV festival that year. Go figure. So far, I've never actually quit a job: the beauty of this work is that there is always an end. If I were confronted with abuse, I would take action and make complaints, but there is nothing you should experience in the workplace that should force you to leave; rather the situation should be corrected. As I mentioned in relation to stunts, but it also applies here, sometimes you're better off staying and making the situation as safe as you can for everyone, rather than walking away.

If you do have to leave, you must give notice (whatever your local laws dictate) and you have to work as hard as you would if you were staying during your last days. Typically, if you don't insist on being paid your notice, you can go straightaway, but as when being fired, it's an opportunity to show class or the lack thereof, and it doesn't have to be the end of your career if you handle it with manners.

Commercials, Music Videos, Corporates, Shorts, Student Films and Demos

I put all of these extremely varied forms together only because I have until now been expressly covering features and TV shows. As I've said elsewhere, the general principles are always the same, but the language may sometimes be a little different.

The biggest difference between **commercials** and other forms is the extraordinary amount of attention paid to each individual shot. You may commonly have three shooting days to produce a 30-second commercial, for example, and you may do literally 25 takes of each setup. Some people from film and TV backgrounds tend to sneer at this process, but in fact it should be respected as a different medium. Pack shots—just as it sounds, pictures of the pack—may be tedious in the extreme and a fascinating display of obsessive attention to detail, but they are also lucrative: commercials are one of the few media where non-union ADs actually get overtime, so in my view if they want to spend 3 hours on a shot of a stick of butter that's fine by me! As long as you've done everything in your power to make things run smoothly, the agency can take as long as they want discussing the logo.

Ah, the agency—they, and the client, are the other big difference between commercials and other formats. On every ad, there will be a video village reminiscent of that on other sets, but on this one the group behind the monitor can be far less reticent about expressing their ideas, and far more comfortable telling the director what to do. Smart directors invite their commentary and collaborate with them; some resent them and tell them to get lost. But ultimately, they're paying all our wages, so they deserve some respect even if they haven't a clue what they're talking about and are thinking more about what their boss will think than whether the shot actually tells the story. People in advertising can be quite nervous about losing their jobs, which explains some of their obsessiveness in relation to elements that may be imperceptible to someone else.

The agency will also be the signatory on the SAG agreement, not the production company, and they will often cast, book and pay the extras, if not the actors, themselves. Because of this, commercials often try to operate without a second AD, and the production company staff will do the call sheet (often, one that covers the whole shoot rather than individual days, and includes the crew list and vendor list) and help get the cast through the works. As it sounds, this system can create more work for the first as you'll have to fill in the gaps, and also can take longer, particularly as everyone from the agency and the client company will want to sign off, yet again, on the characters' "look," and will often change the brief entirely on the morning of the shoot. Some ADs get frustrated by the apparent sloppiness of commercials compared to drama production, but I just try to accept it, enjoy it and contemplate the overtime.

What commercials have in common with **music videos** and the other formats is a distinct lack of paperwork— even the call sheet will probably be created by the production company, which means the second, if there is one, is totally occupied by liaising with cast and transport, but often has time to spend with you on the floor. Aside from the issues discussed regarding playback, music videos tend to have exotic locations and/or elaborate sets and lighting requirements, so it's critical for the first to evaluate how long everyone needs— you don't want to start the three hours of makeup (and if it's a girl band, it could be at least that much) after lighting is ready. Instead of an agency and client, you'll have a record label, who are often as demanding as the artists. It was a record company exec who, when the artist was delayed in traffic, pointed her finger in my face and yelled "You better fire somebody now!" I would have liked to fire her.

What I love about both music videos and commercials is that, at the high end, you get to use all the cutting-edge toys available in the industry. They are pioneers of technology and new visual trends, and you'll often get to use gear that could never be afforded—for either time or money reasons—on a typical drama set. Lenses, cranes, even the cameras are often new and different, and it can educate you about how the various elements work by seeing them in practice. Camera assistants are often happy to share their knowledge with you about how and why the choices are being made (DPs and directors often less so—they seem to worry that you're going to steal their ideas), so I always use them as a mini-film school about the latest gear.

Corporates at the highest end are like glossy, big-budget movies, and at the lowest end I've heard them described as the last step before porno. Either way, they're generally the same as any commercial, with less money but an equally involved client or agency.

Shorts, student films and **demos** or **freebies** need to be approached carefully: the director will often have overambitious ideas, and you need to be realistic without being negative. You need to proceed very carefully if the script involves children, animals, stunts or effects, as the director will be by definition inexperienced, and could be walking into a disaster. You will need to ensure that all of the relevant insurances are in place (more so than you would on a professional job), as well as permits, agreements and contracts. Shorts will typically try to shoot longer days than is advisable, and a lot of that can be avoided if the director understands the options. It can be useful to ask the director to talk you through the shots of every scene, as you can then produce a shotlist to reflect whether that's achievable. A half-hour per setup is as fast as you're ever going to move, so if the shots don't fit, prep is the time to address that. Hopefully, the producer will also understand the restrictions involved; if they don't, you'll need to explain it to them. If you're working on a freebie, that shouldn't affect your professional integrity: it's a job, and you should behave just as you would as if you were getting paid.

How Low Can You Go?

As I've described earlier, whether you're shooting a clip on your phone for YouTube or a 70 mm studio blockbuster, the basic principles are the same: you capture the images, edit them and share them. Many lower-budget pictures try to re-invent the wheel, and while I have a horror of the waste that can go on on bigger-budget pictures, I do believe there is a limit to what can be cut back before the cuts are so deep they have a negative effect on the picture. Obviously, certain elements are invariably expensive—historical or period pieces, obviously, need a lot of money to look acceptable, and the lack of it can lead to unintended comedy. (Imagine a scene—shot for a major cable channel—set in the 1700s, in which the main actors are in a tent, while outside we are supposed to believe there is a major battle raging. Occasionally, a day player will enter and describe the number of dead and wounded. In my view, this is a perfect example of the worst-case scenario: not enough money to shoot the action, and not enough wit to adjust accordingly.) Special effects and stunts are expensive—and this is not an area to make savings: either cut the stunt or pay the price, don't have your buddy do it instead. Visual effects are getting cheaper all the time, depending on your skill or the favors you're able to pull. But typically, if you want to make a film and you don't have much money you want it to be contemporary and have as few characters and locations as possible. On one low-budget film I worked on, the writer had made a virtue of necessity, and combined several characters into one recurring role, whose recurrence became part of the comedy. Either way, having the Receptionist and the Waiter speak is adding hundreds of dollars to the budget with a stroke of a pen—it's not cheap and it's often lazy; sometimes, it's limitations that inspire real creativity.

That said, the following is my list of the minimum shooting crew you need to make a professional film or TV project:

Writer
Director ⎬ These three can all be the same person
Producer
Production Manager
POC
DP
1st Assistant Camera
2nd Assistant Camera
First AD
Second AD
PA
Location Manager
Sound Mixer
Script Supervisor
Hair/Makeup Person
Costume Designer
Art Director
Stand-by Prop

You'll notice that I don't have a single electrician or grip. That's intentional. These are often the most expensive members of the crew, with the most rigid limitations in terms of when and for how long you can shoot. Your DP will hate it, but plenty of great movies—including Oscar winners—have been shot with available light, with no dolly or cranes, and some of them not on film. If you really need lights for a particular scene, you can hire a gaffer and an assistant, but then you'll also need a grip: do you really have the time and the money? When shooting on HD or other digital formats, many of the conventions we consider normal are hangovers from the days when you needed a 10K just to see the actors. Nowadays, even on film, you can control the look with available light, clever use of exposure and filtration, and, above all, the most important element of the DP's craft (in my view)—framing. This is a controversial subject that I won't take up any more time with here, but I would encourage anyone starting out not to assume that you need electricians, grips and lights. You'll be sacrificing a lot of other things—like extras, cars and shooting time—so you need to be sure that you really need them and you're not just getting pushed into having them. You can absolutely make an award-winning feature film with only the crew listed above.

Conclusion

There's no thrill in easy sailing when the skies are clear and blue,
there's no joy in merely doing things which any one can do.
But there is some satisfaction that is mighty sweet to take,
when you reach a destination that you never thought you'd make
Unknown

Sooner or later, whether it has been a pleasure cruise or a perfect storm, it will come to an end. No matter how long you have been yearning for wrap, it always comes suddenly, and like a woman after childbirth, eventually the pain starts to fade and you may even start to feel nostalgic about the fun parts (and there will always be some fun parts!).

I hope it's clear that being a first AD is an exciting adventure, never dull and always full of surprises. It's a job that's challenging, demanding and creative, and will use every cell in your brain and every trace of your diplomatic skills. In fact, the skills you develop as a first are useful in any walk of life: management, logistics and leadership are always useful. Firsting is always a subjective experience and there may be many times throughout this book where you disagree completely about the way to do something, how it should be described or what the purpose is. This isn't a problem: everyone has to evolve their own style, and this book is my very personal opinion, based on my own professional experiences. I look forward to hearing your thoughts on the website (www.runningtheshowbook.com), where you can also find templates for the paperwork discussed throughout the book. I hope, also, that the site and Facebook page can become a forum for firsts from many traditions, where we can compare notes and potentially evolve more productive ways of doing things. The community of assistant directors is just that: we understand each other's lives better than anybody, so our differences should encourage and inspire us to keep learning, and keep rolling. I hope this book will serve its purpose as that friend at the kitchen table and the navigation manual when you're out on the high seas. In my dreams, you can learn from my mistakes so you won't have to find out some of the things in this book the hard way. But every journey is different, so I wish you good luck, and may the trade winds fill your sails!

Appendix 1

SAG Tier Budget Thresholds

50 K – 200 K: Ultra low-budget

200 K – 625 K: Modified low-budget

625 K – 2.5 m: Low budget

2.5 m – 10.2 m: Basic Agreement

More information is available at www.sag.org/productioncenter/theatrical/documents?quicktabs_6=1#quicktabs-6

Appendix 2

Filmmakers' Code of Professional Responsibility

Reprinted with the permission of FilmL.A., Inc.

Dear Neighbors: At FilmL.A., we work to create an environment where on-location filming is conducted with professionalism and courtesy. Our job is to coordinate permits for on-location filming in a way that minimizes the impact of film production on your neighborhood. Production companies are obligated to adhere to this Filmmakers' Code of Professional Responsibility. If you find a production company is not complying with the provisions below, please call us at 213.977.8600, day or night.

Dear Filmmakers: You can count on FilmL.A. to apply our knowledge and expertise to help you film in local neighborhoods. Maintaining a positive working relationship with community members will help ensure continued access to the greatest variety of locations. As a guest in area neighborhoods, you are obligated to treat the public and the location with courtesy. The provisions in this code are a part of your permit.

1. The production company must comply with the provisions of the film permit at all times.
2. The Filmmakers' Code of Professional Responsibility will be attached to every permit, and both must be shown to any member of the public that asks to see them.
3. Productions arriving on-location in or near a residential neighborhood shall enter the area no earlier than the time stipulated on the permit.
4. Moving or towing vehicles is prohibited without the express permission of the local municipality or the vehicle owner.
5. Cast and crew must observe designated parking areas. Parking of cast and crew vehicles on public streets is prohibited unless authorized by the film permit.
6. Parking on both sides of public streets is prohibited unless specifically authorized by the film permit.
7. Production vehicles may not block driveways without the express permission of the local municipality or the driveway owner.
8. Noise levels should be kept as low as possible. Generators and vehicles producing exhaust should be placed as far as practical from residential buildings. Do not let engines run unnecessarily.
9. Cast and crew are to remain on or near the area that has been permitted. Do not trespass onto neighboring residential or commercial property.

10. Designated smoking areas must be observed, and cigarettes must always be extinguished in butt cans.

11. Removing, trimming and/or cutting of vegetation or trees is prohibited unless approved by the owner, or in the case of parkway trees, the local municipality and property owner.

12. If not specified in the permit, an area for meal service and consumption must be designated. All trash must be disposed of properly upon completion of the meal.

13. All members of the production company should wear clothing that conforms to good taste and common sense. Shoes and shirts must be worn at all times.

14. Crew members should not display signs, posters or pictures that do not reflect common sense and good taste.

15. Cast and crew shall refrain from using lewd or offensive language within earshot of the general public.

16. Cast and crew must not bring guests or pets to the location, unless expressly authorized by the permit.

17. All catering, crafts service, construction, strike and personal trash must be removed from the location.

18. All signs removed (or erected) for filming purposes must be replaced (or removed) after use of the location unless otherwise stipulated by the location agreement or permit.

19. When departing the location, all signs posted to direct production company personnel to the location must be removed.

20. When production ID passes are issued, every crew member must wear the pass while on-location.

Appendix 3

Some Filmster Jokes

The Life of a Lightbulb

How many X does it take to change a lightbulb?

DP: One. No, two. Maybe three. How many do we have on the truck?

Director: I asked for a chandelier.

PM: Does it have to be a lightbulb?

Electrician: Three—two to change the bulb and one to fill in the timesheet.

Grip: Two—one to change the bulb and one to talk about how they did it on the last job.

Actors: None, my character wouldn't do that.

First AD: One, it looks good, let's shoot it!

Teamsters

Why is a horse in the Teamsters' logo?

They're the only two animals that can sleep standing up.

How do you know a Teamster's dead?

He drops his donut.

What do you call a Teamster in a suit?

The defendant.

Appendix 3

How can you spot the Teamster's kids in the playground?

They're the ones sitting around watching the other kids play.

What's the Teamster's definition of foreplay?

Back it up, back it up...

Glossary

A Selection of Some Commonly Used Terms

10-100: walkie talk for "in the bathroom"

Abby Singer: the second-last shot of the day

Action vehicle: a car that appears in shot

AFS: After false start, when you have rolled camera but not called action, and then cut

Alan Smithee: a nom de plume used by people who wish to remove their names from the credits

APOC: assistant production office coordinator

Apple box: wooden crates that come in quarter, half, and full sizes

Back to one: reset to first positions

Base camp: also known as unit base, the location where all of the cast trailers, honey wagon, facilities, etc. are parked

Bounce: lighting term; any surface used to reflect, or "bounce" light onto a subject

Butcher's: as in, "to have a butcher's," meaning "have a look," from the Cockney rhyming slang (butcher's hook = look)

Buzz (focus): when a shot goes out of focus for a moment

C-47: a wooden clothes-pin (metal in the UK) used by electricians to clip gels and diffusion to hot lamp "barn doors"

C-Stand: metal stand for hanging flags, nets, gels, etc., and as a point of reference

Cast list: names and representatives for all of the cast; even the generic version should be treated as confidential

Camera wrap: the camera is finished, but the cast and crew may remain to do wild tracks or stills

CGI: computer generated image—any image created in post, not in camera

Contact list: also known as the vendor list, the companies that provide all of the equipment, stock, and other materials required

Cookie: material put in front of a light to make a pattern, such as leaves or a stencil

Copy: walkie talk meaning "understood"

Counter-track: where the camera moves in the opposing direction to the subject

Glossary

Crew list: also known as the Unit List, a list of all crew with phone numbers and addresses

Cutaway: usually a shot of an inanimate object

DFI: different fucking idea, or, change of plan

Drive-to: mileage rate, paid to cast, crew, and extras driving themselves to a local location, calculated as the round-trip distance from the production office to the set, multiplied by a fixed rate per mile (as in, $.50, for example)

Drop/pickup: the time between a cast member's working days

Dutch head: (from "Deutsch") a head that allows the camera to sit at a 45-degree angle from the horizontal

Elbow: as in, "to elbow"—to get rid of, or "lose"

EPK: Electronic press kit, often a one-to-two-person crew shooting "making-of" footage for publicity

Encroach: to break turnaround, known as a "forced call"

Eubange: camera equipment—an arm that extends from the tripod or dolly to position the camera in an otherwise inaccessible position

Expendables: (UK: consumibles) materials such as tape, gels, etc., that are used and discarded during filming

First team: the main actors

Floor plans: maps of the set with symbols marked in for actors and camera positions; de rigeur on multi-camera shoots

Flying in: on the way

Football: the paperwork the second sends back to the production office

Go to makeup: you're in the shot

Got a 20: meaning a location, as in, "has anyone got a 20 on the director?"

High-hat: a base that allows the camera head to be mounted as close to the floor as possible

HMI: Halogen Metal Incandescence—a lamp whose color temperature is the same as daylight

HOD: Head of department

Honey wagon: the toilet truck; sometimes includes the AD's office and some actors' cubicles

Hot set: a set that is being shot on, in which everything is continuity and must not be moved (if lunch happens in the middle of a scene, the first will announce that this is a "hot set" and mustn't be touched)

Insert: like a cutaway, usually a shot of an inanimate object

Joan Collins: the lowest possible *f*-stop, as in, "wide open"

Late call/Split day: a day with a call time later than normal, typically to get night scenes without going past midnight

Lights: baby, blonde, brute, chimera, dedo, midget, joker, junior, inky, kino, leico, redhead, rifa, sky pan, space light, spider, wall-o, wendy, and many more

Magic/Golden hour: the hour before and until sunset

Matt box, filter tray, French flag, eyebrow: camera accessories

Master: a shot that lasts the length of the entire scene

Martini: the last shot of the day

Mickey Rooney: a small tracking move, or a "little creep"

MOS: Without sound

ND: nondescript, as in, 20✕ ND street crowd

Negative fill: the use of any material to absorb light and stop it reflecting back onto a subject

Overcrank: shooting the film at high speed, so that it plays back slow-motion

Overlap: either repeating action from one setup to another, or actors slightly interrupting each other's dialogue

OT: Overtime

Paganini: a one-inch or less piece of wood used by grips to level or adjust height of any object

Per diem: a payment given on overnight locations to cover food costs

Pickup: a shot that is intended to cut into a scene that has already been filmed

Picture car: like an action vehicle, a car that appears in shot

PM: Production manager

POC: Production office coordinator

Poly board: 8′ or 4′ piece of polystyrene or foam, black on one side and white on the other, used to reflect or absorb light

Raw stock: unexposed (unfilmed) film or tape

Reset: everything back to first positions

Reverse: the complementary angle to the one just taken

Room tone: recording of the "silence" of the set, for use in editing

Running all the way: the same as "flying in," it means on the way

Scale: the basic minimum payment for a union member

Scrim: metal nets to cut the intensity of lights

Second team: the stand-ins

Second unit: separate small crew for insert shots, stunts, etc.

Selects: the takes the director likes and wants "printed" or used in the edit

Sequence: a number of shots or scenes to be joined together in the edit to create a single montage

Setup: anytime the camera is repositioned creates a new setup; however, if the lens is changed but the camera doesn't move this is a separate shot and slate, but the same setup

Sharp: in focus

Soft: out of focus

Spanish: to "lose" or get rid of something

Talent: the actors, and sometimes the director (don't take it personally)

Turnaround: the amount of time between wrap and call the following shooting day

Undercrank: shooting the film at slow speed, so that it plays back as fast motion

Unit manager: a bridge between production, locations, and the ADs, who manages set operations

Video Village: On-set video playback area

Walla (rhubarb): indistinct crowd noise, as in a restaurant, background conversations

Walkaway lunch: when the crew is given the opportunity to buy their own lunch locally

Wild tracks: dialogue lines recorded only by sound with no camera rolling

Wrangler: manages animals, etc.

Wrecking crew: makeup and hair department

Websites and Other Resources

Running the Show: An AD Community

Sample schedules, call sheets, production reports; a hub for ADs and other filmmakers at www.runningtheshowbook.com and on our Facebook page

Training

DGA trainee scheme: http://www.trainingplan.org/

http://pabootcamp.com/

http://www.filmskills.com/

Job Search

http://www.media-match.com/

www.Backstage.com

www.hollywoodreporter.com, "movies in pre-production" section, requires registration

www.TheFutonCritic.com

www.FilmStaff.com

www.ProductionHub.com

www.EntertainmentJobs.com

www.Mandy.com

http://www.infolist.com/

All state film commissions have websites that list what productions are coming to town and when

Child Labor

www.sag.org (USA)

http://www.childreninfilm.com/Rules-State-Labor-Info.aspx (USA)

http://www.direct.gov.uk/en/Parents/ParentsRights/DG_4002945 (UK)

Crew Work Practices

http://www.callacrew.co.za/workingconditions.php (South Africa)

DGA www.dga.org (USA)

IATSE http://www.iatse-intl.org/home.html

PACT www.pact.co.uk (UK)

www.screenproducersireland.com (Ireland)

General Code of Safe Practices for Production

www.csatf.org/bulletintro.shtml

Filmmakers Code of Professional Responsibility http://www.filmla.com/neighborhood_filming.php

Filmmakers' Community

Filmmakers' Alliance: http://www.filmmakersalliance.org/Home.html

"On-Set Entertainment": http://www.pajuice.com

Ready, Set, Recycle: http://readysetrecycle.com – Greening the Entertainment Industry

Go For Filming: http://www.goforfilming.com/locations/advanced-search/ – Locations search website

"Overheard on Set" Facebook group: http://www.facebook.com/home.php#!/group.php?gid=205289678723

Youtube videos of crew in-joke animations: http://www.youtube.com/watch?v=05EGkXDUE3c&feature= player_embedded

Sample templates for contracts & other documents: http://www.filmcontracts.net/contracts/form. php?id=1018

The Independent: http://www.aivf.org/

The Independent Feature Project, produces the IFP market and the Spirit awards: http://www.ifp.org/

Scheduling Software

http://www.entertainmentpartners.com/Content/Products/Scheduling.aspx Movie Magic

http://celtx.com/Celtx

http://www.junglesoftware.com/home/Gorilla

https://www.scenechronize.com/ Scenechronize

Breakdown colors: http://en.wikipedia.org/wiki/Breaking_down_the_script

Online Glossary

http://www.imdb.com/glossary/

Recommended Reading

Bruce Block, *Visual Storytelling*

Caleb Clark, *The Production Assistant's Pocket Handbook*

Mike Figgis, *Digital Filmmaking*

Joshua Friedman, *Getting it Done: The Ultimate Production Assistant Guide*

Eve Light Honthaner, *The Complete Film Production Handbook*

Alain Silver and Elizabeth Ward, *The Film Director's Team*

Judith Weston, *Directing Actors*

List of Illustrations

List of Illustrations

Index

Index

Index